CHESAPEAKE STEAMBOATS

By DAVID C. HOLLY

Exodus 1947, 1969

Steamboat on the Chesapeake: Emma Giles *and the Tolchester Line,* 1987

Tidewater by Steamboat: A Saga of the Chesapeake: The Weems Line on the Patuxent, Potomac, and Rappahannock, 1991

CHESAPEAKE STEAMBOATS

Vanished Fleet

DAVID C. HOLLY

TIDEWATER PUBLISHERS
Centreville, Maryland

Library of Congress Cataloging-in-Publication Data

Holly, David C.
    Chesapeake steamboats: vanished fleet / David C. Holly. — 1st
ed.
        p.   cm.
    Includes bibliographical references (p.   ) and index.
    ISBN 0-87033-455-7
    1. Steamboats—Chesapeake Bay (Md. and Va.)—History. 2. Steam-
navigation—Chesapeake Bay (Md. and Va.)—History. 3. Chesapeake
Bay (Md. and Va.)—Navigation.   I. Title.
VM624.M3H65   1994
387.2′044—dc20   94-26450

Manufactured in the United States of America
First edition

To my wife,
Carolyn,
whose love has kept me going
through the years

CONTENTS

ILLUSTRATIONS

ACKNOWLEDGMENTS

The notion for writing this book sprang from a number of impulses. One was the desire to plug a few of the many loopholes in the coverage of the history of the steamboat era on the Chesapeake, areas that I and others left wide open in earlier books. Another was to engage my own interest and that of the reader in the characters of the men who shaped that history. And still another was to say farewell to the steamboats of the Bay and the colorful age they represented.

In furthering these impulses, I certainly encroached on the time and energies of many people, notably the staffs of the Maryland Hall of Records (particularly Ellen Allers and R. J. Rockefeller), the Maryland Room of the Enoch Pratt Free Library, the Hagley Library, the National Archives, and the Anne Arundel County Library. At the last-named library, Phyllis Chansler, Ellen Berkov, and Mary Ellen Bell went past the call of duty in obtaining materials difficult to find. To these patient, willing, and hard-working people, I offer my special thanks. Especially do I owe my gratitude to Charlotte Valentine, Patricia Allen, and Benjamin Trask at the Mariners' Museum; to Peter Lesher at the Chesapeake Bay Maritime Museum; to Paul Berry, Richard Dodds, and Robert Hurry at the Calvert Marine Museum; to Shirley Rittenhouse at the Maryland State Law Library; to Ann Carvel House at the Steamship Historical Society Collection of the University of Baltimore Library.

There are others whose contribution to this book was so important that signal thanks are necessary. Randolph W. Chalfont brought his own research to bear on the history of Charles Reeder and his descendants and on the rival engine works of Watchman and Bratt. William Almy opened his family's collection of documents and valuable memorabilia to tell the story of his grandfather, Captain William C. Almy. Armstrong

Thomas Wallace produced the invaluable family scrapbook and other materials to tell anew the exciting story of his forebear, Richard Thomas Zarvona. At the Chesapeake Beach Railway Museum, Harriet M. Stout, its curator, spent half a day pulling materials together on the resort and explaining in detail its history. John and Angela Vandereedt spent time researching the documentation of *Columbus* and other steamers in the National Archives.

For a day spent discussing the background of the *Express* disaster, for unveiling her own research findings in a generous gesture, and for unbounded hospitality, I salute Grace Anne Koppel. Her contribution was a major one and her own zest for painstaking research inspiring.

To Richard Anderson for his meticulous study of the artifacts from the *Columbus* engine and for sharing his insights on the operation of the parts of an early crosshead engine, I send my thanks. His quiet wit almost masked his scholarship, but his contribution to the line of reasoning on early engineering was substantial.

To the U.S. Army Corps of Engineers I extend with pleasure my congratulations on accomplishing a difficult and challenging task, the raising of the crosshead engine from the wreck of *Columbus* buried in the mud below sixty feet of water. And to my congratulations I add thanks for being permitted to observe the operations and the salvaged artifacts. Special thanks are extended to Jeff McKee, chief, Baltimore Harbor Division, Operations District, and to Mimi Woods, archaeologist, Planning Division, Baltimore District, both of the Corps of Engineers—the first for his generosity in granting the permission and the second for arranging it.

I also extend thanks to Dr. R. Christopher Goodwin and his associates, marine archaeologists, who viewed with me their findings recovered from the bottom of the Bay.

And to Michael Pohuski, photographer, diver, and archaeologist—a man of immense enthusiasm for the maritime history of the Chesapeake — I am most profoundly grateful for arranging access to the *Columbus* operation and study of the findings.

There are others I should thank who helped along the way and brought this project to completion. In a comprehensive work of this sort, inadvertent errors may appear. I offer my apologies. To those who tolerated a researcher, my thanks and good wishes.

CHESAPEAKE STEAMBOATS

PROLOGUE

I haunt the waterfront, and, in turn, the waterfront haunts me. The waterfront is the shoreline of the Chesapeake Bay. Here and there on that vast estuary and its entangling tributaries are bits and pieces of another era. They conjure up the images of a fading past.

At the first light of dawn on a summer's day, I drive down a country road on the Northern Neck of Virginia near the mouth of the Coan River. A small sign directs me to Bundicks, and the road ends beside the narrow channel of the river. On its bank are a couple of dwellings and a small, uninhabited building by the shore. Across the water, not more than a few hundred yards away, are rotting piling and a sagging wharf — vestiges of the landing at Coan.

I am transported back to the 1920s by the scene. In the stillness of early morning, I hear through the mists graying the river and a mind groping for the past the unmistakable swish and beat of an approaching steamboat, then the muffled and melancholy wail of its whistle. Melding with the fog, its shadowy outline moves against the piling on the opposite shore. Figures appear from an imagined warehouse, the agent with a lantern emerges, people arrive by cart and wagon load, and the landing at Coan comes to life in a flurry of activity. Stevedores clatter back and forth with their hand trucks across the gangplank in a rhythmic pattern of silent song and dance. Sleepy passengers appear fleetingly on deck and on the dock. In the latticed windows of the steamer, warm lights glow dimly. And the silent drama of the steamboat's arrival, after an overnight trip from Baltimore, unfolds, until the figure of the captain by the pilot-house signals for departure. The whistle echoes once again across the marshlands of the Coan.

With springlines out, the great, ghostlike steamer, its white sides standing tall in the haze, swings in the narrow channel, and towering

3

over the wharf, ties up at Bundicks. Its wooden rails and gray canvas-covered decks reek with the morning dew. The dock and warehouse and waiting room suddenly throb with people—excited, bustling about, thrilled at the arrival of the vision from Baltimore. It is a country fair all over again, enacted in the morning hours. Cattle are herded aboard. Carts with families waving pull up at the dock. Wagons loaded with produce clatter down the lane. Girls preen and young lads in homespun show off. Dowagers in their finery gossip. Merchants and hawkers husband their wares. And ship's officers strut about in gold braid and self-importance.

It's a sentimental scene: wayfarers coming home to the farms they had known from birth and tearful relatives waiting on the dock; youngsters wrenching themselves from the ties of home for distant schools or hoped-for opportunities; those arriving, those departing, and those left behind. In the shadows, the steamer is another world, a gilded apparition of the city, a touch of glamour that appeared but briefly.

I am awed by the steamer itself—its two decks of white wooden sides punctuated by rows of windows, its name in bold letters emblazoned across the paddle-boxes with a touch of gold leaf and color to brighten them, its tall black stack amidships belching wisps of smoke, its awninged decks and opulent cabin glimpsed through an open door suggesting a world apart in imagined luxury. I sense the engine smell, pungent with oil and steam, and the odor of the cabins, ripe with disinfectant and perfumed soap. And I savor the aroma from the galley, rich with the fried foods of Tidewater. I gaze upward at the captain standing by the rail outside the pilothouse, an omniscient and omnipotent creature, clad in the hallowed braid of his profession. He raises his hand. In the pilothouse, the mate snaps the bellpulls to the engine room. An answering clang sounds far below. Deep inside the boat, the engines sound a faint "whoosh" as they turn the shaft, and the paddle wheels stir up a surge of froth beneath the guards. The steamer moves slowly away from the dock, heading for the open Potomac, a graceful, stately apparition, beguiling and unforgettable.

I haunt the waterfront in search of reminders of steamboating days. The hunt is a restricted one. No one could ever in a lifetime hope to explore the entire shoreline of the Chesapeake. Including all the tortuous rivers and creeks and the Bay itself, the shoreline would measure more than seven thousand miles, twice the width of the Atlantic from Cape Charles to Cherbourg. The navigable waterways alone, those deep enough to float a steamboat, would exceed two thousand miles. But the search is also limited by the number of wharves or landings where the steamboats called. At the peak of the steamboat era, at least three hundred landings on the Bay or throughout Tidewater knew the sound of the steamboat whistle and heard the screech of steamboat guards against the piling. Even this number is impossibly high to visit; and I find that memories are evoked, not by lengthy search, but by stumbling on a site when the sky is right and the weather tells a story. Then the past comes tumbling into the present with an unreal reality.

Some blackened spikes of rotting piling at the end of a lonely lane, a deserted town beside a landing no longer visible, a marina covering the shore where an amusement park once flourished—these are sites stirring up ghosts of the past. Where the past has been reconstructed—a restored landing to resurrect a plantation's history, a restaurant in a former wharf warehouse—the memories seem even more poignant.

Why the mystique about steamboats on the Chesapeake? one may ask. Because the story of their era is finite and infinitely romantic. It spanned 150 years, beginning in 1813 with the launching of *Chesapeake*, a 130-foot craft designed on the lines of a schooner, and ending in 1963 with the departure of the last steamboat from the Bay, an all-steel, streamlined, 300-foot four-decker named *Bay Belle*. The story is rooted in internecine warfare between renowned, related, and talented men either grasping for a monopoly on the Chesapeake or fighting with each other over it. It reached its peak in the early 1900s with the near success of the Pennsylvania Railroad in achieving the monopoly. The Chesapeake steamboat era ended in the wake of the Depression, wartime dislocation, and competition from trucks, automobiles, and a network of fast, hard-surfaced roads. In between, it suffered the pangs of growth through the 1820s, expanded in the pre–Civil War days, rebuilt itself during Reconstruction, and prospered in the golden age at the turn of the century.

More than six hundred steamboats plied the waters of the Bay during the sesquicentennium. At its peak, shortly after the turn of the century, over fifty steamers claimed Baltimore as home port in a given year, and half of that number steamed out of Norfolk and Washington. In summer, on a given day, the horizon on the Bay and its tributaries rarely lacked the smudges of steamboat smoke.

The steamboats at the peak of the era were a sturdy breed, designed by the exigencies of the Bay itself to withstand heavy weather and fend off boarding seas, to carry cargo with easy access to freight decks, and to coddle passengers in the luxury of gilt-adorned public rooms and cuisine-tempting dining rooms. They held up for decades, in contrast to steamers on western rivers built to last only five years. Their engines, unlike those on western boats, functioned faithfully for half a century, even longer. But, most important, they performed a mission that could not be accomplished by any other means at that time: to serve the endless tributaries of the Bay with the essential economic and social link to the supporting cities of the region. They were the lifeline that made possible the development of tidewater Maryland and Virginia. And, equally important, they were singularly graceful, eye-filling, beautifully contoured craft. They bore little resemblance to the waddling boats of the Mississippi, with their raftlike hulls, gingerbread decks, and twin stacks. On the Chesapeake, the steamers showed a distinctly feminine sheer, well-proportioned cabin and deck space, few unnecessary frills, single smoke stacks satisfactorily raked, and clean lines to cleave the seas. Under way, they were apparitions of loveliness.

They came in numerous types—excursion boats, combination excursion and passenger/freight steamers, overnight river packets, swift trans-Bay steamers, and palatial overnight packets between Baltimore (or Washington) and Norfolk. But they enjoyed a general similarity in their white-painted sides punctuated by windows and sideports, and graceful lines.

An overnight trip aboard a steamer on the Bay was never forgotten. I revel in the memory of star-studded nights and the loom of distant lighthouses across the water. The swish of the seas at the bow echoed by the call of the lookout man "All's well!" or the gong of a passing buoy rolling in the swell.

I revel in these images. The sounds in the night. The rhythmic workings of the steamer—the pulsing of its engine far below, the answering creak of the paneling and woodwork. The gentle motion of the boat, cradling and lulling the weary. A deep-throated but remote-sounding blast on the whistle, tapering off in a plaintive wail.

The wheelhouse at night, dark except for the steely gray squares of the windows and the greenish light from the binnacle over the compass. Silhouetted figures of the captain or mate by the starboard windows and the quartermaster behind the five-foot wooden wheel. Quiet except for the terse commands of captain or mate: "Let 'er come to starboard . . . steady . . . meet 'er." Or if maneuvering alongside a dock, the snapping sound of the engine room pull, and a distant gong or jingle from far below. One pull, stop; one more pull, slow ahead; jingle, full ahead; one pull, stop; two pulls, slow astern; jingle, full astern; one pull, stop. On a long reach upon the open Bay, the quiet broken by bits of conversation between master and mate, anecdotes of watermen (Didja hear that one 'bout ol' Abe Mears . . . got lost fishin' up in Hungar Creek . . . given up for lost . . . found him two months later in the marsh . . . livin' off fish he caught . . . said he didn't want to come home to catch hell from Becky, his wife) and of storms (The wind she blew the winders right outta the wheelhouse . . . I looked in the trough and saw bottom) and of incidents (That young buck quartermaster polished the winders so clean in the pilothouse that I near stuck my head through one of 'em . . told him to leave a little dirt next time).

The freight deck at night. The songs of the roustabouts clustered at the open ports. A syncopated rhythm, an off-beat to the clap of hands. Then a croon, a dolorous lament from another time and another place.

A secluded corner beside a crate. The click of rolling dice and a mutter: "C'mon, baby, gimme tha' natchrell . . . seben come 'leben . . . stay 'way, snake eyes."

An upper deck at night. A seductive breeze. A mandolin or ukulele strumming in the shadows, and a few voices softly singing the old refrains, "In the Gloaming" and "Carry Me Back to Ole Virginny." A secluded spot behind the pilothouse. A couple embracing in the light of the stars.

A steamboat knifing through the seas, the waves whispering at her bow, the wind singing in her stays. And cradled below, the people of Tidewater—content within her sheltering embrace.

I can conjure up those days of steamboating on the Bay. Days of tranquility, days of languorous beauty, when time stood still and speed was unnecessary—was even equated to original sin.

In all of my haunts about the Chesapeake, none excites my interest (and exasperation) more than the harbor of Baltimore. I can stand on the grassy green of Federal Hill and imagine the little steamer *Chesapeake* in 1813 setting forth from her wharf at what is now Marketplace across the harbor, daring the British fleet blockading the Bay to stop her. I can look down on Key Highway, near its intersection with Light Street, and watch the smokestacks and weathered buildings of Charles Reeder's foundry emerge from the dreams. I can even hear the sound of his workmen pounding into shape by hand the tools of engine building and the parts for their first crosshead engine.

But my haunting of Harborplace—that brick and concrete monument to the renovations of the late twentieth century—takes me back to the late 1920s and early 1930s, when the same scene was the wharf-ridden stretch of Light Street extending from Pratt Street to Key Highway. The esplanades and squared-off buildings of restaurants and shops and the glass-fronted skyscrapers fade away, and I see Light Street as it was in those days.

The harborside is filled with the wooden false fronts of nearly twenty wharves, some boldly painted with company names and steamboat destinations, others shabby and dilapidated. Cobblestoned Light Street, hemmed in on one side by the wharves and on the other by warehouses of commission merchants, is a cluttered mass of trucks, horse-drawn drays, and automobiles. The din of traffic, the clatter of loading at the wharves, the shouts of stevedores, and the cursing of drivers add to the confusion. Pervading the scene is a scent peculiar to the harbor of Baltimore, a blend of many odors: roasting coffee from the McCormick plant; sulphurous smoke from the steamboats; tar, hemp, vegetables, and cattle from the wharves; and sewage-laden water from the basin itself. The scene on the wharves near sailing time is malodorous, exciting, confused, and colorful.

Between 4:30 and 6:00 P.M., the overnight steamers depart one by one for their destinations in Tidewater. They are lined up, bow first, in their slips along Light Street. As sailing time approaches, the steamers belch smoke, roustabouts shout above the clatter of last-minute freight, passengers scurry across the wharves and gangplanks, in fear of their lives, to the welcoming outstretched hand of the captain, and the evening sun glints on brass rails and gold trim and fresh white paint designed to make each vessel look like a yacht.

At last the time of departure arrives. One by one the steamers sound one long blast on their whistles and back from their piers. A steamboat enthusiast can tell one boat from another by their whistles—some deep and organlike, some shrill and fluted, some two- or three-toned with a plaintive and modulated wail. As each steamer backs into the basin, it digs its paddle wheels or propeller into the harbor filth, shudders as they are reversed, and pivots about, its bow pointed to the Patapsco and the open waters of the Bay.

One by one they emerge: the slim, stately packet for Philadelphia via the Chesapeake and Delaware Canal; the trim and exquisitely proportioned packets controlled by the Pennsylvania Railroad system for the Patuxent, Potomac, and Rappahannock, and for the Eastern Shore; and the largest and finest of them all, the three-deck packets of the Old Bay Line and the Chesapeake Line bound for Norfolk, seeming like small ocean liners on their way to sea.

One by one, they trail one another down the Patapsco. At Seven Foot Knoll they perform a graceful pirouette and take their departures for landings and destinations of Tidewater. In the setting sun, as their lights begin to twinkle, they bring a rush of memories—of long-lost voyages and days of simple wonder and delight.

It is a pageant straight from the past, a parade of steamboats carrying on the traditions of a century and a half of history. For some, it is an anachronism. For others, it is a sentimental link to an unhurried time when the moments were to be savored and treasured.

The steamboat era can be portrayed in vignettes of the past. Its story can be told in the turmoil surrounding the building of the first steamboat and the remarkable ingenuity of the men who devised the engines of the early steamboats. It can be punctuated by the disasters from fire, storm, explosion, and collision that tested the mettle of those who manned them. It can be dramatized by events of the Civil War that turned their decks into scenes of high adventure. It can be enlivened by accounts of amusement parks and resorts where steamboats not only transported the hordes of excursionists but also contributed themselves to the entertainment. It can be humanized in the lives of the men who ran the boats and the eccentric lives of the boats themselves. It can be brought full circle from the battle for monopoly at the beginning of the era to the near achievement of that objective near its end. And it can be climaxed by its tragic end, when the Depression and competition from trucks, automobiles, and fast highways doomed the steamboat to extinction.

The narrative rightfully begins in 1813 with the first steamboat on the Chesapeake, but the story has little meaning without an understanding of the conflicts preceding that event. In those days of tumult, of major consequence for the transportation history of the United States, the stage was set for 150 years of steamboating on the Chesapeake. That era has its own importance in the history of the country.

1

STEAMBOATS ON THE CHESAPEAKE

At the basin of the harbor in Baltimore, only a short distance from Pratt and Light streets, steamboating on the Chesapeake began. The year was 1813. Around the harbor basin, shipyards and smoking foundries, warehouses and wharves, slaughterhouses and glassworks, cheap row houses along mud-pitted alleys, and Federalist-style mansions with gardens to the water's edge melded in companionable confusion. Baltimore in 1813 felt the sharp edge of sudden growth (the population doubled every ten years) and met the contortions, the stench, and the grime with ill-considered grace.

Today, the same setting is overwhelmed by the banality of massive concrete buildings and the spreading esplanade of Harborplace beneath the skyscrapers of a modern city. Adjoining are the angular structure of the National Aquarium and the bulk of a former coal-fired power plant converted into an entertainment center. There is little in the scene to suggest the flavor of a romantic era that began there in 1813.

Haunting that neighborhood as I often do, I found myself haunted, in turn, by that setting as it must have appeared in May of 1813, nearly two centuries ago.

Across the harbor rose Federal Hill, greening in the softness of a Maryland spring. The tranquility of the harbor over which it watched was deceptive. Federal Hill looked down on an unwanted forest of masts. Oceangoing square-rigged ships cluttered the docks and the anchorages where they lay, trapped by the blockade of the Chesapeake Bay imposed by the British in orders-in-council five months earlier. Two months after that, Rear Admiral George Cockburn in pursuance of the order and the blockade thrust his ships of the Royal Navy through the Virginia Capes and began the systematic harassment of communities along the tributaries of the Chesapeake. Pillaging and burning his way along the shores of the Elk and Sassafras rivers in the north, the Chester and the Little Choptank on the Eastern Shore, to the Patuxent and Potomac in the south, he ravaged one town after another, from Frenchtown and Havre de Grace near the head of the Bay to Kinsale in Virginia. By the late spring of 1813, he had reinforced his fleet to eight ships of the line, twelve frigates, and numerous lesser craft. Cruising the Bay with this fleet, he deterred many shipmasters from venturing forth from Baltimore for overseas trade. The threat posed by the British had cut export trade in half by 1811, and in half again by 1813. Hanging in the air around the city was the fear that Baltimore or Washington lay in the sights of the British for direct attack.

Remarkably, the British failed to dampen the spirits or the intrepidity of local sailors of the Chesapeake. Many masters of swift schooners and sloops built on the Bay, with their sharply raked masts and slim hulls, counted on the inability of the British fleet to cover the vast expanse of the Bay and gambled on the probability that, if they were surprised by a British ship, the speed and maneuverability of their craft could outsail any vessel of the Royal Navy. Back and forth across the Bay they sped to carry the produce, tobacco, and other needed wares, in complete defiance of the blockade. And the sailing packets, carrying passengers for Richmond, Petersburg, Norfolk, Annapolis, Washington, Alexandria, Havre de Grace, Port Deposit, and other destinations along the water lifeline, advertised in local newspapers their regularly scheduled departures from various wharves about the harbor in utter contempt for the declarations of the British blockade.

Particularly prominent were the advertisements of the Union Line—the largest and most prestigious of the packet lines—and its daily sailings from Bowley's Wharf (near the Light and Pratt streets intersection) to Frenchtown on the Elk River, with overland stage connections to New Castle on the Delaware River and onward passage by sailing packet up the river to Wilmington and Philadelphia. This line had been formed in 1807 by the merger of two rival and equally prosperous companies.

In 1796, William McDonald and Andrew Fisher Henderson, both Baltimore residents, began operations with four sloops running to Frenchtown, where freight by wagons and passengers by carriage were carried to New Castle for transport by water to Philadelphia. In 1806, Edward Trippe of Dorchester County, John Ferguson of Baltimore, Jonas Owens of Cecil County, and one Captain Taylor started a rival line operating to Courthouse Point on the Elk River, with overland transport to a point near Delaware City and onward travel by sloop to Philadelphia. Both enterprises succeeded, but the competition strained their individual resources. McDonald and Henderson proposed a merger, and Trippe and his supporters agreed. In 1807, the Union Line, as the new company was named, became the largest packet enterprise on the Chesapeake, led by its two progenitors, William McDonald and Edward Trippe.

Somehow, in spite of decided differences in background and personality, the two men found common ground.

William McDonald, fifty-five years old in 1813, still spoke with the burr of Scotland in his teeth. Fleeing the land of his birth and uncertain lineage, he came to America in time to join the forces of the Revolution and by dint of his ingenuity and perseverance became an officer in the Fourth Georgia Line. He was wounded in the Battle of Guilford Courthouse, North Carolina; the name Guilford remained indelible in his memory.

After the war, he settled in Baltimore and began a series of investments in shipping, real estate, banking, and several smaller enterprises, all of which prospered. A small wiry man, white-haired with penetrating eyes, he soon gained a reputation for shrewdness and hard-headed risk-taking in business. Amalgamation and consolidation led to profit. By the turn of the century, he was a wealthy man, among the elite in the commercial world of a burgeoning Baltimore.

When the British fleet finally advanced on Baltimore in September of 1814, McDonald once more donned a uniform to command, as a lieutenant colonel, the Sixth Regiment of Maryland Infantry. He was honored for his participation in the defense of Baltimore by being granted in later life the honorary title of general.

His ventures in real estate brought him to purchase from Ebenezer Smith Thomas a 195-acre farm west of York Road on the outskirts of the city (additional acreage was acquired in 1830). To this estate, McDonald gave the name of Guilford to commemorate his participation in the battle. For twenty-three years he lived on the property, beginning the building of a three-story mansion surmounted by a central cupola, with fifty-two rooms and accommodations for twenty-five guests. Entrances to the estate (near present-day dwellings on Westover Road) were guarded by a porter's lodge and stone lions. (The estate was sold in 1873 to Aranah Shepherdson Abell, publisher of the Baltimore *Sun*, and around 1913, it had developed into the most exclusive and wealthy sector of the city.)

Eighteen months after the purchase of Guilford, McDonald took his second bride, Martha Webb. Six years later, at age seventy, he fathered

William McDonald, Jr. In contrast to his father, who died in 1845, the son "Billy" fled from business and responsibility and devoted his short life of thirty-five years to sport, travel, and the pursuit of pleasure. Guilford, which he inherited, became the site of bacchanalian parties long remembered. Famous was his huge brick stable complete with twenty-five box stalls and marble drinking fountain. Here he kept the finest of Arabian horses, including one Flora Temple, known as "queen of the turf." In the Civil War, he was arrested and incarcerated briefly in Fort McHenry on a charge of signaling agents of the Confederacy from the roof of the house. When his half-brother Samuel died in 1855, William inherited over $1 million and indulged his every fancy, even chartering a yacht to cruise the world with his family and friends to celebrate the adventure in Byronic splendor.

But Samuel, General McDonald's son by his first marriage, showed more interest in his father's business than did Billy. He remained his father's partner in the packet days from 1796 into the early nineteenth century; outsiders often spoke of them as McDonald and Son; a shrewd, hard-headed, and wily pair well remembered.

Edward Trippe, in contrast to McDonald, came to his station in life by lineage and inheritance. The Trippe family, descended from Nicholas Tryppe of County Kent in England who died in 1242, began its history in America when Henry Trippe settled in Dorchester County on the Eastern Shore of Maryland in 1663. Land holdings of the Trippe family extended into Talbot County (one area encompassed Trippe's Creek off the Miles River), but its seat lay at Todd's Point, a few miles west of Cambridge downriver on the Choptank (the promontory can be seen from the present-day Choptank River bridge carrying Route 50 south). The Trippe family proliferated over Dorchester County and other areas of the Eastern Shore. At the ancestral home at Todd's Point, Edward Trippe was born to Captain John Trippe and Elizabeth Noel Trippe on January 29, 1771. The family celebrated his birth in historic Trinity Church on Church Creek off the Little Choptank River.

Edward Trippe grew up in the comforts of plantation life and the sort of feudalistic society that expected tenants to support landowners with their rents and that took as its due the work of slaves to farm the soil and maintain the estates. Educated by family and tutors, Edward arrived at manhood with the self-assurance bred of acceptance among the landed gentry of the Eastern Shore.

In 1813, at age forty-two, he was a handsome man, six feet tall, with a trim physique, fair hair (by then somewhat receding), frank blue eyes, a long and commanding face, and an engaging personality. His friendliness and openness, together with an innate courtesy, recalled to some of his friends the Shakespearean compliment of being "to the manner born." John Quincy Adams, who met him in travel, paid him the tribute of stating that he was a "gentleman alike to president and to slave."

In his late twenties, Trippe's interest in farming had given way to a love for the sea. He moved to Baltimore where he purchased a substantial interest in several vessels engaged profitably in the West Indies trade. He established his residence in a town house between Hanover and Charles streets at Camden. There the waters of the harbor lapped at his garden gate. His fascination with maritime pursuits led him in 1806 to join others of similar interests: Jonas Owen of Cecil County and John Ferguson of Baltimore. The latter with his brother Benjamin operated a new line of sumptuously appointed sailing packets between Baltimore (Bowley's Wharf) and Norfolk (Newton's Wharf) offering passage and "everything found [food] except liquors" for ten dollars. The venture of Owen, Ferguson, and Trippe was to establish a new line via the head of the Bay, overland to the Delaware River, and onward by water passage to Philadelphia. Trippe achieved prominence with the merger of his line with that of McDonald and others in the formation of the Union Line in 1807.

Edward Trippe's interests emerged from innate intelligence and enormous curiosity. He possessed an undivided penchant for science, particularly physics and more particularly mechanics and its application. He plagued local bookshops for publications from abroad dealing with the subject.

In late 1812, Trippe lived an elegant life in Baltimore, excited more by his intellectual pursuit of scientific knowledge than by his business. He moved in a world where he expected his somewhat baronial background to speak for itself and his status to be immediately understood. In this respect, he was not above creating for himself the perquisites. For example, when he wished to visit any of the vessels of the line, a four-oared barge reportedly arrived at his garden gate to deliver him on board in state. In naval parlance, a boat rowed by four to twelve oarsmen became a barge by the elaborateness of its appearance, the smartness of its crew, and its use by admirals (possibly commodores) for ceremonial occasions.

In my habit of haunting the waterfront, I have found myself conjuring up the shadowy image of Edward Trippe's departure from his dwelling at the waterfront. As he stepped through his garden gate, to the curtsy of an attending servant, he would turn to step in the stern sheets of the waiting barge, a figure of consummate dignity. Four sailors would loft their oars in a gesture of salute, while the coxswain near the tiller would touch his forelock and assist Trippe to his seat. Teakwood planking and gilt trim along the gunwale and stern converted the boat into a barge, more fitting a naval officer of flag rank than a part owner of a line of sailing packets serving the Bay. "Bend your oars," the coxswain would order, and the barge would head toward a waiting packet.

In May of 1813, the barge might very well have veered across the basin for a short run to the small shipyard of William Flanigan at 55 St. Patrick's Row, bordering the harbor on Pratt Street near the market house (approximating the position of Long Dock used today as an automobile parking lot for the Aquarium and Harborplace). Alongside the dock lay a vessel whose configuration excited the curiosity of the entire maritime community of Baltimore.

Although her hull superficially resembled that of a medium-sized sailing vessel (length of 137 feet, beam of 21 feet) with clipper bow and bowsprit, mast, yard, and square sail, she added some conspicuous features never before seen on the Chesapeake. Amidships rose a tall black smokestack. Just aft of the smokestack stood an A-frame on either side of the deck; these supported and channeled what appeared to be a guillotinelike crosshead forced up and down from amidships by a rod delving into the bowels of the vessel. The rod connected to a crank rotating a cogwheel, which engaged a shaft running through the vessel. But what seemed most astonishing were the huge half-round paddle-boxes on either side bearing the lettering *Union Line: Chesapeake.*

There she stood—*Chesapeake*—the first steamboat on the Bay. She was an extraordinary revelation for seasoned mariners in and out of Baltimore, the masters of the swift craft sailing the water highways of the Bay and sending forth their rakish clippers to torment the British. That this strange vessel should have been built in the climate of war and blockade seemed audacious and irresponsible. And its capacity to run against wind and tide, although questioned by some, stirred apprehension among owners of sailing craft using established routes and among commission merchants and other business interests profiting from long-standing patterns of commerce.

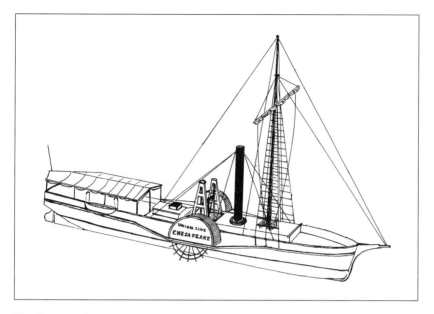

The first steamboat on the Chesapeake Bay, *Chesapeake,* as it might have appeared in 1813. This rendering is based on photographs of the model in the Maryland Historical Society, but corrects that model by placing the smokestack forward of the engine and paddle wheels, and by including the A-frame for the crosshead engine.

Chesapeake in late spring of 1813 lay alongside the dock in the final stages of outfitting for her scheduled maiden runs in June. Shortly, local journals would advertise her projected excursions to Annapolis on June 13 and to Rock Hall on the Eastern Shore. On June 21, she was scheduled to begin her regular run, leaving Bowley's Wharf near the Light and Pratt streets intersection each Monday, Wednesday, and Friday for Frenchtown on the Elk River. There, passengers would cross by stage (freight, by wagon) via the New Castle and Frenchtown Turnpike Company (chartered by Delaware in 1809 and Maryland in 1810, with heavy investment by the Union Line) to the Delaware River for onward passage by the steamer *Delaware* to Philadelphia. *Chesapeake*'s master was advertised as Captain Edward Trippe.

In 1811, he turned away from a role in the management of the Union Line (also termed Citizens Union line) and elected to skipper its first steamboat. Through the years ahead, he continued to follow his chosen profession, the skippering of the line's vessels after acquisition. He served with distinction. On Wednesday, October 6, 1824, the steamer *United States*, with Edward Trippe as master, steamed up the Bay for

17

Frenchtown with a distinguished delegation to receive on board the most celebrated guest of the nation, General Lafayette. When approaching Fort McHenry on the return trip, the steamers *Maryland, Virginia, Eagle,* and *Philadelphia* formed an escort, with flags and bunting streaming from every deck and mast. Captain Trippe continued to serve the Union Line for many years until his retirement to his ancestral seat on Todd's Point, where he died at age 69 on February 2, 1840.

Like most students of steamboat history, I had never questioned the accepted narrative of events leading up to the building of the first steamboat on the Chesapeake and its voyages in 1813. As outlined, the narrative centered very substantially on Edward Trippe as the progenitor of the steamer *Chesapeake* and the father of the steamboat in the waters of the Bay. According to the accepted version of events, Trippe gained the friendship of Robert Fulton, who had launched *North River Steamboat* (commonly known as *Clermont*) in 1807. The meeting, as stated, took place at Clermont, the estate of Robert Livingston on the Hudson. Between Livingston and Trippe there developed a warm friendship and mutual admiration, which led to an exchange of visits, even, as reported, by Livingston to Trippe's estate in Dorchester County.

From this association with Fulton and Livingston, Trippe, according to the account, waxed enthusiastic about the future of the steamboat and in 1811–12 broached the subject of building one on the Chesapeake to McDonald and Henderson. Having confidence in Trippe's knowledge, they agreed to the building of a steamer for the Union Line. Trippe, McDonald, and Henderson agreed to share the costs (about forty thousand dollars), while Trippe would bring to bear his knowledge of mechanics as builder of the vessel. William Flanigan was given the contract, and *Chesapeake* emerged from the shipyard in the spring of 1813, ready to undertake her pioneering role on the Bay.

This account of the birth of *Chesapeake* had its origins many years later in a lecture, "The First Steamboat Built in Baltimore," given by Andrew C. Trippe before the Maryland Historical Society. Andrew C. Trippe (1839–1918), barrister, illustrious hero of the Confederate Maryland volunteers, and wealthy socialite of Worthington Valley, was the great-grandson of Edward of steamboat fame. Notes from this lecture became the basis for one of a series of articles on steamboat history in the Baltimore *Sun* in 1908 and another in 1930. These articles adhered strictly to the Andrew Trippe theme. Several subsequent journal and newspaper articles as well as references in books dealing with the Chesapeake simply repeated the story without question.

18

While there is an element of truth in this story, the actual beginning of steamboat life on the Chesapeake was far removed from the simplistic and rather idealistic version presented by Andrew Trippe in tribute to his forebear. The coming of the steamboat to the Bay and the beginning of the steamboat era in the region had their origins on the Delaware River, in New York, in Washington, even on the Mississippi. The facts present a turbulent picture of conflict: of men larger than life contending with each other in fits of jealousy, anger, and avarice—sometimes viciously—for their assumed rights; and of battles fought but rarely won. Issues of territory, monopoly, patents, inventions, and legality (even those of constitutional law) were contested in a climate of hostility, veiled only by certain codes of civility and assumed family bonds drawn by marriage. Amidst this confusion, the personalities of historic luminaries like Robert Livingston, Robert Fulton, John Stevens, Nicholas J. Roosevelt, and Benjamin Latrobe emerge in dramatic confrontation. It is from this milieu of jealousy and conflict that the era of steamboating on the Chesapeake dawned.

The factual history began in Paris in 1802 when Robert Livingston extended his hand for the first time to Robert Fulton. The introduction, according to some sources, was performed by a mutual friend, Joel Barlow, poet and Connecticut wit, who felt it necessary to bring Fulton's talents to the attention of Livingston. Other sources place the meeting at various mechanical exhibitions in progress about the city, at a demonstration of balloon ascension, or at a social function arranged by an expatriate financier, Daniel Parker. One source emphatically stated that the meeting was arranged by Livingston's brother and occurred at the Panorama, a giant display of the burning of Moscow in the seventeenth century created to amuse the public, painted in large part by Robert Fulton, expatriate artist and would-be inventor.

No matter how the meeting occurred, an unusual and asymmetrical bonding took place. On the one hand, the two men shared an enormous curiosity about the application of certain principles of science, particularly to water transportation, and certain attributes of imaginativeness and purposefulness to achieve their ends. On the other hand, there were many differences, incipient sources of trouble between them. There was the matter of age: Livingston was 56 years old, Fulton barely 36. And more critically, there existed an enormous disparity in status and personality.

Robert Livingston was born in 1746 to a family of Scottish ancestry prominent in New York long before the Revolution. As heir to a large estate on the Hudson, he enjoyed the privileges of wealth and social sta-

Robert Livingston. Drawn from an early portrait.

tion. Conscious of his position, he grew up to expect others to grant him respect without question, and he reacted with unusual sensitivity to criticism or any disparagement of his intentions or his person. At times, he exuded elegance and charm. On other occasions, he revealed his brooding character, a demeanor often cold, avaricious, even rapacious. A tall, thin man—his slender physique was often noted by compatriots—he moved with stately grace. His face suggested his personality: high forehead topped by thick gray hair, arching eyebrows raised in a perpetual question, straight patrician nose, firm chin, wide thin lips suggesting both a smile and a sneer, and unfeeling eyes surveying the world with cold objectivity.

"It is a sad misfortune," one of his biographers quoted him as saying to Alexander Hamilton, "that the more we know of our fellow creatures the less reason we have to esteem them." (Dangerfield, *Chancellor Livingston,* 195).

He valued his legal education, graduating from King's College (later Columbia University) on May 23, 1768, with John Stevens, who later became both brother-in-law and nemesis, as a classmate. He considered himself an expert in both constitutional law and international law, with emphasis on Grotius and Vattel. Legalism in his thinking colored both his diplomatic and commercial life.

Although not a signer of the Declaration of Independence, he served as a delegate to the Continental Congress. At the inauguration of George Washington, Livingston administered the oath of office. In 1781, Congress elected him to the office of secretary of foreign affairs, and he traveled abroad in this capacity for two years. Politically he was ambivalent; a staunch Federalist in 1788, he went through a traumatic conversion to Jeffersonianism in the 1790s. The doctrines of the latter influenced his outlook on the growth of the country and the transportation systems to link its parts. On October 17, 1777, he had been confirmed as chancellor of New York; as such, he headed the state's chancery court, a court of equity. The legal requirements certainly demanded little of him, for he held the job and simultaneously served abroad for years. Nevertheless, he held the title and was known as Chancellor Livingston for the rest of his life. In spite of his professed taste for democracy, he managed his estate of Clermont (rebuilt after its burning by the British) as the lord of the manor—feudalistic, baronial.

Deafness struck him in the 1780s, with unbearable consequences. Livingston loved glamour and reveled in glittering social events. He liked to entertain and be entertained. Frivolity, even vanity, streaked through his nature. With his increasing deafness, he found he could no longer keep up with the gossip flowing around him, and he crept off to grieve in private. In diplomatic circles, where the subtleties of conversation were critical, his disability weighed heavily on his conduct and his disposition.

In 1802 in Paris, Livingston was the minister plenipotentiary of the United States to France to negotiate debts owed by the French government to American citizens. As such, he had access to Napoleon and the highest levels of French bureaucracy. During the year, he had become involved in the tantalizing prospect that the vast holdings of the French in the Louisiana territory, recently transferred from Spain, might by some strange concatenation of international intrigue and the unfathomable intricacies of Napoleon's mind become available for purchase by the United States. Livingston floated in a complicated world of social glitter, intrigue, and deception.

The social and official status of Livingston was far removed from the uncertain status of Robert Fulton when they met for the first time.

At thirty-six, Fulton had yet to make his mark in the world, in spite of a brilliant mind and an acknowledged talent.

Born on November 14, 1765, he grew up on a farm off Conowingo Creek, in Lancaster County, Pennsylvania. His father had emigrated from Scotland; his mother, a woman of superior talents, saw to it that Robert was educated by a Quaker and a Tory. In such an environment, Robert proved to be a poor student. At age seventeen, he set out to find his future in Philadelphia and in particular to apply his artistic talent to portrait and miniature painting and to the drawing of construction plans. With only forty guineas in his pocket, in 1786 he decided to go abroad. In England, with a letter of recommendation he had solicited from Benjamin Franklin, he applied to study under the celebrated painter Benjamin West. In London, he lived a bohemian existence, barely making ends meet with his painting. He interested himself in other pursuits, in particular the design of canals and boats to navigate them. The possibility of steam propulsion for these boats occurred to him in his perusal of the writings of various developers of steam engines in England.

In July 1797, he crossed the Channel to Paris with the idea of presenting his canal concepts to the French government. In Paris, he learned to speak and read the language passably, learned a little Italian and German, and studied higher mathematics, physics, and chemistry. The development of a rope-making machine captivated him for a while. Then he devoted his attention to the creation of the Panorama on boulevard Montmartre, where possibly he met Livingston. He experimented with a torpedo boat designed to sink a ship of the line. By the turn of the century, he had conceived the idea of constructing a four-man submarine able to stay under water for four hours by using compressed air, and he pressed Napoleon to accept it as a means of decimating the British fleet. As long as the notion seemed feasible and promising of early success, Napoleon encouraged Fulton, but he slammed the door in his face when the practicalities proved insurmountable.

Fulton, with incredible versatility, recalled his ideas for canals and canal boats, and he devoted more and more of his energies and time to the notion of using steam propulsion for the latter. He experimented on the Seine with a small craft using an engine of his own design and construction. For one reason or another, it was not successful. In this period of Fulton's frustration, Livingston entered his life. Livingston was captivated by Fulton's intelligence and imagination; with unfailing Livingston charm, he sought to buoy the flagging spirits of the younger man and bring him around to serve his purposes.

At thirty-six, Fulton was an attractive man, whom others instinctively liked at first meeting. He was over six feet tall, slender, and moved with assurance. Square-faced and stern-jawed, he nevertheless spoke quietly, smiled easily, and tended to enliven conversations by his amiability and cheerfulness. His broad forehead was often swept by unruly locks of curly, dark brown hair. Large, dark eyes flashed with humor, intelligence, and wit. His gestures—open, unaffected and often expressive—suggested more of the artist than the engineer or scientist. But he was temperamental, even mercurial, at times; his anger frequently turned violent.

Fulton refused to be intimidated by Livingston's lofty status in the highest reaches of diplomacy and government or by his overweening exhibition of his aristocracy. He decided that a shared interest could be to his benefit. At the same time, Livingston saw in Fulton a talent that he could use and a younger man whom he could dominate.

What the two men found so intriguing was their common interest in developing practical, operating steamboats for navigating the rivers of the world. Both men had followed with avid interest the work of James Rumsey on the upper Potomac in 1785 and the frustrations he had suffered when his jet-type engine produced such meager results. They had watched the steamboat of John Fitch, with its flailing oars like canoe paddles, steam back and forth between Trenton and Philadelphia in 1790, only to stop short when the money ran out and when the somewhat exotic inventor gave up in despair. (Some years later, an observer asserted that on one demonstration run of Fitch's boat, both Fulton and Livingston were on board at the same time, although they did not know each other then.)

Another shared experience was that both men had experimented with building steamboats themselves—Fulton in Paris with his uncertain boat on the Seine, and Livingston in 1797 with a vessel produced at Belleville, New Jersey. The latter vessel incorporated an engine following the designs of the Watt engine of the British and a horizontal, beneath-the-keel paddle wheel devised by Livingston. The boat was testimony to the dilettantism of Livingston and the shallowness of his science. He had learned some mechanical theory at King's College, but the bulk of his knowledge came from superficial reading of pamphlets and tracts when available. When put to the test, the boat failed to move. A second boat of slightly modified design, built because of Livingston's refusal to accept defeat, was no more successful.

At this stage of his experiment of 1797, Livingston was willing to listen to others who offered opinions on steamboat propulsion. One of those was Nicholas J. Roosevelt, scion of a family as distinguished as the Livingstons and experimenter with steam pumps for the Philadelphia Water Company and with various means to cast guns for frigates of the *Constitution* class. What Roosevelt proposed was the use of vertical side-wheels rotated by a shaft connected to the engine. With Dutch stubbornness he pressed his claim that the side-wheels would work. He had little reason to know at the time that his invention—for indeed it was his invention—would revolutionize steamboat history or that it would precipitate internecine warfare between its proponents, involving state legislatures, the national government, and major figures in the maritime commerce of the United States.

Another of those who vouchsafed their knowledge and opinions to Livingston was his brother-in-law John Stevens (Livingston had married Mary Stevens on September 9, 1770) of Hoboken, New Jersey. Livingston and Stevens had known each other since college days.

Stevens enrolled at King's College at age seventeen and graduated in law with Livingston in 1768. Unlike Livingston, he fought in the Revolutionary War and rose to the rank of colonel; the title was often applied by others to his name, so that he and Livingston were frequently referred to respectively as "the colonel" and "the chancellor." After 1788, Stevens's attention was increasingly drawn to the steamboats pioneered by Rumsey and Fitch, and he read with care the various pamphlets and treatises in which each contender bitterly prosecuted his claims for the initial invention. Based on some of the concepts of both the Rumsey engine and the Watt engine and incorporating some of the designs of the Fitch boat, Stevens proceeded to develop an engine of his own. He sought protection for his invention in Albany, but the New York legislature found it not dissimilar from the work of Fitch. Stevens then looked to action by the U.S. Congress to afford protection under the constitutional provisions for the encouragement of the arts and sciences. In his arguments, he rhapsodized on the worldwide benefits of steamboats: "Civilization [as a result of steamboat travel] would spread rapidly over the face of the globe, [and] man [would become] the master of the world, with everything in it subservient to his will" (Turnbull, *John Stevens*, 107).

As a result of his efforts, Congress passed the first Patent Law of the United States in April 1790; the first group of patents included that of Stevens. Oddly, Roosevelt's invention of side paddle wheels in America did not appear. Roosevelt, preoccupied with other projects, simply overlooked applying, and his request for patent protection was not filed until 1814.

Livingston measured his brother-in-law as a man to be reckoned with. Around the turn of the century, in his early fifties and nearly the same age as Livingston, Stevens was a man of moderate height, nearly bald with graying hair fringed about his ears, and sharp-featured with shadowed eyes be-

John Stevens. Drawn from a portrait in Turnbull, *John Stevens,* 1928.

neath heavy eyebrows. More than Livingston, he was a scholar, particularly in the fundamentals of steam; he read every text he could find about the experiments of Newcomen, Watt, and others, raking through the stocks of city book shops and procuring books from London on a regular basis.

By 1797, Livingston, Roosevelt, and Stevens, squabbling among themselves on their relative accomplishments in steamboat propulsion, proposed to pool their ideas. They actually drafted a formal agreement in which they formed a partnership for the production of a steamboat to sail on the Hudson.

Their disagreements stemmed from more than personal jealousy. Stevens, land rich but money poor, needed Livingston's financial support but resented it when proffered. Livingston's vaulting imagination, impracticality, and unwillingness to hear the truth about his shortcomings irritated both associates. And Roosevelt's stubborn "down to earth" demand for tools and foundries dampened the enthusiasm of the others.

Livingston, ever-sensitive to possible encroachment by outsiders, forced the New York legislature to repeal a grant giving John Fitch in 1787 exclusive rights of steamboat navigation on the Hudson and to bestow similar exclusive rights upon himself—this in the face of the fact that Fitch had three years to go on his grant. That Livingston was able to pull off this feat of legislative coercion bore testimony to the weight of family name and wealth on state politics.

Stevens proceeded to build a small twenty-nine-foot operating steamboat in local Jersey waters; while incapable of carrying freight and passengers, it proved the merits of the steamboat—just as John Fitch had done. It abandoned the screw propeller type of propulsion that Stevens had designed in favor of the side-wheel invented by Nicholas Roosevelt. Livingston gave scarce notice to the accomplishment of Stevens and sailed off to France, the hold of the ship laden with his furniture, a large stock of food, and some cattle, hogs, and sheep for the long haul, to undertake his duties as minister plenipotentiary to Napoleon's government.

In 1803, Napoleon suddenly decided to sell the entire Louisiana territory to the United States—a *volte face* completely unexpected to Livingston, who had endured a year of machiavellian intrigue in the labyrinths of French bureaucracy and among the conniving diplomatic corps in Paris. He suffered a severe bout of pique when James Monroe arrived to consummate the deal, when he, Livingston, believed that the credit was his. Nevertheless, the acquisition of the vast territory including the Mississippi and many of its major tributaries opened up vistas that he had not fully envisioned. Earlier, in 1787, while serving as secretary of foreign affairs, he had asserted, from the vantage of his knowledge of international law, that any claims of the United States to navigation on the Mississippi were inadmissible. Now, in 1803, as a newly converted but ardent Jeffersonian, he found that American extension to the Mississippi was "founded in justice." Furthermore, he saw the thousands of miles of rivers as water highways linking the country—not only in the West but also in the East. And, having met Fulton and understood his passion for the development of the steamboat, and taking into account his own self-educated expertise in steamboat design, Livingston was ready to set forth on a literal crusade. Under his own control, of course (perhaps shared with Fulton), he would bring the blessings of the steamboat to his native waters, first in New York and thence to all of America, even to the whole world. His imagination and his vanity soared beyond rational bounds.

Piqued also was Fulton. Rebuffed by Napoleon over the submarine and torpedo boat proposals, he slipped across the Channel and entered England under an assumed name. Somehow regaining his identity, he presented the same proposals to the admiralty in Whitehall to develop his submarine and torpedo boat—but this time against the French fleet. The British turned their backs. However, on this stay in England, Fulton placed an order with the engine manufacturer, Boulton and Watt, for the shipment of an engine constructed according to his dimensions to New York. With Livingston's money, the core of the steamboat project gained tangibility. How Fulton was able to circumvent British restrictions on such exports remains a mystery.

Livingston and Fulton, both having returned to New York, set about the construction of the *North River Steamboat* (popularly called *Clermont* for Livingston's estate). The steamboat was scarcely Fulton's invention. Built with Fulton's skill in bringing together the needed components, Livingston's money and support, a British engine manufactured by Boulton and Watt, the engineering and design of John Stevens, and Nicholas Roosevelt's side-wheels for propulsion (Fulton now claimed them as his own invention), the vessel made her maiden voyage on the Hudson on August 17, 1807. On the afternoon of the eighteenth, she put in to the landing at Clermont, where Livingston, before going ashore, announced the engagement of Fulton to his cousin Harriet Livingston. Through the succeeding years, in spite of their differences and acrimonious exchanges, Livingston and Fulton often addressed each other as "cousin," just as Livingston and Stevens, even under vitriolic circumstances, sometimes called each other "brother."

The launching of *Steamboat*, as it was often called, and Livingston's bold claim by virtue of New York's legislative action to exclusive rights to steamboat navigation on the Hudson, brought forth an eruption from would-be steamboat builders, state legislatures, and the national government.

In the fray that ensued, Livingston's enthusiasm for the steamboat seemed to wane, while that of Fulton waxed. Nevertheless, their arguments, though remarkably different, projected a monopoly of steamboats throughout the navigable waterways of the United States. In essence, the differences, excoriated on either side by Stevens and Livingston as lawyers, struck at interpretations of constitutional law. On one hand, Livingston, a proponent of states' rights, held that the exclusive rights to steamboat navigation on the Hudson granted by New York placed such powers in the hands of the states; since the U.S. Constitution failed to include such controls among the enumerated powers, the Tenth Amendment placed the power of granting navigational rights in the hands of the respective states. But noting the overlap of New York and New Jersey on the Hudson, Livingston declared that the legislative act of New York applied to New Jersey as well. Speculating further, he was moved to consider that since the national government gained its authority from the actions of the states, the monopoly could be extended to western rivers, and, equally important, to the navigable waterways of Ohio, Pennsylvania, Maryland, and Virginia.

Fulton based his theory of monopoly on the power of the federal government to grant patents and, therefore, the implied powers of the inventor to protect his patented inventions—by the control of his inventions wherever they might appear. The area envisioned extended without limit—all of the United States, if not the entire world. The patent Fulton referred to was no less than his "invention" of the side paddle wheel. Clearly, this self-proclaimed patent crossed the steaming path of Nicholas Roosevelt, who rose in righteous anger at the violation of his own, but unpatented, invention of side paddle wheels. It crossed the path of John Stevens, who discovered that no patent by Fulton had been filed in the U.S. Patent Office (it was only filed when Fulton learned that Stevens had uncovered its absence). It stepped across the line of the steam engine patent granted Stevens in 1790, when he instigated the creation of the U.S. Patent Office. Fulton's "patent," along with Livingston's proclamations concerning his exclusive rights on the Hudson to encompass New Jersey, even Delaware (and other states), infuriated Stevens, who saw his future imperiled by the actions of Fulton and Livingston. Roosevelt and Stevens also felt aggrieved because the "patent" summarily destroyed their compact drawn up with Livingston in 1797.

The vicious battle of words waged by Livingston, Fulton, Roosevelt, and Stevens—later joined by many others—lasted for years. It was not settled until Livingston and Fulton died, the court cases multiplied across the nation in waves of protest, and the Supreme Court under Chief Justice John Marshall in 1824 in the *Ogden v. Gibbons* suit declared river monopoly illegal.

In the climate of verbal hostility after 1807, events followed the path of these antipathies.

Livingston and Fulton shared a romantic vision, the transformation of the American river system into a vast water highway traversed by steamboats under their monopoly or control. Under the facade of friendship that they assumed with Nicholas Roosevelt, who labored under the illusion that the agreement of 1797 still could be revived, they persuaded him in 1809 to undertake an investigation of western rivers from the Ohio through the length of the Mississippi. For six months, a flatboat or keel boat became the home of Roosevelt and his indomitable wife on a voyage from Pittsburgh to New Orleans. Based on his favorable experiences and a determination by Livingston and Fulton to proceed, Roosevelt took up residence in Pittsburgh and built the steamer *New Orleans*. She began her voyage on September 27, 1811, for the city of New Orleans, bearing Roosevelt's pregnant wife, an infant son, two servants, and a Newfoundland dog named Tiger. After surviving storms and an earthquake, the steamer reached its destination on January 12, 1812.

In this monopolistic venture on the Mississippi, Fulton got caught up in a defensive maneuver coming from an unexpected quarter. Roosevelt, a compulsive gambler and speculator, faced bankruptcy from unwise investments and turned to Benjamin Latrobe for help, chiefly because Latrobe had recently married Roosevelt's sixteen-year-old daughter. Latrobe, in a spasmodic effort to revitalize the 1797 agreement as a way to help his father-in-law, wrote to Fulton, advising the latter that Roosevelt was the real inventor of the steamboat and stating that if the 1797 agreement between Roosevelt and the others were not acknowledged, he, Latrobe, would seek stern redress. Fulton vacillated in an equivocal reply.

Benjamin Latrobe emerged an implacable foe of Fulton and Livingston. Latrobe's enormous prestige preceded him wherever he went. His name could be attached to the architectural design of the U.S. Capitol, the White House, the cathedral in Baltimore, buildings at Princeton, Dickinson, the University of Pennsylvania, the Baltimore Exchange; to the engineering of the Chesapeake and Delaware Canal, the water supply system of New Orleans and Philadelphia, and other major projects; and even to the design of dinner china. A Latinist and linguist, he was a talented scholar. But Latrobe could be a difficult partner, in spite of his prestige. He was a tempestuous man, given to fits of fury and depression. He worked compulsively and was susceptible to nervous collapse. Petulant, demanding of attention (yet remorseful after bitterly attacking his foes or even his friends), Latrobe also was extravagant and hopelessly impractical in financial matters. When he struck out at his foes, his blow was often trenchant and irrational. His decisions frequently resulted in disaster.

Roosevelt, financially supported by Latrobe, set out on a venture in Pittsburgh to launch steamers for the western rivers, particularly for the Ohio above the fall line but also for the lower Mississippi. *Vesuvius* was built to follow *New Orleans*; others followed, and the monopolistic insistence of Fulton and Livingston was virtually ignored. Costs proved to be staggering, at a time when the foundries of the Monongahela River struggled to begin and machinery arrived with difficulty and at a fancy price. Furthermore, the War of 1812 further pinched off shipments. The venture on the Mississippi failed. Roosevelt found himself deeper in debt and even more embittered. And Latrobe lost nearly his entire fortune, blaming the entire disaster on Fulton and Livingston for their "infernal monopoly." On his trips through Baltimore and Philadelphia and at the head of the Chesapeake, Latrobe set his sights on ways to get even with the two of them, whose monopoly, as he saw it, was stifling the opening of the rivers to free navigation.

As early as January 1808, John Stevens schemed to circumvent the monopoly of Fulton and Livingston on the Hudson. That monopoly, according to their doctrine, extended to the very shoreline of the river; New Jersey steamers, therefore, were excluded from the Hudson. The New Jersey legislature refused to acknowledge a monopoly sanctioned by New York on the river or to grant a monopoly to Fulton and Livingston on any of the waters of the state. Furthermore, the legislature considered measures of reprisal against New York steamers for any New Jersey vessels seized on the Hudson in enforcement of the New York monopoly. Stevens decided to act on his own, in spite of the threats of his brother-in-law.

"Monopolies are very justly held, in every free country, as odious," Stevens stormed. "A monopoly gives an unlimited power to one man or set of men to lay heavy contributions on all the rest of the community" (Philip, *Robert Fulton*, 22).

Accordingly, Stevens built a steamer ironically named *Phoenix*, using a Boulton and Watt modified engine and a design similar to that of the *Clermont* but wider with side paddle wheels—in flagrant disregard of Fulton's claims of exclusive rights—and sailed her defiantly around the Hudson. A hostile standoff occurred, under a guise of family civility. In December 1809, Fulton and Livingston extended a compromise of sorts. In this proposed agreement, Fulton assumed for himself the entire credit for the invention of the steamboat, but he, with Livingston, granted to Stevens the right to build and operate steamboats on the Delaware, Chesapeake, and certain other specified waterways, some far to the south. Stevens refused to sign the agreement but allowed it to stand without protest. Unclear were important issues. Did the agreement continue the Livingston-Fulton monopoly but simply permit Stevens to operate in certain areas under its blanket? Or did it in effect abrogate its own monopoly in those areas and pass the rights of monopoly to Stevens? He chose not to seek an answer and depended on time and events to settle the issues. Fearful that Fulton and Livingston might engage in some form of unannounced move against him if he continued his operations on the Hudson and knowing that their new steamer *Raritan* stood ready to compete with *Phoenix*, Stevens decided to try his luck on the Delaware. His decision was dramatic. The Hudson and the Delaware did not connect; to get *Phoenix* to the Delaware River required an "outside" voyage. On June 10, 1809, he dispatched *Phoenix* on an adventure, unprecedented and fraught with potential danger.

He sent her to sea. Under the command of his twenty-one-year-old son, Robert Livingston Stevens, a highly intelligent and dynamic young man, *Phoenix* steamed out of New York Harbor, and in company with a sailboat that kept pace as a tender, ran down the New Jersey coast on a twelve-day voyage to the Delaware capes and up the Delaware River to Philadelphia. Old-timers said that it couldn't be done. But the little steamer survived the ocean trip in spite of a gale, boarding seas, fog, and dead calm (short on fuel, *Phoenix* ignominiously arrived in Philadelphia by drifting upriver on the tide).

Having started *Phoenix* on her route between Bordentown, New Jersey, and Philadelphia; having located adequate shipyards; and having planned for new boats to operate on the Delaware, Stevens turned his attention at once to the Chesapeake Bay. In a sweep of excited imagination, he envisioned the establishment of steamboat service between Baltimore and Philadelphia via the Head of Elk, as he called it, and Wilmington, and he outlined such a steamboat line in a prospectus dated November 18, 1810. Astonishingly, the subscribers (one hundred dollars a share, ten shares each) included Fulton and Livingston, who were undoubtedly hedging their bets.

In spite of his denunciation of Fulton's avowed monopoly, Stevens foresaw a virtual monopoly operating under his exclusive control from Norfolk and the Carolina sounds below it through the length of the Chesapeake Bay and its tributaries to the Elk River in the north, with overland connections to Wilmington, and steamer travel under the monopoly up the Delaware River to Philadelphia. At Philadelphia, *Phoenix* would provide the water link to Trenton and New Brunswick. The rival *Raritan*, *Clermont*, and new steamers forthcoming under Livingston and Fulton would complete a route to New York and the upper river to Albany. *Phoenix* now was under the command of Captain Moses Rogers, later to gain distinction for commanding *Savannah*.

In January of 1811, Stevens visited Washington, D.C., and attempted to interest members of the government in steamboating on the Chesapeake. He included the president himself, who tactfully declined to subscribe to the Stevens undertaking. Stevens proceeded to advertise the proposal in letters to various newspapers:

It seems to be a prevalent idea that Steam Boats are only calculated for the navigation of smooth waters, than which nothing can be more erroneous. . . . When I first thought of establishing a line of Steam Boats between Philadelphia and Baltimore, before I had taken a view of the navigation of the Chesapeake . . . I must confess I felt somewhat intimidated by the great expanse of water . . . it appeared to contain. When I came to obtain current information . . . I found this . . . extensive sea was, in fact, the far greater part merely shoals. . . . The ebb and flow occasioned little current . . . the wind could never produce such a swell as to prove dangerous to steam navigation.

I have also satisfied myself by an actual survey and taking soundings of the Elk River from Frenchtown to Elkton Landing, that this . . . navigation is perfectly unexceptionable. . . . the steam boat would leave Baltimore at 5 o'clock every morning, arriving at Elkton at 3. Passengers will then cross the Peninsula in stages to Wilmington and, starting from thence in the steamboat between 5 and 7 o'clock, will arrive in Philadelphia between 11 and 12. . . . Again, the steamboat will leave Philadelphia every morning at 10 o'clock, arriving at Wilmington at three. The passengers . . . cross to the other boat at Elkton between 6 and 7, and arrive at Baltimore between 4 and 5 o'clock the next morning. . . . This estimate is justified by the performance of *Phoenix* on the Delaware (Turnbull, *John Stevens*, 302–303).

The advertising of Stevens provoked a sharp response from Fulton and Livingston, the former still outwardly acquiescing in the December 1809 accord granting to Stevens "the exclusive run to Baltimore" but warning that if his (Fulton's) patents were evaded the agreement would terminate and prosecution would follow. Livingston also sounded stern warnings, but his attitude reflected to some extent a waning interest.

Aboard *Phoenix*, Captain Rogers noted the hostility of the New Jersey legislature to encroachments of Fulton and Livingston and stated that "the People have an opinion they can put a Steam Boat on any River they please and make use of any Patent, without any consent whatever" (Turnbull, 307). At the same time, Stevens pushed his plan for the steamboat line by publishing estimates of probable revenues (eighty passengers per day, round trip for day at $1.25, expenses $25, revenue $15, profit $21,000 per year or 85 percent of an investment of $25,000).

As the months of 1811 advanced, war with Britain seemed increasingly imminent. Stevens in his letters attempted to demonstrate the importance of steam transport on inland waters to national defense, particularly in view of the deplorable state of roads connecting the principal population centers of the Chesapeake and the Delaware.

In his trips to the Chesapeake region and to Baltimore, Stevens could not escape travel aboard the sailing packets of the Union Line. In these journeys by packet and in his surveys of the upper Chesapeake, he invariably encountered its principal administrator, William McDonald, accompanied by his son Samuel. With his own ambitions in mind, Stevens began negotiations with McDonald and Son, as he called them, for the transformation of the Union Line, with its sailing packets, to a steamboat line to connect Baltimore and Philadelphia.

The contract that resulted, as reported in the press on January 18, 1812, included McDonald and Son, John Stevens, Henry Craig, George Hand, Levi Hollingsworth (wealthy merchant at Bowley's Wharf, Baltimore), and James LeFevre. At the insistence of William McDonald, who foresaw possible trouble ahead with Fulton and wished to skirt it, the contract contained a clause professing acknowledgment of the patents claimed by both Fulton and Stevens (nothing was mentioned about Nicholas Roosevelt), but nothing in the statement directly addressed any restrictions on new construction. As a wily businessman, McDonald correctly adjudged the prevailing climate. As projected in the contract, the line would link a system extending eventually from Baltimore (perhaps farther south) to Albany. Plans included in the contract called for the construction of a steamboat with a 130-foot keel and 20-foot beam. The shares in the reformed Union Line were set at one hundred dollars each, a thousand in total. John Stevens held a substantial portion.

Exhilarated, Stevens restlessly looked beyond his exploitation of the Union Line to the lower Bay and to the Carolinas. If Fulton could claim a monopoly on the Hudson, why should he, John Stevens, not enjoy the same privilege in southern waters? He traveled through the coastal sounds of North Carolina and eventually reached Beaufort and Charleston, South Carolina. From his inspection, he decided to build and operate three 150-foot steamers: one between Baltimore and Norfolk, a second on the Albemarle and Pamlico sounds, and a third on river systems to Charleston, with part of the connecting route covered by carriage or wagon. He sought monopoly rights from the state of Virginia. Also, he appealed to the North Carolina legislature for exclusive rights; the bill was passed on December 24, 1812.

As he expected, his move brought a storm from the north, generated by Robert Fulton. Declaring that his patents were being infringed, Fulton forbade any use of his "inventions" on the Delaware or elsewhere. How this feud, drawing to a climax, might have culminated must be kept to speculation. The war with Britain brought blockade and land battles too close to the scenes envisioned by Stevens for his grandiose schemes in the South.

Stevens flouted Fulton on many fronts. He enticed workers from Fulton's shipyard to work in the shops on the Delaware that he favored. He looked ahead to the boats he would construct to fulfill his well-publicized plans and established himself familiarly among the hierarchies of government under Fulton's very nose.

Fulton began a process of retaliation. In one of his less volatile moods, Latrobe had intimated that a steamboat route on the Potomac River and Chesapeake Bay from Washington to Norfolk might be profitable. Fulton, also in one of his less volatile moods but steaming with anger at Stevens and ready to resort to any expedient, commissioned Latrobe to file a prospectus and subscription for such a line. In spite of President James Madison's personal purchase of a few shares as a gesture of support, the project failed to arouse popular interest, and Latrobe in 1812 fell short of the needed twenty-five thousand dollars by five thousand dollars. Fulton pouted and looked for ways to build a boat with which to exercise his self-proclaimed monopoly on the Potomac, in spite of Virginia's refusal to grant exclusive rights.

In the midst of these maneuverings, Fulton fought battles on many fronts: with the Livingston family over rights on the Mississippi and with seemingly endless streams of prospective steamboat owners and operators who contested both his patent rights and his assumptions of monopoly. With Latrobe, he entered a period of nasty controversy, punctuated by Latrobe's capriciousness and Fulton's increasingly irritable disposition. Each seemed bent on the other's destruction. Only the war with Britain restrained actions that Fulton might have taken.

During this period, Latrobe, often staying for extended periods in Washington, journeyed frequently to Philadelphia to have machine work done on a forge and block mill he devised in the Washington Navy Yard to be powered by a steam engine. He looked to work he had observed in progress at various yards. On occasion, he declared that the work performed by Daniel Large in his small shop at 508 North Front Street near the Germantown Road, Philadelphia, was eminently satisfactory. From his survey, he also endorsed the shipyard of J. and F. Brice, at Northern Liberties, county of Philadelphia.

During 1812, the contract announced by John Stevens in January establishing the Union Line as a steamboat service between Baltimore and Philadelphia began to materialize. Plans were drawn up to build two boats simultaneously, one in Philadelphia to serve the Delaware River segment from New Castle or Wilmington to Philadelphia, a second in Baltimore to operate the shuttle from that city to Frenchtown on the Elk River. Although he was a shareholder in the Union Line and was committed to its transition to steamboat service, Stevens encountered a stubborn reluctance on the part of the owners in the Chesapeake region to relinquish their interests and control, particularly in the Bay segment. William McDonald, supported by his Baltimore friend Andrew Fisher Henderson, a financier of some distinction, firmly held the reins of control. Edward Trippe, courtly member of the Dorchester Country gentry and a founder along with McDonald, found more interest in the science and application of steam propulsion to a vessel and navigation on the waters of the Chesapeake than in the administration of the business. Other lesser partners (including some original shareholders, John Ferguson and Jonas Owens) viewed the transformation simply as a likely investment.

McDonald, with a hardheaded Scotsman's instinct for profitable ways to circumvent the machinations and power struggles of the commercial world, took careful stock of the situation presented to him in late 1812. First, the country was at war and the British fleet roamed the Chesapeake, creating indiscriminate havoc along its shores. Baltimore and Washington seemed likely targets when the British concentrated their strength. Second, because of the war and the movements of the British inside the Capes, both Fulton and Stevens had temporarily put aside their interest in the Chesapeake for fear of the blockade. Third, Livingston had suffered a stroke (another brought his death on February 26, 1813), and his diminished interest in the extension of a steamboat monopoly had virtually died. Fourth, Fulton was beset on all sides by litigation; the tension had produced remarkable changes in his health, appearance, and disposition, to the point that he would stare into space for long periods or lapse into speech so incoherent as to be incomprehensible. Fifth, Benjamin Latrobe, whom McDonald knew well from association around Baltimore, mouthed his old bitterness about the Fulton-Livingston monopoly and implied that McDonald could simply ignore claims of exclusive rights and patent priorities.

The moves of McDonald and Stevens under the guise of the Union Line were deft. The Union Line placed a contract with J. and F. Brice of Kensington, Philadelphia, for the construction of a 130-foot steamer with a 20-foot-beam crosshead engine, to be named *Delaware*. After launching on the river whose name she bore, she would operate from New Castle or Wilmington to Philadelphia. Funding for the construction came from those Stevens had solicited: Henry Craig, George Hand, Levi Hollingsworth, and James LeFevre. In the choice of J. and F. Brice as the shipyard of construction, the advice of Latrobe featured in the decision. McDonald was fully aware of the enmity that Latrobe, as well as Stevens, harbored for Robert Fulton.

Almost simultaneously, McDonald, acting on behalf of the Chesapeake shareholders of the Union Line, released a contract for the construction of a steamboat in Baltimore, a vessel of very similar dimension and characteristics as the *Delaware*. The new boat would be named *Chesapeake* for the lower half of the route served by the Union Line. McDonald put up one-third of the costs of construction, estimated at forty-five thousand dollars; Andrew Fisher Henderson advanced another third; and Edward Trippe contributed the final third. Furthermore, Trippe was persuaded to overview the construction and to command the *Chesapeake* after she was launched.

McDonald, with Trippe's advice, selected the yard of William Flanigan at Number 10 Pratt Street for the site of construction. But he acceded to the persuasions of Latrobe in selecting Daniel Large as the builder of the engine. Thirty-one years old, Large was an immigrant from England and had been the youngest apprentice of the first steam engine firm, Boulton and Watt of Birmingham. He brought with him the expertise of British engine builders, a knowledge in very short supply in the United States. Latrobe had seen his work on various stationary engines and recommended him highly. At the same time, he knew that Large had a low regard for Fulton's patent claims. In Large's shop, a young man just past apprenticeship, Charles Reeder, showed such engineering skills that Large entrusted him with the installation of the crosshead cogwheel engine shipped by packet and placed in the *Chesapeake*.

Whatever Trippe contributed to the construction of the vessel in Flanigan's shipyard was circumscribed by several factors. First, the pattern of construction was already set by both Fulton and Stevens in *Clermont* and *Phoenix*. Also, the engine had been built on the Boulton and Watt model by Large (who shipped it piecemeal by packet from Philadelphia to Baltimore). The general supervision was provided by Stevens (who even set up a special shop for that purpose on Happy Alley in Fells Point, Baltimore). And last, the general design of the vessel, as understood by Flanigan (the builder), was that of a sailing schooner (to him, the engine was simply an accessory). Certainly, Trippe could scarcely claim the title of "father of the steamboat on the Chesapeake." But his ardent interest in the construction and his venturing forth as the skipper in the face of the threat from the presence of the British fleet in the Bay contributed to the success of the enterprise. There *Chesapeake* steamed— to the surprise, praise, bewilderment, and derision of the maritime and commercial interests of Baltimore and interested spectators along the shores of the upper Bay—a schoonerlike vessel complete with mast and sail, awning on the afterdeck for passengers, tall black smokestack amidships belching wood smoke, crosshead engine slashing up and down like a guillotine cranking the cogwheels and flywheel to turn the side-wheels, and paddle-boxes on either side proclaiming her name and line.

Trippe probably met Fulton on the latter's frequent sallies through Washington. The stately appearance of Trippe and his baronial upbringing probably induced an early introduction to Robert Livingston. Assuredly, Livingston would have been captivated by the similarity in background— the northerner living in semifeudalistic comfort on his estate along the Hudson and the Marylander with similar origins from his estate along the Choptank. Both moved with the assurance of aristocrats and found their tastes remarkably similar. Conceivably, too, the overlap of interest in the science of steam propulsion brought Fulton and Trippe together, although Fulton spoke with practical experience, while Trippe's knowledge came only from his reading; Trippe, therefore, learned from Fulton the means to assemble a working steamboat. But, most importantly, both Fulton and Livingston saw Trippe as a vehicle to further their own interests on the Chesapeake and in the Union Line, in contravention of the independent and monopolistic pursuits of John Stevens in the same direction.

Key to the entire enterprise of building the first steamboat on the Chesapeake was the astute perception of William McDonald. He correctly assessed the intentions and diminishing capabilities of Stevens to effect a monopoly on the Chesapeake. He perceived that Fulton, beset by legal and personal problems, had limited prospects for expanding or even defending his dreams of monopoly. In Livingston he saw a man in failing health, who had long since abandoned his fantasies of a nation linked by water highways. Recognizing Benjamin Latrobe's rather duplicitous attitudes toward Fulton and the others, McDonald held to Latrobe's view that one could do what one chose to do with respect to recognizing patents and exclusive rights. Also following Latrobe's recommendations, he had the engine built by Daniel Large, using his British expertise, in the knowledge that Latrobe's endorsement came as much from contempt for Fulton as from praise for Large.

McDonald also recognized the talent and interest of Trippe as a science enthusiast and a navigator—but not as a business manager. Trippe readily accepted a role in overviewing *Chesapeake*'s construction and serving as her master.

Chesapeake came to life in a gesture of defiance. She began her regular runs in June 1813 to Frenchtown and returned in utter contempt of the British fleet cruising the Bay. On August 8, 1813, she carried an excursion-load of spectators to view the enemy ships lying off the mouth of the Patapsco River. And on September 13, 1814, Captain Trippe anchored her in the line of blockading ships, her white paddle-boxes boldly proclaiming her name, *Chesapeake: Union Line*, to the British men-of-war maneuvering off Fort McHenry toward Fells Point and access thereby to the streets of Baltimore.

But another gesture bore a subtle message. McDonald never gave any practical effect to the Livingston-Fulton-Stevens claims of patent or exclusive navigational rights, nor did the Union Line contribute directly to those rights, except to pay Stevens and his heirs the interest due on their shares in the company. In effect, McDonald conveyed a message through *Chesapeake* and *Delaware*—a message of defiance to the predatory intentions of Livingston, Fulton, and Stevens.

Fulton could not bring himself to abandon his vengeful quest for a Chesapeake monopoly. In 1813, even as *Chesapeake* neared the end of construction, he had the Charles Browne shipyard in New York build the steamer *Washington*. The dimensions of the new steamer were approximately the same as those of *Delaware* and *Chesapeake*, and the configurations were nearly identical. The Robert Fulton Works in New York built the engine for *Washington*. As indicated by her name, her destination was Washington, D.C., for service on the Potomac River to Norfolk. While negotiations dragged in gaining permission to sail *Washington* out of the capital city, the steamer remained in New York after her launching. But an agent of Fulton's, John Devereux Delacey, whom Fulton described as a rogue, succeeded by whatever means in obtaining a special permit for steamboat operations on the Potomac with the express intention of selling the permit to the highest bidder. Fulton exploded.

"You will please try to find Delacey . . . have him arrested . . . put Delacey in prison," he stormed in a letter to his son. "Do not neglect this one moment" (Philip, *Robert Fulton*, 138).

Fulton died in 1815, and Benjamin Latrobe acquired *Washington* for service on the Potomac under the guise of the Potomac Steam Boat Company. Advertisements asserted that she was operating "under patents of Messrs. Livingston and Fulton." It seems clear that Latrobe was granted the sale by Fulton under condition that he acknowledge the patent rights of the latter. His agreement undoubtedly was signed with tongue in cheek.

On May 21, 1815, *Washington* left New York for the Virginia Capes on a perilous voyage for a small river steamer on the open Atlantic. It was the second of such voyages, the first being the historic transit of *Phoenix* from New York to Philadelphia via the Delaware capes under the command of the son of John Stevens. *Washington*, after her arrival in Norfolk on May 24, 1815, but before shoving off for the Potomac, explored the waters of the Elizabeth River, leading south toward the Carolina sounds. The trip had a purpose consonant with Fulton's original dreams: it was a gesture of challenge to the aspirations of Stevens to set up a steamboat route in the southern reaches of the Bay.

To give meaning to his intentions, Fulton, before his death, accompanied the construction of *Washington* at the Charles Browne shipyard with the near simultaneous building of *Richmond* on the adjoining ways of the same company. *Richmond*'s dimensions were somewhat larger (length 154 feet, beam 28 feet) than those of *Washington, Delaware*, and *Chesapeake*, but her appearance was similar. Her engines originated in the Robert Fulton Works. Her destination—clearly designated by Fulton— was the James River, for service between Norfolk and her namesake city, Richmond.

Launched in early 1814, *Richmond* emerged in the face of the barriers placed by the Virginia legislature and local jurisdictions to exclusive rights for navigation—the same difficulties encountered with respect to *Washington*. Not succeeding as his agent had done in obtaining a special permit, Fulton, too exasperated to struggle, left *Richmond* in the Hudson.

There she performed useful services for many years and was affectionately known as "Lady Richmond." However, the naked circumstances of her creation and that of *Washington* exposed the vengefulness of Fulton in striking back at what he perceived as the backbiting of Stevens and the Union Line on the Chesapeake.

Fulton died on February 24, 1815. His widow reportedly secluded herself in mourning, but she recovered sufficiently and expeditiously to remarry in little more than a year. With Fulton's death, and that of Livingston two years earlier, the idea of monopoly over the water highways of the United States—and, indeed over much of the world—expired. It had served only to throttle the legitimate expansion of water transportation in a rapidly growing country that urgently needed its services and held back steamboat builders and owners who had no recourse but to strike out on their own.

Chesapeake, a plucky steamer brought to life in the midst of the machinations of men who featured in the annals of American history, bore testimony to this verdict. She came to life through the canny shrewdness of William McDonald and the dedication of Edward Trippe in her building. As a symbol of the indomitable spirit of Baltimoreans who defied both the British invaders and the greedy interlopers from the north, she stood high in the early history of the state and of steamboat navigation.

A twist to the story of the building of *Chesapeake* in Baltimore in 1813 could be told with the near simultaneous building of *Eagle* in Philadelphia. As discussed before, *Chesapeake*'s construction accompanied a concurrent building of *Delaware* at the J. and F. Brice shipyard on the banks of the Delaware River. Conspicuously placed on the adjoining building ways stood the skeleton of *Eagle* with very similar measurements and appearance. Begun somewhat later in 1813 than *Delaware*, she made her maiden voyage on the Delaware in 1814. Her owners, among others, included Daniel Large and the prestigious captain, Moses Rogers. Skippered by the latter, she operated between Bordentown, New Jersey, and Philadelphia, hence in direct competition with John Stevens on the same route. Rogers had made it clear that, in his opinion, any citizen had the right to use the waterways, even by steamboat, as he chose, and to use patents without prior permission. As he might have expected, hostile pressure by Stevens made continued operations on the Delaware River infeasible, and Rogers came to the same dangerous decision made by Stevens with *Phoenix* and Latrobe with *Washington*—to send his boat via the open sea to seek another life. Rogers, the legendary and visionary navigator who took *Savannah* to Europe in the 1819 crossing of the first steamship on the Atlantic, sailed *Eagle* beyond Cape Henlopen, down the coast, and past Cape Charles at the Chesapeake mouth, sidling up to a dock in Norfolk on June 19, 1815.

He sought a charter and he found one quickly. Samuel Briscoe and John Partridge, sensing the demise of monopoly, started a new line to compete with the Union Line in its operations from Baltimore via Frenchtown to Philadelphia. Chartering *Eagle*, they found their operations so successful in drawing the blood of the Union Line that on August 20, 1817, they decided to buy the vessel. Investors included themselves with the backing of others, Levi and William Hollingsworth among them, both of whom had joined John Stevens in his initial involvement with the Union Line. Vicious rivalry raged on the upper Chesapeake and lower Delaware between the two companies, the Union Line and the Briscoe-Partridge Line, each acquiring new boats to elbow out the other. It ended in 1819 when the Union Line built *United States*. Briscoe-Partridge caved in and sold off their holdings, including *Eagle*. Bought by George Weems, she ran the Bay until her boiler exploded on April 17, 1824, scalding her owner and skipper. Her flames were extinguished by the crew of the passing *Constitution* of the Union Line.

The twist lies in the building and operation of *Eagle*, concurrent with *Delaware*, by so eminent a man as Moses Rogers, in open defiance of the Stevens monopoly and indeed of the Union Line's monopoly on the Delaware—and *Eagle*'s steaming about the Chesapeake in bitter rivalry with the Union Line itself. In the background undoubtedly lurked the fine hand of Latrobe and the enormous curiosity and manipulation of wily William McDonald, who in the end managed to win.

This sequel only serves to highlight the convoluted history of events that brought *Chesapeake* to life and the significance attending *Chesapeake*'s birth on the Bay.

The events preceding and accompanying that birth dramatized the best and the worst of human nature: talent and skill of the highest order; imagination and readiness to explore the limits of a dream; idealism and a romantic perception of the future; avarice, jealousy, duplicity, and rage magnified by the scene itself; and a certain gentility precluding the excesses of passion born in conflict. That the *Chesapeake* symbolized a new age on the Bay for which she was named is testimony to the stature of the men who created her.

2

ENGINE INGENUITY

The ghosts of Daniel Large and Charles Reeder almost certainly haunt the waterfront of Baltimore—even to this very day.

If the modern thunder of four lanes of truck traffic hurtling along Pratt Street could be stilled and the towers of concrete, glass, and polished steel could melt away, today's dreamers might be able to attune their senses to the scene of 1813: a narrow cobblestoned street rattling with the clatter of horse-drawn wagons, a line of ramshackle warehouses, and a shipyard of frame buildings and launching ways bearing the sign of its owner, William Flanigan, sprawled at Number 10 Pratt Street at the foot of St. Patrick's Row, where the market house met the waterfront. At the head of the harbor basin (Bowley's Wharf) just a block or so away at Light Street, there arrived the Union Line's sailing packets from the head of the Bay, bringing passengers and freight from Philadelphia.

On a given day in 1813, a certain scene was repeated. A dray and team of horses being backed to the dockside at Bowley's Wharf challenged the skill and vocabulary of its driver. Beside the wagon, out of reach of the horses struggling in harness and the cursing of the draysman, stood a young man, broad-shouldered, dark-haired, clean-shaven, thin-faced, with heavy eyebrows shadowing eyes as serious as his expression. Twenty-six-year-old Charles Reeder had come to the wharf to meet his employer, who was arriving from Philadelphia, and a precious load of cargo aboard the packet. Over the gangplank came Daniel Large, at thirty-one a sallow-faced man, nearly 5 feet 9 inches tall, with dark hair and blue eyes. He greeted Reeder in the rough tongue of the British Midlands.

Together they stood while the boom of the packet, rigged with block and tackle, hoisted a heavy piece of fabricated metal from the hold, swung it over the side, and lowered it carefully into the waiting wagon.

Charles Reeder, Senior. Redrawn from sketch in Howard, *Monumental City*, 1873.

Together they clambered into the dray and jostled over the cobblestones to the Flanigan shipyard.

Neither displayed the triumph he felt. Yet both had reason to exult. Daniel Large had just passed through a zone of war. He had just sailed through the waters of the upper Chesapeake, patrolled by vessels of the Royal Navy blockading the Bay in 1813. In his pocket he carried a small document, a *laissez-passer*, issued in the name of the American government, stating that he was a British citizen, and therefore not subject to seizure or impressment, and should be allowed to pass through the blockade. How much that statement would have influenced an officer of a British man-of-war seemed questionable, since sailors thought to be of British nationality but serving on American ships that were seized at sea were routinely shoved (on the flimsiest pretext) into His Britannic Majesty's service. Thus, at considerable personal risk, Large had traveled to Baltimore to see for himself how the steam engine he was building in his machine shop in Philadelphia was faring in its installation aboard the first steamboat in Chesapeake waters, the *Chesapeake*. That he was building the engine at all, in spite of tremendous obstacles, and that he had made the journey, along with a part for the engine, without mishap was cause for a moment's pleasure.

For Charles Reeder, the moment could be savored for more personal reasons. At age twenty-six, only five years junior to his employer, he had survived an arduous apprenticeship in the large foundry in Philadelphia, where he had to learn not only the skills of casting iron and steel but also the techniques of using lathes, boring machines, planers, and other equipment to fashion machine parts. Furthermore, he had to learn how to manufacture the machines themselves in order to furnish the foundry itself with its mill. That he had completed his apprenticeship to the praise of Large, a highly skilled and demanding man, was accolade enough. But to be selected by Large to assemble in Baltimore the engine that Large was building in his foundry in Philadelphia was a special tribute.

Dancing in the head of Reeder was a larger vision. Now that *Chesapeake* neared the end of construction and prospects for her success in transiting the upper Bay for the Union Line seemed bright, certainly, as he saw it, there would develop a sudden and insatiable demand for the building of more steamboats on the Chesapeake. Steam engines powered the boats. Someone had to build them. There existed only one millwright in Baltimore, William H. Richardson, experienced only in the placement of factory machinery, who confessed that he had no knowledge of steam engines and their construction. The iron foundry of John Dorsey on Curtis Creek below Fort McHenry produced corronades and cannon shot but had never seen a steamboat engine. The ambition of Reeder reached a point of mentally planning for the future.

The ingenuity of these men, Daniel Large and Charles Reeder, characterized the machinists and foundrymen in the United States from the very beginning of the age of steam in the country. Not that knowledge of what was happening in the mills of England did not reach the more scientifically inclined of the American intelligentsia—they read inventors' pamphlets and the scientific journals arriving from abroad with avidity. Men like John Fitch, James Rumsey, Robert Livingston, Robert Fulton, John Stevens, and many others were well informed. But transposing words, diagrams, and mathematical models into machinery involved skilled foundrymen, millwrights, and engine builders, all in short supply in the United States. Those who attempted the transfer of these trades and skills to the United States faced a mammoth task. What they alone undertook to accomplish was staggering in the context of the times.

The United States at the end of the eighteenth century and start of the nineteenth barely felt the industrial revolution in England and other parts of Europe. Transfer of advancing (though remarkably primitive by modern standards) technology from England to the New World stalled as well-established journeymen in the foundries of Birmingham and elsewhere in England balked at the uncertain prospects of uprooting themselves and relocating in what they deemed to be the wilderness of America. The economy of the fledgling United States, although stirring with newly felt demands, seemingly offered few incentives for transfer of industrial skill.

Yet there emigrated from England enough trained men—men like Daniel Large—to further the process of industrialization begun in the United States. Apprenticed at an early age to the firm of Boulton and Watt of Birmingham, England, Large confronted the tasks of mastering not only the metallurgical and machine trades required for journeyman status but also the technology of James Watt and those who preceded him in the art of steam engine building. By 1806, when Robert Fulton procured his engine from Boulton and Watt for the *North River Steamboat (Clermont)*, James Watt (1735–1819), financially supported by Matthew Boulton (1729–1808), had developed dependable steam engines used in a variety of industrial capacities. Watt's work sprang from a long line of experimenters and inventors, highlighted by the Thomas Savery engine of 1699 and the Thomas Newcomen engine of 1705. A number of British and French patentees thereafter claimed advances in steam engine design. Most of these early engines functioned in pumping water from coal mines or served in powering small factories. Successive patents by Watt through the late 1700s improved his engine for general application and eventually for use in marine propulsion. Boulton shared in the enterprise, not by his technical skill, but by his financial support.

"Watt's engine was, when invented by him, but an ingenious speculation," reported Baron Dupin, a continental intellectual of the period, "when Boulton, with as much courage as foresight, dedicated his whole fortune to its success" (Thomas Tredgold, *History of the Steamboat Engine*, Vol. 1, Sect. 1, 1838, 29). Wealthy from his business successes, Boulton exempted Watt from all the cares of life and allowed him to pursue his mission without restraint.

In this environment, Daniel Large encountered head-on the stiff requirements of learning the arts of steam engine building in the most advanced foundry and machine shop in Britain. Why he decided in 1807 (could it have been related to Fulton's success?), at age twenty-five and as the youngest and most successful apprentice at the firm of Boulton and Watt, to forego his future in England and cross the ocean to Philadelphia he never disclosed.

Near the banks of the Delaware River (later to be described as the Clyde of America), a number of shipyards and other industries had established themselves by the time of Large's arrival. A certain fever of industrial expectancy filled the air. In Philadelphia, he set up shop, first with James Smallman, who, like Large, was an expatriate from Boulton and Watt (where he had advanced to foreman), then after 1810 for himself as foundryman, millwright, and engine builder on Front Street, below the Germantown Road.

In spite of his training, the task confronting Large (with Smallman before 1810) was formidable. Foremost in setting up the plant loomed the problem of manufacturing tools and machines, since lathes, borers, planers, and other shaping equipment needed for fashioning steam engine parts could not be obtained from other sources. Even simple tools such as sledgehammers, clamps, and extruding irons were best produced in the foundry.

Iron and steel production in the early 1800s was more of an art than a science. The difference between cast iron, wrought iron, and steel was not clearly understood in chemical terms, although ironmongers knew their individual properties in terms of hardness and malleability. Laboratory analysis as a means of determining properties of ore and metal in production had yet to develop as a means of control. Molten iron in the early smelting furnaces emerged as a spongelike mass that was beaten with sledgehammers to drive out the slag of impurities. The nature of the resulting metal depended on the residual carbon content: low for the malleable but tough wrought iron, high for hardened steel. Often the result was almost accidental. Skilled ironworkers used forced draft from large bellows to force combustion gases through the molten mass to cause its absorption of carbon. The resulting "pig" iron (named for the stubby, round ingots) could be further refined by heating with charcoal over a period of time to produce steel. These techniques and other methods demanded special skill—almost the artist's touch—in the manufacture of cast iron, wrought iron, and steel. Equally difficult and challenging was the process of casting the molten metal in earthen molds in the shape of machine parts or engine parts, or forming a semimolten mass by hammering it into a desired shape. Some machine tools and, more particularly, some steam engine parts weighed tons.

A foundryman and engine builder had to be a highly intelligent man of many capabilities. He had to sense the difference in the iron he smelted by color and texture, and he needed the artistry to convert the molten mass into the desired hardness of metal. He also had to stand the physical strain of handling the white-hot product and converting it into the rough but heavy components of machinery. Experience, a sixth sense, and skill marked the trade of the successful foundryman.

Basic tools begot machine tools. Like other early manufacturers in the United States, Large had to build his own machine tools, depending on his British experience, before he could begin the fabrication of steam engine parts. Certain machinery was immediately essential: a boring mill for completing the iron casting of a cylinder; a lathe for fabricating shafts, pistons, valves, and other moving parts; a planing machine for refining flat surfaces to an acceptable tolerance; and a punch and toggle device for securing boiler plate.

Probably Large could purchase copper plate from rolling mills in Philadelphia. For many years of sailing ship construction, copper sheathing had protected wooden hulls from worms and fouling, and mills in the United States in the early 1800s were certainly able to manufacture copper sheets of a given weight.

In his own foundry and machine shop, as he had learned during his apprenticeship with James Watt, Large could fashion machine parts made of copper or brass to fairly precise dimensions. A certain pride entered the process, and often the parts displayed a measure of embellishment quite beyond the requirements of their functions.

Large had not steeped himself in the mathematical concepts that engaged the "natural philosophers" of the eighteenth century—their derivation of complex formulas (including the use of the calculus) to describe the "elasticity" of steam and methods to employ its "velocity" in machines. Nor had he grasped their studies of thermal input and output, their analyses of various means of applying power (for more detailed discussion of these technical aspects, see Tredgold). But he carried with him the practical experience of his years with Boulton and Watt. That manufacturing plant, in turn, capitalized on the inventions of the eighteenth century, revolutionized by the expanded production of iron.

The development of the steam engine itself depended on achievements in metalworking. At one time, a distinguished inventor who had built mills and pumps and other metal devices reported to the British Society of Engineers on seeing a model of a proposed steam engine that "neither the tools nor the workmen existed that could manufacture so complex a machine with sufficient precision" (Usher, *A History of Mechanical Invention*, 359). In the late eighteenth century, he was correct.

Errors in cylinders made from rough castings and crude boring machines amounted to as much as a half-inch for a two-foot diameter. Watt was delighted when presented with a cylinder bored accurately enough so that a piston would not go past a shilling. In these early attempts at steam engine building, only packing held steam pressure at all, and the packing was short-lived under friction and heat.

Boring machines used in the making of cannon were crude until an invention by John Wilkinson in 1776 eventually made possible the delivery of suitable cylinders to the firm of Boulton and Watt. The boring machines of the eighteenth century themselves depended on the production of steel hard enough for its use as a cutting edge against softer iron, steel, brass, and other metals.

Lathes had developed from rather primitive turning machines powered by foot or hand (as cord-driven or pole lathes) into the mandrel lathes of 1785 and, finally (with the inventions of Henry Maudsley in 1794), an all-metal lathe with a slide rest. Screw-cutting lathes arrived concomitantly with these inventions. With the development of lathe and boring machines able to cut metal and fashion it into workable parts, planing machines followed around the turn of the century. Punch and toggle devices, depending on manpower, had existed with the use of copper in piping and sheathing.

Given the capabilities of Daniel Large, his shop in Philadelphia probably had its machinery in place and operating in a minimum of time. With power coming initially from hand labor (none of the streams entering the Delaware River at Philadelphia had the current flow necessary for water power), he certainly developed a steam engine of his own manufacture to move the machinery. With his shop operating, he could fabricate the stationary steam engines (constructed generally on the Boulton and Watt model) that excited the attention of Benjamin Latrobe and others on their sojourns in Philadelphia.

Large succeeded, not only in building his factory and steam engines from models carried in his head, but also in overcoming an even more difficult obstacle: training all the men he hired, converting them from unskilled laborers and aspiring apprentices into talented and able journeymen. Much depended on his knowledge of British technology, his talent as a teacher, and his judgment of men.

He did not err in his selection of Charles Reeder as apprentice. Little can be attributed to Reeder's upbringing. He was born April 18, 1787, in Bucks County, Pennsylvania, to Merrick and Elizabeth Reeder, who saw practicality as an expedient and apprenticed Charles at an early age to the trade of millwright and carpenter. He married Elizabeth Clark and moved to Philadelphia, where he met Large and became an apprentice engine builder in the latter's foundry on Front Street off Germantown Road. During his stay in Philadelphia, he lived in a house furnished by Large near the foundry (apprentices were often provided quarters by their employers). By age twenty-six, he had mastered his trade and so impressed his employer that in 1812–13 Large sent him to Baltimore to supervise the installation of the engine built by Large in the steamer *Chesapeake*, which was being built in Baltimore by William Flanigan for the Union Line. Simultaneously, Large was engaged in building an identical engine for *Delaware*, under construction in the J. and F. Brice ship-building yards in Philadelphia, also for the Union Line. As parts for the two engines were completed, those for *Chesapeake* were loaded aboard Union Line sailing packets for Baltimore via the Delaware River, French-town, and the upper Bay. Reeder's job was to receive the parts and assemble them in *Chesapeake*, with the aid of fledgling helpers he could recruit around the docks. His task demanded much of him, and Large often took his own life in his hands, as a British subject, to traverse the upper Bay through the British blockade to visit Reeder and confirm the state of engine installation in *Chesapeake* and his estimate of Reeder as a master engine builder.

The success of *Chesapeake* and the performance of its engine (it steamed without repairs for an extended period) rekindled the fire of ambition in Reeder. With no other engine builders in Baltimore, he wanted to seize the opportunity to meet the expected demand for steam engines certain to follow the pioneer *Chesapeake*. He relished the thought of building the first engine-building yard in the city. With these thoughts, he moved his family to Baltimore and made his plans for the future.

But the sudden glare of war brought his plans to an abrupt halt. The fears of the citizens of Baltimore that their city would become a target of direct attack by the British naval forces in the Chesapeake seemed on the verge of fulfillment. The advance of the British under Vice-Admiral Sir Alexander Cochrane in August 1814 up the Patuxent River in spite of Commodore Joshua Barney's valiant attempt with his barge fleet to hold them back; the landing of British troops under Major General Robert Ross at Benedict and their advance on Washington; the burning of the White House, the Capitol, and other buildings in the nation's capital; and the re-forming of the British squadron after the fall of Washington and the squadron's move up the Bay to a position off the Patapsco's mouth around the end of August aroused the consternation and trepidation of the people of Baltimore. But their fears were countered by a stubborn determination to defend their city against British attack. Calls went out for enlistment in the local militia, a hastily gathered force of "citizen soldiers." Baltimore armed itself to fend off the British by its own unconscripted citizens (in opposition to conscripted soldiers and sailors of the British), men who would temporarily forsake the farm and the forge to place themselves in the path of the invaders.

Charles Reeder joined Captain Benjamin C. Howard's company of the Fifth Regiment and found himself on September 12, 1814, in the thick of battle with the British landing force at North Point on the eastern approaches to Baltimore. At 1 P.M. on that day of engagement, 250 men of the Fifth Regiment under orders moved forward. Not sure of the position of these American "volunteers," Rear Admiral George Cockburn, commander of the British squadron, and General Robert Ross set out personally to reconnoiter in a wooded area. A young sharpshooter among the American militia altered the land conquest plan of the British. A single shot killed General Ross, the ravager of the city of Washington. The land offensive of the British against Baltimore lost momentum. And the failure of the Royal Navy's bombardment of Fort McHenry brought an end to the attack on Baltimore.

Noteworthy is the fact that in the front lines of the unit at North Point (including a company of sharpshooters and Captain Howard's Company of Mechanical Volunteers) stood Charles Reeder, who personally witnessed the end of General Ross. Noteworthy also is the fact that standing in reserve in case the Fifth Regiment might waver was the Sixth Regiment, commanded by Lieutenant-Colonel William McDonald, progenitor of the steamboat *Chesapeake*. And noteworthy, finally, was the presence of that steamboat, which was commanded by Captain Edward Trippe, in a line of blockade vessels (some deliberately sunk) off Fells Point to prevent any British foray into that area or into the city itself. There she stood, the letters *Chesapeake: Union Line* on her paddle-boxes, flaunting her defiance of the British. Because a steamboat was still a novelty to the British (and its technology particularly a thing of mystery to the Royal Navy), the presence of *Chesapeake* under their very noses undoubtedly stirred up both curiosity and jealousy.

With hostilities at an end, Reeder returned swiftly to his ambitious venture: to establish the first steamboat engine factory in Baltimore. By

1815, he had a small foundry and steam engine plant in operation on Honey Alley under the shadow of Federal Hill. Almost incredible is the fact that he was able to complete the building of two steamboat engines —one for *Experiment*, Baltimore's second steamboat, another for *Philadelphia*, the city's fourth—in one year (1816). What he had accomplished within two years spanned what Daniel Large had been forced to produce when he built his foundry and steam engine factory in Philadelphia. Literally, Reeder had to start from scratch—just as Large had done—in fabricating the machine tools, building the equipment, and training his work force from apprentice to laborers. The completion of two steam engines, with their boilers, for steamboats within so short a time and while the plant itself was under construction marked the appearance of a man of considerable skill and energy in the developing industry of Baltimore.

A year later, Reeder had completed the engine for *Norfolk*, the first steamboat permanently to grace that harbor in Virginia. In 1818 came the engine for *United States*, and in 1822, that for *Constitution*, both Union Line boats—Baltimore's sixth and eighth, respectively. (See Appendix B for a listing of representative steamboats mentioned in this chapter, with their specifications and other data.) All of these engines, transported across the harbor, were installed in their vessels by William, Andrew, and Benjamin Flanigan and James Beacham, now associated as partners at a yard in the area where *Chesapeake* came to life in 1813. Each of these steamers, boldly displaying its name on its paddle-boxes, bore on its upper deck the double A-frame characterizing the crosshead engine, variously called steeple, square, gallows, or guillotine engine (so called from the up-and-down action of the athwartships bar carrying the connecting rod attached on either side to the paddle wheels; see Appendix A).

Competition to Reeder arrived almost immediately. Less than a year after the triumphant completion of his foundry near Federal Hill, a rival plant emerged in rented land almost at his doorstep. The firm of Watchman & Bratt, foundrymen and engine builders, began operations in 1816.

Both were Englishmen. John Watchman (born in 1787, the year Reeder was born) hailed from Newcastle-on-Tyne, and, like his partner John Bratt (born in 1790), confused his American listeners with a Welsh accent. Both brought with them the knowledge and skills of their British training in machine construction and steam engine building. By 1822, the business had expanded to the extent that they leased land in perpetuity, in several segments under Federal Hill with access to the harbor, and elaborated the new facility with machinery capable of very heavy construction. The new plant, larger than Reeder's and employing some 250 men (in contrast to Reeder's 200), challenged Reeder on his own turf.

In addition to other massive projects, Watchman & Bratt turned out two Bay steamboats quickly: *Virginia*, to serve the Baltimore–Norfolk route, in 1817; and *Maryland*, to run between Annapolis and the Eastern Shore, in 1819. William Flanigan and his associates built both boats, forming (with *Norfolk, United States*, and *Constitution*) a creditable flotilla in the wake of *Chesapeake*.

Like the engines built by Reeder, the early engines built by Watchman & Bratt were crosshead engines. Unlike *Chesapeake* and *Delaware*, these engines did not require cogwheels to regulate the paddle wheels' rotation. Nor were flywheels, featured in *North River Steamboat (Clermont)*, necessary, since engine experimenters had found that the motion of the paddle wheels themselves in most instances carried the engine past dead center when the steam valves were closed. In fact, constant innovation, experimentation, and the accumulation of empirical data characterized the development of steamboat engines. Remarkably, few of these developments appeared in patents. Most of the changes occurred as a result of rough-and-ready, trial-and-error procedures by practical mechanics.

These early engines were crude but they were massive. The strength of their parts, in spite of major problems from friction, poor vegetable or animal lubrication, and ill-fitting joints, allowed them to function for years.

From the start, the engines of steamboats on the Bay were the *condensing* type, hence low pressure, as distinguished from high-pressure *non-condensing* type engines in which exhaust steam was vented to the atmosphere. The briny waters of the Chesapeake and its tributaries (an estuarine system) dictated the choice. Steam, discharged from the cylinder after it had done its work of pushing the piston, entered the condenser, a cast-iron container half the size of the vertical cast-iron cylinder and located beneath it. There, jets of cold water pumped from the Bay condensed the steam to water, and this condensate became the source of water to replenish the boiler. The water from condensate contained only the salt content introduced by the jets and was certainly far less briny than the water of the Bay itself, if Bay water had been used directly for feed water. The use of condensers and condensate as boiler feed water thus saved engineers the pain of endlessly scraping the boilers and re-

Baltimore Harbor from Federal Hill, from a sketch of 1841. The Reeder factory is at extreme left; that of Watchman & Bratt is to the right. Bowley's Wharf is at the upper corner of the basin or inner harbor. Jones Falls appears behind the steamer to the right of center. Market Place is beside it on the left. Fells Point occupies the cluster of buildings on the right.

lated piping, whenever time could be spared for the task, to remove the salt scales. It also reduced the chance of boiler explosion from inattention to scale accumulation.

Importantly, the condenser served another purpose. The process of condensation in a container, by virtue of the fact that water occupies less space than steam, produces a vacuum. Condensing engines increased their power using the vacuum on one side of the piston to pull while the steam on the other side pushed. A so-called air pump on one stroke withdrew the steam and condensate from the condenser to preserve the vacuum and then on the opposite stroke pumped condensate to the hot well or tank for feeding water to the boiler. The coordinated machinery, rugged as it was, worked remarkably well on the Chesapeake. (See Appendix A for a detailed description and diagram of the crosshead engine.)

On the Mississippi and other western rivers, practice favored the use of high-pressure, or noncondensing engines. Two reasons prevailed: First, the water of the rivers, though holding mud in suspension, was not saline. Second, the current of the rivers required high-powered engines to push against the flow. Sediment held in suspension in the water drawn from the river tended to settle, and the use of auxiliary pumps called "doctors" linked to mud drums provided the means of getting water in a state to replenish the boilers (provided, of course, that the engineers were attentive enough). Boilers in these engines operated at a pressure of around 150 pounds per square inch, sometimes higher, and when explosions occurred, with alarming frequency on the rivers, they destroyed the boat. On the Chesapeake Bay, the boilers ran at 30 to 40 pounds of pressure, capable still of inflicting massive damage if they exploded. Condensers not only helped desalinate the feed water; they also produced a vacuum, as explained above—a highly effective system, well understood by British engine makers from the work of Thomas Newcomen and others before.

On the Bay, because of the exhaust of steam to condensers, engines were quiet, barely whispering with each stroke. On the Mississippi, the steam exhausting to the atmosphere resounded with an explosive sound not unlike that of a locomotive huffing and puffing to pull a long train over a mountain pass. An upstream steamer, pushing against the current, could waken a town miles away.

In other respects, Mississippi steamboat engines and the engines built for steamers on the Chesapeake differed markedly. On the Chesapeake, both side-wheels turned together, propelled from a single source of power, the piston traveling up and down from a single cylinder. On very few boats on the Bay could the paddle wheels operate independently and thus allow maneuverability in docking or swinging around in bends or harbors by the ability of one wheel to "back" while the other went "ahead." A "stick" shaft connected the two paddle wheels. Only a large rudder permitted the control that independent paddle wheels might have provided.

On the Mississippi, early side-wheel boats began with the "stick" shaft, but owners quickly discovered that the single engine mounted in the middle of the main or freight deck (together with the shaft crossing the deck) used up valuable cargo space and that rapid swings in uncharted channels to avoid snags, bars, and floating timber required maneuverability that independently propelled wheels offered.

Side-wheelers, with separately propelled wheels, steamed in company with stern-wheelers. Conjecture on the reason for the apparent dominance of the latter on western waters has often focused on early attempts to circumvent the monopoly claimed by Robert Fulton for his self-proclaimed invention of the side paddle wheel. This argument is weakened in light of the fact that *New Orleans*, built in 1811 by Nicholas Roosevelt (the actual inventor of the side paddle wheel) and the first steamboat to navigate the Father of Waters, carried a stern wheel for propulsion. Whatever the reason, stern-wheelers flourished from the very beginning of steamboat manufacture on the Monongahela and other western rivers.

In spite of the enormous logistical problems of building foundries and steam engine plants near Pittsburgh and down the Ohio, these early iron foundrymen and engine builders managed to bring the basic materials over the mountains from the East, use the raw materials in plentiful supply in their own regions, and build the shops sorely needed in the Midwest. While the first boats were stern-wheelers, production of side-wheelers picked up momentum. All carried independently operated paddle wheels. Each paddle wheel was propelled by a long-stroke horizontal engine. Boilers on each side accompanied each engine, and the tall, thin, black smokestacks—twin, athwartships, often ornamented with a gilded emblem suspended between them—became the hallmark of steamers on the Mississippi. In western waters, steamboatmen referring to the stacks and boilers and other equipment, as well as the navigation of the boat, used the term "larboard" for "port" (as used in the East), meaning the left side of the boat; the term "starboard" for the right side persisted in both areas.

With the introduction of the balanced rudder, stern-wheelers on western waters became more maneuverable and attractive to owners. These huge rudders, placed at the back of the hull but forward of the stern-wheel, projected under the wheel itself, but a substantial section reached forward of the steering post and extended under the stern; thus, when turned, these massive rudders offered resistance to the water both fore and aft of the rudder post and succeeded in furnishing acceptable steering control. With their ability to back off bars and sidle up to a bank or levee and to provide uncluttered deck space for enormous cargoes, the stern-wheelers offered advantages over side-wheelers. The latter had the unfortunate propensity of drawing mud under the boat when it attempted to back off from an offending bar, of chewing up a raft and its occupants if they ventured too near its overhang, or of grounding the inboard wheel on a bank when the steamer lay overnight and the current swung it parallel to shore. On encounters with the shoreline, logs, rafts, and human occupants, the side-wheel simply ground its way into the offending material, rearing up the side where the collision took place and sending a shudder through the boat and a resounding crash through the air. That owners of Mississippi steamboats considered them expendable, to last no more than four or five years (some did not last that long), seems understandable.

The construction of Mississippi River steamboats contributed to their short lives. Extreme lengthening to provide for enormous cotton (or other) cargo-carrying capacity, hull flattening to reduce draft, and the use of light framing and scantling (sometimes decking was only one-quarter inch to one-half inch thick) led to early hogging, requiring extensive bracing, and rapid deterioration.

Those rattling vessels, in spite of their poor hull construction and dangerously crude engines, captured the imagination of romantic America. With their white gingerbread superstructure, gilded saloons, glassed-in top-deck cabins called "the Texas," pilothouses where braided officers strutted about, and cotton bales stacked to the overhead, they ran the rivers of the West like misshapen swans and touched the landings along the way to the shouts of crowds and the music of bands and minstrels. A certain mystique about these boats threaded through the fabric of American culture and history.

Their propensity to wear out could be attributed, in part, to their engines. Horizontal engines, in which the piston must travel through the length of an extended cylinder, required not only a ready means of replacing packing but also lubricants able to stand up well under intense heat and high pressure and against uneven friction applied to the lower surface of the piston, where gravity forced it to bear its weight against the bottom of the cylinder. Neither of these requirements was met. Engines simply wore out. And so did the boats.

The horizontal engine met only disdain among the first engine builders in the East. Crosshead engines, as built by Charles Reeder and Watchman & Bratt, used a vertical piston moving in a vertical cylinder, thereby eliminating or substantially reducing the friction of the piston in the cylinder. Rugged, though crude, these early low-pressure crosshead engines lasted for many years.

However, crosshead engines had their faults. The dual A-frames carrying the tracks guiding the crossbar in its vertical motion added little to the appearance of the boat and, more importantly, often went out of alignment. The unequal action of waves on opposite sides of the boat introduced forces causing, over the years, the two crankshafts to lose the synchrony required of their performance. Longer-stroke crosshead engines, deemed more efficient, meant added separation between port and starboard crankshafts and A-frames, space not available in boats of the period. The paddle wheel shaft between port and starboard cranks and crankshafts went by necessity directly beneath the cylinder, thereby restricting any further increase in cylinder size and, accordingly, in the length of the piston stroke. Larger and more powerful engines could thus not be built on the crosshead model. All of these factors led to doubts about installation of crosshead engines in steamboats, even though many of the original engines continued to operate from the day they were built in the 1820s until after the Civil War. However, in the late 1820s and 1830s, over the inland waters of the Eastern Seaboard, from the Hudson River and Long Island Sound to the Delaware and the Chesapeake, the move toward the development and use of the vertical (or walking) beam engines became inevitable.

The steamboat engine developed by invention and improvisation. Machinists tinkered with the moving parts and perfected them, most often without recognition for their skill and ingenuity. News of unpatented changes spread around the waterfront. Gaskets and packing around piston rings at first were made of paper or canvas or even rope, but new materials created from iron filings treated with acid became effective molded substitutes applied to metal rings and served as adhesive applied to various joints. Single stem valves in earlier engines, difficult to fabricate to the close-fitting clearances required to hold steam, were replaced by double valves, which were able to withstand the pressure and guide the valve action more effectively. In 1828, Robert Livingston Stevens, the talented son of John, introduced the double-poppet valve. This consisted of two disc valves (connected by a valve spindle) of unequal size, thereby permitting steam pressure itself to assist in the working of the valve. Applied both to steam input and to exhaust output, the double poppet system made the hand-gear operation of the engine much easier. In addition, the younger Stevens and Frederick E. Sickels patented versions of the "cut-off" valve, designed to stop the entry of steam into the cylinder before the piston completed its stroke, thereby utilizing the expansion of the steam without wasting it. Other inventions and improvisations accompanied the emergence of the vertical beam, or walking beam, engine in the mid-1800s.

Who actually invented the walking beam engine remained in doubt. One Colonel Aaron Ogden (1756–1834), quartermaster under Lafayette, in conjunction with Daniel Dod (1758–1823), engine builder, constructed an engine for *Sea Horse*, which was designed for ferry service between Elizabeth, New Jersey, and New York. The engine was reputed to be the first of the walking beam type; Dod sometimes is credited with its invention. Robert Stevens had one built around 1822, and he too is credited with its invention. By the 1820s and early 1830s, the engines were commonplace. On the Chesapeake, their teetering beam above the cabin space became a virtual hallmark.

Centrally placed in the vessel, with its footing on the keel and adjacent framing, the vertical beam engine reared as much as three stories high to the great walking beam in the open air above the top deck. This diamond-shaped, cast-iron monster, mounted vertically and fore-and-aft in huge supporting frames, weighed (on average) about fifteen tons. It pivoted—or teetered like a seesaw—from these supports. The forward end carried the piston rod, driven up and down by the piston in the cylinder. The after end drove a huge crank around the paddle wheel shaft, in itself a solid iron piece one foot or more in diameter running across the entire vessel and divided only at the middle where the crank rotated it. In the engine room rose the cylinder, taller than the stroke of the piston moving vertically within it (as much as ten or more feet), with the condenser, half the length, mounted underneath. The air pump and other auxiliary machinery functioned by the vertical pull of rods reaching to the walking beam far above.

Around the paddle wheel shaft, where the huge crank propelled it, were eccentric plates whose off-center rotation produced fore-and-aft motion in horizontal eccentric rods leading to the steam chest mounted vertically in front of the cylinder. These eccentric rods, through a system of "toes and wipers," caused the valves to open and close, admitting steam from the boiler to the cylinder, or releasing steam when it had performed its work to the condenser beneath the cylinder. All cylinders and steam chests were dual in function, providing power on both the up and the down stroke of the piston. In the middle of the control room, a lever called the "start bar" could be used to control the valves manually, in starting up the engine from stop or in maneuvering where bells from the pilothouse were frequent. When fully under way on a long reach, the engineer "dropped the hooks," in effect connecting the eccentric rods to the "toes and wipers" for automatic operation.

Boilers—often there were several to supply steam to these mammoth engines—were the *fire tube* type. Most early boilers were formed from copper plate. Heat (hot gases) from the grates underneath traveled through coiled tubes inside the boiler filled with water and hot steam, was recirculated through flues and eventually exited through the smoke stack. Boilers on Bay steamers were approximately ten to twenty feet, both in length and in breadth, depending on the tonnage of the boat and the capacity of its engine. (See Appendix A for a detailed description and diagram of the vertical beam engine.)

The walking beam engine's overpowering massiveness in motion staggered the uninitiated observer. Its sheer weight—mounted vertically— invited the incredulous inquiry: How does the steamboat stay upright? Why doesn't it roll over and sink? Early designers feared the effect of this weight on the metacentric height (the relation of the center of gravity to the center of buoyancy), and took it into account in their planning. Nevertheless, only by careful ballasting and balancing of fuel (wood or coal) and cargo could equilibrium and stability be assured. Yet never in the history of steamboating on the Chesapeake did a paddle wheel steamboat, even in rough weather, simply capsize. Top-heavy these steamboats were not. The vertical, or walking beam, engine powered these boats to the very end of the steamboat era.

Changes in engine construction accompanied developmental changes in steamboat design and construction. From hulls that looked like schooners—even to masts, sails, bowsprits, and tillers—emerged, step-by-step from the shipyards around Baltimore, the steamers of a new generation. Clipper or spoon bows gave way to knifelike stems; hulls became nearly flat-bottomed with high dead-rise under the counter for the long rudder assembly; the main deck extended ten or more feet over each side beyond the hull to encompass the paddle-boxes and greatly increase the cargo space; an upper deck appeared with cabin space and staterooms; a pilothouse, even officers' staterooms aft of it, followed; enclosures guarded cargo forward on the main deck; and the white superstructure dotted with windows became the familiar symbol of steamboats on the Bay.

The yards of Charles Reeder and Watchman & Bratt kept pace with the times. Crosshead engines of their manufacture powered early boats, but these men met the challenge of the shift to vertical beam engines, not only in building them but in improving them at the same time. The habits of a lifetime of practicality and improvisation stood them in good stead.

Reeder's plant, where it stood beneath Federal Hill, remained in the family during its long history. For a brief period, Reeder formed a partnership with William H. Richardson, the foundryman who preceded him in Baltimore but knew little about steam engines; together they operated a small plant at Paca and Camden streets, while Reeder maintained his own factory under Federal Hill. The Reeder plant expanded at various times as business demanded, but it never reached the proportions of the rival next door, Watchman & Bratt. In 1838, fire nearly destroyed the Reeder plant and sent the family into a financial slump from which it had difficulty recovering. But it emerged and advertised itself to the world as the manufacturer of low- and high-pressure steam engines for steamboats and propelling machinery and other steam engine–related machinery: boilers and tanks; iron and brass castings; rolling, grist, and saw mills; pumping engines for waterworks or mines; and hydraulic presses and blowing cylinders.

During the plant's history, the Reeders established many benchmarks. In 1832, for example, they collaborated in the building of the "York," a more practical railroad locomotive than Peter Cooper's "Tom Thumb" and later the "American" and "Antelope" locomotives of the fledgling Baltimore and Ohio Railroad. For the Baltimore Water Company, the Reeders built the machinery to pump water into the reservoir. Other major machinery projects of the company went unheralded.

Most noteworthy were the engines for steamboats (even steamships) they constructed. Most of these engines went in steamers built in Baltimore for Chesapeake service. However, some were built for boats (high pressure, no less!) on the Mississippi and other western waters, for steamers operating out of Gulf ports, and for oceangoing vessels engaged in transatlantic or coastal trade. At full count, Reeder built engines for fifty-seven steam vessels, from tugs and steamboats to oceangoing ships. Of these vessels, Reeder built seven of them from the keel up.

The list of Chesapeake Bay steamers propelled by Reeder engines (or built entirely by Reeder) is extensive. Among the Chesapeake steamers carrying the Reeder trademark and punctuating the history of the steamboat era were the following: *Chesapeake* (1813), *Philadelphia* (1816), *United States* (1816), *Constitution* (1822), *Thomas Jefferson* (1827), *Columbus* (1829), *Georgia* (1830), *Juniata* (1848), *Hugh Jenkins* (1849), *Louisiana* (1854), *George Weems* (1858), *Matilda* (1864), *Theodore Weems* (1872), *Minnie Wheeler* (1881), *Danville* (1882), *Choptank* (1883), *Tockwogh* (1889), *Sassafras* (1892), *Easton* (1896), *Susquehanna* (1898), and *Queen Anne* (1899). (See Appendix B for a list of representative boats with specifications, enrollment, and other data.)

Technology advanced rapidly during the later years. For example, the graceful *Susquehanna* (1898), a vessel of symmetry and style built entirely by Reeder, was propeller-driven by a compound (two-cylinder) engine using high-pressure steam (125 pounds per square inch) from an advanced type of water tube boiler, in which water was turned into nearly super-heated steam as it passed through tubes inside the boiler hot with the gases of combustion. Compound and triple-expansion engines, with the superficial appearance of huge internal-combustion engines (like those in automobiles) and with driving rods rotating the propeller shaft, represented the last inventions fabricated by Reeder. Inclined engines for small paddle wheels—like railroad locomotive engines—used in several later steamers on the Bay (*Talbot* and *Dorchester*, for example) were not within the Reeder repertory.

Of the nearly sixty vessels equipped with Reeder engines or built by the Reeders, forty-one were Chesapeake steamers. The contribution of the Reeders to the maritime life of the Bay was prodigious. Charles Reeder, Jr., son of the founder, died on December 1, 1900. With his death and the turn of the century, the firm dwindled and finally expired. Its passing marked a milestone in the history of steamboating on the Chesapeake.

The accomplishments of the Reeder foundry were matched but never overshadowed by the work of the neighboring rival, Watchman & Bratt. The two created a thriving plant by the harbor basin under Federal Hill on a large site leased in 1822. At the beginning of the enterprise, in 1816, John Watchman had attempted an experimental operation on a small plot in the same vicinity. His first efforts surrounded the building of an engine for the steamboat *Virginia* under construction by William Flanigan and associates in the year that had launched *Chesapeake:* 1813. Later, in 1816, John Bratt joined Watchman as a partner, although the management remained in the hands of Watchman. The difficulties that had confronted Daniel Large and Charles Reeder in building a foundry and engine-building shop from the ground up posed the same challenge to Watchman and Bratt. That they thrived within so short a time testified to the skill and stubborn brawn of these men.

Through the years Watchman & Bratt earned a nationwide reputation. They were able to advertise their work, not only on engines for steamboats, but also on engines for mills of all descriptions, on heavy machinery, and on all sorts of cast iron and brass works. They could say with a note of pride that their establishment was very extensive and supplied with heavy turning lathes, iron planing machines, and tools of every description. Its capacity exceeded that of Charles Reeder.

The successful dredging of Baltimore Harbor in 1827 could be attributed in large measure to the engine and mud-dredging machinery the firm built for that purpose. The first iron vessel built in Baltimore, the *Ironette*, moved through the water by paddle wheels and engine constructed by Watchman & Bratt. And Watchman's interest in steam-powered fire engines led him to become one of the incorporators of the Watchman Fire Company, an outfit formed to protect the environs of Federal Hill from incineration (but equally to hold its own in frequent brawls with rival fire companies).

Above all, in the building of engines for steamboats, Watchman & Bratt achieved an enviable notoriety. During the company's existence, including the period when it was owned exclusively by the senior partner, the firm built engines for a total of approximately thirty-four steamboats, many designed for service as oceangoing coastal ships or as steamboats operating in areas beyond the Chesapeake. Representative of Bay steamers among them were the following: *Virginia* (1817), *Maryland* (1819), *Port Deposit* (1822), *Susquehanna* (the first, 1825), *Fredericksburg* (1827), *Patuxent* (1827), *Rappahannock* (1830), *Medora* (1842), *Planter* (1845), *Powhatan* (1845), and *Mary Washington* (1846). (See Appendix B for representative steamboats with their specifications, enrollment, and other data.)

Beginning in 1824, the firm had called itself the Eagle Works of Watchman & Bratt. The "eagle" part of the name traced its source to the wooden carved eagle taken from the pilothouse of the ill-fated *Eagle*, which challenged the Union Line's attempted monopoly on the Chesapeake in 1815 and blew up in 1824, scalding George Weems and endangering the future of the Weems line.

On February 24, 1841, John Bratt, Sr., withdrew from the partnership, leaving his sons (John, Jr., William, and Samuel) in the employ of the company. Even after his withdrawal, the senior Bratt seemed to play a hand in the operation of the firm. The joint name of the partnership persisted for some time. And John Bratt's independent enterprise in the steamboat world, particularly with respect to the extraordinary events surrounding the *Mary Washington* (discussed later in this chapter), often tied him to the original organization.

Watchman suffered through a dramatic and tragic disaster on April 14, 1842, an event that punctuated steamboat history on the Chesapeake. On that day, the steamer *Medora*, built in the Brown & Collyer shipyard adjoining the Watchman & Bratt plant and carrying the engine and boiler designed and built by Watchman, prepared to move from the wharf of the engine builder for her first trial run. *Medora*, the first steamboat built for the fledgling Baltimore Steam Packet Company (nicknamed the Old Bay Line), carried the pride and aspirations of the founders of the company. Principal among those who incorporated it in December 1839 were Colonel (General) William McDonald and his son Samuel (the managers of the Union Line and those who embarked on the building of *Chesapeake*), John S. McKim (copper manufacturer and owner of the famous Baltimore clipper *Ann McKim*), and Andrew F. Henderson (codirector of the Union Line and participant in the financing of *Chesapeake*). The last-named official on this day of April 14, 1842, Henderson was also the president of the line proudly displaying *Medora* on her first trial run.

Most of the steamers (*Powhatan, South Carolina, Georgia, Jewess,* and *Alabama*) acquired by the Baltimore Steam Packet Line as its initial fleet suffered from service and, in some instances, from approaching senility. Consequently, the directors placed their hopes and ambitions in the first vessel they commissioned to be built for the Old Bay Line. *Medora*'s white-sided sleekness, with a length of 130 feet, beam of 24 feet, and depth of hold of 8 feet, impressed her designers and builders.

For the occasion of her trial run, arranged to test machinery and boiler, the company invited numerous dignitaries and visitors aboard. A large number of carpenters from Brown & Collyer, as well as boilermakers and engine mechanics from Watchman's company, mingled with the dignitaries to observe. Approximately one hundred people surged about the decks and crowded in the engine room. On the dock, another one hundred or so stood by to watch, a colorful crowd in a holiday mood. Youngsters gaped from the slopes of Federal Hill.

At 3:00 P.M., *Medora* drew in the gangplank and signaled her departure. The walking beam began to rock. Water frothed under her paddle wheels as she began to back from the wharf. The paddle wheels made two revolutions and started on a third.

Suddenly, a violent explosion rent the air. The huge iron boiler burst through the upper deck and rose thirty feet in the air, then rolled and fell into the wreckage of the forward part of the vessel. The smokestack flew upward and dropped in the debris with a crash. Scalding steam enveloped the boat. Heavy wooden framing splintered; decking shattered in tiny fragments. And the boat abruptly sank in thirty feet of water.

People on board died when hit by fragments of the boiler or decking. Some were blown high in the air and fell on shore, in the water, or on boats nearby. Severed limbs flew through the air. Many of the visitors were scalded beyond recognition. Those who inhaled the scalding steam had little chance of survival. A few of the injured jumped overboard and drowned.

Confusion prevailed. People on shore ran about, not knowing what to do. Some attempted to help the wounded and dying. When a count could be made, twenty-six had lost their lives; some thirty-eight had suffered major injuries, some of whom died within weeks. The explosion of the *Medora* marked the greatest disaster in steamboat history on the Bay; even annals of maritime disasters to the end of the twentieth century have failed to minimize it.

For days after the explosion, cannon boomed at intervals, a procedure believed to cause submerged corpses to rise to the surface. Flags flew at half-mast throughout the city.

Among those who lost their lives were Andrew F. Henderson, president of the Baltimore Steam Packet Company and contributor to the birth of *Chesapeake;* John C. Moale, general agent of the company, along with William, one of his two sons; William Lewis, clerk of the steamer *Rappahannock*; and a host of others, including guests of the company and apprentices and workmen from both the Watchman & Bratt and the Brown & Collyer plants. Captain Sutton was standing over the boiler when it exploded. He suffered head injuries, and many doubted that he would recover. But the doughty skipper survived and later commanded many Old Bay Line steamers on the Baltimore–Norfolk route.

What caused the boiler to explode became a matter of urgent conjecture. An inquest held three days after the disaster produced a congeries of opinion. Watchman believed that some unspecified individual or individuals had weighted down the safety valve and that too many machinists had crowded the engine room so that the boiler pressure gauge could not be seen. The engineer of the *Constitution* who came aboard *Medora* as a guest stated that he had finally squeezed through the crowd and seen the gauge; the pressure reading was so high that he had barely time to reach the stern of the vessel before the explosion.

Some months later, Benjamin H. Latrobe, the somewhat eccentric but brilliant architect, engineer, and manipulator of William McDonald and Son in the choice of engine builder for *Chesapeake*, reported his theories about the cause of the explosion to the Franklin Institute in Philadelphia. He believed that not only was the boiler too large for the expected pressure but also that the plate used in its construction was too thin. He criticized the thickness for boiler plate as some magic dimension automatically accepted by boilermakers, certainly inadequate, in his opinion, to the massive diameter and pressure of *Medora*'s boiler and inadequate, also, at the connections and joints.

The battered hulk of *Medora* was raised from the bottom on May 9, 1842. To the dismay and utter embarrassment and chagrin of Watchman, the Old Bay Line awarded a contract to a competitor to fabricate a boiler (or boilers) of a different design and to reinstall the engine (fortunately, the latter sustained little damage). The competitor was none other than Charles Reeder.

Rebuilt, the steamer emerged from the yard with a new name, *Herald*, which she wore through many years of service on the Bay. After the Civil War, she left the Chesapeake and worked her final years (until 1885) as a tug in New York Harbor. In spite of her catastrophic birth, she enjoyed a long and useful life.

Like many shipbuilders in the early decades of the steamboat era on the Chesapeake, John Watchman and John Bratt invested in steamboats —most often, steamboats for which they had built the engine. In many instances, taking shares in a particular steamboat or the company that owned it served as part payment for the bills incurred in the building of the engine. A certain secrecy often attended these acquisitions of steamboat interests, and the public disclosure of these interests at some later time occasionally led to verbal explosions and accusations of backstabbing when the interests collided.

Such was the experience of John Watchman and John Bratt in their dealings with the Baltimore and Rappahannock Steam Packet Line in 1829. The line had been created with the avowed purpose of expelling the Weems line from the Rappahannock River. Watchman & Bratt built the engines for both the *Rappahannock* of the Baltimore and Rappahannock Steam Packet Line and the *Patuxent* of the Weems line. Furthermore, Watchman & Bratt held one-sixth of the shares in *Rappahannock*. *Patuxent*, under George Weems, had pioneered steamboat service on the Rappahannock in July 1828, and Weems held to the view that the risk he took in venturing on the river gave him some priority. Jealousy among the planters around the Virginia river and greed of merchants in Fredericksburg and Baltimore impelled them in January 1829 to form the aggressive rival company, the Baltimore and Rappahannock Steam Packet Company. Nearly two hundred stockholders subscribed. To the astonishment and anger of Weems, the list of stockholders when published contained the names of John Watchman and John Bratt, builders of the engines in both rival steamboats. The vicious competition between the rivals for the meager trade on the Rappahannock approached open warfare. In May 1830, Weems, profoundly discouraged by the rate cutting and slashing attacks of his opponent, withdrew *Patuxent* from the Rappahannock. He smoldered with anger and frustration.

But he was not content to surrender so easily, and from 1832 through the season of 1834, he tried again with *Patuxent* on the Rappahannock. Once again the flames of trade warfare flared between the rivals, fanned by the Baltimore and Virginia owners of *Rappahannock*. Once again, Weems withdrew, deeply hurt by those who, in his view, had stabbed him in the back. These included, most particularly, John Watchman and John Bratt.

The tempest over trade on the Rappahannock (a virtual monopoly) did not end with the retreat of *Patuxent*. It revived in 1845 when the Baltimore and Rappahannock Steam Packet Company faced a profound financial crisis created by its mercurial president, James Harwood of Fair Haven, Maryland. The company faced bankruptcy, at a time when its fleet of two boats disintegrated. *Rappahannock* limped about in dire need of boiler and engine repairs. An even older vessel, *Fredericksburg*, acquired to relieve *Rappahannock*, sank at her moorings. Impetuously, the directors, led by Harwood, voted to build a new steamboat from the keel up as a means of reviving the company. Her name would be the *Mary Washington* and her engine would be built by John Watchman. The directors of the steamboat company failed to take into account a patently obvious fact: the company was stone broke. John Bratt, a director, was one of a special committee appointed to recommend the construction of the new boat.

When launched, *Mary Washington*, as well as her parent company, stood beneath the shadow of court action and bankruptcy. By order of the court, *Mary Washington* was placed on the block. Astonishingly, she was bought on February 3, 1847, for only twenty-six thousand dollars by a suddenly created new corporation, the Maryland and Virginia Steam Packet Company. Among its stockholders were John A. Robb, builder of the steamer—and none other than John Bratt. The shadowy maneuvering behind the scenes to acquire a boat for half its price—when the new company finally proclaimed itself—at first baffled, then disgusted many members of the steamboat circle around Baltimore.

Mary Washington and the Maryland and Virginia Steam Packet Company fared badly. Other steamboats ventured on the Rappahannock and offered stiff competition; depletion of financial resources, general mismanagement, and incipient bankruptcy forced the steamer and its parent company to surrender; and *Mary Washington*, up for sale, ended up in the hands of the Weems line after all. The Weems family triumphed. *Mary Washington* served through the Civil War and became the stage for the denouement of the drama of the "French lady spy" that riveted attention on both sides of the lines during the early days of the conflict (see Chapter 4).

John Watchman retired in 1846 in the heat of the battle over *Mary Washington*. He died in 1865. The Watchman plant, sold in 1846 to Murray and Hazlehurst, continued operations until 1860, when a new company, Hazlehurst and Wiegand, bought it and produced engines for vessels, many oceangoing and experimental, until the turn of the century.

John Bratt died in 1850. His withdrawal in 1841 from the partnership with Watchman has been attributed to disagreement between the two over the insecurity of the investments in the Rappahannock enterprise. Certainly Bratt registered no repugnance in playing both sides against the middle, as long as some advantage could be gained. His advantage on the Rappahannock ventures was short-lived, however. George Weems had little reason to forgive him. Not surprisingly, in 1849, when *Patuxent*'s engine, built by Watchman & Bratt in 1826, needed replacement, the Weems line conspicuously turned to Charles Reeder & Sons to build the new one.

As the nineteenth century matured, the business of building steamboats (with their engines) shifted from the banks of Baltimore Harbor to Sparrows Point (Maryland Steel Company) at the mouth of the Patapsco and then, more and more, to the shores of the Delaware, the so-called Clyde of America. Shipyards like Pusey & Jones, Neafie & Levy, and Harlan & Hollingsworth on the Delaware took the place of Skinner, Woodall, and Brown & Collyer in Baltimore. But the place of Charles Reeder and Watchman & Bratt in the record of the steamboat era on the Chesapeake is a firm and historic one. They, like Daniel Large, overcame almost impossible barriers to create the means of building the machinery to propel the first generation of steamboats, even as crude as they were, on the waters of the Chesapeake.

3

GHOSTS REVISITED

The ghosts of sunken ships haunt the bottom of the Chesapeake. During the long history of the navigation of the Bay, from the eighteenth century to the present, perhaps as many as two thousand vessels sank as the result of disasters from weather, fire, collision, grounding, scuttling, or naval engagement. Most of the hulls have disappeared in the muck, but a number remain in various states of decay, tantalizing divers, archaeologists, and those historians sensitive to their touch.

In his assessment of the Chesapeake Bay in 1811, John Stevens wrote that "this extensive sea was, in fact, the far greater part merely shoals . . . the ebb and flow occasioned little current, [and] the wind could never produce such a swell as to prove dangerous to steam navigation" (see Chapter 1). How wrong he was! He never witnessed the savagery of the Bay in a storm, the mountainous seas, the dangerous currents, and the high winds. Steamers disintegrated or were driven onto the shoals.

Of the 2,000 or more recorded disasters, perhaps as many as 150 are those of steamboats once regularly plying the waters of the Bay. A few of the wrecks are still distinguishable as sites on the bottom. Their locations are often known by local watermen; legends persist about their fate.

The Bay near the mouth of the Potomac River has earned a reputation as the graveyard of vessels plying those waters. The seas could be placid on a calm day. But a reach of thirty miles from Pocomoke Sound across the Bay to the mouth of the Potomac—the widest part of the Chesapeake—allowed the open seas to build up in high winds to a vicious chop. Coupled with eccentric currents and a tidal flow at this juncture, wind-driven seas far too often spelled disaster. Fogs in the vicinity frequently blanketed the busy shipping lanes between Baltimore and Norfolk. Furthermore, the lower reaches of the Potomac and the neighboring waters of the open Bay seemed to be a breeding ground for catastrophe of all sorts: burnings, explosions, groundings, and collisions. The setting brewed disaster with little warning.

Probably as many as forty wrecks litter the bottom of the Bay off the mouth of the Potomac. Point Lookout (north) and Smith Point (south), though widely separated by the width of the mouth, bore witness to tragedies as they unfolded before them.

Among the wrecks near the Potomac's mouth were those of several steamboats, their locations generally known. Sometimes fishermen snagged the wreckage and even brought artifacts to the surface, but the wrecks remained in depths of water ranging from sixty to seventy feet. Among the watermen and the more superstitious of the residents of southern Maryland, the passing along of these legends through the years has kept alive their locations and tragic endings.

Three of these wrecks held a particular fascination, not entirely for their disastrous finales, but for the aura surrounding their endings. The three catastrophes nearly spanned the steamboat era, and each symbolized a segment of it.

Steamboat *City of Annapolis,* as she might have appeared at the time of her sinking. Drawn from contemporary advertising and photographs.

The most recent catastrophe of the three occurred on February 24, 1927, when the *City of Richmond* rammed and sank her sister ship, the *City of Annapolis,* off Smith Point in a fog.

Identical twins, the steamers, owned by the Chesapeake Steamship Company and operated in 1927 between Richmond, York River landings, and Baltimore, were born in 1913 at the Bethlehem Steel Company in Baltimore. Handsome, steel-hulled, 262-foot vessels, with triple expansion engines capable of driving each boat at better than fourteen miles per hour, they resembled high-sided oceangoing passenger ships, sleek in glistening white paint from waterline to hurricane deck.

The Chesapeake Line gloated with pride in these twin steamers built on the model of the *City of Baltimore*, launched two years before. In its rivalry with the Old Bay Line (the Baltimore Steam Packet Company), the Chesapeake Line paraded its splendid steamers as worthy competitors. Their sumptuousness shone in glittering dining rooms and balconied saloons with grand stairways and frescoed ceilings.

The press had lauded the steamers' actions in major accidents on the Bay when they stood by to take passengers from doomed vessels. In 1915, the *City of Richmond*, along with the *City of Baltimore*, rescued 76 passengers and 34 crewmen from the burning *Maryland* at the mouth of the Magothy River. In the same year, the *City of Annapolis* with the *City of Baltimore* took aboard 83 persons from the *Tivoli* on fire off Bloody Point. When *Three Rivers* burned off Cove Point on July 5, 1924, and 10 persons lost their lives, including 5 of 54 members of the Evening *Sun* Newsboys' Band returning from the annual Chesapeake Bay workboat races, the *City of Annapolis* and the *City of Baltimore* assisted in the rescue and searched for survivors. And when the steamer *Virginia* burned to the water's edge off the mouth of the Potomac in May 1919, most of the 219 persons on board, many bound for Newport News to welcome loved ones returning from service in World War I, were saved in a harrowing rescue by the lifeboats of the *City of Annapolis*.

Every other night, the twins passed each other near the Potomac mouth, one going south, the other north. They exchanged whistle salutes, plaintive calls in the dark of the night. Each stayed to the designated side of the channel, northbound to the left of the southbound. Each expected to see the running lights of the other at the same time and place. The *City of Annapolis* and the *City of Richmond* shuttled back and forth through the years on their voyages through the length of the Bay, each voyage an adventure for the passengers aboard.

A bank of fog shrouded the mouth of the Potomac in the early morning hours of Thursday, February 24, 1927. *City of Annapolis*, northbound off Smith Point, groped her way into the gathering post-midnight mist. Captain George C. Claytor, in the pilothouse, heard fog signals from various directions in the deceptive grayness that surrounded him. He ordered fog signals sounded on the whistle (a prolonged blast every two minutes) and rang the annunciator to the engine room from full to half-speed ahead.

71

A whistle sounded close aboard, and out of the mist ahead loomed a tramp steamer headed south, well out of the established shipping lane. At Captain Claytor's order, the quartermaster threw the wheel hard over, and *City of Annapolis* spun on her heel and headed away from the path of the tramp and eastward athwart the shipping lanes north and south. The captain continued the fog signals and speed, with the objective of swinging his ship back on her northward course as soon as the tramp steamer cleared his way. He could hear whistles of other vessels in the fog but could not make out their distance or course. Somewhere among them, he knew, was the *City of Richmond*, southward bound.

Aboard the *City of Richmond*, Captain Howard C. Willing was restless. Unable to sleep, he left his stateroom and entered the wheelhouse just before midnight. Peering through the windows of the pilothouse, he saw ahead the gray eminence of the fog bank blanketing the Bay off Smith Point. As the vessel entered the fog, he immediately ordered signals sounded and blew the whistle once or twice himself. The engine room annunciator read "full speed ahead" (about fourteen miles per hour). The captain did not order it changed. The pilothouse clock read 12:25 A.M.

On the bow of *City of Richmond*, the lookoutman, Charles Walter of Cumberland, heard the whistle signal of *City of Annapolis* in an ill-defined area ahead and shouted his report to the wheelhouse. The wheelhouse acknowledged with a tap on the bell.

Suddenly, the long white shape of *City of Annapolis* appeared like an apparition in the mist—straight across the bow of *City of Richmond*. Captain Willing sprang for the annunciator and rang for "full astern."

In the engine room, an order from "full ahead" to "full astern" could only be interpreted as an emergency call, and Frederick G. Greenfield, second assistant engineer, leaped at the throttles.

"When he threw the indicator over all the way," he said later, "I gave them all that we had, for it means business when they do that."

The order to go astern was received in the engine room by Greenfield at 12:27. At 12:28 he felt his vessel strike. After a brief delay, he received orders to set the engine for "slow ahead."

Aboard the *City of Annapolis*, just before the collision, Captain Claytor stopped the engines and listened for the fog signals of *City of Richmond*. Assuring himself from the sounds in the fog that there was no danger of collision, he ordered the engines ahead at half-speed. Immediately afterward, the *City of Richmond* parted the fog bank and drove her bow into the port side of the *City of Annapolis*.

"The moment we sighted the *Richmond,* I ordered the engines reversed and changed our course in an effort to avoid a crash," he declared. "It came on though, and cut through our port side, forward . . . tore through the saloon and stopped only when its bow had touched the stairway."

Roused by the emergency signals (four blasts on the ship's whistle) and by crew members, passengers on *City of Annapolis* rushed from their staterooms, donned life jackets, and stood by. Shortly afterwards, they were led to the port side, where the bow of the *City of Richmond* had impaled the hull and decking of *Annapolis.* The engines of *Richmond* turning slowly ahead kept the bow firmly in the rupture. All of the passengers, except one, and the crew of *Annapolis* were able to step to the deck of *Richmond.* Many were clad in night clothing, and some of the crew had only blankets to cover themselves.

One passenger failed to survive. Virginia Nice Starker of Govans (a Baltimore suburb), who had boarded the steamer at West Point, Virginia, occupied the portside stateroom where the prow of *Richmond* struck. The stateroom disintegrated in the impact. Her body was never recovered. Three years beforehand, she had escaped from the burning of the steamer *Ontario* of the Merchants and Miners Transportation Company off Block Island, while en route from Baltimore to Boston. She suffered from exposure and shock. This time, aboard *City of Annapolis,* her fortunes at sea ran out.

Survivors had harrowing stories to tell. One man from the *City of Annapolis* actually saw the *City of Richmond* strike:

I had just prepared for bed, when I heard the series of whistle blasts which warned me of impending danger. Not greatly alarmed, but uneasy, I stepped to the port [window] and looked out. There before my eyes was a great wall of white rushing at me. It was—although I did not know it at the time—the *City of Richmond.* My eyes had barely focused enough to let me see that it was the prow of a ship when it crashed into us. My stateroom crumpled in from the impact, and a part of my berth was smashed. If I had been in it, I would have been badly hurt, perhaps killed. . . . All about me was wreckage. The door was splintered, and I seized some of the pieces and pulled out enough of them so I could get my head and one arm through. There I stuck until one of the ship's officers came along and pulled me the rest of the way (Baltimore *Sun,* February 25–27, 1927).

Passengers aboard the *City of Richmond* had equally disturbing stories to tell. One passenger related the following experience:

When the foghorn sounded, I opened the [stateroom] window and peered out. . . . The fog was one of the worst I have ever seen. It was so thick one could not see ten feet ahead. The searchlight of the *Richmond* . . . could not penetrate it. Around us other foghorns sounded but in such weather one can't tell if such a horn is a mile away or very close. As I was trying to see through the fog the collision came. We were upon the *Annapolis* before anybody could see her. The cracking of wood and breaking of timbers made a terrific noise.

Just as the *Richmond* dug its prow through one of the forward staterooms of the *Annapolis* there was a penetrating scream of a woman, heard distinctly above the roar caused by the breaking and splintering timbers of both ships. There was only one scream. . . .

Taking a life preserver and in pajamas—the air was quite warm—I went on deck. . . . Immediately after the collision several steamers came up and covered us with their searchlights. The prow of the *Richmond* was locked tight in the side of the *Annapolis*, holding the latter vessel up. For a time, because of the *Annapolis* list to starboard, I feared she would pull us down with her.

There was no undue excitement on either vessel. . . . Lifeboats were lowered, but there was no need for them. The crews of both steamers assisted the passengers of the *Annapolis* to step across the deck rail from her to the *Richmond*. When the last of the passengers and crew were off the *Annapolis*, the *Richmond* backed out. . . . I shall never forget the way the *Annapolis* went down. The *Richmond* was standing off a bit with her searchlight on the *Annapolis*. Some time before, all lights on the *Annapolis* went out, leaving the ship in total darkness. . . . Suddenly the prow of the *Annapolis* dived into the water, leaving the propeller high in the air and the ship nearly at right angles to the water. She disappeared within a minute. . . . (Baltimore *Sun*, February 25–27, 1927).

Forty-seven passengers and fifty-three crew members stepped from the doomed ship to the deck of *Richmond*. Standing by was the *City of Baltimore*, bound from Baltimore to Norfolk. Circling off *Annapolis*, she came so close to the doomed vessel that she smashed a portion of her superstructure on the port side. She, along with *City of Richmond,* watched the sinking of *City of Annapolis,* the dramatic and wrenching ending of decades of partnership.

City of Annapolis sank in seventy feet of water off Smith Point at the mouth of the Potomac. Among the watermen of southern Maryland and the Northern Neck of Virginia she remained the subject of legends passed along from generation to generation. And there have been those who would tell, wide-eyed, that once a year, on a fogbound winter's night, when the minutes after midnight reached the half-hour point, a single piercing shriek had penetrated the gloom and echoed across the waters of the Bay.

A ghostly legend has persisted for more than a century concerning the sinking of the steamer *Express* off the mouth of the Potomac in the violent storm of October 22–23, 1878. That storm, an unheralded hurricane marching straight up the Bay from the Capes to the Susquehanna, created untold havoc in its path. It devastated Tidewater country; inundated the shoreline, farmlands, and low-lying towns; and scattered shipping before it, including a number of steamboats, like wooden toys.

The steamer *Express,* a veteran of over forty years of service, bound from Baltimore to Potomac landings and Washington, became its most notorious victim. Her life had never been a happy one, and she expired in the midst of untold tragedy.

Express, built in the early 1840s, bore little of the grace that described many steamers of the period. She had a checkered career and survived the ravages of the Civil War to carry on her trade for more than a decade afterward. A vessel of 150-foot length, she carried a crosshead engine —somewhat of an anomaly, at a time when vertical or walking beam engines were being introduced.

Beginning her career in Norwich, Connecticut, she steamed in abortive opposition to the New York and Albany Night Line on the Hudson. She managed to collide with the *Empire of Troy* on June 4, 1845, and suffered extensive damage. For a time she ran excursions from Boston to Plymouth, but on January 18, 1848, she arrived in Philadelphia from Boston, towing the bark *Elk* behind her. Lengthened some twenty-five feet and embellished with a depiction of a horse and rider on her wheelhouse to symbolize her name, she returned briefly to New York waters before being dispatched to Baltimore. Dissatisfied with her capacity, her new owner, Anthony Reybold, had her cut in two, lengthened, and rebuilt.

Steamboat *Express*. Edited from enrollment and other data and redrawn from sketch in the Mariners' Museum.

At the outbreak of the Civil War, when the monopoly of the Weems line on the Patuxent River seemed broken by the seizure of its steamers by the federal authorities, Reybold decided on a bold stroke by creating the Patuxent Steam Express Company as a challenge, with *Express* running in opposition to the monopoly. The Weems family quietly enjoyed the moment when *Express* burned at the dock and went off to Baltimore for repairs. She emerged over two hundred feet long, still slim with the original beam of twenty-three feet, and worn by twenty years of service. Promptly she was requisitioned by USQMD (the U.S. Quartermaster Department, sometimes Depot) and became a Union transport, shuttling troops to Virginia waters as the fortunes of battle dictated and loading Confederate prisoners-of-war aboard for transportation to various camps or sites for exchange with federal prisoners.

On January 6, 1865, upon her release from federal service, Reybold sold her as a battered and abused but still functioning veteran to the Potomac Transportation Company of Baltimore. Two months later, before being delivered north, she sank off Hilton Head, South Carolina, stove in by ice. Badly damaged above the main deck, she was raised and repaired in Baltimore. Reportedly, her superstructure above the main deck remained structurally weak from the damage sustained by wear, ice, and sinking. Nevertheless, she began her chore for the Potomac Transportation Company of shuttling passengers and freight between Washington and Baltimore (and landings in between), a routine she would follow for another thirteen years.

The moments before midnight of Tuesday, October 22, 1878, would test her mettle.

During the afternoon of that day, passengers boarded the steamer at the Light Street wharf of the Potomac Transportation Company, in expectation of her four o'clock departure for Washington and Potomac landings. The passenger list was short, as vacationers rarely ventured forth in October. There were only ten names on the list:

MRS. MARY A. BACON, a portly woman of forty, was returning from a shopping expedition in Baltimore to replenish the stock of the store operated by her son at Bacon's Wharf in St. Mary's County. She was the widow of Dr. James Bacon, who had practiced medicine in Baltimore.

DR. D. C. BURCH, thirty-six, a native of Bryantown, Charles County, had graduated from the School of Medicine of the University of Maryland in 1864, practiced at Chaptico in St. Mary's County, but elected to open a store in Milestown, where he served also as postmaster. He was widely esteemed in the county. On boarding in Baltimore, he brought with him a quantity of general merchandise for his store and expected to join his wife and three children on arrival.

HENRY B. ULLMAN, Baltimore cattle dealer, came aboard with a western-style flourish, a revolver at his side, a sweeping overcoat over his shoulder, and eight-hundred dollars in silver in his pocket. On Lee Street in Baltimore, his wife and five children awaited his return.

CAPTAIN JOHN T. WALMSLEY of Fredericktown on the Sassafras River, Cecil County, boarded without biography or expressed purpose.

M. LEVITAN, forty, a traveling salesman, had a family in Baltimore.

MRS. J. P. TARLETON of St. Mary's County, a young mother with her six-year-old child, had just visited her brother-in-law, George R. Tarleton of Hill Street, Baltimore.

MRS. DR. (or CAPT.) RANDOLPH JONES, reported to be about twenty-five years old, stylishly dressed wife from Cross Manor, St. Inigoes, St. Mary's County, was reportedly returning from a visit to her family in Philadelphia. In the news reports, she was variously titled "Mrs. Captain" or "Mrs. Dr." Randolph Jones.

Two black women bought second-class passage: CHLOE DYSON of St. Mary's County, and a MRS. THOMAS of Lancaster Wharf, Rappahannock County, Virginia.

Another black passenger was JAMES H. LEE.

Twice as many crew as passengers were on board, including the following:

CAPTAIN JAMES T. BARKER, about forty years old, an experienced waterman and steamboat skipper of Baltimore

FIRST OFFICER LEONARD J. HOWARD of west Baltimore

SECOND OFFICER JOSEPH HANEY of Virginia

CHIEF ENGINEER CHARLES W. BAILEY of south Baltimore

SECOND ENGINEER EDWARD PRYOR of south Baltimore

F. J. STONE, clerk, forty-five, of St. Mary's County

QUARTERMASTERS JOHN and JAMES DOUGLASS, brothers, of Virginia

FILLMORE RICE, lookoutman, of Northhampton County, Virginia

STEWARD THOMAS CARRINGTON, son-in-law of George L. Seaton, highly respected among the black residents of Alexandria, Virginia

NATHANIEL CARRINGTON and GEORGE WALKER, waiters

MATILDA ISAACS, chambermaid

ROBERT HAWKINS and DAVID WYATT, firemen

WILLIAM GAUNT, cook

WILLIAM HOLT, deckhand

CHARLES CASSELL, deckhand

HIRAM JONES, deckhand

GEORGE GREEN, baggage master

Several unnamed and recently hired deckhands, all from Baltimore

WILLIAM ("WILLIE") BARKER, sixteen, son of the captain, who rode as a supernumerary, ostensibly serving as bartender.

While greeting the passengers at the gangplank with the handshake and bow expected of a host, Captain Barker mentally digested telegraphic weather bulletins coming into the U.S. Signal Service in Baltimore. A "gale coming from the tropics," as reports stated, had swept toward the Florida Keys. At eleven o'clock on the morning of October 20, the signal service ordered storm signals flown at Key West. On the morning of the twenty-first, the storm had moved southeast. The latest reports on the morning of the twenty-second placed the center of the storm to the east of southern Georgia. Wind velocity stood at sixty miles an hour, higher over open water, and heavy rains drenched the lower Eastern Seaboard.

Nevertheless, the 11 P.M. report of the U.S. Signal Service in Baltimore on October 21 (the latest tidings Captain Barker himself had been able to see) announced fair weather at Cape Hatteras, North Carolina, wind velocity at eighteen miles per hour, and a light swell from the east. Norfolk enjoyed fair weather, with only light winds. The forecast of the chief signal officer in Washington called for "warm, clear weather, followed by increasing cloudiness, southerly winds, becoming variable, and a falling barometer." The captain glanced at the afternoon sky. The low, swiftly moving clouds spoiled the golden glow of a sunny afternoon.

Although he was not an oceangoing mariner, Captain Barker had known what had previously happened to "gales coming from the tropics" as they swept up the coast. Many had followed the path of the Gulf Stream and dissipated in the North Atlantic, wreaking havoc along the New England coast but leaving the Tidewater country of Maryland and Virginia unmolested except for torrential rains. Based on the optimistic forecast of the signal service and the heartening fact that other steamboats out of Baltimore would be engaged in their normal pursuits on the Bay, he decided to depart as usual from Baltimore at 4:00 P.M. and take *Express* down the Bay to Potomac River landings and Washington. At the appointed time, *Express,* with a trailing trill on her whistle, backed clear of her Light Street pier and headed down the Patapsco.

As *Express* rounded Seven Foot Knoll and lined up for the long reach down the Bay, Captain Barker noted with a sense of apprehension that the sky had darkened with low, scudding clouds and the beginnings of a thick overcast, and that, underfoot, the waters of the Bay moved with an unfamiliar rhythm—not the usual short chop but a long swell cresting in foam near the shallows. *Express* began to work in the swells, her framework creaking. But, aside from a freshening breeze and the slightly sickening pitch of the steamer in the swells, nothing disturbed the passage of *Express* down the Bay toward the Potomac.

By midnight, Barker could see the distant light of Cove Point above the mouth of the Patuxent, far off the starboard bow, but the loom was dimmed in the settling haze. The breeze on the trip down the Bay had picked up strength. The rain came and with it the power of the wind. First in gusts, it mounted by the half-hour in force and intensity.

By 2:00 A.M., the wind from the south and east had reached the force of a gale. The swells became monstrous waves with wind-driven breakers curling at their crests. They broke over the superstructure of *Express* in savage fury. In the predawn of October 23, Captain Barker knew that he and *Express* fought a battle of survival against the full force of a hurricane thundering its way up the middle of the Bay.

The choices were unpalatable. Barker could seek the shelter of the Patuxent, once past the formidable cliffs of Calvert on the western shore. But swinging *Express* into the trough and broadside of the mountainous seas could be suicidal. Eastward lay the treacherous shoals and islands guarding the mouth of the Choptank and Little Choptank rivers; seeking haven meant not only the palpable risk of turning broadside to the seas but also the danger of breaking up in shallow water far from safety. Southward was a possible lee in Hooper's Straits, or, still farther, near the Potomac mouth. Barker pressed southward—the only acceptable choice, in his view—the vessel under him barely manageable as the paddle wheels lifted from the rolling seas and deepening troughs, and the rudder lost its bite.

The seas boarded the steamer at the bow and pounded the superstructure below the wheelhouse, straining the joiner work and draining into the fireroom and coal bunkers. The steamer, under the weight of water in the hull, listed sharply to starboard.

In this desperate situation, Barker called for the crew and male passengers to throw the cargo and loose gear overboard. Hiram Jones, one of the deckhands, by a lurch of the boat, was carried overboard with a hogshead of bacon but was swept back aboard by the next wave.

Reckoning that *Express* had blown somewhat to the east of the shipping channels and hence into shallow water, Barker ordered the anchor let go. Several crewmen risked their lives in the waves breaking over the bow to swing the davit supporting the anchor overboard and cast the anchor itself into the surging water. The flukes grabbed the bottom; the chain pulled taut and in the next great wave—snapped. Barker ordered the engines ahead, and *Express* scarcely stood in place with her paddle wheels flailing the crests and seas breaking over her. Her upper works groaned as timbers labored and swayed in the shrieking winds and sea. Barker estimated his position, as best he could determine it, as being south of Barren Island and off Hooper Island, but well north of Point No Point marking the turn into the mouth of the Potomac at Point Lookout.

The wind continued to veer around, until at about 5:00 A.M. it roared in from the southeast, bringing the full force of the hurricane from the mouth of the Bay across the open reaches of Pocomoke Sound and the Potomac mouth. The seas rolled under *Express* in such heights that she became totally unmanageable, her paddle wheels and rudder unable to engage the water. Barker entertained the thought of attempting to reverse course, but he knew that *Express* could not turn in the trough and would be left at the mercy of the storm.

He left the pilothouse and looked to the welfare of his passengers. Procuring life jackets, he distributed them with words of assurance. He placed the women in what he considered the most secure place in the saloon, and instructed them to remain there, promising in the event of disaster to be on hand to render assistance. Then he returned to the wheelhouse to tend to his ship.

In a few minutes the climax came with unexpected suddenness. *Express*, caught by a series of enormous seas boarding her bows and crashing at her superstructure, turned on her side. The saloon disintegrated into timbers and splinters.

Passengers and crew were left in the raging seas to seek their own salvation. Some clung to the hull and then slid off, grabbing at pieces of timber to stay afloat. Captain Barker had lashed his son, Willie, to pieces of the saloon and then started to the assistance of Second Officer Haney, who had fallen through a skylight as the saloon collapsed. Assuming that Haney had drowned, Barker turned back to aid his son and saw the woodwork to which the boy had been attached floating off. He concluded that his son, too, had drowned. Captain Barker and a black passenger together grabbed a piece of timber and stayed afloat.

When the steamer capsized, four of the crew were below, two white, two black; they drowned. Matilda Isaacs, the chambermaid, clung to the overturning hull until she slipped off into the surging water. She caught a mattress in the debris and climbed on it, but the next wave swamped it and plunged her into the sea. Clerk F. J. Stone, still in his nightclothes, without a life jacket but wearing an overcoat, dove from the wreck. His overcoat dragged him under, but one of the crew floating on some timber helped him free himself and climb aboard the makeshift raft. In the process, he was struck repeatedly by large sections of debris from the wreck, becoming bruised and lamed.

A yawl floated free of the wreck, and an attempt was made to get Mrs. Bacon and Mrs. Jones inside it, but no boat could live in such a sea. The portly Mrs. Bacon drowned immediately. Mrs. Jones clasped a bundle of laths in her arms but lost her hold and disappeared.

Mrs. Tarleton with her six-year-old child on her left arm clung to a frail raft of sorts, but succumbed to the pounding of the waves. Henry

Ullman, the cattle dealer, emptied his pockets of eight hundred dollars in silver, withdrew his revolver, and threw off his overcoat, before plunging into the water. He was not seen again. James Douglass, quartermaster, adrift on some lumber five miles from the wreck noticed in passing debris the piano from the steamer and some of her furniture, along with a hat box abandoned in his stateroom. When it floated within reach, he grabbed it and donned his best dress hat to celebrate his survival.

Dr. D.C. Burch clung to the edge of a section of the saloon floating by with Clerk F. J. Stone and two crew members, David Wyatt and Hiram Jones, on top. Burch was washed off several times but was pulled back by the others on the raft. Struck on the head by a timber of the wreck and bleeding freely, he lost his grip in a surging wave, threw up his hands, and disappeared. Fragments of the wreck—timbers, doors, large objects —were picked up by the combing of the waves and hurled with great velocity for fifty to a hundred yards before hitting the water again; danger from these missiles added to the horror of the scene.

The stranding in the storm of the Clyde line steamer *Shirley* near Barren Island was a providential disaster. Under Captain Travers, *Shirley* left Baltimore on Tuesday evening bound for West Point on the York River with 150 tons of freight. Off Point No Point, the waves drove a hawser into her paddle wheels. Her machinery disabled, she hoisted sail and ran before the wind. Once on that hurricane-driven course northward, there was no "coming about." She was driven high upon the shore in Tar Bay, between Hooper's Island and Barren Island. Drawing nine feet of water aft, she rested at low tide with bow out of the water and three feet around the stern. The offending hawser, 100 fathoms in length, had been swept from the hurricane deck, 23 feet above the water, by a wave and carried under the paddle wheels. Had it not been for this accident and the broaching of the *Shirley* near the scene of the *Express* disaster, most of the people aboard the latter would have perished. When picked up by the boats of the *Shirley*, the survivors of the *Express* were in a state of utter exhaustion. F. J. Stone could not help himself and had to be hoisted by chair into the stranded *Shirley*.

Captain Travers first knew of the tragedy when barrels and broken cabin sections drifted by his vessel. After sweeping the seas with his binoculars for some time, he saw one of the shipwrecked crew on a section of the wreck. From him, he learned the details and magnitude of the disaster. He dispatched the two boats of the *Shirley* in the direction of the wreck, and plucked ten of the survivors from the sea.

Those rescued by *Shirley* were John T. Walmsley, F. J. Stone (clerk), John Douglass (quartermaster), Robert Hawkins and David Wyatt (firemen), William Gaunt (cook), Hiram Jones (deckhand), Charles W. Bailey (chief engineer), Willie Barker, and George Walker (saloon waiter). Miraculously, Willie Barker had survived on top of a piece of the saloon deck with George Barker, who had held tightly to the boy during the ordeal.

A wrecking expedition for assisting *Shirley* arrived in Tar Bay on October 26; it consisted of the propeller steamer *George H. Stout*, a barge, and a crew of boatmen and stevedores, whose mission was to offload the cargo of *Shirley* and additionally to search for bodies from the ill-fated *Express*. As the exploring party went down the beach, they noticed in the distance what might have been taken for the carcass of a huge whale on which vultures were feeding but which proved to be about seventy-five feet of the starboard side of the lost steamer's hull. It lay in Hooper's Straits, near the mouth of the Honga River. Local wreckers (like vultures) swarmed over it, hacking with axes to lighten the fragments for floating to shore. They were busily gathering up remnants of the cargo strewn about the beach. The timbers showed the evidence of the fury of the storm, which literally tore the steamer apart and dumped its boiler and machinery into the water when the steamer overturned and broke up. The explorers from the wrecking expedition found no bodies from the wreck.

The schooner *Samuel T. Waite* (Captain Jesse J. Parks) rescued Captain Barker, James Douglass (the other quartermaster), and James H. Lee, a black passenger. They had clung to planks in the water for seven hours. Captain Barker suffered injuries from the flying debris and physical exhaustion; he was overcome with grief at what he believed at the moment to be the loss of his son, Willie. Later, the captain and the boy met on Light Street wharf in an emotional reunion spectators never forgot.

William Holt and Charles Cassell, black deckhands, were plucked from the floating debris by a passing three-masted schooner and brought to safety in the Patuxent River.

In all, fifteen people survived the *Express* disaster. The remainder of the passengers and crew perished. Some of the remains washed up on the beaches of the Eastern Shore.

Captain J. J. Parks of the schooner *Samuel T. Waite*, who rescued Captain Barker and others, discovered two bodies from the steamer and buried them at the site. The body of First Officer Howard had washed ashore and been temporarily buried, to be disinterred and removed to Balti-more. The bodies of Second Officer Haney, Second Engineer Pryor, Mrs. Tarleton and her child, and Nathaniel Carrington were identified and buried. Mrs. Tarleton's body was found fifteen miles from where the re-mains of her child came ashore. Other bodies were discovered and buried.

Captain Robert J. W. Powley of Pone Island found a body on Adams Island—that of Mrs. Jones or Mrs. Bacon. The body was lying face down-ward, still wearing a life preserver, a black silk dress, an open-faced gold watch, a chased gold ring, and a set ring on the same finger. He buried the body. Later, Edward Bacon came down to search the small islands off Kedges Straits to the south of Holland Straits for the body of his mother, Mary A. Bacon, temporarily buried there; he found the body, identified it, and shipped the remains to St. Mary's County for interment. The body discovered and buried by Captain Powley, therefore, was that of Mrs. Randolph Jones.

The hurricane that struck *Express* wreaked havoc all along the Atlantic seaboard and particularly in the Tidewater region of the Chesapeake. Damage to crops, buildings, bridges, even to whole communities, was staggering. Shipping suffered enormous losses.

The storm struck steamboats on the Bay and its tributaries with feroc-ity. *Planter* of the Weems line met the storm in the Patuxent River and survived, but Captain Thomas B. Gourley brought back harrowing tales of schooners and pungies driven ashore and, in some instances, demol-ished. *Massachusetts* on the Bay succeeded in finding shelter in the Patuxent at the height of the storm. She lost part of her rudder and grounded, but remained intact.

Theodore Weems made safe harbor at Crisfield, where she was towed by *Tangier*. The former lost her rudder and sustained considerable damage to her upper works. *Tangier* as the rescuer lost her anchor, and the storm stove in the port side of the main deck from the stern to the forward gangway. *Mary Washington* went to Crisfield to tow *Theodore Weems* to Bal-timore.

Fear mounted about the fate of *Matilda* of the Weems line under the command of Captain James Gourley when she failed to appear after her departure from Fredericksburg on Monday at midnight. Henry Williams, general manager of the Weems line, dispatched *Mary Washington* to search for her.

Matilda had left Fredericksburg at 2 A.M. Tuesday, met enough fog on the river to slow her down, and stopped at Riverview, fourteen miles from the mouth of the Rappahannock, to await moonrise to illuminate a return upriver to landings on the river she had missed on the downriver passage. The hurricane burst upon her. She was driven onto the beach. On Saturday morning, her freight was transferred to *Mary Washington*. At high tide, *Mary Washington* pulled her free, and she resumed her journey to Baltimore, to be greeted on arrival with great relief by the Weems family, who had anticipated her loss.

The Chesapeake proved once again that she was not to be taken for granted. Far from being the placid lake described by John Stevens, she was a vicious tyrant that made fools of men who dared to tame her.

Legends about the *Express* disaster have lingered through the years in St. Mary's County. One of them concerns Mrs. Randolph Jones of stately Cross Manor, a plantation replete with colonial history. The manor house overlooked St. Inigoes Creek, where a steamboat wharf (Jones' Wharf then, Grason's Wharf later) served the manor and the community. Steamers like *Express* running the Potomac to Washington had stopped there for years.

According to legend, Captain Jones, sitting with relatives in the parlor of the Cross Manor mansion and awaiting the arrival of his wife from Baltimore, heard a knock on the front door. Looking through a nearby

The river front of Cross Manor. Through the window at center of lower porch, Randolph Jones saw his wife's apparition on the night of October 22–23, 1878.

85

window at the storm-streaked porch, he saw what appeared to be his wife beckoning to him to come to the door. Struggling against the fury of the wind, he opened the door. No one was there. The time coincided with her disappearance in the tumult as *Express* capsized and disintegrated in the hurricane.

A certain eeriness and sense of unreality surround the available facts concerning Randolph Jones and his spectral wife. He was the oldest son of Caleb Morris Jones, M.D., a physician who had practiced for years from his estate at Cross Manor. Born in 1788, Caleb had graduated from the University of Pennsylvania Medical College in 1813 and married Rebecca Davis on March 17, 1815. They had five children: one died at birth; another, Alexander, died at age twenty-three while in medical school; the remaining three were Randolph and his two younger sisters, Emily (born in 1829) and Elvira Ann (born in 1831). The latter married James Fox Ellicott and had a daughter who married Senator Charles Grason (sometimes spelled Grayson), thus the change of name from Jones' Wharf to Grason's Wharf.

Caleb Jones, the patriarch, during his long lifetime certainly dominated life at Cross Manor. He was a man of opinion and zeal. When the Civil War began, he openly declared his enthusiasm for the Union cause, a position not consonant with the southern sympathies rampant in St. Mary's County. Furthermore, he put his expressed opinions into action. For only twenty-five dollars, he rented land in March 1864 to the federal government in order for the Potomac River Flotilla to build shops, warehouses, ammunition magazines, and coal storage sheds to service the vessels of the flotilla. Naval officers frequented the manor house itself, and, according to rumor, shared the loot (silver and other valuables stolen from manor houses along the river in raids) with Dr. Jones and his wife, Rebecca. The officers and crew of the vessels developed quite a bond of affection for Cross Manor.

One of the gunboats based at the St. Inigoes coaling station, as the base established at Cross Manor was called, was the U.S.S. *Tulip*. Like others of her class, she was a misshapen craft designed for other duties. Schooner-rigged (the masts, sails, and bowsprit were later removed) and steam-powered as a gunboat, she was originally built in 1862 in the United States for the Tzu Hsi government in China in its efforts to quell the semireligious T'ai-ping rebellion. When the boat was stranded in the United States for lack of funds, the U.S. Navy acquired her and re-armed her for blockade and patrol duties on the Potomac. Her machinery, particularly her starboard boiler, was defective from the start. In spite of repairs, which were often haphazard and ill-conceived, she limped about her duties under the steam of the other boiler.

Ordered to the Washington Navy Yard on November 11, 1864, for further boiler repairs, she set forth from St. Inigoes on the port boiler—with a firm injunction from the flotilla authorities not to fire up the starboard boiler. Stories varied on the reaction of Acting Master William H. Smith to this injunction. One account showed Smith as boasting to his officers at the midday meal that he intended to put both boilers on the line as soon she entered the Potomac in order to hasten the trip to Washington. Another version had Smith worrying that the limping *Tulip* would present a ready target to Confederate batteries on the Virginia shore. A rumor (even a legend) in St. Mary's County persisted that Smith hurried to meet a "date" with his wife in Washington. Engineers, protesting the firing up of the defective boiler, were relieved on the spot—even, according to legend, chained by Smith to the after-rail.

Near Piney Point, Smith ordered the defective boiler fired up and placed on line to furnish steam to the engine. Off Ragged Point, the boiler exploded. The boat disintegrated. Only ten of fifty-nine officers and men of the crew survived, and some of them subsequently died. Eight unidentified bodies were buried in a small graveyard beside Cross Manor. (Today, the site is a half-acre national cemetery marked by a white marble monument duly inscribed to those who perished in 1864.)

Caleb Jones presided at Cross Manor at the time of the tragedy. It left an imprint on his children. Randolph, the oldest son, remained a man of mystery. A certain disparity appears in the date of his birth. A chronicler of Caleb Jones places the son's birth at about 1816, thereby conforming to the conventions of the marriage in 1815 of Caleb and Rebecca. But the headstone of Randolph Jones in the graveyard of St. Ignatius Church in St. Inigoes states flatly that he was born on March 17, 1813 (died April 15, 1896). The headstone states, also, that Randolph married Matilda Cross of New Jersey. The chronicler of Caleb states that her name was Matilda Gross of Pennsylvania. Of considerable relevance is the press report on November 1, 1878, that the body of Mrs. Randolph Jones was located, disinterred, identified, and shipped to Philadelphia for burial.

The character of Randolph is of interest. He did not seem to develop a particular career. When the Civil War threatened, he followed the lead of his father, Caleb, and enthusiastically embraced the Union cause, a position not popular in St. Mary's County, where southern sympathies abounded. Randolph was chosen captain of the St. Mary's Dragoons, a company of forty men organized in 1860 but disbanded when their sympathies led them to join the ranks of the gray across the Potomac. One report states that Randolph served as a captain of cavalry under McClellan in Virginia; he visited Cross Manor at intervals, riding a white horse but turning aside questions about the war (understandable in view of McClellan's inactivity). Randolph was described as "taciturn."

In 1861, Randolph became the enrollment officer and provost marshal for the county, a post others refused because of the hazards of the office in the presence of a hostile population. He was bullied, forced to arrest men for resisting enrollment, and threatened with murder. Undoubtedly, his rank, carried on in titular form after the war, gave rise to Matilda's designation as Mrs. Captain Randolph Jones. The title of Mrs. Doctor Randolph Jones is less easy to explain—perhaps associated with the reputation of the father, Dr. Caleb Jones at Cross Manor.

At the time of the *Express* disaster in 1878, Randolph's age cannot be established with certainty; a chronicler would place it at age sixty-two; his tombstone would set it at sixty-five; but the August 1870 census (his age then sixty-four) would confirm it at sixty-two. Matilda, his wife, was described on boarding *Express* in Baltimore as being an attractive twenty-five or twenty-six. But the 1870 consensus, setting her age as thirty-five, would make her forty-two or forty-three in October 1878: hardly an ingenue, but certainly a winsome bride for the older Randolph. The 1870 census confirmed her birthplace as Pennsylvania.

Something appeared to be troubling Randolph—something mental, physical, or emotional—because Caleb, his father, at first almost excluded him in his will. The father, who died on March 19, 1878 (seven months before the *Express* disaster), had drawn up his will shortly before he died. He did not leave Cross Manor to his son but willed it to his daughters, Emily and Elvira Ann. The husband of the latter, James Fox Ellicott, probably lame and a Quaker, certainly a noncombatant forced to endure a naval base under his very nose and the aftermath of the carnage aboard U.S.S. *Tulip*, was named as executor. Caleb left a smaller farm, Rake's Lodge, to his daughter-in-law, Matilda, as guardian to Randolph. Subsequently, Caleb redesignated Randolph and his two sisters as co-executors of Cross Manor. Randolph lived until 1896, eighteen years after Matilda's death. On October 5, 1880, he signed a will bequeathing all his possessions to his two sisters, who had already inherited Cross Manor. His signature was a bare scrawl, totally illegible.

James Ellicott and his wife separated, and he reportedly moved to Baltimore. Elvira and Emily, who never married, remained at Cross Manor.

Randolph's presence in the parlor of Cross Manor on that stormy night in 1878 must have been in the company of his two sisters in the wake of the death of their father, Caleb. The condition of Randolph, when he saw the apparition of his wife, can only be a matter of speculation. But the incident got bruited about and formed part of the ghostly heritage of the Bay.

The exploration in 1991 of the wreck of a steamboat built in 1828 and sunk in 1850 near the mouth of the Potomac—and the resurrection of important components of its crosshead engine in 1992–93—have stirred up eerie visions of the distant past in the steamboat history of the Chesapeake.

In 1991, the U.S. Army Corps of Engineers explored the projected path of a channel to be dredged from the Chesapeake Capes to Baltimore. The study was necessitated by the Baltimore Harbor and Channels Fifty-foot Project in the Chesapeake Bay. Several shipwreck sites presented obstacles to the planned dredging, those sites having been located previously by archaeologists exploring the region. One site in particular, located off the mouth of the Potomac, focused the attention of archaeologists on the possibility that it constituted the remains of an early nineteenth-century steamboat with significant engine parts intact. Furthermore, parts of the hull could be traced by divers, and this shape plus notable engine parts and a paddle wheel shaft could be measured, or their dimensions estimated. The measurements, compared with archival data from steamboat enrollments, could lead to identification of the vessel and a determination of its historical significance.

Divers with archaeological experience groped in waters nearly sixty feet deep in murk so thick that strong lights barely revealed the diver's hand in front of his helmet. Despite poor visibility, they managed to trace most of the hull, measuring as they went, and to ascertain the diameter of the cylinder, clearly identifiable as it protruded from the wreckage, along with the stroke of the piston rod. They established the length of the hulk as 174 feet, its beam as approximately 30 feet, the diameter of the cylinder as 50 inches, and the stroke as 78 inches. Their finds excited the world of history and science: their measurements coincided precisely with the archival data on the paddle wheel steamboat *Columbus*, built in 1828. She burned and sank off the Potomac mouth in 1850. Even more dramatic, the engine was square or crosshead, built in 1828 by Charles Reeder. In the wreck at the bottom of the Bay near the Potomac mouth lay the only crosshead engine in existence—an enormously important link in the industrial history of steamboat development in the United States. The site immediately became a candidate for the National Register of Historic Places.

The biography of the steamboat *Columbus* began when the Maryland and Virginia Steamboat Company contracted for her construction in 1828 by James Beacham and George Gardiner in Baltimore. On May 18, 1829, she set forth on her trial run from Baltimore Harbor down the Patapsco to its mouth and up the Bay to Poole's Island. On her return, she clocked a speed of twelve miles per hour, a testimonial to her design and the quality of machinery built and installed by Charles Reeder.

The engine was a crosshead (square or steeple) type. Observers noted that it was remarkably quiet and smooth running, creating little vibration in the vessel even at top speed. The vertical cylinder, as previously noted, measured fifty inches in diameter, and the thrust of the piston driving the crosshead up and down was seventy-eight inches. Rated at one hundred horsepower, the engine drew praise from officials and observers alike for the excellent workmanship of Reeder.

Columbus met the test of the trial, and the president and directors of the company expressed their gratification at her performance and appearance. She was a handsome steamer for the times. As originally built, she was 137 feet long, with a copper-sheathed hull more than 30 feet wide, and a depth of hold of 10 feet 9 inches. The main deck extended 10 feet on either side beyond the hull to accommodate the paddle wheels and provide additional cargo space. Built primarily to transport merchandise between Baltimore and Norfolk, she had the capacity of two thousand barrels in her hold, and, in addition, she had space for cattle, tobacco hogsheads, and cotton bales forward on the main deck.

As a freight carrier, she had less passenger space than many other packets of the period, but the accommodations, nevertheless, were elegant. Cabin space on the main deck and below aft was quite luxurious.

"The forward or gentlemen's cabin," wrote a journalist, "contains 18 births [*sic*], and the after or ladies' cabin the same number. In the latter (which is fitted up in very handsome style, ornamented with rich carved and gilt work, the doors and pannel [*sic*] work of mahogany and curled

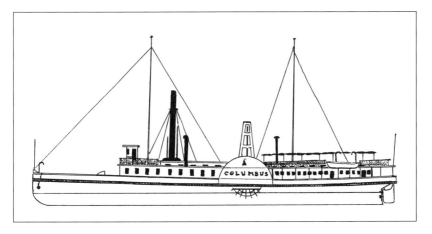

Steamboat *Columbus* as she might have appeared prior to 1850. Drawn from depictions of comparable steamboats of the same period and archival data.

maple, and richly carpeted) there are eight state rooms, each having two births [*sic*], a wash stand [and writing desk and other conveniences]; the curtains are of white dimity, neatly and tastefully arranged" (Norfolk *Herald* in Emmerson, *Steamboat Comes to Norfolk*, 97–98).

Ten days after her trial run, *Columbus* began her three-day-a-week service between Baltimore, Norfolk, City Point, and Richmond. On her initial run down the Bay, she completed the trip from Baltimore to Norfolk in nineteen and one-half hours. Fares from Norfolk to Baltimore cost seven dollars; from Norfolk to Richmond, three dollars. In between her shuttling, Captain John D. Turner carried excursionists, as many as four hundred to five hundred at a time, to resorts within a day's run from Richmond or Norfolk. In July, *Columbus* offered transport to President Andrew Jackson at Old Point Comfort, but other plans interfered with his acceptance. Like other steamboats, *Columbus* had her share of minor calamities, except, in her case, they occurred almost immediately. On an excursion run on July 29 out of Richmond, Captain Turner managed to ground her on a bar and kept some one hundred passengers aboard overnight; the excursionists enjoyed the novelty. On August 9, she suffered sabotage to her boiler. Soon after leaving Baltimore, engineers discovered that the key to the discharge cock had been forced out and stolen. A week later in Baltimore, a man offered for sale the very nut that had been removed; he was arrested, and evidence before the magistrate disclosed that the man was known for other unexplained acts of sabotage.

On March 13, 1831, she was rammed by the steamer *Rappahannock* off Smith Point at the mouth of the Potomac and suffered damage to her wheelhouse; the passengers praised Captain Turner for his solicitude and seamanship. Ice blocking the upper Bay to some fourteen miles below Baltimore in the freeze of 1831 almost brought *Columbus* to a halt, but the perseverance of Captain Turner in navigating through the packs and reaching Norfolk in record time impelled his passengers to bestow upon him a "tribute of merit" and a silver urn inscribed to the captain for "his skill and intrepidity . . . on the passage thro' [*sic*] the Ice, and in a violent storm, from Baltimore to Norfolk, the 10th day of December, 1831" (Emmerson, 199).

Again, in October 1833, passengers offered a public testimonial to the skipper of *Columbus*, this time Captain James Holmes, for bringing the steamboat safely through a gale off the Potomac mouth. And later, for his "judgment and skill displayed during a dangerous passage through the Ice from Norfolk to Annapolis [where *Columbus* could proceed no further] on the 16th and 17th, February, 1835," the passengers presented to Captain Holmes a silver pitcher suitably engraved.

Columbus participated in numerous historical celebrations and events. She celebrated the fifteenth anniversary of the Battle of North Point with a display of troops and bands on board. In June 1833, she carried Black Hawk, the Sauk chief, and his braves to Baltimore after their release from custody at Fortress Monroe and their tour of the Navy Yard at Norfolk, where they declared the ship of the line *Delaware* to be a "great canoe" and marveled at its Indian figurehead.

Newspapers in the 1830s advertised "through service" from Richmond and Norfolk to Philadelphia and New York. In 1833, for example, the Maryland and Virginia Steamboat Company boasted that it could provide service from Norfolk to New York in thirty-three hours.

"The new arrangement," stated the advertising, "of the . . . *Columbus* . . . proposed to give a degree of despatch [*sic*] unexampled, to the conveyance between Richmond, Norfolk, and New York, transporting the passengers from Richmond to New York in 41 hours, and from Norfolk to the great commercial emporiums, in 33 hours. This is really next to flying, and we are bound to believe that it is the ultimate point of expedition to which the ordinary means of transportation can arrive" (Emmerson, 223).

The means for such a "flight" meant the use of the barges through the new Chesapeake and Delaware Canal (or, alternatively, a ride on the new sixteen-mile Frenchtown New Castle Railway) and the risky transfer from steamboat to steamboat on the open Bay off the entrance to the Patapsco River. There the steamer on the run between Baltimore and Frenchtown at the lower end of the canal met the steamer running between Norfolk and Baltimore, and alongside each other in the chop of the Bay, the steamers managed to move passengers from one vessel to the other. North of the canal, passengers went by steamer up the Delaware River for passage via New Jersey landings to New York.

Tyrone Power, Irish comedian and great-grandfather of the late movie star of the same name, witnessed such a transfer in open water between the steamer *George Washington* and the steamer *Columbus* in September 1834:

> Whilst steering through the waters of the Chesapeake, [we] perceived a large steamer right for us, with a signal flying. Learned that this was the *Columbus*, bound for Norfolk, Virginia, for which place we had several passengers, who were now to be transshipped to the approaching steamer.
>
> We were out in the open bay, with half a gale of wind blowing, and some sea on; it therefore became a matter of interest to observe how two large ships of this class would approach each other.
>
> The way they managed this ticklish affair was really admirable: before we neared, I observed the Norfolk ship was laid head to wind, and just enough way kept on to steer her; our ship held her course, gradually lessening her speed, until, as she approached the *Columbus*, it barely sufficed to lay and keep her alongside, when they fell together, gangway to gangway: warps were immediately passed, and made secure at both head and stern: and in a minute the huge vessels became as one.
>
> Here was no want of help; the luggage and the passengers were ready at the proper station, so that in a handful of minutes the transfer was completed without bustle or alarm . . .
>
> As we thus lay together, I noticed that the upper or promenade deck of the *Columbus* was completely taken up by a double row of flashy-looking covered carts, or tilt-waggons [*sic*], as they were called. Upon inquiry, I found that these contained the goods, and were, indeed the movable stores, or shops, of that much enduring class, the Yankee pedlars [*sic*], just setting forth for the annual winter cruise among the plantations of the South; where, however their keen dealing may be held in awe, they are looked for with

lively anxiety, and their arrival greeted as an advent of no little moment. . . .

Our business being completed, the hissing sound of the waste-steam pipe ceased . . . the paddles began to move, the lashings were cast off, and away the boats darted from each other with startling rapidity: the *Columbus*, with the gale aft, rushing down the great bay of the Chesapeake, and the *Washington* breasting its force right for Baltimore (T. Power, *Impressions of America*, 1836-38, Vol. 2, 42–45; Brown, *The Old Bay Line*, 1940, 21–22).

Through the years *Columbus* trundled faithfully on her route between Baltimore, Norfolk, and Richmond. In early 1836, she underwent major alterations in the shipyard of Gooding & Company, Baltimore, to increase her length to 174 feet, suitable for use on the line between Norfolk and Charleston, South Carolina. A new boat, *Georgia*, being built especially for that route by the Maryland and Virginia Steamboat Company, would replace her. *Columbus*, relaunched on April 25, 1836, began her new duties in the South, carrying mail, freight, and passengers.

The final years of the Maryland and Virginia Steamboat Company were marred by increasing competition from rival steamboat lines and from newly built railroads appearing on the scene around the lower Bay, with connections reaching into North Carolina, Washington, and the North. The venerable company teetered on the edge of bankruptcy.

In December 1839, the General Assembly of Maryland passed an act incorporating the Baltimore Steam Packet Company (known later as the Old Bay Line), which would assume the assets of the defunct Maryland and Virginia Steamboat Company. Leaders in the new corporation were William McDonald, his son Samuel, and Andrew F. Henderson, all key to the building of the *Chesapeake* for the Union Line in 1813. *Columbus*, still skippered by Captain James Holmes, joined the Old Bay Line fleet, but her tenure was short. In 1845, an affiliated unit of the company was formed for the express purpose of serving the James River. This new company, represented by its president, John W. McKim, a board member of the Baltimore Steam Packet Company, was the Powhatan Line. It acquired *Columbus*. Initially, she was designated to run between Baltimore and Lumpkin's Landing, Mathews County, Virginia. But then her assignment was changed, and it was a welcome one. Her new route carried her over the waters she had navigated from her youth: up and down the Bay between Baltimore and Norfolk, and up the James River to Richmond. Over this familiar path,

Columbus traveled patiently for another five years, enduring the gales, the icing, and the treachery of the Bay, while at other times basking in its serenity. And the crosshead engine of Charles Reeder faithfully cranked the paddle wheels as they cut a pattern of squares in their frothy wake.

The dramatic climax of the career of *Columbus* came on November 27, 1850. Around four o'clock on that Wednesday afternoon, *Columbus* backed as usual from the Powhatan Steamboat Company's slip at Pier 5, Light Street, for her run to Petersburg and Richmond. She carried one regular passenger and an impoverished German named L. [David] Seligman, who had been given free passage. Freight was light; six horses, the property of Mr. C. Leadbetter, the paying passenger, were tethered forward. Into a cold and blustery night steamed *Columbus.* Past midnight, nearing the mouth of the Potomac River, where the Bay widened to thirty miles, she felt the unsettling chop of ruffled seas from a stiff southwest wind. About three o'clock on Thursday morning, she stood off Smith Point Lightship, which marked the southern extremity of the Potomac as it met the Bay.

Suddenly there were shouts and screams from the engine room echoing through the ship. As told by Lloyd Lecompte, engineer, who survived, a fire virtually exploded from the furnace door in the fireroom:

Prior to the outbreak of the fire, I had been troubled by the failure of the furnace to draw properly and instructed one of the firemen not to put much wood in it. I couldn't figure out what was wrong. To prime the bilge pump, I went aft to draw a bucket of water, but returned immediately, in my worry, to the fireroom. Looking down, I saw a sudden sheet of flame shoot from the furnace doors, striking down a deckhand working there, chasing the fireman, Daniel Stevens, up the ladder, and swallowing up the machinery itself in flames. The wood pile caught fire, and then the dry paneling and timbers of the deckhouse. Pretty soon, the whole cabin was ablaze. I flew up the cabin stairs to the pilothouse and collared Captain John Hollingshead standing near the wheel.

"She's on fire," I shouted. "The whole fireroom and engineroom are on fire—and the flames have caught the cabin. She's gone—there's no way, captain. We've got to take to the boats to save ourselves. Now."

Then I leaped over the rail to the main deck and ran to the forecastle beneath it to stir up the deckhands asleep there. Then I figured I had to save myself and raced through the flames and smoke in the cabin to the starboard lifeboat on the quarter and slid down the tackle. In the boat were six men, frantically trying to stop off the hole in the bottom where the drain plug had been removed. We managed to get the plug back in, bailed with our caps, and cast off. Captain Hollingshead stood above us on deck directing the launching of the boat; then he shouted, "Hold on!" and ran back into the cabin flames, to search for others on board; then he reappeared and with two deckhands jumped overboard in the frigid waters. We were unable to rescue them.

The steamer by now had gone off some distance. Her machinery ran for a while, then she stopped and drifted. I was shocked to see that the port lifeboat was still in its davits and that the flames had spread so rapidly that no one could reach it. We rowed in the wake of the burning steamer, hoping that we could rescue anyone trying to save themselves. When the upper works collapsed, we turned toward the Smith Point Lightship and reached it after much effort. There we stayed, because of the rough weather, until the next day, when the *Georgia*, coming up from Norfolk, took us off for Baltimore. In the meantime, the wreck, a mass of flames, drifted so close to the lightship that we could feel the intense heat. At 8 o'clock in the morning, the wreck was still puffing steam or smoke and drifting about, and we watched her with binoculars, but around 11 A.M. she disappeared. We assumed that she sank (quoted from accounts in the Baltimore *Sun* following the disaster).

In the wheelhouse, another drama had been enacted. In the half-hour before the fire began, the captain had relieved the mate, Littleton Goodwin, who retired to his bunk nearby. When the engineer, Lecompte, burst into the wheelhouse with his cries of fire, Goodwin sprang from his bunk and ran off to search for his nine-year-old son, asleep in the captain's office in the cabin. Neither was seen again.

Levin Pearson, the helmsman, managed to throw over the rudder and turn the steamer downwind while the engine was still running, before he raced off to save himself in the lifeboat. But the engine stopped and the burning steamer drifted about in the shifting current and tide.

The *Columbus* catastrophe became headline news. Nine people lost their lives, including the captain, mate, the mate's much-loved small son,

L. [David] Seligman (the nonpaying passenger), and several crew members. Six horses perished. Seven people survived. The speed with which the fire spread, its intense heat, and the bad weather were contributing factors to the tragedy. But the direct cause seemed to be the malfunctioning of a new spark arrestor in the smokestack, blocking the draft when it failed and causing a blow-back in the furnace.

At the time of the tragedy, *Columbus* joined the list of shipwrecks on the Chesapeake. Nearly a century and a half later, her wreckage assumed particular significance. In its midst was her crosshead engine, the only one known to exist, a maritime monument of exceptional historical importance.

The location of the wreck, but not its identity, was known from surveys conducted in the 1970s, notably by the National Oceanic and Atmospheric Administration (NOAA). In 1990, the U.S. Army Corps of Engineers, commissioned to deepen a shipping channel to fifty feet, decided that the mass of machinery on the bottom bordering the channel posed a special danger to deep-draft tankers and other Baltimore-bound ships for which the channel was being deepened. Before the debris could be removed by demolition, the engineers had to obey federal injunctions to conduct a preliminary archaeological survey.

At that point, the exploration and documentation of the wreck assumed critical importance. Not only the Corps of Engineers, as the principal participant and leader of the project, but also other organizations called in by the corps or under its contract became involved, notably Dr. R. Christopher Goodwin and his associates, who employed archaeological divers to study, measure, and sketch the wreck and its engine; Michael Pohuski, diver, photographer, and archaeologist, and his team engaged by Goodwin to document the operation (Pohuski's work was crucial in identifying the wreck); a group of U.S. Army reservists, to contribute in manning the equipment; a team of U.S. Army divers from Fort Eustis, to ascertain the means of salvaging the artifacts; and collateral units and individuals gathered for related purposes. Contributors to the project included the Maryland Historical Trust, the Maryland Port Administration, and other sponsoring organizations.

The initial detailed survey by archaeologists began in earnest in 1991. For them, diving to the wreck nearly sixty feet below the surface meant exploring it at times in nearly total darkness; strong lights helped very little. Sediment, the opaqueness of the water at that depth, and the half-buried condition of the relics required the divers to learn the configuration of the wreck and the components of its engine by touching them and tracing them painstakingly by hand.

They discovered that the port side of the hull was largely missing, but that the starboard side, copper sheathed, could be traced from the bow practically to the stern, which was buried in the bottom silt. Because the stern was covered up, the length of the hull was originally over-estimated as being more than 200 feet. However, when the remains of the rudder (some gudgeons and pintles intact) were located, the archaeologists knew they could measure the correct length, somewhere between 170 and 180 feet. Along the length of the hull, they drove metal stakes at intervals to provide reference points. Given the contour of the hull, they were able to estimate its beam at approximately 30 feet.

Studies of the machinery conducted in the murky depths were in the early stages confusing. The cylinder was readily identifiable, lying as it did on its side with the piston rod protruding and the condenser beneath it. The cylinder's diameter, initially measured externally as sixty inches, was corrected to an internal measurement of fifty inches in order to compare it with possible historic data on the vessel. Its stroke (distance traveled by the piston in the cylinder) was estimated to be seventy-eight inches (determined from the dimension of the cylinder itself). Other pieces of machinery (a smaller cylinder considered to be the air pump, two steam chests with valve assembly protruding, a cast-iron box possibly associated with the fireroom, and pieces of piping) lay nearby among a half-buried mound of unidentifiable metal. One of the paddle wheel shafts, hub intact but minus the buckets, could be seen. All of these artifacts were heavily layered with concretion after lying at the bottom of the Bay for more than 140 years.

Two small items were brought up by the divers—a packet of hooks and eyes used on ladies' dresses of the period and a jar of facial cream, which only the most fastidious of female passengers would have preferred.

With the data on the length of the hull, its probable beam, and the diameter and stroke of the cylinder in hand, researchers turned to the archives to identify the wreck. *City of Annapolis* and U.S.S. *Tulip* were summarily eliminated by location and description. *Express*, seriously considered, failed the test when her dimensions and the accounts of her sinking were studied. *North Carolina* burned and sank in 1859 off Smith Point, but her vertical beam engine and the presumed site of her sinking eliminated her from the list. The wreck of *Louisiana* brought some attention, but the location of her sinking and her configuration dismissed her

Silhouetted against the morning sun across the Bay, equipment of the U.S. Army Corps of Engineers prepares for the day's work in the salvage of the crosshead engine of the *Columbus*. BD (barge derrick) in center with receiving barge alongside, army tugs at left, LCU (landing craft, utility) at right with bow door open for divers to use. Drawn from author's photograph.

from consideration. However, the evidence fell heavily on the side of *Columbus*. Hull length and beam, cylinder diameter and stroke—these coincided precisely with enrollment data in the National Archives. Even the site of the wreck squared with the story of her burning and sinking, as reported in the press at the time.

In the summer of 1992 and extending into the fall, the Corps of Engineers began the process of bringing the parts of the crosshead engine to the surface. The equipment was impressive. At the buoyed site, they anchored a BD (an enormous derrick mounted on a barge), moored a substantial steel barge, placed two or more tugs in the immediate vicinity to maneuver both BD and barge as necessary, and manned an LCU (105-foot landing craft utility) with a team of divers and engineers (with quantities of related equipment). At the site, one boat carrying corps officials and another bearing the diving team of archaeologists under contract assembled. Work went on for weeks in the shadowy darkness at the bottom of the Bay. Sudden gusts of wind built up a chop, hampering diving operations. The open waters of the Bay, nine miles off Point Lookout and nearly out of sight of land, could be calm, but they could also boil up quickly in nasty, crested seas. Divers summoned the courage to sink to the murky depth in these waters and to attempt to attach the frames from the derrick which were designed to lift the machinery weighing tons from the wreck.

On August 26 came the first success. From the depths emerged one of the paddle wheel shafts, about twenty feet in length and ten inches in diameter, of cast iron heavily loaded with concretion, with the six-foot hubs for the framing and buckets, as well as the crank at the inner end, still intact. Cheers went up as the derrick lowered it to the deck of the barge.

Success was short-lived. In the worsening weather of the fall, the tribulations of the engineers mounted. One dilemma after another plagued their efforts: sudden storms; anchors dragging, requiring draconian maneuvering to put the barge precisely back in place among the buoys; equipment failures; and the shortening season. In November, the corps reached the decision to suspend operations until the spring of 1993.

Members of the archaeological team survey the artifacts from the crosshead engine of *Columbus* aboard a barge in Curtis Bay, Baltimore. The principal parts are named. Drawn from author's photograph.

In place over the site once again, the corps began operations to lift the machinery in May. With some heavier lifting frames and resort to cutting some of the machinery components on the bottom into smaller pieces, the engineers gained confidence in their final success. Their hopes were shattered on Thursday, May 20, when, with equipment in place and the derrick poised, the engineers watched the seas mount in a vicious chop. As suddenly as they rose, however, the waves died down in a calm during the night. On Friday, the condenser of *Columbus*, attached to a frame from the derrick's cable, broke the surface and rested on the barge.

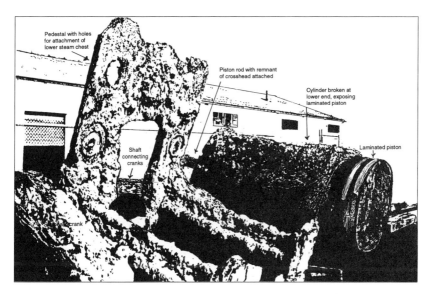

Covered with concretion, the massive pedestal, crank, cylinder (with piston rod and piston exposed) rest on a barge in Curtis Bay. Drawn from author's photograph.

Sunday, May 23, was the long-waited day of triumph. From the depths came the cylinder (broken in two pieces but exposing the piston and shaft inside), the air pump, and quantities of piping. The next day saw the two steam chests join the other components on the barge, as well as the massive pedestal supporting the cylinder and holding the shaft and crank in place.

Alongside a military dock in Curtis Bay, Baltimore, the barge displayed the artifacts of the engine of *Columbus*, sprayed with water to prevent immediate deterioration, destined by truck for the International Artifact Conservation and Research Laboratory in New Orleans, where they would be subjected to a lengthy process involving electrolysis to remove the concretion and preserve the metal. According to its plans, the corps would donate the engine components to the Maryland Historical Trust for exhibition, probably as a centerpiece in the atrium of the Columbus Center for Marine Research and Exploration in the inner harbor at Baltimore. There it would stand as a major contribution to the industrial and shipbuilding history of the United States. (See Appendix A for a detailed description and analysis of the crosshead engine as extrapolated from the components of the engine of *Columbus*.)

Strange stories accompanied the raising of the engine. Divers in the gloomy depths reported feeling the grasp of a hand on their shoulders when they were alone. Watchmen aboard the derrick barge above the wreck heard, in the dark of night, unexplained noises coming from beneath the deck. And then, one night, a chair used by the derrick operator in an enclosed cabin near the top of the rig somersaulted (as though hurled in anger) down a long enclosed stairwell used to reach the enclosure; there was no apparent reason for the displacement of the chair, and nothing like that had occurred before. Among the superstitious of the army's crew, there were mutterings about disturbing the dead at the bottom of the Bay.

The experience of touching the cylinder and its piston, as well as the other artifacts from *Columbus*, conjured up the eerie presence of Charles Reeder, touching the engine he had just completed with such pride in 1828. This crosshead engine, the only one in existence, even in partial form, is destined to carry his presence into succeeding generations.

4

CHESAPEAKE CORSAIR

The passions of civil war inflamed the Chesapeake. They burned for decades after hostilities ceased, and in some regions they left scars long in healing and a mystique carried on through the years. Seen in perspective, the Chesapeake, by its position, could not escape the ravages of war or the upheaval of its citizens. At the Potomac, North and South drew the line; Washington and Baltimore lay to the north, Richmond and Norfolk to the south. The strategy of war perceived the Bay as the water highway over which passed the munitions of war. From Norfolk south lay Albemarle and Pamlico sounds for access to the Confederacy. Up the James lay Richmond, the ultimate Union target. Where Union and Confederate armies met in battle in northern Virginia, the tributaries of the Chesapeake served as vital channels of logistics. In its northern reaches, the Bay linked the industrial might of the North to Union armies in the field. Baltimore at Locust Point became a major supply center, and steamboats steamed out of the harbor laden with ordnance, food, and the necessities of war, bound for the battlefields and the areas of siege in the Tidewater.

Both Union and Confederate forces confiscated—under enforced charter provisions—any steamboats that they needed. For the Confederates, the ability to grab steamers was short-lived. With all of the channels of the Bay, the Potomac River to Washington, and the vast anchorage of Norfolk and Hampton Roads controlled by Union forces, the Confederate quartermaster was hard put to find steamers to confiscate, except a residual few on the upper James and the Rappahannock. Most of the steamboats on the Bay—homeported in Baltimore—fell to the grasp of the USQMD (the Union army's quartermaster department), which seized them without warning, forced a leasing contract on their owners, varying from eighty-five to two hundred dollars per day, ran them hard, abused them, released them occasionally and whimsically when the need dropped off, then quixotically seized them again, and in the end turned them back to their owners in a dilapidated condition that nearly defied restoration.

The boats of the Baltimore Steam Packet Company, the Eastern Shore Steamboat Company, the Weems line, the Slaughter line, the Individual Enterprise Company, and other independently operated lines felt the grasp of the USQMD. The circumstances under which the vessels operated after chartering varied. Some were directly controlled, even manned, by Union army personnel; many operated with their original civilian crews, but under army direction; and some were allowed to run on their routes but were subject to army intervention at any time for specific missions and to surveillance of their activities. They were searched for contraband at any time. Because of the logistical demands of Union forces in the Chesapeake, all felt the pressure of constant steaming, often under arduous and even dangerous circumstances.

Some steamers operated in the vicinity of General Ambrose Burnside's campaign to blockade Pamlico and Albemarle sounds and to close off Confederate access to Norfolk. Operations in the James River, as Union pressure mounted on Richmond, engaged many of the boats; as transports, they carried the troops for City Point and the siege of Petersburg.

The Union generals exercising control over the Chesapeake region from Baltimore regarded some of the steamers and their crews with outright suspicion. Rebel sympathizers manned many of these boats; their activities sometimes escaped scrutiny. For example, the Weems line steamer *George Weems*, a relatively new boat when the war began, spent much of her time while under USQMD control in the shipyard, having her boiler repaired. Charles Reeder, Jr., worked on her boiler through a series of lay-ups: June–December 1861, March–July 1862, April–May 1863, and June–August 1864; she spent as much time with Charles Reeder, Jr., as she spent on supply and transport missions about the Bay. Oddly enough, she had suffered no boiler disability prior to her confiscation, nor did she experience any boiler affliction after her release. Perhaps rough handling under enforced contract could explain her boiler distress, but there persisted an underlying suspicion that her malingering was occasioned by those crew members so disposed to the Confederate cause that they saw to it that she sailed for her Union masters as little as possible.

In spite of the ruthless treatment the steamers received at the hands of the Union army, they made money for their owners from the federal contracts. During the "hospital" period of *George Weems*, for example, her repairs cost less than $2,000, yet her net earnings were $28,058.78. Similar profits accrued to the accounts of other vessels. Nevertheless, when USQMD released the steamboats, many faced extensive renovation, if not virtual rebuilding. Some were summarily scrapped; their wartime earnings barely met the costs sustained by their owners.

Passions ran deep in Maryland throughout the war. In the southern counties, sympathy for the Confederate cause ran strong among the planters. Even in Baltimore, feeling for the South coursed through much of the population and broke out occasionally in open defiance of federal authority. Beneath the surface were many individuals ready to undertake ventures for the rebel cause.

Along the Potomac, where North and South eyed each other across the river, the tension never eased. Shore batteries, moving from place to place on the Virginia side, let fly at passing vessels. From the Maryland shore, at appropriate promontories and points, the Union army unleashed a similar barrage. Federal gunboats prowled the length of the Potomac, even the lower reaches of the Rappahannock and the Piankatank, attempting to enforce a declared blockade but also seeking to stem the flow of covert and nocturnal activity across the rivers.

Crossing the Potomac, even tempestuous as it often was near its mouth, became the means of linking an active network of spies, informers, smugglers, and undercover crusaders working for either side and often for both. These men, and sometimes women, frequently came down from the North on steamers (like *Mary Washington* and *George Weems*, before her confiscation) to Millstone or other landings on the Patuxent. Thence, they went overland to the Potomac, where at Leonardtown or Point Lookout they sought passage at night to Kinsale or other landings in Virginia.

Kinsale, a picturesque and orderly town on the West Yeocomico River, which empties into the Potomac, and Leonardtown, a shipping port on Breton Bay, also a Potomac tributary, earned unsavory reputations and considerable profit as havens for covert spying and smuggling. Their warehouses and wharves at night, darkened from inquiring eyes, placed cargoes of munitions and passengers aboard small sailing craft, which left with muffled oars for the winds of the river and the opposite shore. The somewhat sleazy hotels of these towns provided the setting for exchanges of intelligence by informers and for pillow secrets elicited by ladies of the night.

A dramatic episode occurring in June and July of 1861 startled the populations on both sides of the Potomac. At its center played the principal actor, whom the South proclaimed as a national hero and symbol of the romantic days of chivalry, but whom the North branded as a traitor and pirate. Emotions erupted on both sides, and the flamboyant actor on center stage became a suffering victim of the passions stirred by the event.

It all began when Confederate lookouts along the Virginia shore, watching river traffic passing in the Potomac (and, more particularly, the movements of patrolling Union gunboats), noted a certain pattern of activity surrounding one gunboat, the U.S.S. *Pawnee*. She was known to be commanded by a Lieutenant Ward, USN. *Pawnee* was a small, hastily outfitted vessel commandeered to engage mobile Confederate shore batteries (if they didn't sink her first) and to intercept smugglers and spies crossing the river furtively by small boat. To the rebels strung out along the Northern Neck, she was a thorn to be plucked at the first opportunity.

Intriguing to them was the way in which the mail and some stores were delivered to the vessel, sometimes off Aquia Creek but frequently elsewhere on the Potomac. Under the cover of darkness, U.S.S. *Pawnee* anchored, while a steamer from Baltimore, the *St. Nicholas*, came alongside to pass the mail and goods awaited by the gunboat. Because the approach of *St. Nicholas* became a routine, *Pawnee* accepted her arrival without challenge and without any special security precautions (see Appendix A for data on *St. Nicholas*).

To several shrewd observers, the routine provided an unprecedented opportunity to seize *Pawnee*. The idea, daring and dangerous, involved somehow seizing the unarmed *St. Nicholas* by a band of men in disguise, who would board in Baltimore, and capturing *Pawnee* in a surprise attack from the decks of the mail steamer as it came alongside without challenge in the Potomac.

Several fertile minds in the Virginia militia apparently toyed with the notion of seizing *Pawnee* by this means about the same time, but none seemed to have a practical plan for putting it to the test. In June, Lieutenant H.H. Lewis, CSN, stationed at Aquia Creek, proposed to his regional superior, Brigadier General Thomas [Theophilus] H. Holmes in Fredericksburg, that a force of three hundred men from the Tennessee regiment be used to seize *St. Nicholas* at a landing downriver. The general deemed such a direct attack too risky. He refused to give his permission even when pressured by the Confederate secretary of war, L. P. Walker.

Commander George N. Hollins, CSN, claimed credit for a similar idea. Hollins had enjoyed a promising career in the U.S. Navy, commanding the U.S. frigate *Susquehanna* in the Mediterranean squadron with the rank of captain. Ordered to Washington, he arrived on June 6, 1861, and promptly tendered his resignation in order to join the Southern cause. He approached his duties in the Confederacy by boarding *Mary Washington* in civilian clothes in Baltimore and debarking at Millstone landing on the Patuxent River. Resting at the estate of a friend in St. Mary's County, he learned of the movements of U.S.S. *Pawnee* and *St. Nicholas* and, on his own, hatched up a scheme not unlike that concocted by Lieutenant Lewis. Crossing the peninsula to the Potomac and riding a small boat under darkened skies to the Virginia shore, he made his way to Richmond. There he proposed to the Confederate secretary of the navy that U.S.S. *Pawnee* be captured by a surprise boarding party from the decks of *St. Nicholas*. He was told of the refusal of both General Holmes and the secretaries of war and the navy to allow the plan to proceed. But then he was informed that Virginia Governor John Letcher, a man with a bit of fire in his eye, would undertake on his own to approve a plan presented to him by still another individual and would advance one thousand dollars for the undertaking.

Governor Letcher at that point introduced Holmes to Richard Thomas, who had offered his services to the Confederacy and was prepared to implement a means for capturing *Pawnee*.

Richard Thomas was well known in the social circles of southern Maryland and northern Virginia. A scion of a family of Maryland landed gentry, he was the son of Richard Thomas, Sr., former speaker of the House of Delegates, former president of the Maryland Senate, and brother of Governor James Thomas of Maryland.

Born on October 27, 1833, Richard, Jr., was the eldest of three sons. All three fought for the Confederacy: Richard, Jr., in the episode of *St. Nicholas*, and both George and James William in Company A, Second Maryland Regiment, CSA (George as captain, James William as first sergeant). The latter two fought in Pickett's charge at Gettysburg. George was twice wounded: shot in the face at Cold Harbor and grievously injured at Gettysburg.

The manor house at Mattapany, ancestral home of Richard Thomas Zarvona, presently the official residence of the Commander, Naval Air Warfare Center, Aircraft Division. Courtesy of the Public Relations Officer, U.S. Naval Air Station, Patuxent.

All three grew up under the sheltering maples of Mattapany, the family plantation on the south shore of the Patuxent River, five miles from its mouth and abreast of Solomons Island on the opposite side. The mansion, a long, stately building of brick, stood on level ground above a fifty-foot bluff at the river's edge, with three hundred feet of grassy park extending from the veranda. (The mansion is now the official residence of the Commander, Naval Air Warfare Center, Aircraft Division, U.S. Naval Air Station, Patuxent.) Mattapany enjoyed a long history of entertaining the gentry of southern Maryland. In colonial days, the lord proprietor of Maryland often vacationed there in summertime, accompanied by a retinue of servants. Charles Calvert, third Lord Baltimore, came riding from St. Inigoes to court the beautiful daughter of the house, and the wedding that followed was remembered as a grand affair in the annals of St. Mary's County. In the Revolution, the ancestors of the Thomas brothers stood in the Maryland line in the charge at the battle of Long Island.

Of the three Thomas brothers, Richard, Jr., was the most spirited and daring. Even as a boy among the hard-riding, hard-drinking young blades of the county, he gained a reputation for his near reckless courage and dash. An excellent sailor, marksman, hunter, and skilled horseman, he reveled in the sports that excited the young gentry of southern Maryland.

In early life, he was sent off to Charlotte Hall Academy, a military boarding school, and to a similar institution at Oxford in Talbot County. At age sixteen, he sought (with his political connections assured) and won an appointment to West Point. More interested in the martial arts than in the prescribed studies of the academy, his academic performance was not outstanding. He stood fifty-fifth in a class of seventy-one in his first-class year (thirty-ninth in mathematics, fifty-ninth in French, fiftieth in English studies), and he accumulated 189 demerits for the year. He resigned from the military academy on October 21, 1851.

His spirit of adventure carried him far. Family legend has it that he engaged for a considerable time in government surveys of California and other western territories, and that subsequently he went to China and joined forces with those protecting coastal shipping from the depredations of local pirates. Although no records exist of his Italian service, he reportedly joined the army of Giuseppe Garibaldi to fight for the freedom of a people oppressed by foreign rule. An exuberant and militant idealism drove him to undertake revolutionary adventures more characteristic of a soldier of fortune.

Richard (as determined by later correspondence) certainly witnessed the red-shirted battalions of Garibaldi as they triumphantly entered Naples in September 1860. He probably played some part in the rout of the remnant Bourbon army in the Volturno a month later and accompanied Victor Emmanuel on the latter's entry into Naples. Shortly thereafter, Richard Thomas returned to the United States.

How he initially became interested in Garibaldi could be easily explained. When the great liberator in 1849 retreated through central Italy, pursued by the armies of France, Austria, Spain, and Naples, he eventually found sanctuary by escape to America. During his stay in the United States, the press worldwide glorified him for his past exploits in the defense of freedom in Uruguay in 1834–36 and, after his return to Italy in 1854, for his defense of Italy against Austrian invasion. Richard Thomas, with his head in the clouds of romantic adventure, could only have been stimulated by these stirring accounts of military achievement in the face of nearly insurmountable odds for a crusading cause.

Unexplained was the fascination of Richard Thomas for the Zouaves. These were certain segments of the regular French army, first formed in Algeria in 1831 from a tribe of Berbers (Zouaves) dwelling in the mountains of the Jerjura range. The Zouaves gained a reputation for their strict discipline, fighting capabilities, and oriental uniforms consisting of red, flared-out pantaloons, blue doublet, crimson cap with gold tassel, white gaiters, and scimitarlike saber.

Richard Thomas on his return to the United States in early 1861 soon exhibited his utter obsession with the Zouaves. Interestingly, Thomas spoke fluent French on his arrival. Such fluency did not coincide with his rather poor showing in the one-year study of the language at West Point and could only be attributed to continuous use of the language during his stay in Europe. Furthermore, a certain fluency in Italian could be expected from his reported association with the forces of Garibaldi; but he never evidenced any command of the Italian language after his return to the United States. These links to the French stood in contrast to the avowed animosity of Garibaldi toward France and its allies. Finally, family legend held that Richard Thomas fell in love with a French girl, who died. He mourned her loss so deeply that he took her name as his own and chose to be called Richard Thomas Zarvona. The evidence would suggest that, sometime during his stay in Europe, he served with the Zouaves and brought back with him a romantic notion that he sought to translate into reality in service to the Confederacy. (The National Archives and the Service Archives of the Ministry of Defense of France were neither able to confirm nor deny his service with the Zouaves.)

On April 26, 1861, Zarvona addressed a letter to a cousin in which he outlined his plans for serving the Confederacy:

> To avoid the fatigue of a private's life—which I admit I am little prepared for, I wrote for information as to means necessary to pursue a commission on the staff either as engineer or topographical engineer. Is it possible to get either of these [or] armed ship of Maryland or any Southern State, private armed vessel bearing the Confederate flag? . . . I probably would be better afloat. If Maryland raises no navy, will not someone be willing to fit out a small, strong and swift propeller [vessel] carrying two (or even one) 10 or 11 inch guns up the patent carriage? . . . As for men I believe that I can get 150 in one day, . . . revolvers (I can get them in the North), cutlasses, knives, and about two dozen carbines. . . . (quoted from the manuscript scrapbook compiled by Armstrong Thomas, *The Thomas Brothers of Mattapany*, 1963. Document is in the Library of Congress. All further quotations

cited as *Thomas* in this chapter refer to undated newspaper clippings and journal entries in this scrapbook.).

In May 1861, he formed the nucleus of what he hoped would be a Confederate Zouave regiment. Fifty men began training under his direction on the shores of the Coan River near the mouth of the Potomac. In this encampment he learned from information surreptitiously exchanged from both sides of the river about the movements of U.S.S. *Pawnee* and the supply runs of the steamer *St. Nicholas.* The opportunity that their movements presented for the seizure of both vessels by ruse and attack was perceived by the wily Richard Thomas Zarvona, just as it had been seen by Commander Hollins and Lieutenant Lewis. There was one difference, however: Richard Thomas had in hand a quickly formulated and defined plan for accomplishing the mission.

Accompanied by his friend and kindred spirit, George W. Alexander, a former engineer in the U.S. Navy, Zarvona went to Richmond to tender his services to Governor John Letcher.

Governor Letcher saw before him a young gentleman dressed in the height of fashion, a slender figure with a boyish face. Others described Zarvona as "fragile in form, with sharp irregular features, sharp indentations in his cheeks, blue eyes, aquiline nose and closely shaved in the head and face. There was a deep-seated melancholy about the man. . . . He seemed downcast . . . in the extreme. . . . He seemed to be extremely gentle and spoke in a low, weak voice. . . . Some years ago he formed a tender attachment but . . . the object of his regard expired in his arms while endeavouring [*sic*] to revive her from drowning. Ever since . . . he [was] said to be erratic and gloomy" (Samuel Phillips Day's *Down South*). Another reported that he wore a scar across his cheek, testimony to his frontline combat at some point in his career. Some observers saw him as short but slender, others as tall and thin. But the unusual appearance he presented impressed everyone.

Letcher at first viewed Zarvona as an eccentric but revised his opinion as the latter presented his plan, a few days later, for the seizure of *Pawnee* from the decks of *St. Nicholas.* Letcher, before he reached a decision, invited Commodore Matthew Fontaine Maury to join in a discussion of the plan.

Maury had served as superintendent of the U.S. Naval Observatory, where as a naval lieutenant he performed his work so well that Simon Newcomb, the astronomer, declared that "the institution bode fair to take a high place in science." Then Maury turned his attention to studying ocean winds and currents. On April 26, 1861, Maury left his post and joined the cause of the Confederacy with the rank of commodore.

In the meeting that occurred in the governor's office following Zarvona's initial contact, the plan was unfolded. Zarvona proposed to go to Baltimore, enlist the services of a dozen or more adventurous young men, whom he could recruit from the ranks of southern sympathizers ready to undertake a bold mission against the North. They would board the *St. Nicholas* as passengers, and at a proper moment in the Potomac River and on a given signal, seize the vessel from her officers and crew, assume command under Zarvona, and steam into the Coan River to gather up reinforcements from Confederate units, including Zarvona's Zouaves, before proceeding alongside *Pawnee* to effect her capture by ruse. Those present at the meeting arrived at the conclusion that the plan was feasible.

Governor Letcher called upon the secretary of the navy to furnish pistols, ammunition, and cutlasses for the party boarding U.S.S. *Pawnee.* He also prevailed on L.P. Walker, secretary of war, to order General Holmes at Fredericksburg to send a force of six hundred men drawn from the Tennessee regiment to the Coan River to support the operation and to transport the needed arms.

Walker agreed, reluctantly, under the stipulation that the troops were not to engage in the seizure of the civilian vessel, *St. Nicholas*, an operation he still considered harebrained.

Governor Letcher presented Zarvona with an advance of one thousand dollars to be used in procuring arms in Baltimore and possibly for encouraging a few young adventurers to join in a bold strike at the foes of the Confederacy. At the same time, he promised Zarvona the rank of colonel (Alexander and George, the rank of captain) if the plan succeeded, and told Zarvona to use the title in recruitment.

Zarvona, accompanied by Alexander, set out for Baltimore, traveling the usual route: by furtively crossing the Potomac, traversing the peninsula to the Patuxent, and (as an apparent farm worker) boarding *Mary Washington* for passage up the Bay. In Baltimore, the two let it be known in certain covert circles that they were seeking men for a bold but rewarding enterprise for the Southern cause.

One of the men, George W. Watts, late lieutenant, CSA, recruited by Zarvona, recounted his enlistment:

We were all strong Southern sympathizers, and one day the information was quietly circulated among those true to the cause that a Colonel Thomas, who had served in foreign wars, was planning a desperate expedition. I nosed around and got wind of what was up, and then one night I met Colonel Thomas and fifteen other men.

Well, Sir, at first I was mighty disappointed with the Colonel. He looked like one of them slick floorwalkers in a department store. I think the other men felt the same way that I did, but pretty soon we found we were all fooled. Believe me, Sir, that man had the quickest brain I ever ran across, and his eyes were just as quick. Eyes? Why, when that man looked at you [they looked right through you]. It didn't take us long to learn who was boss around there. So we got all our plans ready ("Last Survivor of a Gallant Band," *Evening Sun*, August 27, 1910).

On the evening of June 28, 1861, the men engaged by Zarvona boarded *St. Nicholas* in Baltimore. They arrived at the wharf one by one or in pairs at intervals, passing themselves off as harvest hands in search of employment in the fields of southern Maryland. They paid their fares and were duly searched for contraband, as required by military authorities, who found nothing.

Among a total of nearly sixty passengers coming aboard *St. Nicholas* just before departure was a very stylishly dressed young lady, speaking only broken English with a marked French accent. Her brother (a fierce-looking bearded man) accompanied her, so she said, and helped translate her wishes. Her name was Madame LaForte, she said, and she had a number of large trunks to take with her, in order to establish her millinery business in Washington. Entranced by her smile, the purser assigned her to a commodious stateroom off the main deck and had deckhands haul her trunks to her cabin.

When the steamer departed, the lady emerged from her stateroom and flirted shamelessly with the most attractive males among the passengers and ship's officers. Captain Jacob Kirwan, who prided himself on his knowledge of French, tried out his vocabulary on the lady, who proved herself a native of France with a voluble stream of coquettish language that quite overwhelmed him. Fluent French gushed from her lips. She radiated charm. A veil covered her eyes and cheeks but not her reddened lips. She tossed her fan about and cocked her head at an angle toward any gentleman who occupied her attention at the moment. With her bearded brother at her arm, she meandered from saloon to dance hall, flirting as she went with the ship's officers. Captain Kirwan was disturbed.

"I didn't like the appearance of that French woman at all," he said later. "She sat next to me at table and so close that our legs touched. I thought she looked mighty queer" (Day).

She swished about the deck, waving a large fan like a Spanish dancer.

"That young woman behaved so scandalously that all the other women on the boat were in a terrible state over it," said George Watts. One crew member, utterly mesmerized by the lady, leaned over to kiss her and straightened up abruptly with the mark of a hand slap on his cheek.

For some reason, which the crew did not understand, most of the passengers elected to wander about the decks on into the night as the steamer plowed her way south toward the Potomac. About midnight, the steamer rounded Point Lookout and sidled alongside the dock just inside the spit of land at the point. Coming aboard were several men including an elderly gentleman, all seeking passage to Washington.

George Watts, member of the recruits boarding in Baltimore, was upset:

Among [the passengers] I counted my 15 comrades. We all kept separated, however, and didn't let anyone know we knew each other. But what worried me a lot was I couldn't find the colonel or anyone that looked like him. I could see the failure of the whole expedition, and also I could see myself behind bars at Fort McHenry, and the picture didn't look a bit good for me.

I was on deck a-wondering where it was all going to end and whether I'd be hung as a Rebel spy when someone touched me on the arm. I whirled around like somebody had stuck a knife in me and saw Alexander [the bearded brother]. He grinned at the way he had scared me and said, "You're wanted in the second cabin."

I hurried below decks [to the second cabin] and nearly had a fit when I found all our boys gathered around that frisky French lady. She looked at me when I came in, and, Lordy, I knew those eyes in a minute! It was the Colonel. Then he shed his bonnet, wig, and dress and stepped forth clad in a brilliant new Zouave uniform. In a jiffy the "French" lady's three big trunks were dragged out and opened. One was filled with cutlasses, another with Colt revolvers, and the third with carbines. Each man buckled on a sword and pistol and grabbed a gun, and then the Colonel told us what to do ("Last Survivor . . .").

The colonel and two men proceeded to the captain's cabin and confronted Kirwan, who, when apprised of the force seizing his ship, readily surrendered. George Watts, former sailor in the U.S. Navy, and John Frazier, a Baltimore pilot who had been briefed on Zarvona's plans, entered the pilothouse and placed a pistol at the head of the black quartermaster at the wheel. He gave in meekly enough, and Frazier, with Watts as quartermaster, wheeled the steamer about and pointed her bow for the mouth of the Coan River on the Virginia side of the Potomac. Elsewhere on *St. Nicholas,* the crew and passengers were informed of the capture of the vessel by Confederate men and assured of kind treatment when the steamer reached its immediate destination in the Coan River.

When Colonel Zarvona appeared on deck in full Zouave uniform and gave the signal for the capture of the vessel, the elderly gentleman who had boarded at Point Lookout shed his white wig and cane and emerged as Commander George N. Hollins, CSN. He had been ordered to board *St. Nicholas* with a few additional recruits to help insure the success of Zarvona's mission.

In the early morning hours of June 29, 1861, *St. Nicholas* docked on the Coan River and took aboard some thirty well-armed soldiers led by Captain Lewis. The large unit of the Tennessee regiment supposedly dispatched by General Holmes under orders of the secretary of war had been delayed, administratively or logistically. Not too far away was the small encampment of Zouaves still under training by Zarvona. From the decks of *St. Nicholas* trooped the passengers and crew taken captive the preceding night.

The passengers were permitted to leave with all their possessions. Many started off to seek conveyance by carriage or cart and boat to their homes. Several had missed their breakfast aboard the steamer and found it in a neighboring farmhouse. Upon asking how they should pay, they received a particularly hospitable reply, "Gentlemen, recollect that you are in Virginia!"

With a force of well-armed men aboard the captured prize, Zarvona prepared to undertake the next and more critical phase of his adventure.

The climactic news came with frustrating suddenness. U.S.S. *Pawnee* had eluded his grasp and had left her station on the Potomac to proceed to Washington. Her skipper, Lieutenant Ward, had been killed by a rebel sharpshooter the day before in an artillery exchange with Confederate batteries off Point Mathias, and the vessel had returned to the Washington Navy Yard for the funeral.

How Zarvona learned of these tidings is not clear. Some reports indicated that Commander (later Commodore) Hollins had gathered the information before boarding *St. Nicholas* at Point Lookout. One account stated that Hollins learned of the event from newspapers at Coan. Still other accounts place *St. Nicholas* steaming fruitlessly up the Potomac in search of *Pawnee* before the news reached Zarvona on board from intelligence operations on shore.

However the critical information reached Zarvona, he reacted, first with an explosion of frustration, and second with a resolve to make the most of the capture of *St. Nicholas* before the federal authorities learned of her seizure.

St. Nicholas, now manned entirely by men loyal to the Confederacy and commanded by Zarvona and Hollins, headed for the Chesapeake Bay, bent on a raid to compensate for the lost opportunity.

A large brig, the *Monticello,* bringing thirty-five thousand bags of coffee from Brazil to Baltimore, hove into view. *St. Nicholas* ranged alongside and confiscated it in the name of the Confederacy. A boarding party was placed aboard it in command of Lieutenant Rimms, who set sail for Fredericksburg, where coffee was in short supply and hard to obtain. In less than a hour, *St. Nicholas,* still in the Bay, captured and boarded a schooner, *Mary Pierce,* ten days out of Boston, bound for Washington and laden with ice. A prize crew, Lieutenant Robert D. Minor, CSN, in charge, took her to Fredericksburg where the hospitals welcomed the ice.

During these operations, both Hollins and Zarvona grew apprehensive about the dwindling bunker of coal. *St. Nicholas* had steamed about her limit without replenishment since leaving Baltimore, and Hollins readied the engineers to burn cabin furniture or any combustibles if the fuel ran low. Fate took a hand.

The schooner *Margaret,* coming out of the Potomac into the Bay, fell in the sights of Zarvona and Hollins aboard *St. Nicholas*. She was loaded with coal, bound from Alexandria to New York. A crew member from the schooner later wrote about the event:

On Saturday, the 29th of June, we passed Smith Point, at the mouth of the Potomac. We saw the steamer *St. Nicholas* come out of a river on the Virginia shore, called Cone [*sic*] River. She passed us, and paid no attention to us, we thinking all the while it was rather strange for her to be sailing down the Bay, as it was out of her course. Her object, as we soon found out, was to seize the brig

Monticello, and the schooner *Mary Pierce*, which were bound up the Bay, as we were going out.

In a few minutes, the *St. Nicholas* headed up the Bay again; she came up and passed us; then turned again and bore down on us; Captain Hollins hailed us, and asked what schooner it was. We told him the schooner *Margaret*. He then inquired what it was loaded with, and we told him. He then sung [*sic*] out that we were a prize to the Southern Confederacy. The *St. Nicholas* was then run close alongside; then about twenty-five armed men jumped on board and drove all hands on board the steamer. . . . They then took the schooner in tow, and took us up the Rappahannock river as far as the depth of the water would permit. That night they came along-side, and coaled the *St. Nicholas* from our cargo. Next morning we started for Fredericksburg (Thomas).

Lieutenant Thorburn, part of the Virginia contingent on board *St. Nicholas*, commanded the prize crew.

Hollins and Zarvona, fearful that news of the capture of *St. Nicholas* and the sailing vessels would bring the power of the Union naval vessels on the Potomac around their heels, had decided to high-tail it up the Rappahannock. With the coal schooner in tow (and *Mary Pierce*, which they overtook), they proceeded to Fredericksburg.

In line with the policy of the Confederate government with respect to fair treatment for the people of Baltimore (whom they hoped to entice), at Fredericksburg the *St. Nicholas* was first processed in the Richmond District Court in Admiralty and was put up for sale for $18,924.17. The proceeds went to her original owners. She was purchased, in effect, by the Confederate Navy and became the C.S.S. *Rappahannock* (she was burned in the evacuation of Fredericksburg in April 1862 to prevent her capture by Union forces). The flag at her staff when she was seized was the first American flag captured in the War between the States.

In Fredericksburg, Zarvona and his men received the enthusiastic welcome of a city greatly excited and overjoyed by their exploits. A ball was given in their honor, and Zarvona to the utter devastation and de-light of those present appeared in the hoops and skirts of the lady milli-ner from Paris.

In Richmond, also, Zarvona was feted and idolized. Governor Letcher, with the hearty approval of the Virginia legislature, commissioned the hero as Colonel Richard Thomas Zarvona, thereby officially recognizing not only his rank but also his chosen name. George Alexander was simultaneously commissioned captain. Zarvona was the hero of the day; more parties were held in his honor.

When he appeared in uniform, as he often did, he presented a dramatic illusion of oriental splendor: blue (not the red of the original Zouaves) pantaloons, embroidered vest, white gaiters, crimson cloth cap with gold tassel, and a light, beautifully crafted sword.

"What a strange looking man he was," extolled one British observer, "as he walked into the dining room in his Zouave costume and red cap on his closely shaven head! The tassel hung low down on his shoulders, his neck was bare and scraggy, and his manner silent, reserved, and gloomy. Poor man!" (Thomas).

On the Fourth of July, lavishly celebrated in Richmond, the Zouave units of Zarvona paraded with great flair, among other troops, through the streets. They fired twelve rounds on Capitol Square, eleven being in honor of the Confederate states, and one for the legislature of Maryland. The guard, as they were called, was accompanied by a brass band, which enthused the audience by playing the Marseillaise, as Zarvona, treated with great respect, looked on from the capitol steps.

One amusing incident was duly but belatedly reported in the press:

At the Spottswood House, surrounded by his friends, they insisted on seeing him in his female costume as he appeared on *St. Nicholas*. To gratify them he left the room, promising to return promptly, provided the company was not enlarged, as the joke was to be strictly private. Unfortunately, the circle was shortly after disturbed by the entrance of a strange lady, for whom, however, room was made and to whom a seat was tendered with customary Virginia gallantry. The rest of the company broke into knots, leaving the stranger to herself, and discussed in whispers the propriety of keeping the Colonel out, until a favorable opportunity presented itself. Suddenly their embarrassment was relieved by the action of the lady, who, lifting her skirts to a modest height, displayed a soldier's uniform and end of cutlass. The effect was astonishing. (Thomas)

Vast numbers of the citizens of Richmond called to pay their respects, and Zarvona's room at the Executive Mansion, where he was a guest, was often crowded with visitors clamoring to see him. He swept about in great style, his Zouave uniform flashing red and blue among the gray.

By now, accounts of his adventure had reached the northern press, which denounced him roundly as a traitor and spy. But on the Union army, the effect was sobering. The skill with which Zarvona had pursued his objectives and the imaginative boldness, even audacity, of his attack caused fear that he would try again—with equal success.

Telegrams went out from local naval commanders to the secretary of the navy in Washington. Stated one: "A man of notoriously bad character . . . has formed a plan for the capture, during the present week, of one of the steamboats plying between Baltimore and the Patuxent River, either by putting his men on board the boat at Baltimore, or at Millstone Landing. . . . Small vessels are constantly plying between that position and the Rappahannock and Coan Rivers, chiefly to the latter, where a Tennessee regiment is posted" (*Official Records of the Union and Confederate Navies*).

Their fears were well founded. Richard Thomas Zarvona was a restless man, even more depressed and restive than usual in the social adulation of Richmond society. He planned for the next venture.

Given the success of the last mission, he decided to undertake the seizure of another steamboat out of Baltimore. In this instance, the warnings of federal authorities gleaned from intelligence agents on both sides of the Potomac and in Baltimore were remarkably accurate and continued to come in. U.S.S. *Pocahontas* in the Potomac reported on July 9 ". . . that a pungy had come over from Coan River and landed crews of the three vessels captured by the *St. Nicholas*. The crews proceeded by land to Millstone Landing [on the Patuxent] . . . and the pungy went up the Chesapeake Bay. She was manned by well-armed men, variously estimated from eighteen to thirty. . . . The overland men arrived safely and had taken passage in the steamer *Mary Washington* for Baltimore. . . . The notorious Thomas went up in disguise, the idea of him and the armed party . . . is to capture the next steamer from Baltimore, which will be the *George Weems*" (*Official Records of the Union and Confederate Navies*).

These observations were generally correct, except that Zarvona, after gaining the permission of Governor Letcher for another venture, cast about for options on how to proceed. Governor Letcher, at the time, believed that Zarvona also considered going to New York to procure arms incident to seizing some vessel with which to go to sea and raid the shipping lanes for the Confederacy. In either contingency, Zarvona faced the immediate problem of how to proceed.

He could transport a force of armed men directly up the Bay aboard the pungy he now owned, the *Georgeanna*, and effect the capture of a steamer in Baltimore. However, alerted as the Union forces must be to his possible movements, interception seemed not only possible but probable. Alternatively, he could adopt some form of disguise or civilian camouflage and with his men (unarmed to avoid detection by search) travel by steamer from a Patuxent or another landing on the steamer route to Baltimore, and thus escape scrutiny on the Bay. The latter plan entailed the procurement of weapons in Baltimore to arm his comrades. To Zarvona, the second choice seemed the more feasible. He decided to land from the pungy with a few trusted and able men and board the steamer for Baltimore.

His decision was star-crossed from the start. A number of events occurred simultaneously, which he could not have anticipated.

First, on July 8, Union troops commandeered the steamer *Chester* at her Light Street wharf, put her passengers ashore before sailing, and moved her to Fort McHenry. There, two twenty-two-pound guns, a company of artillery and infantry, and a squad of police were put aboard, prior to her dispatch, to search for the vessel in which Zarvona was reportedly embarked. *Chester* sailed down the Bay but returned after midnight, having failed to contact the boat under suspicion, and steamed about six miles up the Patuxent to Millstone Landing. In spite of her failure to intercept the boat, her captain did learn that the pungy had been there in the morning and had debarked about thirty men, some armed.

Second, the steamer *George Weems* was taken over by federal troops in Baltimore and not permitted to leave her slip. The purpose was to preempt any attempt by Zarvona to capture her.

Third, Lieutenant Thomas Carmichael and a small detachment of men departed for Fair Haven on a tug under orders from Provost Marshal Kenly of the military police in Baltimore to arrest a man there by the name of Neill Green, who was charged with engaging in the riots of April 19 in Baltimore. (On that day occurred the first real bloodshed of the Civil War, when the Sixth Massachusetts Regiment, in changing from one train station to another, bore the attack of a mob on Pratt Street.) Thirst for revenge among Union forces ran strong. Carmichael and his men arrived at Fair Haven, arrested Green, and arranged to return with him and his wife to Baltimore aboard the steamer *Mary Washington* on July 8.

Fourth, an unexpected coincidence of passengers boarding *Mary Washington* at Fair Haven occurred. The coincidence concerned Edward

Case, master of *Margaret*, which had been seized by Zarvona aboard *St. Nicholas*. Case narrated what occurred after his schooner was towed to Fredericksburg by *St. Nicholas*:

> We were put on the cars [train] for Richmond . . . and were taken direct to jail. . . . After going to the Mayor's office and obtaining a permit to pass out of Virginia, the whole of us—thirty eight in number [the crews of all three sailing vessels seized by *St. Nicholas*, plus the original crew of the steamer itself]—were permitted to depart. . . . We were taken back again to Fredericksburg. . . . At 1 o'clock Friday morning, 5th July, we were put on board a boat and . . . landed down river at a place called Mahassen [Monaskon on the Northern Neck?]; we staid [*sic*] and slept in a barn there. The people here were kind to us. . . . On Saturday [July 6] we started and walked twenty-three miles before we could reach the banks of the Potomac, at the head of the Cone [*sic*] River.
>
> Captain [Jacob] Kirwan, the late Captain of the *St. Nicholas*, got a wagon and drove four miles, where he managed to [contact] a schooner that would take us across the following morning. We walked the next morning for the boat, which was of the Confederate Army, and named the *Georgeanna*, owned by Colonel Thomas; Col. T. was on board with a crew of about twelve in number. We sailed for Point Lookout, on the Maryland shore, and landed about 5 o'clock on Sunday [July 7]. Directly we landed she [the schooner] started and sailed up the Chesapeake Bay.
>
> We . . . walk[ed] the 30 miles to Millstone Wharf on the Patuxent River, to meet the steamer *Mary Washington*. We reached there about 6 o'clock in the morning, Monday [July 8]. The captain of the *Mary Washington* [Mason Locke Weems] . . . gave us all a passage to Baltimore, and furnished us all with a splendid dinner.
>
> At Millstone Wharf who should come aboard but Col. Thomas, the same man who seized the steamer *St. Nicholas* (Thomas).

Among other passengers and crew members of *Mary Washington* were some individuals who knew Zarvona well. Southern sympathizers and admirers of the Confederate hero, they quietly warned him that he was in danger and urged him to flee while he had a chance. He laughed them off.

The steamer, after clearing the Patuxent mouth, turned to the western shore for a scheduled landing at Fair Haven, a resort south of An-

napolis established by the Weems line. Boarding at Fair Haven were
Lieutenant Carmichael, John Horner, and a few police, along with their
prisoner, Neill Green.

Captain Kirwan and the original crews of *St. Nicholas* and the captured
sailing vessels very quickly tipped off the police. Zarvona was spotted but
not immediately arrested in order to avoid a possible armed confrontation on board. But Zarvona grew increasingly uneasy as the steamer approached Baltimore:

> Before we arrived at North Point [Patapsco mouth], Colonel
> Thomas imagined that somebody was on the lookout for him, and
> endeavored to lower the quarter boat of the steamer, but he was
> caught in the act by the officers, and stopped. He drew a pistol,
> and the officers drew their revolvers; they told him they would take
> him dead or alive. He called out for his "boys," and by that the
> officers found out who the rebels were that were with him
> (Thomas).

In the meantime, Carmichael had approached Captain Mason Locke
Weems and ordered him to take *Mary Washington* alongside the wharf at
Fort McHenry, so that federal troops could be brought aboard to seize
the rebels. The order had become common knowledge very quickly. Zarvona demanded to know by what authority the *Mary Washington* was being directed to Fort McHenry. Carmichael replied that the diversion was
under police orders.

In the commotion that the armed confrontation caused among the
passengers (some of whom stepped forward to shield the rebels, others
to remonstrate with them), the police officers, better armed than the
rebels, persuaded those rebels whom they had in sight to surrender. A
number of witnesses were summarily arrested, including John L. Hebb
(who had exhibited friendliness for Zarvona), a Dr. Edward Johnson, a
Colonel Forbes, and lighthouse keeper James Tongue (these witnesses
were released shortly afterward); other witnesses were detained. In the
excitement, women went screaming from the saloon and retreated into
the ladies' cabin.

When *Mary Washington* tied up to the dock at Fort McHenry, one of the
police officers reported immediately to General Banks in command, who in
turn ordered a detachment of Massachusetts infantry on board. The sus-
pects (and the witnesses) were rounded up and marched off to prison.

But Zarvona had disappeared, vanishing into thin air. Some conjectured that he had jumped overboard, but then countered that he would have been seen in the attempt. After an hour and a half of searching the vessel from hold to hurricane deck, the police were prepared to release the vessel and allow Captain Weems to proceed to Baltimore Harbor.

Then they found him. He had been stuffed into a bureau in the ladies' cabin. Among the female passengers were several who found the colonel irresistible. Removing the bottoms from the drawers in the bureau, they had fitted the slender chap in place. But one of the ladies tipped off the police. And the immaculately dressed "French lady spy," as he was known throughout the land, was a sad spectacle as he was dragged, cramped and drenched with perspiration, off to prison.

Zarvona was placed in close confinement in Fort McHenry. In his baggage, the police found his Zouave uniform, some letters confirming his mission of depredation on Chesapeake shipping, his commission in the volunteer forces of Virginia, and the letter of credit for one thousand dollars drawn up by B. H. Maury and Company of Richmond on a prominent Baltimore bank. These were subsequently used as evidence against him.

His capture sparked a furor of excitement in the press, both North and South. In the North, newspapers denounced Zarvona as a traitor and treacherous spy, but beneath the rancor the journalists divulged a grudging admiration for the plucky soldier of fortune, the "French lady spy." In the South, the press rhapsodized over the colonel, portrayed him romantically as the hero of the hour, and demanded his release by exchange from Union confinement.

Zarvona's imprisonment was a blight on the reputation of the government for decent treatment of those incarcerated in wartime. Union authorities refused to accept him as a prisoner of war. Instead, they chose to perceive him as a civilian accused of major crimes, or, indeed as someone held under capital charges by the Department of State rather than the War Department.

He was held in solitary confinement at Fort McHenry, allowed to cross the yard only for sanitary reasons under armed guard, and locked up at night in a partially underground cell. Under their refusals to accept him as a prisoner of war, both Major General Nathaniel Banks and his replacement, Major General John A. Dix, holding jurisdiction over him in Baltimore, rejected his demand for release on parole. Behind their rejections was the vengeance of Secretary of War Edwin M. Stanton, determined to reflect the wrath of the North in his punishment of Zarvona. Talk of hanging him circulated in official circles. Furthermore, witnesses against him (some former crew members of *St. Nicholas* and others) were confined for more than a year in Fort McHenry, awaiting a trial that failed to take place.

Zarvona's health deteriorated under the stress of confinement. Somewhat physically frail, he suffered increasingly from nervous debility. Even Major General John A. Dix, a hard-nosed patriot exercising military authority with an iron hand, was moved to address General McClellan on Zarvona's behalf, citing the fact that "his nervous system is much broken by confinement and want of active occupation and he has made earnest appeals to me for the privilege of walking about the garrison within the walls on his parole of honor not to attempt to escape" (Earp, "The Amazing Colonel Zarvona"). The request was ignored.

On December 2, 1861, Zarvona was transferred by steamboat under heavy guard headed by Major D. P. DeWitt to Fort Lafayette in New York Harbor at the Narrows. The move accompanied a further refusal of Major General Dix to consider transferring Zarvona to the list of prisoners of war, his rejection being a response to an inquiry from the secretary of war. At Fort Lafayette, surveillance of his every move continued; his correspondence was intercepted and read. Some letters of his attracted more than usual attention:

> Fort Lafayette
> February 25, 1862
>
> Box received. Box inclosed for Mr. H. delivered. Your letters not received. Have you signed in language?
>
> R.
>
> Fort Lafayette
> February 26, 1862
>
> See to-day's Herald, column 6, pages 1 and 2. Please inform me if any books or letters from France for me addressed to care of J. have arrived.
>
> R.

(*Official Records of the Union and Confederate Navies*)

A day later, Adjutant General L. Thomas addressed a report to Lieutenant Colonel Martin Burke, commander of Fort Lafayette:

I have been informed that Thomas, the French lady, imprisoned at Fort Lafayette, has a cipher by which his correspondence with a Mrs. Norris and others in Baltimore passes without suspicion. For instance, his quotation of a line of poetry will in some way convey a request for acids, files, or anything he may desire and which will be conveyed to him under the case of a breast-pin or something apparently harmless. He is a desperate man and very restless under his confinement, and designs escaping if he can. My informant was lately released from Fort Lafayette . . . where he says he became acquainted with the above facts (*Official Records of the Union and Confederate Navies*).

Lieutenant Colonel Burke transmitted papers to the adjutant general of the army that purported to support the allegation of "secret writing." Stated Burke, "His peculiarity in writing has been noticed here for some time" (Thomas).

In April, Zarvona's mother pleaded in a series of letters to Lieutenant Colonel Burke to permit her to visit her son in prison. At one point, it seemed that her pleas were winning a favorable response. At the last moment, however, her requests were refused. On April 22, Burke received the following report:

At half past 9 o'clock last night Richard Thomas Zarvona, the French lady, a prisoner in close confinement at this post, informed the sergeant of the guard that he wanted to go to the water closet. The sergeant sent him out attended by a member of the guard; when he reached the water closet (which is situated at the sea wall) instead of entering it he jumped overboard [into stormy waters] and attempted to escape by swimming to the Long Island shore. The guard immediately gave the alarm, when the barge belonging to post was manned and he was recaptured before he had succeeded in getting but a short distance. To prevent a reoccurrence of this, I have had a police tub placed in his room (*Official Records of the Union and Confederate Navies*).

According to one source, Zarvona, unable to swim, had attached a belt of tin cans to his waist to keep him afloat. His efforts failed, and his confinement became more stringent than ever: he was not permitted to leave his casemate cell under any circumstance and was constantly guarded by a sergeant known for his harshness (or three tough privates when the sergeant had to leave temporarily). Another request by Zarvona's mother to visit her son was at first summarily refused.

Then the refusal was rescinded, and Mrs. Richard Thomas visited Fort Lafayette:

> When he [Zarvona] came in [to the commander's office], she did not recognize him at first he was so changed. He looked so tall and was very thin and emaciated and had hardly strength to speak. His hand which you know was short and plump is now long and bony. He held her hand all the time. She asked him how he was. He said he was as well as could be expected shut up without light or air, his cell partly under water, with a place about the size of a dollar to admit the light; on cloudy days he could not see to walk about his room. . . . (Correspondence from Captain George Thomas to General T. J. [Stonewall] Jackson, November 18, 1862, in which Thomas pleaded with Jackson to intercede; in Thomas).

Zarvona continued to languish in solitary confinement. Aroused by the stories reaching him about the colonel's condition, Governor Letcher of Virginia undertook to address a letter to President Abraham Lincoln himself:

> Executive Department
> Richmond, Virginia
> January 2, 1863

> Sir:

> On the 19th of April, 1861, the convention of the Commonwealth of Virginia . . . passed "An ordinance to repeal the ratification of the Constitution of the United States. . . ." Against this Confederacy, the Government of the United States declared war. In the prosecution of this purpose, Col. Richard Thomas Zarvona . . . was arrested . . . and is now confined at Fort Lafayette. Right of a prisoner of war is denied [even] holding as he did the military commission. If he is regarded in any other light, [he is] entitled to a speedy and a public trial. . . . Notwithstanding this express clause he has now been confined for eighteen months. . . . Why Colonel Zarvona has not been exchanged . . . it is for the Government of the United States to explain. . . . It is proper under all the circumstances of this case that I should inform you distinctly of the course that I have taken and the policy I intend to pursue. . . . From these prisoners [those expressly captured in pursuance of

the policy] I have taken two of the officers [a captain and a lieu-
tenant] and [five privates] . . . to be kept in the penitentiary in
solitary confinement. All of them there to remain until Colonel
Zarvona is properly exchanged under suitable agreement or
discharged and permitted to return to this city (various official
sources and Thomas).

In Washington, this letter, in spite of diminishing interest in Zarvona as
the war mounted in intensity on many fronts, stirred a response. The threat
of Letcher to reciprocate in double for the treatment of Zarvona had to be
taken seriously. Under orders to investigate the condition of Zarvona's
health, Dr. W. H. Studley, surgeon, U.S. Army, reported that "his health
[was] generally good . . . social and rational." Others who saw Zarvona dis-
agreed and privately concluded that the surgeon's report was a deliberate lie.

In Richmond, the military hostages held by Letcher suffered also. On
February 5, 1863, they addressed a letter to Washington:

> Penitentiary of Virginia
> Richmond
>
> Your petitioners are prisoners of war confined in the penitentiary
> of this city. We are held as hostages for one Colonel Thomas. . . .
> We have been prisoners for more than three months, one and half
> of which has been in this loathsome place where we have suffered
> extremely . . . rooms small . . . diet same as convicts. . . . There are
> seven of us held for the release of one man. We should think our
> government ought to make the exchange without hesitation. . . .
> Our officers among us are very gallant men, too. . . . We have
> written several letters to Secretary Stanton . . . received no reply.
> . . . Governor Letcher has long since notified our government of
> his readiness to exchange us . . . (Thomas).

Wives, relatives, and friends of the hostages, as well as detained witnesses,
deluged the War Department and the State Department with petitions. A
Mrs. C. A. Wilson wrote to Secretary of State Seward on January 3, 1863:

> Please excuse me, but necessity compels me to call to your atten-
> tion once more to the case of Charles Wilson, my husband, now in
> prison to await the trial of Thomas, the rebel. He is witness against
> him, and has been in prison in Baltimore since July last. Wilson was a
> hand on board of the schooner *Margaret*, of Boston, when taken by
> Thomas. . . . For God's sake, let my husband come home (Thomas).

While the correspondence mounted, the U.S. Senate, moved by appeals from its constituents, resolved that the Committee on Military Affairs and the Militia be instructed "to inquire for the purpose of extending such relief as the circumstances may require into the case of Mr. Thomas of Maryland. . . ." (Resolution of U.S. Senate, January 28, 1863).

The pressure to release Zarvona mounted. By mid-March, the secretaries of war and state had concluded that his continued confinement would serve no purpose except to induce reprisal from Virginia. Lieutenant Colonel Martin Burke, apprised of these developments, approached Zarvona. Burke wrote to the adjutant general in Washington:

> I wrote to you some days since in regard to a parole for R. T. Zarvona (the French Lady). He now desires to say that if released he will leave the country and give his parole of honor not to return to the United States or the Confederate States during the war, and that he will not take part in the rebellion. He says he will do this because his health is destroyed by the confinement he has undergone (from the official records quoted in Earp, "The Amazing Colonel Zarvona").

On April 11, 1863, the army commissioner general of prisoners at Fort Monroe, Virginia, notified the authorities in New York that Secretary of War Stanton had authorized the exchange of Zarvona. The military commands in Washington and Fort Monroe were notified that Zarvona left Fort Lafayette on April 16.

Zarvona reached Richmond on May 6, 1863, "his nervous system completely broken down." Greeted by family and friends, and Governor Letcher, he had difficulty regaining his poise and composure. Nevertheless, Zarvona proposed that he be given command of the united Maryland line, even though he was obviously unfit for duty and such an appointment would violate the terms of his parole. General Bradley T. Johnson instead received the appointment. Zarvona, broken in body and spirit, departed for France.

The three Thomas brothers, at the close of the war, found themselves in financial duress. Union forces had occupied Mattapany and confiscated anything that could be removed—cattle, horses, farm equipment, furniture, and produce. James William worked as a civil engineer on the transcontinental railway system, but returned to St. Mary's County and died in 1901. George returned to Mattapany, farmed, and conducted a school in the mansion for his own and neighboring children. He died much respected as a scholar, orator, and genial host at the manor.

Zarvona returned to St. Mary's in 1870 but left the country again. Back again in 1872, he faced the grim task of coping not only with failing health but near financial disaster.

In 1873, he penned a rather disconnected account of his status and misfortunes. It appeared that he had gone abroad the second time to invest in some sort of enterprise to insure himself with an income for the rest of his life. After waiting for two years—with considerable loss of time and money—for the project to bear fruit, he came to the conclusion that his venture would not succeed. The nature of the venture was not clear. At that point, he realized that he would be entirely without money and considered seeking some sort of temporary employment to defray expenses on his return to the States. In addition to his financial troubles, he was beset by health problems that stood in the way of active efforts to relieve his difficulties. Particularly poignant were his references to Mattapany, where he had lived for a short time, having been left the estate by his mother, and then its subdivision under suit by his brother, James William.

Zarvona lived his last few years in anguish over the state of his health and his fortunes. He never lost the feeling that he had been abandoned by those closest to him, his gallantry forgotten in the larger events of the war.

Zarvona died on March 17, 1875. He was buried at Deep Falls, the family estate near Chaptico in St. Mary's County, where he had lived with the family of James William for a short time before his death.

The shadow of Zarvona lingering over the site would have been surprised and gratified by the accolades pouring in to commemorate his life. Among them was a memorial written by John Letcher, ex-governor of Virginia:

> Colonel Zarvona was a most . . . extraordinary man [with] a fine intellect, . . . a good conversationalist, and a most pleasant and agreeable gentleman. . . . If any man has ever lived of whom it must be said "he was insensible to fear," Zarvona was undoubtedly that man. He . . . sought the most hazardous undertaking, and fearlessly exposed himself to the most formidable dangers. And yet modesty, candor, and sincerity, . . . gentleness, kindness, [and] tenderness were predominant traits in his character. He was a sincere and devoted friend, a true and tried citizen, and a patriotic

and gallant soldier. He was somewhat eccentric, but his eccentricities did not render him disagreeable; on the contrary, tended rather to inspire regard for and excite interest in him. . . . I became very much attached to him, and appreciated him most highly for his integrity and his intellect, for his coolness, his courage, for his public and private virtues, and for the possession of all those qualities that make up the man (Thomas).

Two steamers of the Chesapeake bore witness to the daring exploits of this colorful man. The decks of *St. Nicholas* and *Mary Washington* knew his step. They set the stage for the dramatic events of his brief wartime career—his quixotic triumph and his exotic downfall. The shadows may lie long at Deep Falls, but they still quiver with excitement at the memory of the gallant corsair of the Chesapeake.

5

DREAMLAND

Dreams of the past make up the stuff of today's pleasures. I haunt the waterfront in search of dreams and find them in obscure spots long forgotten in the shoveling-over process of modern development.

Here and there about the shores of the Bay are vestiges of resorts and amusement parks where the city-weary came to refresh their zest for living and cherish their pleasures when the visits ended. Each trip meant an excursion by steamboat. Memories of these resorts and steamboat excursions conjure up dreams, indeed a kind of special dreamland created from the fantasies of the past. One steamboat, together with the resort that it served, even adopted *Dreamland* as its name, but those who dreamed applied the name generally to all the resorts they remembered so vividly. I search the waterfront to revive those memories and those dreams.

A back road, little traveled, leads from Chestertown on the Chester River to a marina on the sandy beach of the Eastern Shore of the Chesapeake. Across the Bay, the upper works of the steel plant at Sparrows Point at the mouth of the Patapsco can be seen on a clear day. The marina nestles in a forest of trees running up a bluff and into the shadows of a ravine. The present-day workings of a yacht marina and its inhabitants create their own sounds and smells. Only the lapping of the wavelets on the beach and the continuous whisper of the pines in the woods speak of a time unlimited, reaching back to a scene dramatically different.

I am transported back to the scene in the 1920s, when the same groves were filled with hundreds of picnickers gorging themselves from hampers laden with fried chicken and ham and pies and jugs of frosted lemonade. The amusement park rattled to the clatter of the wooden Whirlpool Dips and thrilled to the screams of its riders whipping about the tracks of the most fearsome roller coaster on the Bay. Both young and old revolved in blissful abandon on the camels, giraffes, and horses of the calliope-playing carousel. The sedate rode the miniature steam railway across the bridges and through the tunnels to the delight of the elders and the near exclusion of the children who were meant to ride it. Signs everywhere forbade the drinking of liquor on the premises (but paper cups hid their contents), and the shooting galleries tempted patrons to try their skill with prizes of celluloid dolls. While lovers romanced and danced in the pavilion, the wide hotel porch entertained the more sedentary with rocking chairs overlooking the Bay and the beach. The beach itself pealed to the clamor of bathers frolicking in the waves, tossing balls in uproarious games about the sand, or preening in increasingly skimpy bathing suits set apart from the baggy black one-piece, nondescript ones rented at the bathhouse with the words "Tolchester Beach" emblazoned fore and aft.

I remember using up my hoard of nickels and pennies on Ferriswheel rides, on a five-cent ice cream stick called a hokey-pokey, and in the penny arcade, where I dropped a copper into the slot of a stereopticon to view slapstick comedy and "chase-and-pursuit" drama of doubtful quality. Even after stuffing myself on the ham and potato salad of the picnic, I still found room for quantities of taffy and other sweets gathered from concessions or won in the midway. I still own a very bad and yellowing photo of our family shot for a quarter in a flimsy booth.

The ghosts of Tolchester, Maryland, have haunted me and others of my generation through the years. I remember how my mother and other ladies in our family in the heat of the summer slaved for days before the planned picnic, preparing huge quantities of food to load into baskets to be lugged aboard Baltimore trolley cars and then aboard the boat to Tolchester. As a little boy and fleet of foot, I know what it was to be singled out for a stellar performance: As the steamer from Baltimore docked at the wharf at Tolchester, I, like a drove of other little boys so designated, was to leap (even before the gangway was over) to the dock and race headlong down the long pier. Up the walkway through the park and into the picnic grove I would dash. I would quickly locate a desirable table and sit on it, thus reserving it for the rest of the family proceeding behind, laden with food hampers and jugs and, in the case of the ladies, hampered by skirts and stays. Among the hundreds of excursionists in one steamer-load from Baltimore, competition for the most desirable tables inspired a theatrical race—and woe be to the less fleet of foot.

Tolchester Beach as viewed from the steamboat landing in the 1920s. A crowd waits to board the arriving evening steamboat from Baltimore. Drawn from a series of contemporary photographs.

I still recall my envy of the bearded engineer who ran the little brass-studded steam engine leading the miniature open cars around the tracks through the park. Next to a steamboat captain, I could think of no job on earth nearer heaven. The sun-filled days at Tolchester, the utter contentment with which they were savored, linger like a golden mist, shimmering and warm.

On the evening trip by steamer back to Baltimore, when the setting sun silhouetted the bow and the sky astern purpled, the little orchestra in the social hall serenaded with waltzes and dancers dreamed. Passengers on the upper decks took to singing, and harmonicas hummed away. A sensuous breeze invited lovers to meld in the languorous beauty of the Bay. For a brief moment, at least, excursionists forgot the anxieties and rigors of their daily lives. Tolchester, even for a day, was a life-restoring vacation.

There were those who saw it as pure honky-tonk—boisterous, noisome, gaudy, smacking too much of Coney Island. But Marylanders flocked to it by the hundreds, even thousands, as the excursion steamers shuttled back and forth during the days of warmth from Pier 16, Light Street, to the long dock at Tolchester.

Steamboats marked the beginning of Tolchester and the Tolchester line in 1877. Founded by a pair of aging Quakers (Calvin and his son E.

133

B. Taggart), pushed by an entrepreneur named John M. Armbruster, and galvanized into action by a young employee, William Conlyn Eliason, who rose from clerk to president, the resort and steamboat line overcame initial adversity to become the prized amusement park on the Chesapeake. Like other amusement parks starting up in the late 1870s, it partly owed its inspiration to the display of attractions at the Philadelphia Centennial Exhibition of 1876.

Steamboats serving Tolchester through the years brought a touch of romance to the lives of their passengers. The early boats *Pilot Boy* (she had seen service in Albemarle and Pamlico sounds in the Civil War) and *Nelly White* (she collided with a schooner in 1886 and sank at Sandy Point) were followed by a series of steamers. *Emma Giles,* using the engine of *Nelly White* (she got it from *Alice C. Price,* which was blown up in the Civil War), became the darling not only of the excursionists to Tolchester but also of the passengers, tradesmen, watermen, and planters on the landings of the Little Choptank, Sassafras, Chester, South, and West rivers and other tributaries of the Bay. She was a veritable and venerable workhorse, steaming for half a century in the lives of the residents of Tidewater. *Louise,* a large side-wheeler built during the Civil War, was purchased by the company and remodeled with huge open but sheltered decks and a dance floor to feature the big bands of the 1920s. She could carry twenty-five hundred excursionists per trip to Tolchester. *Susquehanna,* a propeller-driven vessel of exquisite grace built for the line by Charles Reeder, became the link to the Susquehanna River and serviced the overflow crowds at Tolchester. Also, on her trips to the Susquehanna River and the head of the Bay, she put in to Betterton, a resort above Tolchester on the Bay near the mouth of the Sassafras River (see discussion of Betterton in this chapter).

Other steamers followed. As the decades of the twentieth century marched inexorably to the Great Depression and the approach of World War II, the Tolchester line added even larger excursion boats: an ill-fated double-ended ferryboat renamed *Express* and converted to carry hundreds of vacationers, and then a series of steel-hulled, open-air side-wheelers named *Tolchester,* which were capable of entertaining thousands of resort-seeking passengers on board and disgorging them on the pier at Tolchester. The resort held the affection of Marylanders for over eighty years. And the steamboats transported them not only from the sidewalks of Baltimore to the vacationland of Tolchester but also from the prosaic to a fantasy world of their own.

Along the shoreline just fourteen miles north of Tolchester lay the hotel resort of Betterton at the mouth of the Sassafras River. Today, Betterton is a community of newly constructed condominiums with a fishing pier and private accommodations for overnight guests. Its beach is crowded once again in the summertime. Until its recent renovation, Betterton was a sad sight indeed. Only ghosts could inhabit the decaying remains of the frame-structured, wide-porched hotels and rooming houses fronting the Bay from the bluff above the pier. Only sagging buildings, unsafe to enter, flapping shutters, broken banisters, and collapsed flooring remained to call to mind the fashionable resort that flourished there in the early decades of the century. Ragged piling formed a line of decaying teeth extending from the beach and defined the site of the pier where the steamers from Baltimore or Philadelphia docked in the grand days of the resort. Very little was visible of the dance pavilion, where the great bands of the 1920s and 1930s performed to crowds of vacationers and to the sons and daughters of nearby planters who came to revel in the sinful pleasures of the city folk.

Betterton began as a resort in the 1850s when Richard Townsend Turner, business partner of Enoch Pratt of Baltimore, built the steamboat wharf below the bluff on the land originally owned by a planter named Edward Crew. In time, twelve hotels, a dance pavilion, and various forms of beach entertainment attracted throngs to enjoy not the carnival capers of Tolchester but the atmosphere of a residential resort overlooking the expanse of Bay from Aberdeen Army Proving Ground on the western shore to the Susquehanna in the north and the Sassafras at the water's edge on the Eastern Shore. Not that the throng at Betterton was more sedate than the crowd at Tolchester—it wasn't. On Saturday nights, the rhythm of "Eight to the Bar" rattled the windows of the boardinghouses. But vacationers came to Betterton not for the day but for a week, even for a summer. Among the middle class of Baltimore, Philadelphia, and Wilmington, a vacation at Betterton was the acceptable, even the expected, thing to do. The Hotel Rigbie, an ample, shingled four-story building with the comfortable look of a private residence, filled its wide shady veranda with rocking chairs and a magnificent view of the upper Bay. A number of smaller hotels overlooked the beach, like the Price Cottage or Jewell Cottage, with an old-fashioned two-seater lawn swing in the front yard. On it, four ladies could sit comfortably facing each other and keep the swing in motion by a gentle movement of their feet on the connecting platform—a favorite rendezvous spot for gossip, knitting, and critiquing the scenery and the sultry activities on the beach. When the ladies withdrew, little boys, standing inside on the platform, could pretend that the swing was a locomotive engine and get it moving back and forth at increasingly dangerous speeds as they whooped the sounds of an engine whistle.

The vacationers overwhelmingly arrived by steamboat. In the 1890s, the Tolchester line became increasingly interested in Betterton and acquired its own wharfage. Its steamer *Susquehanna* with the "perfect sheer" (seen by some connoisseurs as analogous to a "perfect thirty-six") called routinely on runs to the north of the Bay. But chiefly, the steamers bound to and from Philadelphia and Baltimore via the Chesapeake and Delaware Canal provided the essential link between these major cities and the resort.

Until 1927, when the Chesapeake and Delaware Canal became a wide, sea-level canal, the steamers passing through it could not exceed a mere twenty-six feet in beam in order to fit in the three narrow locks of the canal. Most of the early steamboats run by the Baltimore and Philadelphia Steamboat Company (nicknamed the Ericsson line, since its boats at first had to use the propellers of John Ericsson) were nearly two hundred feet long, but, with an average beam of barely twenty-four feet, they presented the appearance of a needle, viewed point first. The steamers running overnight between Baltimore and Philadelphia carried staterooms reached by a narrow corridor between them on the passenger deck. These overnight steamers included the *Anthony Groves, Jr.* and *Ericsson*, both of which called at Betterton on their journeys north and south. By the turn of the century the Ericsson line ventured an astounding daylight run: departure from one city at 5 A.M., arrival at the other city at 6 P.M., in spite of delays of over three hours in transiting the canal locks. Because of their incredibly thin lines and excessive power plants, the steamers won a reputation for speed—the fastest on the Bay—averaging better than twenty miles per hour, one clocking twenty-four. But they raised a wake that created havoc along the shoreline and stirred up such a storm of disapproval that their speed was used sparingly. *Penn* and *Lord Baltimore* joined the fleet with the same old configuration. Most wags bet that sooner or later the wind would blow one of them right over. They were right. *Ericsson* ran into a gale near Wilmington and capsized; some of her upper deck had to be removed to restore stability.

With clockwork regularity, the Philadelphia–Baltimore boats in summertime pulled into the landing at Betterton. Porters cluttered the dock, shouting the names of their hotels and boarding houses and trundling the trunks and baggage of arriving or departing vacationers. Nearby at the dance pavilion, if the steamer arrived in the evening, the band might pause when the whistle of the steamer sounded, to allow the dancers to view the long white boat glide alongside the dock and then begin the circus of activity. With the long whistle of departure, the band resumed, and the evening sang. Those who frequented Betterton remembered all too well the music, the flirting, the long days of warmth by the beach, and the quiet rocking-chair evenings on the porches to watch the ritual of the sun setting across the reaches of the upper Bay.

A similar resort flourished on the western shore south of Annapolis. Fair Haven was established in 1839 to fulfill George Weems's dream of providing an escape for pleasure-loving city dwellers in an idyllic setting on the shore of the Bay and, at the same time, on the route of the Weems line steamers. The resort had earned a reputation through the years for its accommodations and fine cuisine, including an amply filled cellar of wines and liquors. Vacationers came to Fair Haven to fish in the sometimes rewarding waters of the Bay, to hunt in neighboring glens, and to gorge on the tempting fare of seafood served up on verandas where the Bay's expanse stretched to the horizon. Although Fair Haven as a resort remained in the hands of the Weems family, the hotel changed management at various times after the Civil War. But its reputation remained unaltered. Some picnickers arrived for the day, frolicked briefly in the surf (on the exposed western shores, the waves carrying the force of the winds coming up the Bay were not simply wavelets as described on the opposite shore), stuffed down the contents of their hampers and pails, and scurried back to the homeward-bound steamer. Without carousel, roller coaster, or midway, Fair Haven rested on its laurels as a resort to be relished for the sumptuousness of its hotel and its fare, and for its tree-shaded groves where the wind murmured and the waves splashed distantly. And the trip from Baltimore on the Weems line steamer turned a day's excursion into a brief voyage at sea.

Theodore Weems, the steamer succeeding *George Weems* in 1871 when the latter burned at the dock on Light Street, stopped on her Patuxent River route to deposit vacationers or picnickers at Fair Haven and retrieve them on the return. Although she carried staterooms for the Patuxent run, she wore the festive air of an excursion boat, with pennants flying and bands playing. Her expansive deck space (open to the sky from end to end on the top deck, and, except for the cabin space, open from side to side on the passenger deck) invited her passengers to lounge in shady comfort on one deck or bake in the sun on the upper. Her cabin decor reflected a taste for Victorian plushiness and overcarving, and her dining room cuisine was intended to match that of the finest restaurants in Baltimore. Professors Itzel's Fifth Regiment Band often played for listening and dancing, both on board and at the hotel.

Several other Weems line steamers assisted *Theodore Weems* in peak season, but vacationers at Fair Haven equated her to the pleasures of the resort. If chiggers, biting flies, and mosquitoes in the groves at times plagued the picnickers, the cool breezes sweeping the decks of *Theodore Weems* offered consolation. When rain or cold wind caught the boat under way on the Bay, the deck crew unfurled canvas curtains rolled up under the overhead, while the passengers huddled on deck chairs, without a view of the Bay or any comprehension of the storm engulfing them. But the band played on, the bar functioned with remarkable efficiency, and the passengers, who may have endured certain moments of doubt and discomfort in the buggy woods of Fair Haven or the rigors of rain-swept decks, all arrived in Baltimore with the uplifting tidings that all was well on the Chesapeake.

In the summer season, *Theodore Weems* had a busy schedule. For eight years, beginning with the 1881 season, she stopped at Bay Ridge, a resort at the mouth of the Severn River close to Annapolis. In 1879, under the leadership of James H. Van Sant, the Bay Ridge Company began operations with the purchase of Tolly Point, where the Severn met the Bay, and erected a large hotel. The resort expanded, until travelers coming by steamer and rail felt rewarded for the journey with the luxuries of a grand hotel, a restaurant pavilion, and scheduled entertainment, including concerts, dances, and variety shows. It came to be known as "the queen resort of the Chesapeake." In July 1881, *Theodore Weems* shuttled nearly four thousand excursionists from Baltimore to attend a jousting tournament, followed by fireworks and dancing. The Chautauqua Literary and Scientific Circle managed Bay Ridge for a time around the turn of the century, the beach briefly took the name of the society, and cultural programs attuned to the purposes of the group offered uplifting themes designed to attract large numbers from the city.

Steamers other than the *Theodore Weems* pulled into the resort at Tolly Point. *Columbia*, bought by the Bay Ridge Company itself, had the capacity to shuttle large crowds with its 260-foot length and ample deck space. *Jane Moseley*, the comely *Tred Avon*, and *Tockwogh* served the beach. The deep-draft *Empire State* called and embarrassingly grounded within sight of the pier. And *Emma Giles*, the faithful workhorse of the Tolchester line, included the resort on her rounds to Annapolis and the South, West and Rhode rivers.

Bay Ridge survived through cycles of profit and loss and was admired by a certain coterie of the self-professed elite but deprecated by those who lost money on its undertakings.

The inhabitants of Tidewater—except for the privileged who needed no escape and the underprivileged who could not afford it—played hard when they could get away from the grinding labor of factory, farm, and countinghouse. Often the respite they sought in play could be found in the resorts and amusements parks reached by boat. From Washington, the resort at Colonial Beach, Virginia, with its seafood restaurants, somewhat steamy atmosphere, tolerable fishing, and superb beach at the bend in the Potomac, beckoned, and the steamer *St. Johns* shuttled. Other steamboats followed in later years, especially the huge 315-foot *Potomac* (with three stacks athwartships, completely unique and perceived as alien on the Bay). At twenty-three miles per hour it was capable of transporting hundreds of passengers in considerable splendor, including mahogany-paneled saloons decorated with sculptures, oil paintings, and water-playing fountains. On a string of special occasions, Paul Whiteman or Benny Goodman played for dancing as the steamer headed for Chapel Point, Liverpool Point, and Colonial Beach.

The venerable *Charles Macalester* plied the Potomac for a generation (and that generation venerated her) between Washington, Mount Vernon, and Marshall Hall, where the roller coaster, midway, dance hall, and free-wheeling beer halls released the tensions of Washingtonians. *River Queen* serviced Marshall Hall in its early days as an amusement park, but the doughty steamer later moved its service to Notley Hall, a park with amusements similar to those at Marshall Hall but catering to black clientele.

In contrast to the amusement parks, the resort at Piney Point, only a few miles from the Potomac mouth and Point Lookout, catered to a special clientele—or at least that was the hoped-for objective. Occupying a narrow, sandy neck of land with pine trees combing its interior, the resort featured a rather elegant hotel and rows of quaint cottages appealing to the fashionable and politically or socially prominent residents of Washington. At times in its history it welcomed James Monroe, Franklin Pierce, Theodore Roosevelt, John C. Calhoun, Henry Clay, and Daniel

Webster as vacationers. Notables at Piney Point expected to see their names listed in the society columns of the Washington newspapers. Nationally known bands and orchestras serenaded all summer long. Vacationers bathed near well-appointed bathhouses, rowed in the river for exercise (and fought for it if the wind came up), fished for perch, bumped about on horse-drawn hay rides, sang in the gazebos after dark, and danced through the night under Japanese lanterns. And the lighthouse keeper, guardian of the thirty-foot lighthouse built in 1836, told lengthy stories to visitors willing to listen. The two-story wharf contained an upholstered waiting room, a paneled smoking room, and a well-stocked bar to entertain the vacationers awaiting the arrival of a steamboat.

The Weems line steamers, running between Baltimore and Washington on the Potomac, served Piney Point through the years. These steamboats, the classics of overnight packets on the Chesapeake, included *Anne Arundel, Calvert, Lancaster, Middlesex, Northumberland, Sue,* and *Potomac,* some of the handsomest vessels of the steamboat era. On board these vessels at times, in staterooms, at secluded areas of the deck, or in the bars, the politics and affairs of the nation were debated, and often decided, among the passengers traveling to or from Piney Point.

In the period before the Civil War, the prestigious Piney Point Hotel held glittering balls for its distinguished guests, who had come to the resort, partially to relax and escape the pressures of their official life but also paradoxically, to be seen among the elite, where an important word or two could be uttered. Franklin Pierce entertained the Russian ambassador rather lavishly. Transactions of state by many of Washington's bureaucracy could be conducted in the shadows of the potted palms.

Other vacationers at Piney Point came for a brief stay to sample the atmosphere and frolic as best they could. These were the secretaries, the clerks, the middle-rank employees, and the groups of fraternal organizations, church members, bicycle enthusiasts, and Hibernian societies. They stayed for a few days, reddened in the sun, and sailed away, never having penetrated the inner sanctums of the privileged.

The steamer called at Piney Point three days a week in season, more frequently in peak periods. Hotels and rented cottages emptied as guests flocked to the pier to watch the steamer's arrival, and "folks from up-country" came by cart and wagon and Model-T to meet and socialize on the dock. The status and importance of each passenger crossing the gangplank was weighed, and the prestige of each lady judged by the number, quality, and size of her "steamer trunks" lugged ashore by the stevedores.

In later days, a large dance hall on the beach (highlighted by revolving colored mirrors in the center of the ceiling reflecting the light from spotlights in each corner of the room) attracted the active set, particularly when orchestras from Washington or Baltimore came to play. Square dancing was popular, also, and the dance hall became the scene for masquerades, vaudeville shows, and impromptu performances by visiting guests.

The atmosphere of Piney Point differed sharply from the abandonment to unbridled and rollicking pleasure in the amusement parks south of Washington on the Potomac (Marshall Hall, Colonial Beach, Notley Hall, and the others served by steamboats from the city). Around Baltimore, similar amusements flourished and were served primarily by steamboats on short hauls from the harbor basin or from the foot of Broadway. Tivoli, Rockaway Beach, Fairview Beach, Brown's Grove, all on the shores of the Patapsco or in creeks near its mouth, were among those local parks deluged by Baltimoreans who boarded the steamboats on hot summer days for a quick escape to the breezes of the Bay.

But the prime contenders, combining both amusements and the amenities of resorts, were Tolchester on the Eastern Shore and Chesapeake Beach (later called Seaside Park) on the western shore. Chesapeake Beach lay below Herring Bay, some fifty miles south of Baltimore on the sandy shores of the Bay backed by the bluffs near Calvert Cliffs.

Chesapeake Beach occasionally bore the nickname "Dreamland." It came partly from the steamboat *Dreamland*, which unloaded three thousand excursionists each day on the resort's pier, and from the expectations of its patrons, who came by train from Washington and by boat from Baltimore to indulge in its pleasures.

A short generation of Washingtonians and Baltimoreans knew these pleasures intimately. The notion of building Chesapeake Beach emerged from the grandiose schemes of a group of men in 1891 who wanted to build a railroad from the sweaty streets of Washington to the breeze-swept shores of the Chesapeake Bay. Their prospectus of 1894 for the Washington and Chesapeake Beach Railway was a masterpiece of hyperbole and exaggeration. It boasted that the construction of the railroad had already begun, even to the building of a drawbridge ("the largest single-span girder bridge in the country") to span the Patuxent River, and that a fishing and steamboat pier neared completion at Chesapeake

Beach, the newly named but uninhabited terminus on the Bay. None of these statements was true, and, in fact, the newly chartered company was nearly bankrupt. Reorganized, with an infusion of modest capital, the company set about to advertise the dreams of the original founders.

Brochures proclaimed that the resort would be "The Great Seaside Suburb of the National Capital, situated only thirty miles from Washington, and fifty-two miles from Baltimore." Promoters promised a railroad furnishing rapid transit and connections, with chair and observation cars for passengers' special comfort. At the beach, as projected by promoters and their hired architects, the lavishness of hotels and amusements would rival Monte Carlo. Hotel Chesapeake, with six hundred rooms overlooking a boulevard fronting on the Bay and an architect's elevation (drawing) reminiscent of the great houses and castles of Britain (even to portcullis and battlement), would entertain guests with bowling alleys, billiard rooms, bars, ballrooms, and a dining room large enough to accommodate one thousand at a sitting. It was designed to surpass anything that Newport or Bar Harbor or even Monte Carlo had to offer. Another hotel, the Patuxent, offering less expensive accommodations, would cater to the less affluent. All sorts of amusements were projected: bathing beaches and bathhouses, scenic railways (roller coasters, with restrained dips), carousels, pavilions for dancing and concerts, and a circular racetrack designed for year-round trotting races.

Again, financial ruin struck. In the ensuing bankruptcy proceedings, the court appointed Lincoln M. Hyer, chief engineer of the railway, as receiver. Hyer's first task was to find someone willing to purchase the residue of the corporation and proceed with the building of the railroad and the resort. He landed on Colonel Ambrose C. Dunn, of Confederate persuasion and a self-professed consulting engineer. They met at the Willard bar in Washington, discussed the project, met again in New York to gather up Charles Popper, an interested financier, and then once more in Washington to meet still another interested person, Otto Mears, a man who had earned a widely respected reputation for railroad building in the rugged terrain of Colorado. On August 21, 1897, the three men purchased the capital stock of the railroad and set about its construction. One of the additional investors was David H. Moffat, a steady hand in the negotiations.

Otto Mears, a little man with a heavy accent, was a resourceful and determined man who learned to engineer his own future. Orphaned at age two from his Russian homeland and raised in England for part of his life, he was packed off alone to America at a tender age to relatives in San

Schematic drawing of Chesapeake Beach as it was planned at the turn of the century. Drawn from contemporary depictions.

Francisco who did not claim him, and was forced to fend for himself by selling newspapers on the street. At age twenty he joined the Union forces for the defense of California and emerged with a little change in his pocket and the will to start his own business in New Mexico. His various enterprises and investments prospered, and he turned to the daunting task of building railroads in the mountains of Colorado. When some of these spectacular railroads fell on difficult financial times, Mears turned his attention to railroads in the East. His ear caught the blandishments of Dunn and Popper.

Ambrose C. Dunn, in spite of professed talents in engineering, was a smooth-tongued rogue. A Georgian, he resigned as a cadet from West Point after he failed in mathematics and English in his first midterm examination. Three times he was either court-martialled or cashiered (or escaped by resignation) from the Confederate Army: once as a captain with the Georgia Volunteers (he fought at Bull Run), twice as a lieutenant colonel with the Virginia Cavalry. Each time he managed to evade or falsify his past record and elude the inquirers. Sometime after the Civil War he managed to convince some investors of his expertise in railroad construction. Throughout the stormy early history of the development of Chesapeake Beach, Dunn proved to be a conniving hindrance.

Charles Popper, a native of Baden, Germany, bred cattle in Colorado in partnership with Otto Mears and prospered in mining and other pursuits. He followed his wife to New York, became restive, and yielded to the urgings of Hyer to join the Chesapeake Beach enterprise.

David Halliday Moffat, a close friend of Mears, was a skillful banker who brought his financial wisdom to bear on the building and incorporation of major rail lines in the United States. Mears obtained his support for the fledgling enterprise, and Moffat proved to be loyal to his friend and to the undertaking. Mears assumed the role of president, Dunn vice president, Hopper treasurer and general manager.

In the first phase of the ambitious plan, the building of the railroad to serve the rich farm country beyond Washington and into the Maryland counties of Prince George and Anne Arundel took immediate priority. The first objective was to entice the farmers and regional businesses to use the railroad. From these expected revenues, the railroad's construction toward the Bay could be financed. Almost forgotten was the original goal—the building of a palatial resort at Chesapeake Beach.

From October 1897 to March 1899, the railroad track crept eastward from the District of Columbia to the terminal at Chesapeake Beach. Its progress was checkered with misfortunes, financial setbacks, internal friction between Mears and Dunn, and altercations over the quality of construction.

A major point of contention arose between steamboat and steam train at the crossing of the Patuxent River. The issue turned on the right of passage of the Weems line steamboats proceeding upriver to Bristol, a landing serving a considerable community. The Maryland general assembly, in chartering the Washington and Chesapeake Beach Railway Company, forbade any construction that would obstruct navigating the river to Bristol. The side-wheel packet steamers, *Richmond, Westmoreland*, and, occasionally, *St. Mary's* of the Weems line, with beams measuring up to fifty-six feet, sailed up the river several times a week on regular schedules, laden with cargo and passengers. With the railroad moving toward them, the residents of Bristol, disturbed by the prospect of losing Weems line service, petitioned the Maryland legislature to require the tracks to be laid across a bridge above Bristol, not below it. Bills introduced simultaneously in both houses of the legislature differed so markedly that deadlock resulted. Henry Williams, general manager of the Weems line, worn by his attempts to goad the legislature into action, despaired and looked toward legal action to curb the objectives of the railroad.

A new drawbridge was proposed, approved by the U.S. Army Corps of Engineers. The contract awarded to the Youngstown Bridge Company required the building of a plate-girder drawbridge swinging from a center island with manually controlled machinery. In 1899, the span was in place, but the machinery was not. Cables were required to open the draw. When the cable equipment was not manned, steamers waited, sometimes overnight. Construction of bulkheading seemed at one point to so restrict the space for steamers to pass through the draw that Weems line masters doubted that their side-wheel steamers could make it; only propeller-driven steamers like *Potomac* would fit, and the diversion of Weems steamers from their established routes posed massive rescheduling problems.

Tempers broke. Henry Williams and his senior captains stormed the offices of the Army Corps of Engineers and threatened suit. Quickly Mears and his engineers refocused their priorities and completed the draw with sufficient space for the side-wheelers to pass without difficulty. (Today, one path through Jug Bay Wetlands Sanctuary is the former right-of-way of the old railway. It terminates at the Patuxent River, where midstream one can see the round turning island where the drawspan once stood, a ghostly reminder of the battle between steamboat and steam train.)

Toward the close of 1898, the realization of Mears and others set in that the real goal of the enterprise—the creation of the "celestial" amusement resort at Chesapeake Beach—was being neglected, if not forgotten, in the tribulations of building a railroad.

Mears pressed for the completion of the principal hotel, the boardwalk and pier, and a building designated as a casino. He beckoned for prospective concessionaires to set up various amusements, fund a half-mile racetrack with grandstand and stables, and operate the gambling casino. Power, ice, and water plants were nearing completion. The impetus to erect the resort in record time worked, but the immediate result was far short of the grandiose design originally conceived.

With financial disasters rearing up intermittently that year, the resort opened on June 9, 1900. The first trains bearing picnickers arrived from Washington, and the steamer *J. S. Warden* from Baltimore, chartered from the Port Steamboat Company, pulled into the half-finished wooden pier.

The opening had been well publicized. Because of the crowds buying railroad tickets for the beach, the Baltimore and Ohio Railroad added special trains from Baltimore to connect with the trains to Chesapeake Beach. The steamer *J. S. Warden*, overflowing with passengers, was supplemented by the Weems line steamer *St. Mary's*. In the summer of 1899, Henry Williams had tried to prod the developers to complete the resort by routing his steamer biweekly to the landing there while en route to the Patuxent River or to Fair Haven. He designated *St. Mary's* to assist with the first crowds of the 1900 season, but as the resort contracted for other steamers, he withdrew.

What the first visitors encountered was both exhilarating and dismaying.

Their arrival by steamboat was not exactly propitious. They looked down the length of a half-mile pier that they had to hike, a pier made of half-sawn, rough planks without any sort of guard rail to prevent the unwary from fetching up in the water. The pier, so long that it made the beach look distant, was necessitated by the depth of the water, so shallow that bathers could walk a hundred yards from the shoreline before the water lapped their chins.

Once having tramped down the pier from steamer to beach, the excursionist or vacationer discovered the joys of a mile-long boardwalk (a most unusual one, built three hundred feet out from the shoreline itself and running parallel to it for its entire length). A few concession stands—others were advertised but not yet opened—dotted its sides. The beach itself, with some bathhouses as concessions, lay inside the boardwalk, so that bathers (mostly children) splashed in the wavelets with a view of the Bay through the piling supporting the boardwalk. At the extreme lower end of this boardwalk, the cliffs of Calvert reared up vertically, the hunting ground for amateur paleontologists gathering fossils.

A short way down the boardwalk spiraled the "scenic railway," a giant roller coaster, built partly over the water and partly over land; it sold its first nickel-a-ride tickets on opening day. In the picnic groves ashore, the public found tables, concession-operated refreshment stands, and a German beer garden selling beer at five cents a glass, the same price charged on the steamer from Baltimore. A handsome merry-go-round built by Gustav A. Deutzel sent its wooden animals (including a purple kangaroo) and animated passengers revolving under a mirrored canopy to the pumping of Strauss waltzes and lesser tunes of the day. Electricity—generated by the local plant—powered the carousel and illuminated the boardwalk with a few light bulbs in the evening, to the astonishment and delight of the uninitiated. Electricity also powered the pumping station to feed water to locomotive boilers.

All sorts of special performances highlighted that opening week at Chesapeake Beach: dancing bears, death-defying trapeze artists and balloon riders, the serenading by a succession of dance orchestras in the pavilion, and fireworks over the water.

But notably missing were important components of the Monte Carlo dream of Otto Mears and his compatriots. The racetrack, with its elaborate clubhouse, stables, and grandstand, stood at an impasse, the victim of public sentiment (notably religious) in Calvert County against granting a license for gambling. The grandstand and stables were demolished, and the materials were used for concessions along the boardwalk. For many years, the pattern of the racetrack showed, until it disappeared in the encroachment of marshland.

The gambling casino, handsomely appointed, became a restaurant where dinners were served on the bluff overlooking the Bay. And with the demise of its original purpose, the grand design of the Monte Carlo of the East Coast came to an end.

The two magnificent hotels (the Chesapeake and the Patuxent), planned to entertain the wealthy in lavish, even baronial style, had not materialized and never would. In their stead, Otto Mears erected his clubhouse, which was intended as an elegant substitute, but instead sat on the hill overlooking the Bay as a somewhat ordinary-looking four-story wooden building with a wide porch, two Victorian-style turrets, and accommodations already outmoded. It was renamed the Belvedere Hotel, but nothing about it could reconstruct the fantasy of a fashionable spa devoted principally to the pleasures of the privileged. It was to remain as the only hotel of any consequence in Chesapeake Beach until it burned to the ground in 1923.

In the meantime, Chesapeake Beach, in spite of periods of near financial catastrophe, developed into an amusement park and playground totally different from the dreams of its founders. It became the escape from the cities of a host of excursionists, not the well-heeled leisure class traveling by luxurious club or observation car on the train, but the workers from factory or office, with their families and hordes of youngsters, bent on a one-day frolic on the beach, along the boardwalk, in the dance hall, aboard the roller coaster and carousel, and in the beer halls everywhere.

And with this remarkable shift in tone came a surprising reversal—the advent of slot machines. Otto Mears, taken aback by the local opprobrium on gambling and the resultant wrecking of his plans for racetrack and casino, would have been stunned. Slot machines appeared everywhere: on the boardwalk, in the bars, in restaurants, in lodging houses—some say, even in grocery stores and public buildings. Chesapeake Beach gained a reputation as a place of gambling and drinking, but also where families could still play in the sun and thrill in the amusement park. Real estate developers sold waterfront plots for little summer cottages, rooming houses opened up, a town sprang up, and the trains and steamboats brought throngs in the morning and took them home in the evening, leaving the town to indulge in its own bacchanalian pleasures until the invasion began on another day.

The pleasures of Chesapeake Beach during the 1920s and 1930s excited the tastes of boardwalk lovers, picnickers, and hustlers. The boardwalk stood until 1928, offshore by one hundred yards, a mile-long honky-tonk of vendors, refreshment stands, beer halls, shooting galleries, dancing pavilion, carousel, roller coaster, and gambling parlors. The parlors were replete with pinball machines, bingo games, smart hucksters of weight-guessing and other tricks to capture the vacationer's dime, chance stands with various prizes (canaries in a cage, hosiery [including men's pure silk stockings], onyx, stuffed dogs, and china), and the ubiquitous slot machines. A rather ornate band shell engaged

The boardwalk at Chesapeake Beach in the early 1930s. Drawn from a series of contemporary photographs.

prominent orchestras and bands to perform at certain times. John Phillip Sousa led his band off the train toward the band shell to the strains of "The Washington Post March." Both Tommy and Jimmy Dorsey played, and Charlie Spivak made the youngsters dance in front of the bandstand and on the floor of the dance hall.

In 1928, under new management (there was a long succession of interests and administrations from the days of Otto Mears), the long boardwalk was deemed unsafe: The piling was rotting beneath it. Whereupon there began an enormous undertaking, to move all of the concessions and amusements—even the huge roller coaster—to the park on dry land and to dismantle the boardwalk. In a year's time, the transformation was complete, and the former boardwalk amusements joined the Ferris wheel, the only original thriller on the hill. Shortly thereafter, the resort gained a new name, Seaside Park, although most Baltimoreans continued to call it Chesapeake Beach.

Costumed characters walked through the park, teasing the children, mimicking the adults, and whistling at the girls: "Billy Jean" dressed like Davy Crockett, an Indian warrior, a ten-foot clown on stilts. German bands oom-pahed in the beer garden with a slap on the lederhosen calculated to stir up the ethnic loyalties of groups that came often from Baltimore.

In the town of Chesapeake Beach, the carpenters, bricklayers, foundrymen, and tradesmen, and their families often sought accommodations in the cheap hotels and rooming houses further down the beach. Aside from gambling, the principal sport was drinking. Chesapeake Beach and its developing neighbor, North Beach, attempted to enforce a code of conduct. Rowdyism was prohibited. On the weekends, North Beach jail, the only one near the boardwalk, was full.

"If you came down here and you didn't behave yourself," said William (Buster) Fortler, an old-timer, "they didn't put you in jail for a week or anything. They locked you up till the next train left, then the police put you on the train and told you not to come back. Your fine was usually the amount of money you had in your pocket."

John Donald, superintendent of Chesapeake Beach, earned the title "czar of the boardwalk." He demanded strict compliance with his rules: no bathing suits on the boardwalk, no alcoholic drinks except in certain beer gardens or bars, coat and tie on the dance floor, and "orderly" conduct throughout the park. A covey of police patrolled the grounds to enforce his rules and dress code, but he himself paraded through the place to make his heavy presence felt.

When Prohibition came along after World War I, speakeasies became almost a way of life in Chesapeake Beach and North Beach. Raids by "revenuers" were frequent. Townspeople worked up a warning system to alert each other if suspicious automobiles or official-looking men arrived from Washington. The network of tips paid off in profits, and Chesapeake Beach (and North Beach) survived on a reputation for free-flowing beer and uninhibited pleasure.

Baltimoreans as a lot brought to their pleasure a heap of baggage— often their ethnic origins (many were first- or second-generation immigrants and tended to cluster) and a life of determined struggle to win out against the odds. But they were also a family-oriented, fun-living crowd as a rule, calling anyone "hon" for "honey" whether they knew the person or not, loving to sing and dance and to extract a bit of humor out of the driest situation. They were a sentimental lot, too, and susceptible to touches of romance.

Their trips to Chesapeake Beach aboard a steamboat brought them to the fun of the park, but the steamboat ride itself, lasting for several hours down the Bay, smacked of a glamorous voyage, almost beyond dreaming for many of them.

At the beginning of the 1909 summer season, the managers of Chesapeake Beach chartered a large excursion steamer from its owner, the

Queenstown and Love Point Transportation and Development Company. The steamer had been used in opposition to the Baltimore, Chesapeake, and Atlantic Railway Company in runs between Baltimore and Love Point. The manager of the opposition line, John C. Bosley, proceeded to buy the steamer on his own for thirty thousand dollars, and to serve as its general manager. From 1909 until 1925, the steamer ran between Baltimore and Chesapeake Beach and gave the beach itself another name.

The steamer had been born as *Republic* in 1878 and had run excursions between Philadelphia and Cape May, New Jersey, until 1904. She suffered a name change to *Cape May* in 1902. Just before beginning excursion duty between New York and Coney Island for the Dreamland Transportation Company, she gained another name: *Dreamland.*

The name, for Baltimoreans, came to mean both the boat and the park itself on the Bay.

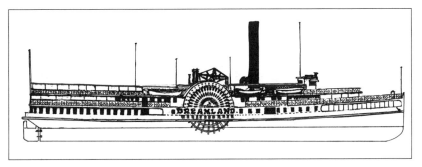

Steamboat *Dreamland.* Drawn from numerous photographs, including one by the author.

She was the largest excursion boat on the Chesapeake, and her ample decks welcomed three thousand passengers at a time. She was fast. On the Delaware she clocked twenty miles per hour between Philadelphia and Cape May; on the Chesapeake, with somewhat aging boilers, she slowed her pace to fourteen miles per hour, still enabling her to serve the beach with timely regularity. Her decks on each trip swarmed with excursionists; her hurricane deck, canopied for most of its length except forward of the pilothouse, accommodated folding chairs and their occupants from rail to rail. The passenger deck below, except for the enclosed and windowed cabin area, overflowed with picnickers, children scurrying about, and settled passengers who had scrambled for chairs and favored spots in the shade or sun even before the boat left Baltimore. And the main deck, mostly enclosed, provided deck space for the overflow from the decks above. On the passenger deck, just inside the main cabin, was the dining room, where substantial meals could be purchased for fifty cents and would be served by white-coated waiters on snow-white tables with formal silver. A lounge adjoining the dining room boasted upholstered furniture, dark paneling, and retreats for the ladies. A wide carved stairway connected the decks. Amidships on the main deck stood a comfortable bar where beer flowed at five cents a glass, while music spilled over from the dance hall aft.

The entire third of the main deck aft was a grand, hundred-foot, wedge-shaped dance floor, enclosed by windows looking out from both sides at the panorama of the Bay; entertainment during the daily runs was provided by an eight-piece orchestra playing the fox-trots, waltzes, and two-steps of the times.

Over 284 feet long and 66 feet wide, with a long, white, graceful sheer and a stout black stack raked at an appropriate angle, *Dreamland* showed her happiness when she curled back the waves of the Bay and steamed along, flags and bunting whipping in the breeze, crowds singing, cavorting, and basking about her decks, and music swelling from her dance floor. For a generation of Baltimoreans, she made dreams come true.

When the day's run to Chesapeake Beach ended, *Dreamland*'s life began anew. With the setting sun silhouetting the church spires and warehouses of Baltimore, she backed from her wharf laden with the young lovers of the city on a biweekly "moonlight cruise." For several hours, she steamed out of the Patapsco, around Seven Foot Knoll, and back to her pier, while the dance floor swayed to the rhythms of hundreds of dancing couples and the "smoothest" music on the Bay. On well-advertised occasions, some of the nationally known name bands played. Invariably, as the steamer slid quietly toward her berth near midnight, the band played the old favorite, "Meet Me Tonight in Dreamland," the theme song of the cruise, the steamer, and even the park on the Bay.

At Chesapeake Beach (or Seaside Park, as it was called), *Dreamland* tied up to a wooden pier extending more than a half-mile in length to the shore: quite a hike for the long-skirted, hamper-laden picnicker or luggage-burdened vacationer. About 1930, the company built a miniature railroad on the pier, with terminals at the T-landing where the steamer docked and one-half mile away at the beach. Narrow tracks were laid on the boards, and a gasoline-powered engine pulled a train of open

Steamboat *Bay Belle* at end of the half-mile pier at Chesapeake Beach with miniature railroad in foreground. Drawn from contemporary photographs.

cars with board seats. The engine, although sputtering gasoline fumes, looked like a small brass-bound steam locomotive of the 1930s and later like a streamliner, and it tooted merrily to scoot the hikers from its path as it trundled down the pier, fare ten cents one way.

That ten-cent fare was a fair price, considering that a round trip on *Dreamland* cost fifty cents. Even the steamer fare might have stretched a working man's budget in the 1930s. Consider that the engineer on the Chesapeake Beach Railway made 37.5 cents per hour, and, when he became temporarily demoted at the Washington, D.C., terminal and cleaned up the coaches, as he was often called upon to do, he earned only thirty cents per hour. His wages represented the average working man's salary at the time; fares for a family aboard the steamer to the beach coupled with the outlay for entertainment deemed necessary when they got there could dent the budget of any working man.

The miniature railroad ran on the pier for a number of years. It saw steamers other than *Dreamland* arrive and depart. But the pier took the name of *Dreamland*'s pier, and, because of it, people often spoke of Chesapeake Beach as Dreamland. Even a song was written, often played by the Chesapeake Beach Orchestra led by John B. Bovello:

On the pier at Dreamland,
Merry, happy Dreamland,
Off you ride and by your side
  is one most dear.

On the pier at Dreamland,
Blissful, dazzling Dreamland,
Through wonders you roam,
and you hate to go home.

Saccharine as it may sound, the bit of very bad verse spoke to the generations of Marylanders who waxed sentimental over the days of roller coasters, carousels, splashing waves, and blissful days on the Bay. The inconveniences, the drudgery, and the biting mosquitoes were somehow forgotten.

The steamer for Baltimore left at 4:00 P.M. The deep-throated whistle sounded at 3:30, again at 3:45, and just before departure. The pier thundered with the race of picnickers toward the distant gangplank. A few were too late. On occasions, the boat turned around and rescued the frantic from the dock.

The last train for Washington left at 10:00 P.M. It, too, sounded warning blasts from the engine whistle. At 9:30 the orchestra in the dance pavilion abruptly stopped playing, packed up its instruments, and fled to the station platform. Crowds boarded the coaches. A few always seemed to miss the train, and sought a place to roost in the town wherever they could find it.

The steamer left its wake on the Bay. The train left a trail of smoke in the air. Both eventually were no more than ghostly memories.

6

STEAMBOAT PERSONALITIES

A steamboat was a living thing. Each had a personality of its own. Some seemed to wear an air of sweet contentment. They pulsed along with a quiet rhythm, undisturbed by the forces of wind and sea and man that surrounded them. They handled well. Their masters praised and loved them. And they held on for years, even decades, serenely spanning the Bay with their grace. A beloved example was the *Emma Giles.*

Others (like *Eastern Shore*) were plodding, patient, buxom work-horses, the width of their freight decks nearly one-third their length, their passenger decks tiered with spartan staterooms. They would steam slowly but steadily along the reach of the Bay and pull up to distant wharves in the far bends of the tributaries by night and day, in faithful and constant service. The farmers, watermen, and merchants of Tide-water could scarcely imagine what life would be like without them.

A particular few were winsome dancers—lithe, graceful, exquisitely sheered—performing a solo ballet in knifing through the seas of the lower Bay. A certain aesthetic gentility of balance and proportion governed the design of these steamers by the naval architects who conceived them. In contrast to a number of features in more utilitarian vessels that often jarred the sensibilities of Bay-boat aesthetes, these se-lect few of the Chesapeake steamboats preened themselves in yacht-like style, with an uplifting and sweeping sheer that gave a feminine grace to the superstructure and hull; a neatly raked stack, neither too tall, nor too fat, nor too slim, placed precisely amidships; a propor-tional allocation of open decks to cabin space; a well-mounted and spacious pilothouse above the hurricane deck; and a sprinkling of windows along the sides of the main and passenger decks spaced regu-larly and in proportion. These vessels entranced steamboat lovers for

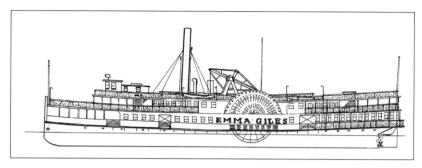

Steamboat *Emma Giles* of the Tolchester line. Drawn from contemporary photographs, including one by the author, and enrollment data.

generations. The *Susquehanna, Tred Avon,* and *Potomac* were some of the long remembered.

Then there were the Philadelphia packets, thin enough to fit the locks of the canal they had to transit—so slim that their beams measured only a tenth of their length, a gust of wind could threaten to capsize them, and their staterooms were constricted and freight capacity limited. Some medical wags called them anorexic. But they cut through the water like a blade and sped to their destinations on trainlike schedules.

And then there were the cranky and spiteful steamers. Some were so difficult to handle—and willful in their own way—that when such a vessel (like *Florida*) refused to meet (halt) a hard swing to port or starboard, masters and quartermasters often would let the boat "box the compass," or revolve through an entire circle, rather than fight her. Contrarily, boats rattled and banged (like *Annapolis*), sought out sandbars with suspicious frequency (like *Westmoreland*), were too underpowered to clear a dock with any alacrity (like *Anne Arundel*), or were so overpowered and badly designed (like *Mason L. Weems*) that their hulls scraped the bottom when they maneuvered in shallow creeks. Several (like *Cambridge*) flexed in the middle when put to speed. Others (like *Middlesex*) maddened their skippers and owners with exorbitant fuel bills and poor performance. A few (like *Columbus*) blew up or burned without warning.

But the steamboats of the Chesapeake, by and large, were a sturdy and colorful lot. They set a pace for life on the Chesapeake, and the Chesapeake itself dictated the life they themselves led.

The shadowy shapes of these vessels continued to haunt the Bay long after the boats departed. Their biographies became legends, and the legends intertwined with the history of Tidewater.

156

Over the years, from 1813, when the steamboat era began, to 1963, when it ended, the steamboats themselves went through stages of metamorphosis. The little 137-foot pioneer, *Chesapeake*, would almost have fitted in the freight deck of the 330-foot *President Warfield* (queen of the Bay in 1940) of the Old Bay Line, if the former could have been jockeyed through the cargo ports of the latter. The ghosts of William McDonald and Edward Trippe aboard the former would have faded at the sight of the latter towering in white-walled steel above them. To the shade of Legh Powell (president of the Old Bay Line), that of William McDonald would have sputtered in Scottish dismay. To that of William Almy, square-jawed, gold-striped, salt-stained skipper of the latter, that of the aristocratic Edward Trippe of the former would have communed in the tribulations of navigating the capricious and unforgiving Bay.

Steamboats and the men who manned and managed them gave meaning to the era of 150 years.

The fires of ambition, greed, and passion were spent in the lives of John Stevens, Robert Fulton, Robert Livingston, Nicholas Roosevelt, and Benjamin Latrobe in the beginnings of the steamboat saga on the Chesapeake (see Chapter 1). The steamboats they created were crude contraptions, contrived on the accepted lines of sailing craft and powered by engines created by ingenuity and remarkable skill but rudimentary by later standards. Although advertised flamboyantly as luxurious and catering to every comfort of their passengers, travel on one of them must have been a trying experience.

Imagine, if you will, boarding one of the early boats—*Eagle* or *Constitution*, for example—for passage from the upper Bay to Baltimore, an overnight journey at five miles per hour. Your first impression as you stepped aboard was the paucity of space allotted to passengers on the main deck: a space at the rounded stern measuring twenty-two feet wide by about thirty feet long, covered with a canvas awning if the weather grew inclement but not too breezy, otherwise left uncovered if sparks flew from the smokestack and threatened ignition of the canvas. Here all the passengers—and there could be several dozen—gathered to breathe fresh air mixed with wood smoke and cinders. Wooden benches, straight-backed enough to meet the prim standards of the times and to satisfy the corseted stance of ladies in stays, lined the rails. Forward of this passenger space intruded the upper works of the engine: the top of the cylinder with the piston rod throbbing up and down when the boat was underway, and the crosshead knifing the air like a guillotine and cranking the paddle wheels on either side. There stood the captain under a stovepipe hat and on a mounted grating, so that he could see forward, relay his rudder orders to the steersman at the stern, and bang his foot on the deck to signal the engineer at the throttle below.

When the boat was under way, the paddle wheels on either side threw up spume that sprayed over the passengers in full force if the wind was up. Soot from the smokestack powdered the passengers' garments with black. At night, the stack glowed a menacing red and belched hot cinders to the deck below. The tall stack stood forward of the machinery and above the boiler. An enormous pile of cut logs filled the deck forward—needed to satisfy the appetite of the furnace beneath the boiler. Stevedores, who had hauled aboard whatever freight could be carried—and this was limited by the pile of stacked logs—became firemen, lugging the heavy wood in an almost continuous chain to feed the grates. Hot, smelly, and dirty, they often kept their spirits alive in a kind of chant, rhythmic and incomprehensible.

If you were a woman, and fastidious, you viewed with apprehension, if not distaste, the prospects of sleeping as best you could on a cotlike bunk in a cubicle below the main deck, with only a curtain to shield your privacy. Only a few portholes kept the air from becoming stifling, and these had to be closed if the waves picked up. You slept in your shift and performed whatever ablutions were possible from a washbasin at the end of the compartment.

If you were a man, you quickly discovered that your sleeping compartment in the hold beneath the main deck doubled as the dining room. You could not retire until the tables of the evening meal had been cleared, folded up, and stacked with the chairs in an appropriate closet. Bunks folded out from the bulkhead, and passengers managed as best they could to sleep in public, with the din of the engines and neighborly snoring all about. Before dawn a bell rousted them out. Whether they liked it or not, their bunks disappeared in the woodwork, and tables were reset by the ubiquitous stevedores doubling as waiters, preparing to serve breakfast. Woe be to the lonely bridegroom, hankering for his bride in the ladies' compartment: a steamboat was not a place for a honeymoon.

The early boats had to earn their place on the Chesapeake. Not universally viewed with favor, in spite of their obvious advantages over sailing vessels in flat calm or stormy seas and their unpredictable schedules, they had to overcome the worries of planters and watermen of Tidewater in displacing their long-standing patterns of commerce with commission merchants in the cities, and they had to placate the travelers' fears of instant elevation from bursting boilers. The fire-breathing, steaming, clanking contraption hurling water behind it was viewed with alarm and suspicion. Except for *Chesapeake*, which on an established packet route and as a pioneer returned 40 percent on its investment, most early steamboats as they multiplied and competed earned a meager income. Only as steamboats and their channels of commerce gained acceptance in the 1820s and 1830s did the owners and operators realize a worthy profit.

To gain acceptance, steamboat builders radically changed steamboat design. Gone were the schooner hulls as well as bowsprits, mast, and sails (early precautionary measures if engines failed). Instead, steamboat design reflected the needs of the patrons and the physical facts of steaming on the Chesapeake and its tributaries. In the decades before the Civil War, the steamboat evolved in a general form familiar for the remainder of the steamboat era. Classic examples were *Columbus, Mary Washington,* and *Express.*

Passengers who boarded a steamer in the 1830s or 1840s at any of a number of wharves around Baltimore Harbor encountered a far different setting than that seen by the traveler in the early days. The main deck, running continuously from bow to stern in a gentle sheer, was sheathed completely in a white-walled, cabinlike superstructure, with cargo ports (where the gangplanks entered) and a row of windows along the entire length. The deck flared out as much as ten or more feet in a long curve from bow to stern along the hull, the extension allowing space for the paddle wheels and their gilt-painted and ornate paddleboxes to protrude and providing additional area for cargo forward and passenger accommodations aft. Staterooms on either side of a plushy saloon (from French salon) were furnished with iron beds, washstand, and perhaps a chair. Wooden shutters covered glass windows, which could be lowered. In the absence of individual drains, passengers simply shot the soiled contents of a washbasin out the window, with the hope that the wind was right.

Aft of the saloon was the dining room. In the tradition of hospitality—long-standing on the Bay, where steamers competed for culinary reputations—the tables sparkled with white linen, silver service, and suitable flowers or other decorations. The menus reflected the tradition and the bounty of the Bay and Tidewater country. They also taxed the skill of black cooks who were called upon to prepare full-course meals on short notice in a cramped galley, on a wood stove, below decks, with little or no ventilation. How they and the waiters, white-shirted with napkin over left arm, kept their aplomb in hot weather remains a mystery.

Second-class passengers, separated by race and gender, occupied bunks in a compartment in the stern below the main deck, with portholes that could rarely be opened because of the splash from the paddle wheels. A so-called water closet for passengers simply emptied directly into the waters of the Bay. Ashes from the fireroom grate were carried in hoppers to the cargo port on the main deck and dumped overboard. Frequently, the colored wake of a steamer could be traced for miles.

Black crew members—stevedores, roustabouts, deckhands, stokers, waiters, cooks—bunked beneath the freight deck in a crowded and jumbled space shared with anchor chain, hardware, and the "boatswain's stores." On some lines, many of the black men were slaves. Some gained manumission and promotion. Although a few rose to lookout men and quartermasters, none became officers.

Officers occupied staterooms near the passengers on the main deck. Only the master had quarters aft of the pilothouse mounted on the hurricane deck forward. In the first steamers of the 1820s and 1830s, even into the 1840s, the pilothouse was a square box with a few windows fore and aft, and the steering wheel centered within. As the voyages lengthened, the pilothouse increased in size, becoming rounded forward, with seven or eight windows across the front, and with generous space for a quartermaster at the five-foot wheel, the mate alongside, the master if he chose to appear, and any visitor on a bench along the rear wall. In later versions, the deck space behind the wheelhouse came to be occupied not only by the master's cabin but also by an extended deckhouse containing staterooms for the officers.

Amidships rose the stout black funnel, throwing soot in the air. Just aft of this stack were the A-frames (port and starboard), covered in sheathing to support the tracks in which the crosshead of the engine rose and fell as its connecting rods and cranks rotated the paddle wheels on either side. Later, these crossheads disappeared, and the fifteen-ton vertical or walking beam teetered to crank the paddle wheels. At the stern, awnings covered a promenade deck for the passengers. Protective railings consisted of narrow horizontal planks. From staffs flew banners and flags proclaiming the steamer's name, company, and destination.

In early boats, swivel guns and bells signaled landings, other vessels, and alarms. Steam whistles arrived in the late 1830s via Narragansett Bay, where a steamboat owner thought the sound of a locomotive whistle would be useful on a steamboat. A storm of protest from steamboatmen, who hated trains, greeted the proposal, but the idea persisted, and steamboat whistles cropped up everywhere. Not until the mid-1850s, however, was there any uniformity in their use, and earlier masters pulled on the whistle cord in any variety of shorts and longs for any purpose imagined.

Steamboats appeared on the Bay in the period before the Civil War in many shapes and sizes and personalities. Their passengers appeared in the same variety. They traveled, not for convenience or utility, but for necessity or adventure. With the discomforts, it took a hardy soul to set forth by steamboat. But far worse were long, slow trips by stage or wagon over muddy, powdery, or rocky dirt roads meandering through fields and forests and spending nights in inns where the beds were shared and the vermin trenchant. A trip by steamboat, for the planters and their families boarding at the country landings as well as for the merchants and their wives coming aboard at the city wharves, meant dressing up in the very best they could afford. The ladies simpered aboard in voluminous skirts sweeping the deck, hoisted in the rear in late deference to the bustle, their silk, muslin, fauns, and belgerines chastely covering their arms and necklines. Their swept-up coiffures were anchored by brimmed hats trimmed with imitation flowers and gewgaws. A prim parasol guarded against the ravages of the sun. Men boarded in frock coats and stocks, irrespective of season, complete with waistcoat, often brocaded and laced with gold chain and watch fob. Starched shirts and high, stiff collars marked the gentleman, as well as the stovepipe hat, which he wore with aplomb in spite of the wind and doffed only in an elaborate salute to a passing lady or to her escort when the latter doffed his in greeting. In the pre-Victorian era, these rituals divided the classes, but even the bumpkin boarding in homespun might try an acceptable imitation of these rituals.

Bathing of the complete person, except for the most fastidious and self-indulgent, remained a Saturday night chore, accomplished at home in a portable metal tub (bedroom or kitchen) filled with hot water by servants or by the wife of the planter or city worker. Crowded steamboat saloons or the second-class quarters below decks on hot summer nights reeked of stale air and the odor of sweat-stained clothing. Dances, frequent on the decks of the steamers carrying parties of excursionists, were not only vigorous to the rhythms of the two-step and new-fangled waltz but also redolent with the scent of unwashed bodies and quantities of cologne.

Prudishness, derived from early Puritanism, Quakerism, and Catholicism and the restraints of rising Methodism, set the outward mores. Newspaper advertising was circumspect about clothing; advertising for bathing suits or beachside attire did not appear. If audacious people entered the water at resorts, they went fully clothed; for the ladies not even an ankle was exposed.

Beneath the facade of propriety, vulgarity, profanity, and rough behavior remained unbridled. Drinking, roistering parties, clandestine stateroom trysts, and brawls were all too common. Captains and mates often settled battles with their fists and kept the peace among the crew with ready clubs. Gambling prevailed. Some professionals traveled in search of suckers. Large holdings, even plantations, changed hands in the flick of the cards.

In the traumatic years following the Civil War, the owners of steamboats about the Bay dealt as best they could with the ravages that the forced and careless operation by the federal authorities had dealt their boats, and with the myriad problems of resurrecting the steamboat industry on the Bay torn by the divisions of conflict. But out of the upheaval and the tribulation, there came eventually a remarkable transformation in the steamboat itself. Industrial expansion brought changes in design and engineering. The tastes of the times changed, and steamboat companies moved to provide the comforts and amenities for a demanding public.

While many of the prewar boats stubbornly continued to function in the postwar years—even some, like *Express*, with crosshead engines—new construction set the pattern. Although the white-sided, knife-bowed, stack-amidships style prevailed, the steamers were larger, ranging from 175 to 250 feet in length, with corresponding increases in beam, tonnage, freight capacity, and passenger accommodations.

Wooden hulls, although still built even in later years, were increasingly replaced by iron hulls, then by steel hulls, as the shipbuilding plants around Baltimore, at Sparrows Point, and on the Delaware, fell in stride. Composite hull construction remained popular to the end of the century. *Emma Giles*, built in 1887, had a hull of timbers held together by an iron and steel framework. But the hulls and machinery reflected the sophistication of a new age of engineering and technology.

The fleet of overnight packets running the tributaries of Tidewater made up the bulk of the postwar construction. Most of them, as they evolved, were two-deckers, as they were called. In fact, they utilized the space of four decks: the deck in the hull itself, the enclosed main deck running from bow to stern and guard rail to guard rail in beam, the passenger deck including a stretch of open deck space fore and aft and the saloon with staterooms on either side, and the hurricane deck holding the pilothouse with officers' quarters aft and a long, covered space for promenading and reclining.

A typical and especially appealing steamboat of the later period was *Lancaster* of the Weems line, held in favor by steamboat aesthetes through the years. She was built in 1892 at a cost of $113,307.37 by the Maryland Steel Company (see Appendix B). Her hull was of three-eighth-inch-thick mild steel, fashioned to form a waterway at the keel and with heavy framing for rigidity. Except for the steel of the hull and steel enclosing the engine and boiler, her structure was made of wood.

In the hull itself were accommodations aft for ninety-seven second-class passengers, segregated by gender and race: small compartments containing only basic beds and amenities, curtained off for privacy, and communal washrooms and water closets. A stair led to the main deck above. Portholes spaced under the counter beneath the overhang of the main deck could be opened if the waves or the wash of the paddle wheels did not threaten. Forward in the hold or hull were the engine and boiler spaces, occupying nearly one-third of the length and one-half of the width amidships. In the bow area of the hull were boatswain's stores, chain locker, and a rather large compartment set aside for the crew (separated by race), and containing bunks lined up in rows, a few cubicles for boatswain and quartermaster, and basic sanitary facilities. It was entered by a stairway from the freight area of the main deck above.

The main deck, running uninterrupted from bow to stern, served as the freight deck for half of its length, with side ports on both sides for loading. However, amidships, opposite the fire walls containing the engine and boiler spaces, were a mail room (the steamer delivered and received the mail at tributary landings), double staterooms for senior crew members, the purser's office, a package room for passengers' excess luggage, a barroom paneled in walnut like an English pub, the men's toilet complete with stalls and adequate plumbing, and the dining room galley, which had to be large enough to meet the demands of the first-class dining room above (a dumbwaiter hoisted the food) and of those other passengers who ate in the main deck saloon aft. This saloon, thirty feet in length and twenty feet in breadth and paneled in hardwood, formed a capacious, airy space surrounded by a gallery about the stern and lighted by closely spaced windows affording a panorama of the

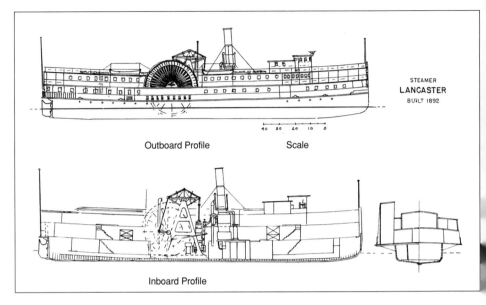

STEAMER
LANCASTER
BUILT 1892

Outboard Profile   Scale

Inboard Profile

Steamboat *Lancaster,* inboard and outboard profiles, reconstructed and redrawn from builder's drawings and data from archives and contemporary photographs.

passing Bay. A few tables sat in the middle; a banquette of upholstered leather continued on either side beneath the windows. At the very stern was a small water closet, which, like all other similar facilities on board, emptied its contents directly into the Bay. With a small orchestra serenading, the after saloon was a favored spot for dancing. A handsomely carved, double-width cherrywood stairway led to the main saloon above.

The passenger deck, except for the engineroom, boiler room, and paddle wheel casings, was devoted to a saloon (salon), with forty staterooms on either side, and to the dining room forward. With joiner work in basswood and sycamore, carved molding, ornamental alcoves, paneled doorways, ceiling in white and gold, and heavily upholstered furniture in green leather, the saloon presented the appearance of a Victorian drawing room.

The staterooms, equipped with comfortable beds or double bunks, were no longer spartan but furnished with chairs, small desks, bureaus, and washstands with hot and cold running water. Four staterooms (bridal suites?) aft were embellished with brass bedsteads and painted in white, gold, and blue pastels. Staterooms and saloon were carpeted in body Brussels carpet. Gold-framed mirrors adorned saloon and some staterooms. Special washrooms and toilets for ladies and gentlemen boasted marble fixtures. Not a single bathtub or bathing facility found a place aboard the vessel.

Forward in the saloon stretched the main dining room, an expanse of white tablecloths, swan-folded napkins, and silver embossed with the company seal. Two broad, converging stairways in carved cherry and basswood led to the main deck below. Open decks at bow and stern afforded passengers breezy places to absorb the beauties of the Bay and Tidewater. On the hurricane deck was the pilothouse, with room for the quartermaster on a wooden grating behind the five-foot wooden wheel, the captain and mate, and as many as five spectators (if invited). Aft, but connected with the pilothouse by its door, was the captain's cabin (in basswood and sycamore with a luxurious built-in bedstead) and separate cabins for first and second mates. Four lifeboats in davits flanked the vertical (walking) beam rocking in its A-frame and the tops of the enormous paddle-boxes, gleaming from the exterior in gold and bright colors. Sporting flags and bunting, *Lancaster* drew sighs of admiration from those who saw and rode her near the turn of the century.

Not all overnight packets matched *Lancaster* in comfort and splendor. Many were cramped, slow, unpredictable, and malodorous. Others surpassed her in contrived grandeur and advertised gestures to passengers. The personalities of the boats differed so markedly that passengers established their own preferences, if possible, and patronized, often at some inconvenience, the lines and steamers they liked. Steamboat reputations mattered, and some owners and masters, acting as grand hosts, exerted themselves to extend the gracious hand. Others, when they monopolized the trade, were indifferent, even arrogant.

Technology and design affected the appearance and characteristics of the later overnight packets. Inclined short-stroke engines, much like those on railroad locomotives, turned small, fast paddle wheels, so recessed and faired into the superstructure that the vessels looked like they were screw driven. And compound (two-cylinder) and triple expansion (three-cylinder) engines driving propellers at the stern revolutionized the performance of the vessels, their speed and maneuverability, and their appearance. Not that the steamers enjoyed some uniform magic as a result. *Middlesex*, with inclined engines, looked like a propeller-driven vessel and, with a decided sheer, fairly danced on the water, but she had a voracious appetite for coal—to the extent that her owners, who had designed her, sold her off. *Anne Arundel*, sleek, propeller-driven, and graceful, bore an engine built for a tug; her operators tied her up at the end of a dock rather than on the side, because she was too slow in backing clear. *Potomac* bounced around from owner to owner at birth, was nearly orphaned in the process, and finally became the idol of steamboat lovers on the Bay: an apparition of loveliness as she steamed past on a cloudless day. She served as an icebreaker for other steamboats when the Bay froze over and proved to be a tough fighter in a seaway and heavy wind. These later boats marked the climax of overnight packet service on the Chesapeake.

When amusement parks and resorts began to flourish around the Bay, steamboats adapted to the times. Like *Louise* and *Dreamland*, they cast aside their cabin space and staterooms for great expanses of deck—either open all around and covered by the deck above, or open to the sun and skies above. With bands playing, dancers swinging, and picnickers crowding the decks, they turned each voyage into a holiday (see Chapter 5). After the turn of the century, they led the way to the design and construction of all-steel steamboat behemoths whose purpose was identical to their predecessors. But somehow in the steel encasement, they lost personality, and patrons forgot themselves and used the names of the boats they affectionately remembered.

These old boats had their eccentricities. *Louise* got so accustomed to her runs to Tolchester that on one unusual excursion to the head of the Bay she flatly refused to change course to the north; three steersmen had to fight her wheel and her master had to scold her: "C'mon, you ole fool! You ain't goin' to Tolchester today. Come about!"

With amusement parks, excursions, and river trade (passengers and freight) competing with each other for the attention of steamboat operators (who, to make a profit, had to tend to each), there appeared a kind of steamer that would combine all three functions. *Emma Giles* of the Tolchester line was such a boat. She was designed for the task.

She was needed to supplement *Louise* on the run to Tolchester with hordes of picnickers and merrymakers crowding her decks. But the demands of planters, watermen, and merchants required her services to carry freight between the landings on the Little Choptank, Chester, Sassafras, South, West, and Rhode rivers and Baltimore. Furthermore, regular service for passengers (irrespective of season)—travelers, drummers, vacationers, youngsters off to boarding school, families, even corpses shipped off for distant burial—was a clear necessity. And, at the same time, city-worn excursionists yearned for one-day voyages down the Bay, either on charter or in coordination with regular service to the tributaries.

Emma Giles, launched in 1887, by design met all of these demands. With a length of 178 feet, a bosomy beam of 50 feet out to the guards, she could accommodate a large freight area forward on her main deck, as well as a handsome social hall in the triangular area near the stern. The hall, surrounded by closely spaced windows, provided a spectacular view of the Bay. Here a piano played, even when the steamer plied the rivers for trade. Here, also, an orchestra serenaded for excursions, and patrons danced away the day and the spell of evening.

A grand stairway of carved cherry led to the saloon above. Much shorter than that aboard the overnight packets like *Lancaster*, the saloon, constrained by the engine and boiler room casings and the paddle-box intrusions, nevertheless displayed some of the elegance of the packets, with rich carpeting, French mirrors, piano, heavy upholstered furniture, and carved paneling. Only six staterooms adjoined the saloon, three re-served for the ship's officers, three for passengers with small children for an extra fare.

But the huge forward and after portions of the passenger deck, as well as the expanse of the hurricane deck, were designed to please not only the excursionists but also the picnicking crowd headed for the beaches and groves of Tolchester. They were intended to accommodate the "moon-light cruise" trade, when the youngsters of Baltimore set out for a few hours of romance to the lulling beat of the old boat's engines and the caress of the breeze and the waves of the Bay. Families boasted later that many proposals of marriage occurred aboard *Emma Giles* (see Holly, *Steamboat on the Chesapeake*).

The Tolchester line was not alone in designing steamboats for multi-ple uses. In many varieties and with individual personalities, steamboats served Tidewater.

For the country crowd that came down to the landings to punctuate their lives with the spectacle of the arrival of *Emma Giles*, the sight had the effect of a carnival—and a touch of unreality. Stevedores clattered back and forth over the gangplank with freight on their hand trucks while they chanted and jigged to lighten the work. Some carried sheep bodily on board. Others forced cattle to cross the plank by mass shoving and a twist of the tail. The freight deck smelled of crated fruit and vegetables and the dung of cattle. On the passenger deck, well-dressed passengers stood at the rail sedately watching the scene on the wharf below, while a piano tinkled away in the saloon or the social hall aft. What the country specta-tors on the dock could see of the paneled interior of the saloon or the expanse of the social hall—or hear of the latest tunes played on the piano or even by a small orchestra—convinced them that they had glimpsed another world, far removed from the prosaic routine they endured on the farms.

Apart from the overnight river packets and the excursion boats was a class of steamer designed for a specific purpose, the transportation of passengers and freight between the major ports of the Bay: Baltimore and Norfolk.

The Old Bay Line (Baltimore Steam Packet Company) and the Chesapeake Line ran luxurious, fast, overnight steamers between the two ports for decades. The former company began operations in 1840. Around the turn of the century and into the late 1920s, large (three hundred feet or more in length), commodious, screw-propelled steamers, steel-hulled and most often three-deckers, evolved. Because they traversed the roughest part of the Bay, their lower decks were completely enclosed, and they resembled white-hulled ocean liners. Because they carried heavy freight (other than bulk cargo), their freight decks and holds measured a third of their length. Because they catered to the fur-clad, cloche-hatted, bejeweled, spats-shanked, Florida-bound clientele in the winter season and the well-heeled vacationers bound for Virginia Beach and other Atlantic resorts in the summer season, their appointments were sumptuous: cuisine that matched Rennert's, and other first-class hotels in Baltimore, palatial dining rooms, more than a hundred staterooms (some with private bath), palm rooms for entertainment and dancing, publike barrooms, shuffleboard decks, grand stairways, and galleried saloons rich with oil paintings, chandeliers, and gilded carving. Because they met trains at either end and because their patrons were travelers rather than excursionists, they ran with clocklike precision (except when the weather interfered). They were the unquestioned "queens of the Bay." (See *The Old Bay Line, 1840–1940*, by Alexander Crosby Brown.)

Like other steamers they had individual personalities. *Florida*, in spite of lavish, late Victorian overdecoration, had a nasty disposition: she was difficult to handle in close quarters and rebellious to engine orders. *Alabama*, her near sister, ran sweetly, but banged and rattled in a head sea. *State of Maryland* ate up fuel but showed her teeth in a heavy gale. She plowed through the hurricane of 1933 and arrived in Norfolk from Baltimore only scarred and weary after a fierce battle with enormous seas and winds that tore away her boats and railings and smashed her sideports. She was something of a heroine in the eyes of steamboatmen. *President*

Warfield, the flagship of the Old Bay Line, ran with destiny (see Holly, *Exodus 1947* and Chapter 8).

From the turn of the century to the Great Depression and the start of World War II, steamboating on the Chesapeake reached its peak. Gallant steamers had formed a picturesque if disparate parade through the preceding century.

The personalities of people who manned these boats were equally disparate. Most conspicuous were the captains, who were venerated, pinnacled, or reviled.

Most of the early skippers gained a reputation for toughness, bluster, adventurism, and—surprisingly—a certain gentility. Such a man was Mason Locke Weems (1814–1874), long-time manager of the Weems line and master of its principal steamboats through the years. His lineage should have bestowed gentility. Descended from the Earl of Wemyss (created lord high admiral of Scotland by Queen Anne) and David Weems (third son, who emigrated with his mother to Maryland in 1715), he was the oldest of four sons of George Weems (1784–1853), progenitor of the Weems line, which came into existence with his purchase of *Surprise* in 1819. Mason Locke Weems was named for his uncle, the itinerant and eccentric clergyman who became the first biographer of George Washington. George Weems saw to it that his four sons learned the business of managing, operating, and navigating his early steamboats, *Planter* and *Patuxent.* Mason Locke at the tender age of seventeen was handed the keys to *Planter* and commanded every Weems line steamer until his death. When his father, George, died in 1853, Mason Locke had long beforehand assumed control of the line; his brothers served the line in various capacities but reserved interests for themselves in separate enterprises. Under Mason Locke, the line survived the rigors of the Civil War, the savage fighting of an ulterior sort with conniving rivals, and the transition to a postwar economy. By the time of his death in 1874, he had brought a fleet of elegant steamers to the Weems line, prosperity to the family, and wealth to his two daughters, who succeeded him in the ownership of the company.

But in spite of his lineage and his success, he was not known for his courtliness or forbearance. He inherited few of the visionary and often impractical characteristics of his father, who swallowed the blandishments of George Stiles (defender in 1814, manufacturer, mayor of Baltimore) in selling him the trouble-ridden, rotary-engined *Surprise* and who fought a losing battle with the competition on the Rappahannock and with his supposed best friend, James Harwood. Mason Locke, unlike his father, appraised the world with the eye of a businessman, measuring the gain against the investment. A heavy-set man with a broad face wrinkled in a perpetual frown and a lip curled in disapproval, he often overpowered those he met. He nevertheless loved the Bay and particularly the Patuxent, a passion which he shared with his attachment to steamboats. As a master, he was authoritative, even dictatorial. But in his relations with the crew and particularly with his family, he forged a bond of affection that lasted through the years.

His brusqueness annoyed patrons of the steamboats he skippered. On the Rappahannock, he and his father George were compared unfavorably with Noah Fairbank, popular master of vessels on that river. "Captain [George] Weems appeared as a stern navigator [and] neither he nor his son [Mason Locke] was much given to urbanity. Indeed, the idea that they were unaccommodating, rude and illiberal generally extended, until they became quite unpopular. . . . Captain Noah Fairbank was of different turn—polite and accommodating" (B. B. Minor, Fredericksburg *Star,* August 2, 1890).

Mason Locke Weems tolerated little nonsense from his crew or, for that matter, from his passengers. Some years later, Judge James A. C. Bond, a noted Maryland jurist, recalled an event occurring on a trip from a Patuxent landing to Baltimore. Mason Locke skippered the steamer. At eight years of age and dressed in a velvet suit and white collar as befitted a young gentleman of means, the future judge took a stance at the rail to observe the monarch of the wheelhouse, as he bellowed his orders to maneuver the steamer away from the dock. Noticing brown mud in the water frothed up by the paddle wheels, he yelled at the brass-buttoned skipper, "Hey! Don't you see you're running her into the bank?" Weems swung about to check astern. Finding all was well, he glared down at the foppish imp who had dared to challenge his seamanship. "Why you little . . ." he began, took a fresh breath, and launched into a verbal blast that could be heard across the marshes. As the judge told it seventy years later, "Before he had finished, I was debating whether I should kill him right there on his own ship. But I decided not to. Instead, I retired to the cabin, leaving the entire responsibility for that ship's guidance in the hands of that inexperienced captain" (Mark S. Watson, "Motor Horns . . .").

Mason Locke Weems inherited his father's tenacity. He overcame years of adversity to build one of the most respected steamboat lines on the Bay and the outline of a steamboat empire as the means of developing the Tidewater from the Patuxent and the Potomac to the Rappahannock.

Weems trained many men to become steamboatmen. Some became the most renowned skippers on the Bay, often passing on to their sons the skills they had learned on the Weems line.

One of the most revered was James Russell Gourley. For sixty-one years he skippered steamboats, first of the Weems line, then of the successor, the Maryland, Delaware, and Virginia Railway Company (MD&V). He was born in Ireland on July 19, 1836, and never shook the brogue in his teeth. Before he had turned sixteen, he had arrived in Baltimore. On his own, he sought out employment. George Weems, aging but with a soft touch for enterprising youngsters, hired him as a deckhand aboard *Patuxent*, discovered that the boy had an aptitude for figures, and promoted him to purser. Discovering, also, that the lad thirsted for a chance at the wheel and the knowledge to navigate the Bay and its endlessly winding rivers, Mason Locke, into whose care the boy was placed, undertook the tutelage necessary to transform him into a pilot. On Gourley's twenty-first birthday in 1857, Mason Locke Weems presented the young man with his master's license. At that time, the issuance of a license depended entirely upon the judgment of the sponsoring captain. In this instance, the judgment was well founded. Enthusiastic, high-spirited but remarkably intelligent, James Russell Gourley embarked on a lifetime career aboard steamboats on the Bay. Even before he acquired his license, he had discovered his bride, age sixteen, and married her when he turned eighteen; they honeymooned on the anniversary every year thereafter.

During his long years of service with the Weems line and the MD&V, Gourley skippered *Planter, Mary Washington, Theodore Weems (St. Mary's* when she burned), *Essex, Mason L. Weems* (named for his sponsor), *Richmond, Potomac, Westmoreland,* and *Anne Arundel.* He held the record for the longest continuous master's license on the Chesapeake, earned the title of commodore of the Weems line, and supervised the building of its finest steamers. His triumph could not be deduced from his appearance: a small, frail, quiet man, with a low voice and self-deprecating manner. Nevertheless, his skill in shipbuilding, encyclopedic knowledge of the Bay, years of experience with wind and sea, confident but low-keyed exuberance, and personal warmth inspired confidence and affection.

Gourley's technical skill matched that of his brother, who settled in Rome, New York, and founded a shop specializing in the manufacture of precision instruments. Surveyors favored the Gourley transit over other instruments for many years.

James Russell Gourley had a way with women, At the end of a three-hour stop at Bay Ridge with *St. Mary's* in 1892, he blew the whistle to summon the passengers, who had gone ashore to sample the thrills of the resort. He sounded a series of blasts at departure and pulled out from the wharf, only to discover a large group of women frantically waving on the wharf—left behind through failure to hear or heed the whistle. Although the steamer stood several hundred yards from the pier and had lined up for the Patuxent, Gourley wagged his head in pity and gave the order to turn back. "I cannot ignore the plaintive wails of ladies," he said. Declared the ladies, "He is the most gallant mariner that ever trod a deck" (Baltimore *Sun*, April 18, 1892).

Through the years, rumors had persisted that Gourley was somehow connected with the episode of the French lady spy, Colonel Richard Thomas Zarvona, in the opening year of the Civil War (see Chapter 4). Gourley was certainly on board *Mary Washington*, most likely as mate, when Zarvona boarded the vessel at Millstone Wharf on the Patuxent. Mason Locke Weems was master. As an eyewitness, Gourley reported the encounter.

"When Colonel Thomas stepped on board the steamer . . . I, *who knew him personally* [emphasis added], warned him against remaining on board, telling him he would certainly be recognized and arrested. He laughed my warning to scorn, but when it became whispered about who he was and the boat, according to police orders, was headed for Fort McHenry, he realized his mistake."

The admission, "I, who knew him personally," suggested much more than casual acquaintanceship. Newspaper accounts of Gourley's death on April 17, 1912, brought to light that as an impressionable young man, sympathetic to the Confederate cause, he enthusiastically joined Zarvona in the scheme to capture *St. Nicholas*. According to these accounts, Gourley himself was held prisoner at Fort McHenry but gained release for lack of evidence and through the intercession of Weems. Certainly, Mason Lock Weems, as skipper of *Mary Washington* at the time, had an odd task of dissembling—disclaiming any knowledge he may have had of Gourley's activities and his undoubted bond to the young man (Brooks, "Co-injock Roberts"; Baltimore *Sun*, April 18, 1912; and *Official Records of the Union and Confederate Navies*).

When James Russell Gourley died at his home in Halethorpe, outside Baltimore, after bringing *Anne Arundel* to her slip in Baltimore the previous day, he left behind his son, Mason Weems Gourley, to command a variety of Bay steamers in his father's wake.

The senior Gourley in his later years skippered both *Potomac* and *Anne Arundel,* the prime propeller packets of the Weems line and the MD&V. Association with *Potomac* evoked an odd assortment of stories.

Potomac came into the world star-crossed. In a sense, her creation was an act of revenge.

Charles R. Lewis, who with his brothers had started a steamboat operation on the Potomac River with the purchase of an awkward little steamer named *John E. Tygert* and had expanded it singlehandedly with the purchase of the pretty side-wheeler *Sue,* attempted in 1893 to challenge the monopoly of the Weems line on the Rappahannock with the acquisition of the *Lady of the Lake,* a disheveled vessel much the worse for wear. Weems retaliated by preparing the resplendent steamer *Lancaster* for operations on the Potomac, thus dangerously undercutting what trade Lewis enjoyed on that river. The *Lady of the Lake* venture was a disaster, and Lewis vowed revenge against the Weems line.

His tack was to build a steamer so handsome—the finest of its class—that it would proclaim that Lewis's company, the Maryland and Virginia Steamboat Company, was an outfit to be reckoned with.

The steamer was built by Neafie and Levy in Philadelphia and was named the *Potomac*—indeed the best of the propeller-driven overnight packets on the Bay—a gracious and comely vessel, maneuverable and sturdy in a seaway. Financing for her building depended on the profits earned by *Sue* and *John E. Tygert* plus the acceptance of mortgage arrangements with the builders in excess of one hundred thousand dollars. But aging *Sue* required extensive repairs, and *John E. Tygert* was too small to support the company. In desperation, Lewis looked for a buyer to bail him out. He toyed with the Baltimore, Chesapeake and Atlantic Railway Company (BC&A), a subsidiary of the Pennsylvania Railroad Company (PRR). Abruptly, his old nemesis, the Weems line, appeared on the scene. Its president, Henry Williams, was determined to preempt any advance of the PRR into his "territory" on the Potomac or Rappahannock.

The Weems line bought the tottering Maryland and Virginia Steamboat Company in January 1895, thus acquiring *Sue, John E. Tygert* (which it promptly sold), and *Potomac,* just as the latter was undertaking its maiden voyage to the Potomac.

Lewis scuttled off to Lewisetta, at the mouth of the Coan River, to tend to a cannery that he owned there. A rather colorful but mercurial individual, he responded quite dramatically to competition from rival canneries by simply burning them to the ground in the middle of the night—and enjoyed a tenure in the Virginia penal system as a result. Fearful of the clamor his release to Virginia might create, he settled upon his return to freedom at Wynne, Maryland, not far from Point Lookout, where he owned a general store.

Legends persisted about the theatrical later life of Charles R. Lewis. In his store, he stocked a shelf of filled castor oil bottles and tomato cans—ready for instant tapping in the days of Prohibition. He was a skilled marksman and enjoyed using his rifle ("Long Tom") to hit the halyards of a passing schooner, sending the sails rattling to the decks before a startled crew. A ready wit and yarn-spinner, he reveled in the company of children, gave them penny candy, and brought down from Baltimore the first ice cream seen in St. Mary's County. In spite of his eccentricities and somewhat elfish behavior, he was beloved by his neighbors and was extolled on his death at age eighty-one: ". . . having given Southern Maryland and Virginia the first real freight and passenger service . . . the largest oyster packer in the east . . . a man of quick and broad interests and great gentleness . . . intelligence, integrity, and talent." He was respected, somewhat feared, but regarded as the source of legends in southern Maryland and the Northern Neck of Virginia (for a detailed account see Holly, *Tidewater by Steamboat*).

When *Potomac* sailed briefly for Lewis and almost immediately found herself flying the red ball flag of the Weems line, her skipper was William C. Geoghegan, for most of his life a captain of steamboats on the Chesapeake Bay and Potomac River. His son Charles was first mate.

A native of Dorchester County, Maryland, William C. Geoghegan was born on December 20, 1838, and soon followed the water, steadily working his way from cabin boy aboard a sailing ship to mate aboard the *George Peabody* of the Powhatan Steamboat Company. At twenty-four, he was appointed master of the *Pocahontas* of the same line. He became an avowed Unionist after a boat he owned was seized by the Confederate raider *Alabama*. Under this Unionist affiliation (anathema to most steamboat captains who wore their rebel sympathies on their sleeves and derided Geoghegan for his), he continued to serve the Powhatan line through the war and beyond. During that time he commanded *Petersburg, State of Maryland* (the first), and *Ellen Knight,* running between Baltimore and Richmond. He interrupted his wartime service to marry on May 12, 1862.

In 1874, he followed Reuben Foster, general manager, into service with the York River line as master of *John S. Ide*. At the end of eighteen months, he became master of *Sue* on the Potomac River route, a vessel with which he maintained an intermittent but established connection for the next twenty years.

In 1884, he was undoubtedly master of *Sue* when the Stewart sisters brought their celebrated suit against the Potomac Transportation Company. The four sisters—Martha, Mary, Lucy, and Winnie, black passengers bound for Kinsale—bought first-class stateroom tickets but found themselves assigned to inferior accommodations relegated to black passengers and spent the night on chairs in a segregated portion of the saloon. A district court judged that accommodations must be free from discrimination and awarded one hundred dollars to each of the plaintiffs.

This occurrence preceded the Maryland segregation (Jim Crow) laws of 1904 (preceded in 1901 in Virginia), which imposed stiff penalties against ship's officers for not enforcing segregation by race and enjoined others (presumably passengers) to assist in ejecting any passengers who refused to occupy an assigned (segregated) location (see Bibliography for pertinent law).

Geoghegan was master of *Sue* on November 8, 1874, when she rammed Fort Carroll in Baltimore Harbor in fog and spent time in the repair yard nursing a bent nose. His service for the Potomac Transportation Company brought him the command of other steamers, the *Charlotte* and the *Baltimore*. At one point, he broke his service to command the new *Pocahontas* for the James River Steamboat Company of Richmond. But he left that company after six months to skipper *Washington* of the Washington and Norfolk Steamboat Company. Such was the life of many skippers of Bay steamers who transferred from line to line when opportunities seemed to present themselves.

Then, in February 1894, Charles R. Lewis engaged Geoghegan to supervise the construction of *Potomac* at the yards of Neafie and Levy. At the launching and on the maiden voyage, Geoghegan stood in command. And when Henry Williams of the Weems line finalized the sale, *Potomac*, flying the red ball flag, sailed with William C. Geoghegan as master.

Geoghegan commanded other Weems line steamers: *Northumberland*, *Middlesex*, and *Calvert*. When the last-named steamer, on her maiden trip to the Patuxent, arrived at Solomons, Maryland, the whole town turned out to greet her. Flowers were presented to an embarrassed Geoghegan, who blew the whistle in a tuneful salute.

In 1904, *Anne Arundel,* as a Weems line steamer, made her first run from Baltimore to Washington. Geoghegan proudly skippered her, the triumph of overnight packets on the Chesapeake and a splendid running mate for *Potomac.* Little did Geoghegan realize that the new boat would be the last—the end of a long line of white packets on the Bay.

On January 14, 1909, aboard *Anne Arundel,* then under the keystone symbol of the MD&V, Geoghegan received a medal from the secretary of the treasury for a rescue on December 10, 1876. On that icy night, he personally pulled a midshipman and sixteen other men of the flagship *Hartford* from an open and drifting boat in Hampton Roads, Virginia, and saved them from an icy grave. Captains were heroes but a stoic lot. Portly, genial, rather dignified and unassuming, Geoghegan played down the drama of the occasion. But around the Bay, he assumed a stature larger than life from the incident and the award.

Heroes abounded among the steamboat masters of the Bay. The Old Bay Line earned a reputation for producing them. One was John L. Marshall, the "youngster" of the line, when with only twenty-five years of service (as quartermaster and second and first mate) he became master of the *State of Maryland* in 1932. Except for the *President Warfield,* she was the ultimate in steamboat travel on the Bay. His first officer was Patrick L. Parker, destined to transfer *President Warfield* to the War Shipping Administration and wartime service sometime later.

Captain Marshall took the *State of Maryland* through the worst hurricane to ravage the East Coast in many years. The steamer sailed from her Light Street wharf on the evening of August 22, 1933. Telegraphic warnings reported a storm off Hatteras, North Carolina, but the path of such disturbances normally carried them out to sea in the Gulf Stream. In a stiff breeze, *State of Maryland* headed down the Bay, followed by *City of Norfolk* of the Chesapeake Line. Only the lookoutman found the waves disturbing, as he fought off spray over the bow.

At two o'clock in the morning, the hurricane, which had violated the normal rules of behavior and marched straight through the Virginia Capes and directly up the Chesapeake, struck with full force. In its circular path, it first mounted a following sea, which lifted the 330-foot steamer on each swell and plunged it bow first in the trough, the propeller spinning in the air until it found a bite in the next wave. The steamer wallowed in sickening dives, while the wind shrieked through the stays, blew off lifeboat covers, and hurled spray over the decks. In the cabins, havoc prevailed: furniture was thrown asunder, dishes in the dining room and galley were smashed, and passengers huddled together in fear and resignation. The steersman in the pilothouse fought to keep the vessel from broaching in the troughs. Then the wind shifted around to the east, and *State of Maryland* found herself in a vicious quartering sea and in winds that drove her inexorably toward a lee shore on the western banks of the Bay.

Captain Marshall faced some unpalatable and life-threatening options. He could breast the sea and hope for shelter close to land on the Eastern Shore, but the steamer would be entering shallow water, difficult to navigate between the shoals on a clear day. Astern, *City of Norfolk* seized that option and promptly went hard aground—so firmly that it took days to drag her off.

Another option was to swing *State of Maryland* around to the west and head for shelter in the Potomac or Rappahannock. This option was unacceptable for several reasons: The steamer would be dangerously exposed on the flank as it turned. Furthermore, the rivers themselves would be lashed by the storm. Finally, the vessel would be heading toward a lee shore, a precarious undertaking in a wicked blow.

The third option seemed the most auspicious: plow on into the night and into the storm, bound for Norfolk, and pray that she could make safe haven in the vicinity of the Norfolk terminal. The storm through which she steamed wreaked havoc on the Chesapeake—wharves were destroyed, whole areas around the rivers and creeks were flooded, and some steamers at their Baltimore wharves found their bows in Light Street before the flooding and gale winds subsided.

State of Maryland proved that she was sturdy. She fought the hurricane with her own studied fury, and Captain Marshall in the wheelhouse nursed her along with cool courage. When the lights of Old Point Comfort showed close aboard, he heaved a sigh of relief—shelter at last. But the pier, as he discovered, was under water. In the gray morning, he turned *State of Maryland* across the white-flecked waters of Hampton Roads, to discover that the wharf at Norfolk was also flooded. But the piling still showed, and, with some daring and much skill, Marshall maneuvered near enough to tie up and bring an end to the ordeal. A few passengers debarked by rowboat; others remained aboard until the waters quieted.

Marshall found himself the center of adulation for his courage and seamanship. He was venerated in the legends of the Old Bay Line. All of the attention embarrassed him. A quiet, slender man—clean-shaven, boyish looking—he scarcely looked the hero. But the Old Bay Line people thought he was and poured on their praise.

William C. Almy. Drawn from photograph in *Norfolk Ledger,* November 22, 1932.

Marshall was first officer aboard the *President Warfield,* the flagship of the line, when Captain William C. Almy, senior skipper and commodore, brought her down from her construction yard (Pusey and Jones on the Christiana River, Wilmington, Delaware) on her maiden voyage to Baltimore on Friday, July 13, 1928 (a portentous day, that Friday the thirteenth!). On board, also, for the brief Atlantic transit was Holder Almy, Jr., the captain's brother and master mariner.

Captain William C. Almy earned a medal as a hero. He won esteem, also, for long service aboard the steamers of the Old Bay Line.

Born in Portsmouth, Virginia, in 1859, he came from a line of New England watermen, going back to the first William Almy in America, who arrived as a mariner with his family aboard *Abigail* in 1632. The father of the Old Bay Line captain was Holder Almy, Sr., of Tiverton, Rhode Island, who served as a government pilot during the Civil War and navigated some of General Ambrose Burnside's vessels in the vicinity of Hatteras. Later he worked with a salvage company off the coast of North Carolina, and established his residence in Portsmouth, Virginia.

Young William C. Almy was born with salt water in his blood, and put aside his school books at the age of thirteen to become deckhand and cook on the tug *Commodore S. F. DuPont* in Baltimore Harbor. How the crew fared with his ministrations at the galley stove was questionable, but his zest for a life on the water remained undiminished. A year or so later, he signed on with a wrecking crew out of Norfolk, thus following in his father's footsteps. He then elected to sample the life of a blue-water sailor by becoming quartermaster, then second officer, aboard the ocean-going Baltimore-to-Boston ships *William C. Crane* and *Decatur H. Miller* of the Merchants and Miners Transportation Company. Unlike most officers of Bay steamboats, young Almy learned the use of a sextant and the rudiments of celestial navigation. For a time he worked on the railroad-car transfer ferry *Canton* between Locust Point and Canton in Baltimore Harbor, then aboard the tug *Spring Garden* in Norfolk, where he earned his master's papers at the phenomenal age of twenty. After a stint as pilot on the side-wheeler *John Romer* running between Norfolk and Newport News, he joined the ranks of the New York, Philadelphia, and Norfolk Railroad (NYP&N) as captain of *Norfolk*, its first tug. When the company's passenger steamers, *Cape Charles, Old Point Comfort*, and *New York* (see Chapter 7) were put in service, Captain Almy commanded each in turn. Finally, he elected a career with the Old Bay Line. On November 1, 1888, he joined the company as master of the iron side-wheeler *Carolina*, an 1877 vessel, 250 feet long, whose vertical beam engine built by Charles Reeder had been salvaged from *Louisiana* after the latter had been rammed and sunk by *Falcon* in 1874. William C. Almy prized the history.

Recognition of his competence and loyalty led to his captaincy of the best of the Old Bay Line fleet: *Virginia, Georgia* (the first propeller ship of the line; Almy was picked because he knew how to handle screw-propelled vessels), *Alabama, Tennessee, Virginia* (the second), *Florida* (magnificently furnished in Victorian splendor but difficult to handle), *State of Maryland* (where he taught John L. Marshall a thing or two), *State of Virginia*, and, finally, *President Warfield* (the proclaimed queen of the Bay).

He lived aboard ships for sixty-one years and served with the Old Bay Line for forty-four of them. At the time of his retirement in 1932, his service had extended over nearly half the life of the Old Bay Line itself. He estimated that during that time he had traveled more than five million miles by water between Baltimore and Norfolk. He knew those waters like the back of his hand.

On two occasions, Captain Almy was cited for heroism and skillful seamanship.

Early in 1911, when coming up the Bay aboard the old *Florida*, he sighted a burning schooner, apparently abandoned, off Sharps Island

Light at the approach to the Choptank River. Ahead in the ship channel to Baltimore, he sighted the lights of other vessels, which had apparently passed the schooner without pausing. Captain Almy was not satisfied. Swinging *Florida* (with much effort on the part of two steersmen when she balked at being diverted from her regular route) to starboard, he entered the Choptank mouth and approached the schooner some four miles away. Four men were clinging desperately to a makeshift raft near the vessel they had been forced to abandon.

Later in the same year, Captain Almy and six members of his crew on *Florida* made names for themselves again by rescuing five men in the lower Patapsco. On that cold and dark evening, as *Florida* headed for the open Bay in a forty-five-mile-per-hour gale, Almy saw a dim red lantern waving in the wide stretch off Sparrows Point. At first thinking that it came from a sloop that had foundered several days previously, he decided not to investigate. But a seaman's precautionary instinct impelled him to slow down, approach the light, and have a look. Turning on *Florida*'s searchlight, he swept the wind-tossed water. The light picked up an open launch with five men precariously hanging on and desperately waving for help. Maneuvering the cranky *Florida* near the launch alarmed Almy with the possibility that the little boat could be caught in the wash of the vessel and swept under its mammoth paddle wheels. He elected to drift past the launch and attempt another tactic. The men in the boat shrieked in fear that *Florida* would pass them by. For a time, the little boat disappeared from Almy's view in the trough. But it reappeared, and crew members from the main deck tried to cast heaving lines to it without success.

Then Almy ordered the engines to back slowly. His maneuver flattened the seas close by and afforded a lee to the beleaguered boat. Suddenly *Florida* backed into a sandbar. Almy ordered her engine stopped. But his maneuver brought success. A line reached the launch, a winch on *Florida* hauled it in, and the five men gained the safety of the steamer's deck when crew members dragged them aboard. Gently, Almy coaxed *Florida* off the bar, and she proceeded on her way, as impudent as ever but cocky in success.

On August 5, 1912, a ceremony was held both in the executive offices of the Old Bay Line at Pier 14, Light Street, Baltimore, and on board *Florida* moored pretentiously at her slip. At noon, the directors of the company assembled in the office of Captain John R. Sherwood, president, there to be joined by a number of distinguished guests, including the presidents of other steamboat lines. A few minutes after 1:00 P.M., the group marched across the pier and boarded *Florida*, where Captain Almy and five members of the crew waited under an awning in front of the pilothouse. To Captain Almy, William R. Hurst, director, presented a massive octagonal gold medal, with bars displaying a life buoy and crossed oars, and the face showing the house flag enameled in red and the white-enameled "B" encrusted with diamonds. The reverse side bore the captain's name and the inscription: "In recognition of faithfulness in service and heroism in action. Saving life May 11, 1911; November 12, 1911." Except for the diamonds, similar medals were awarded to First Officer R. S. Foster, Second Officer George U. McGrath, Lookoutman Floyd Miles, Ernest Selson (black waiter), and Albert White (black deck-hand). Following the awards, the recipients, directors, and invited guests gorged themselves at midday dinner.

Captain Almy was a heavy-set, square-jawed, weathered, mustached man with a pudgy nose and a mouth that seemed on the verge of a per-petual smile. His eyes bespoke years of searching the waters of the Bay, yet welcomed the newcomer with warmth and friendliness.

He was known for his hospitality aboard the boats he skippered, and entertained at his table a number of distinguished passengers: Presidents Taft, Wilson, and Theodore Roosevelt, Governor Albert C. Ritchie of Maryland, Cardinal James Gibbons, and others.

On the other side of his character, he was a man who expected much of his officers and crew and got it. With his depth of knowledge and experience, there was little about steamboating that he did not know and the men who served under him knew that he knew it. They performed accordingly. At the same time, they knew that he had a temper, slow-ris-ing but trenchant, and that he possessed a vocabulary to match it—a seaman's vocabulary, rich and often profane. He became a legend, not only as dean of Bay steamboat masters but also for being what he was, a sturdy, competent, but often colorful man of the sea.

Although he served the Old Bay Line loyally for many years, he was not averse to taking on the company in open conflict if he felt that he had been wronged. Such a situation developed in midcareer.

"Left Bay line Apr 24th 1909," he wrote with a flourish in his personal log, "because of dissatisfaction at being suspended 60 days for leaving mate in charge of str. to move from one wharf to another wharf in the harbor and he [the mate] backing str. into a wharf. This was not violating any marine law." He took the matter to court and won, not only his case but also honorable reinstatement with the Old Bay Line.

Although he lived comfortably, with residences in Baltimore (on Broadway near Johns Hopkins Hospital, in Roland Park, and in Mount Washington), and owned a farm near the South River bridge, his salaries through the years reflected the standards of the times: as a sailor with the Merchants and Miners, $25 per month; as master of the tug *Spring Garden*, $70 per month; as master of the Cape Charles steamer *New York*, $83.33 per month; as master of *Georgia*, $154 per month; as master of *Florida*, $179 per month. By the time he was master of *President Warfield* in the early 1930s, he had doubled his last salary.

He held passes for free transportation and accommodations on a number of railroads (Southern, Seaboard Air Line, Pennsylvania, Atlantic Coast Line, and the Richmond, Fredericksburg, and Potomac), testifying to the interlocking interests of these systems, particularly with those of the Pennsylvania Railroad. Several steamboat lines extended courtesies, including the rival Chesapeake Steamship Company, itself held in the interlocking railroad net (see Chapter 7).

Captain Almy's death on July 19, 1939, brought a wave of accolades and expressions of nostalgia. He was among the most respected masters in the long line of captains of steamboats on the Chesapeake.

Captains came in many sizes, interests, and temperaments, but they shared one quality: their knowledge of the Bay and its two thousand miles of navigable waters. Like Horace Bixby, who tyrannized young Samuel Clemens on the Mississippi, the masters demanded that the aspiring pilots who apprenticed themselves to learn the Bay commit to memory the entire tangle of wandering rivers, convoluted sounds, twisting and narrow creeks, and the expanse of the Bay itself, with its treacherous shoals and cantankerous disposition. Although charts existed, they offered no substitute for the image of the bluff ahead when the channel curved beneath it, for the deceptive shadowing of the shoreline where headland masked headland, for the miles of marshland where the shallow channel wound in tortuous confusion, for the mouth of the Potomac and the breadth of Pocomoke Sound where the Bay seemed like an ocean with no land in sight.

Captains were directly responsible for the licensing of young pilots and masters in the earlier days and, in later days, recommended them for licensing by responsible boards. But the captains alone carried the weight of training, and they exercised it with firmness—even with the arrogance paralleling the stellar performance of Horace Bixby.

Navigational instruments and publications for deep-water steaming (the nautical almanac, Bowditch, reduction and azimuth tables, sextant, chronometer) had little practical value on the Chesapeake, and Bay watermen scarcely knew of their existence. The only aids were a good pocket watch to time the transit in fog and low visibility from buoy to buoy, headland to headland, or lighthouse to lighthouse, and a compass mounted and dimly lit on the binnacle in the pilothouse. Even with the compass, some old-time watermen either ignored or failed to learn the difference between magnetic and true north, and used the former for all their readings.

Skippers made mistakes and paid for them. Most of the collisions resulted from judgmental errors. Few of the groundings came from the weather; most occurred because skippers miscalculated. One skipper on the Potomac awoke in the middle of the night and, befuddled by sleep, rushed to the wheelhouse and demanded that the wheel be thrown over and the steamer headed for what he believed was the mouth of a creek where the vessel was scheduled to make a landing. The mate and quartermaster remonstrated with him—"It ain't time to make the turn. We have to wait." But the skipper seized the wheel in his own hands, spun it over, and headed toward shore. Promptly, the steamer ran aground. It took two days of pulling by a tug—and the loss of a month's pay by the captain—to extract the steamer from its predicament.

Skippers took pride in their seamanship and preened themselves over their prowess in bringing a steamer alongside a dock. But their failures, when they occurred, were conspicuous. The currents on the Patuxent and Rappahannock swept steamers "backing full" right past their wharves, and skippers hid their chagrin when they had to turn around in narrow confines to try again.

Skippers could be vain, pompous, quiet, explosive, cold and withdrawn, intellectual and studious, and hospitable and generous. But on board their ships, within the limits of the law, they were monarchs, and the public viewed them at least with respect, if not awe. Like the steamboats they ran, their personalities tempered the spirit of the steamboat era.

7

THE KEYSTONE FLEET

In the 1920s, employees of the Pennsylvania Railroad (PRR), especially those in the operating divisions, found their service with the company a mixed blessing. On the one hand, they lived in the presence of steam locomotives, those monstrous romantic behemoths with the flailing driving rods pulling freight trains of one hundred cars or hurtling down the tracks leading pullman trains in elegant procession between the major cities. The clicking of the telegraph from block tower to distant station—a lonesome wailing whistle in the dark of night—these moments were savored and remembered. And with the romance of railroading were the rewards of faithful service: a modest retirement and a gold watch suitably engraved.

On the other hand, the PRR demanded much of its men. For operating employees (telegraph operators, dispatchers, agents, engineers, firemen), the work week had no meaning. Each employee was required to work seven days a week throughout the year without vacation—except for exactly two consecutive days per month granted him as "relief days." This allowance of only two days per month per operating employee (Sundays, Christmas, and other holidays were work days unless they fell on "relief days") would seem barbaric today, but it followed standard practice in the 1920s on the railroads of the United States, including the Pennsylvania Railroad.

Those two relief days climaxed every month for each employee. For him and for his family they assumed a holiday importance irrespective of date, weather, or the state of health or wealth.

Most employees and their families chose to travel. The magic wand was the company pass. A senior operating employee held a red-banded card (his wife, as a courtesy, had one, too) entitling him to travel free throughout the entire "Pennsy" system, not only on the main lines but also on the widespread network of railroads and steamboat lines controlled directly (or even indirectly) by the PRR. By application, a dependent minor enjoyed the same privileges with the issuance of a special pass for each trip.

With only two days allowed, the extent of the journey was clearly circumscribed, but employees and their families made the most of it. Children were taken out of school (with the flimsiest excuses to the principal for the absence). Days of preparation and anticipation preoccupied the parents.

For a certain employee who lived in Baltimore, the journeys by train invariably led to cities within a comfortable day's radius. He could travel to New York by express: to thrill when the great steam locomotive puffed away from the standing train at Manhattan Transfer to allow an electric engine to take its place for the trip in the tube beneath the Hudson River into Penn Station in the heart of the city, to ride on top of the double-deck bus for a nickel's fare up Fifth Avenue to Central Park, to reach the top of the tallest building in the world (the Woolworth Tower), to gape at the glitz of vaudeville at the Paramount Theater for thirty-five cents, to eat dinner at Horne and Horne's Cafeteria for fifty cents. He could go to Richmond to view the capitol of the Confederacy and the crater on the battlefield at Petersburg and to renew family connections and a certain visceral allegiance to the Stars and Bars. Or he could visit Philadelphia —to touch the Liberty Bell and join the parade of youngsters solicited to contribute fifteen cents apiece to rebuild the Betsy Ross house, birthplace of the Stars and Stripes.

But for that certain employee who lived in Baltimore, the trips in spring, summer, and fall carried him aboard the steamboats of the Chesapeake.

Like most Baltimoreans, he found it necessary at least once or twice a season to perform the ritual of dipping his feet in the surf at Ocean City or Rehoboth Beach. In the early 1920s, he had a choice. He could board the steamer in early morning at the Light Street wharf for a two-hour trip across the Bay to Claiborne, a quiet, tree-shaded town on the Eastern Shore, there to board a waiting train for Rehoboth. Several hours later, after clattering behind a chugging and cinder-shedding engine across the peninsula through Maryland into Delaware, he beheld the glint of the ocean spreading before him from Rehoboth Avenue. Or he could board the steamer in Baltimore, cross the Bay to Love Point on the northern tip of Kent Island, and cross the Delmarva Peninsula by train to

Ocean City for a day's sojourn by the sea and family accommodations in a rooming house at two dollars. After the midtwenties, with the cancellation of the Claiborne–Rehoboth route, only the Love Point route to Ocean City remained.

The experience of riding the steamer *Cambridge* to Love Point was unforgettable. She was a graceful vessel, questionably reputed to be the fastest on the Bay, with a decided sheer and a rake to her funnel. On the top deck, a passenger could feel the pulsing of the triple-expansion engine far below and, most remarkably, note the flexing of her upper deck with each thrust of her propeller. Cutting through the water, out of the Patapsco and across the Bay, she stirred up a sensuous breeze across her open deck, a vacation in itself for the street-weary passengers from Baltimore. On the beach, they would wade in the surf or flop in the sand, tilting their straw hats for shade, and listen to the music of the sea. Women, with their long skirts gathered to midcalf in one hand, often shed their shoes and padded along the edge of the incoming surf, their other hand gripping their cartwheel hats against the breeze. Youngsters gathered shells in the sand—and there were many in those days—and darted back and forth with the lapping waves. In an expansive mood, the employee might reserve pullman seats for the return trip—at three dollars each.

Another trip beckoned: from Baltimore overnight to landings on the Potomac River, where, to meet the schedule, the employee and his family left the palatial *Dorchester* at Morgantown and boarded the train at Pope's Creek for a smoky, slow ride on benchlike seats across the farmland of southern Maryland. They would stop every few minutes at little country stations, to arrive in due course at Bowie, and there they would change trains for a Washington–Baltimore express.

Frequently, the employee and his family indulged in the luxury of an overnight trip—free, of course—aboard one of the packet steamers of the Old Bay Line from Baltimore to Norfolk. In the early 1920s, they rode the *Alabama* or *Florida;* in later years they traveled in style aboard the *State of Maryland* or the *President Warfield.* On board, the free-pass passengers rubbed shoulders with the social elite bound for Florida or Virginia Beach. Children were often scooted away by their parents from the sight of the bar, where men were said to gamble and carouse, and from the obvious parties, sometimes a bit bawdy, spilling over from the staterooms. Unlike the well-heeled festive passengers, the less well endowed, on arrival in Norfolk, spent a day at Ocean View Amusement Park, riding the roller coaster and strolling the boardwalk before returning on the steamer the following night. Stepping off the boat in Baltimore, the returning passenger felt in the cold morning light that he had spent two days in another world, far removed from the dull routine of daily life.

At least once a year, the employee yielded to the yearning he felt for his old home in Accomac County, Virginia. Accordingly, he boarded the steamer *Eastern Shore* at her Light Street wharf before evening sailing time, listened to her sonorous whistle signal departure, watched her sturdy paddle wheels throw up spume as she pivoted in the basin, and viewed the receding skyline of Baltimore in the setting sun. Through the night she churned her way south, her bosomy bulk as stable as a church in the choppy seas, her vertical beam engine sighing in the darkness with each thrust of the piston and each quiver of the paddle wheel. Just before dawn, thunderous knocks on the adjoining stateroom door awakened the occupants, the tremor of paddle wheels reversed, and the scraping of the guards along the piling of a wharf announced the arrival of the steamer at Crisfield on the Eastern Shore. By midmorning, the steamer had moved through Pocomoke Sound and reached Onancock, its white houses and churches encircling the creek. There on the wharf were gathered hordes of relatives (everybody on the Eastern Shore of Virginia was related—all of them had to be kissed), forming an escort to the family home, where a country-style picnic on the lawn awaited. Here the visitor enjoyed the divided blessings of staying in a huge but drafty house with outdoor plumbing. Late the next evening, a train stopping at Keller, Hallwood, or Makemie Park bore the employee north. Because of the flatness of the terrain and the straightness of the track, the headlights of the train ten miles away were visible. Northbound passengers traveled to Wilmington, a three-hour ride, to await an express from New York to the end of the journey in Baltimore.

As an alternative route from the Eastern Shore to Baltimore, the passenger could take the southbound train traveling down the peninsula to Cape Charles. There he could board the *Maryland*, a sleek, swift vessel, for a run across the mouth of the Chesapeake to Norfolk. From that city, he could ride by train to Petersburg, shuttle to Richmond and, via Washington by train, arrive in Baltimore by train. Overall the trip tried his endurance of bench-seated coaches and nearly matched in time the overnight trip by steamboat alone out of Baltimore.

In fact, upon due consideration by the thoughtful passenger, the dominance of the Pennsylvania Railroad on the transportation system of the Chesapeake appeared to be overwhelming. The rail network from New York, Philadelphia, and Wilmington south swept from the Susquehanna in the north through Baltimore, Washington, and Richmond to Norfolk. On the Eastern Shore, it reached from Wilmington through the spine of the Delmarva Peninsula to Cape Charles and via steamer service to Norfolk; it crossed the Eastern Shore from the Chesapeake to the Atlantic. On the Bay, the sizeable fleet of steamboats the PRR owned or controlled reached far into the tributaries where the railroads could not profitably penetrate—on the Chester, Choptank, Wicomico, Nanticoke, Pocomoke, and Occahannock rivers of the Eastern Shore; to the Patuxent, Potomac, Rappahannock, York, and Piankatank rivers of the western shore; and behind the scenes, it operated a swift service of packet steamers between Baltimore and Norfolk. In effect, most of the principal tributaries of the Bay were served by steamboats under PRR control, and the Bay was encircled by a railroad system governed directly or indirectly by the company.

These observations were borne out in fact. The Pennsylvania Railroad by the 1920s had nearly completed a task that it had set for itself much earlier—the acquisition of railroads and steamboat lines (to complement the rail network) to serve the entire region of the Chesapeake and to squeeze out the competition. The fact that it had entered the game too late to prosper from it and brought into focus its own fallacious judgment of the economics of the times did not diminish the tentaclelike grasp the PRR held over the Tidewater region.

The policy was long-standing. As stated by authoritative observers, "it rested upon the reasoned conviction . . . that a railroad system could not attain its greatest effectiveness and utility until it had rounded out its contours to include its logical sphere of territory. A natural corollary was that this should be accomplished as promptly as possible" (Burgess and Kennedy, *The Pennsylvania Railroad Company*, vi).

As constituted after its full expansion, the PRR owned over 600 companies (railroad, steamboat, ferry, bridge, real estate, warehouse, and other). By later consolidation and amalgamation, the number of companies it owned was reduced to sixty-three active transportation lines, but it held strong if not dominant stock positions in ninety-five others—a network of 158 companies embracing much of the commercial, agricultural, and industrial center of the country. At its peak, the system was the largest in the world.

This mammoth system of the 1920s had its inception in a much more modest goal a century beforehand in the notion of building a railroad from Philadelphia (still perceived by its residents as the traditional center of the United States) to Pittsburgh. None other than Colonel John Stevens, the behind-the-scenes progenitor of the Union Line's steamers *Chesapeake* and *Delaware* in 1813, petitioned the Pennsylvania legislature in 1818 on the "Expediency of a Railroad from Philadelphia to Pittsburgh." In 1823, he gained partial success. His request was granted, addressed to "The President, Directors and Company of the Pennsylvania Rail Road," to build a railroad from Philadelphia to Columbia (on the way to Pittsburgh). Stevens himself explored the route on horseback. For lack of support for a scheme that everyone at the time deemed too radical, the plan was not implemented.

The interest of John Stevens in railroads began somewhat earlier. Notably, Stevens, at the time of his moves to underwrite the conversion of the Union Line to steamboat service, petitioned the New Jersey legislature for a charter to build a railroad connecting Trenton on the Delaware River to New Brunswick on the Raritan River, hence opening traffic to New York and the Hudson. Shortly afterward, John Stevens passed to his son Robert Livingston Stevens his interest in the steamers *Phoenix* and *Delaware*, operating from New Castle to Trenton. In 1825, the Union Line itself passed into the ownership of Robert Livingston Stevens (along with his brother Edwin). The proposal of John Stevens to build a railroad matured in the 1830 construction of the Camden and Amboy Railroad and Transportation Company. John Stevens had much to do with inspiring the Philadelphians to view the railroad as the important transportation link of the future.

However, it took the threat of competition to stir the Philadelphians, prideful of their perception of their city as the most important in the Americas, to action. When they saw the menace of the New York & Erie Rail Road Company creeping out of the growing metropolis of New York and—most compelling—the open challenge of the Baltimore and Ohio Railroad moving from Baltimore westward to Pittsburgh, they rose from their silk-padded posteriors in outrage. A group of wealthy Philadelphians decided to incorporate the proposed Pennsylvania Railroad on April 13, 1846. From the very beginning, the company had financial backing, and its success can be attributed to the wealth that sustained it.

During the regime of the first two presidents, the line moved to acquire land and smaller rail lines in its march toward Pittsburgh. But it remained for its third and much renowned president, J. Edgar Thomson, who administered the company from 1852 to 1874, to create the vast system that operated for another century under its own name. A native of Pennsylvania, born in 1808 of Quaker stock, he entered railroading as a profession in early life, surveying for roadbed in New Jersey and Georgia. In 1830, he headed the engineering division of the Camden and Amboy Railroad. He studied railroad engineering in Europe for two years, returned to become engineer of the Georgia Railroad, and then joined the PRR as chief engineer. A brilliant engineer, hard-nosed manager, and visionary, he brought vigor to his job and earned advancement to the presidency of the company.

A stocky, broad-shouldered man, with a firm jaw, gray hair and side whiskers framing his square face and high forehead, he presented an aspect of authority that few were willing to question. He was known as a difficult man at times, temperamental, taciturn, abrupt, and even rude, and was disposed to making sudden decisions on his own without consultation. But he was devoted to the interests of the company and pursued his vision of its future with nearly fanatical zeal. His foresight found its own reward in the system that he established, which remained intact through the years before his death in 1874. In this empire, which he created, the monopolistic grasp of the Pennsy reached fulfillment in the territory that it served.

During his administration and that of his successor, Thomas A. Scott, the PRR not only consolidated its network to the Mississippi and the Great Lakes but also reached southward to Baltimore, Washington, and beyond. In this process, the PRR eventually and inescapably challenged its archrival, the Baltimore and Ohio Railroad, on its own turf.

The building of rail links from Philadelphia toward Wilmington and the head of the Chesapeake began much earlier than the advent of the PRR on the scene. These separate rail links, including the Philadelphia, Wilmington and Baltimore Railroad Company, were landmark acquisitions by the PRR. Buried within these acquisitions lay the title to the old New Castle and Frenchtown Turnpike Company (incorporated in 1809) to provide the means of connecting the segments of the old Union Line steamed by *Delaware* and *Chesapeake*.

With the PRR established in Baltimore, its attention focused on access to Washington, where its nemesis, the Baltimore and Ohio Railroad (B&O), took a determined stance to prevent any encroachment on its monopoly of rail traffic in or out of the nation's capital. Thomas A. Scott, the PRR president, appeared before one congressional committee after another to break the B&O's hold, without success. But Scott was firmly

190

determined—not only to gain access to Washington but also to reach further south. "To make this enterprise complete," he threatened, "arrangements have been made to extend the road across the Potomac, through Alexandria, to junction with the Richmond, Fredericksburg, and Potomac Railroad northeast of Fredericksburg, thus forming a direct and continuous line of railway between all important points to the southern Atlantic States with those of the north and east" (Burgess and Kennedy, *The Pennsylvania Railroad*, 273).

In spite of the bravado of this declaration, the obstacle of B&O obdurance remained, particularly as the Maryland legislature openly displayed its bias in favor of the B&O, which was perceived by the legislators as the founder of railroading in the United States. There seemed to be little hope for the Pennsy's entrance into Washington.

Then the prying nose of the PRR's agents discovered a loophole—in fact, a very wide breach—in the B&O ramparts through which the PRR could march. The loophole centered on an unusual provision in the charter of a little railroad planned by some planters of southern Maryland to connect their farmland not only with Baltimore but also with the Potomac River, south of Washington, for possible connections by water to the South. In 1853, the Maryland legislature had granted a charter to this projected rail line, the Baltimore and Potomac Railroad, as it was tentatively named. But the planters, somewhat less than aggressive, failed to move ahead quickly and allowed the events of the Civil War to preclude its construction.

Immediately after hostilities ended, the PRR agents, still smarting under the success enjoyed by the B&O in resisting penetration of its monopoly in Washington, discovered the charter of the never-built Baltimore and Potomac Railroad—and a fascinating provision within it. Under the general terms of the charter, the projected railroad was authorized to construct a main line from Baltimore to Pope's Creek, a point on the Potomac River near Morgantown, Maryland. But, most surprising to the PRR, it also was authorized to build lateral branches from the main line. These lateral branches could not exceed twenty miles in length.

The PRR saw its chance. In 1866, the PRR underwrote the construction of the Baltimore and Potomac Railroad, in effect becoming its owner, and built the main line through the town of Bowie, Maryland, on the way to Pope's Creek. Washington, by careful calculation, lay within the twenty-mile radius of Bowie. A lateral branch from Bowie to Washington, therefore, had the advance approval of the Maryland legislature and, by act of Congress in 1867, the District of Columbia.

The opposition of the B&O caved in. In due course, the main line of the Pennsy ran directly to Washington. At one point in its history, the B&O itself, in financial difficulty, was owned by the PRR, but the PRR relinquished its stock holdings for other enterprises.

As a matter of interest, the original "main line" of the Pennsy from Bowie (a community created by the railroad and named for Ogden Bowie, the only president of the line and later governor of Maryland) to Pope's Creek functioned as a single-track branch line through most of the later history of the PRR. Its once-a-day passenger train with freight cars attached puffed its way south through the rich fields of southern Maryland to its terminal on the banks of the Potomac at Pope's Creek. To make the journey was an adventure for passengers, if they were willing to accept soot and cinders through the open windows of the coach, lengthy stops at every crossroad, an average speed reckoned at less than twenty miles per hour, and boarding passengers ranging from drummers peddling their wares to Amish in bonnets and plain suits to fishermen carrying their smelly catch in open baskets. Today, little remains at Pope's Creek (numerous crab houses excluded) to remind the visitor of the southern terminus of the "main line" of the Pennsy—only some rusting metal in a thicket and a skeleton of a brick building probably constituting a power station. Along the highway (U.S. Route 301) toward the present-day Potomac River bridge (just downriver from Pope's Creek), railroad tracks on the surface of the road at Upper Marlboro and Waldorf call to mind the pygmy railroad that produced a giant.

South of Washington, the reach of the PRR groped through the years into the affairs of various railroad lines. Particularly important to the transportation network surrounding the Chesapeake Bay was the interest that the PRR developed in the Richmond, Fredericksburg, and Potomac Railway (RF&P) to Richmond; the Norfolk and Western Railroad (N&W) bringing Norfolk, Petersburg, and the James River basin in touch with the North and the West; the Southern Railway; the Atlantic Coast Line Railroad; and the Seaboard Air Line Railroad. The last three railroads connected Washington with the South. The interest of the PRR in these railroads, particularly the last three, was not overt. It existed in the form of stock holdings, loans, and other forms of financial backing, which left the companies subservient in most decisions to the preferences of the PRR. In turn, these companies' substantial holdings in steamboat lines on the Bay placed the steamboat companies in the position of being manipulated, or subject to indirect control, by the PRR. A case in point was the ownership of the Old Bay Line (the Baltimore Steam Packet Company) by the Seaboard Air Line Railroad. Another case in point was its rival, the Chesapeake Line, which felt the weight of the Southern Railway behind its back. And behind both steamboat lines and their railroad controllers lay the grip of the Pennsylvania Railroad.

Encirclement of the Chesapeake Bay by a rail network required the creation of a system running the length (and breadth) of the Delmarva Peninsula. This one-hundred-mile-long stretch of land separating the Chesapeake Bay from the Atlantic Ocean and including Delaware and the eastern shores of Maryland and Virginia contained some of the richest farm country on the Eastern Seaboard. As it developed from a tobacco-growing area to a region of a diversified economy based on truck farming, peach growing, and a thriving oystering and fishing industry, the Eastern Shore attracted the attention of railroad planners.

The process started with the acquisition in 1830 by the PRR of the New Castle and Frenchtown Turnpike Company (renamed the New Castle Turnpike and Railroad Company), a line running the land route of the stagecoaches connecting the segments of the old Union Line on the Chesapeake Bay and the Delaware River. Over the years, various lines constructed around the northern portion of the Eastern Shore became targets of interest to the PRR. With the arrival of railroads as far south as Tangier Sound, the notion of running steamboats from the Eastern Shore to Norfolk reached the stage of direct planning, which was interrupted by the outbreak of the Civil War.

The ascendancy of Alexander J. Cassatt in the administration of the PRR focused attention on the Delmarva Peninsula largely because of his personal interest in the development of a railroad to link Philadelphia and Wilmington with Cape Charles, Virginia, and, via a steamer line across the Bay's mouth, with Norfolk and the South. It was Cassatt's nature to pursue his interests to a conclusion satisfactory to him, irrespective of such ephemeral considerations as loyalty to a company or additional accumulation of personal wealth.

At the outset, Cassatt was a very wealthy man by inheritance. And, because of his family's wealth, he had the advantage of an education in engineering available to only the very few. Born on December 8, 1839, in Pittsburgh, he traveled at an early age to Europe with his parents, where he attended continental schools reserved for the upper classes and then

A. J. Cassatt, seventh president (1899-1906) of the Pennsylvania Railroad. Drawn from a portrait in *Centennial History,* 1949.

Darmstadt University, Germany. When his family returned to the United States, he entered Rensselaer Polytechnic Institute and received an advanced degree in civil engineering at the precocious age of twenty. Beginning his career in railroad engineering in Georgia, he fled north with the opening shot of the war and started as a rodman with the Pennsylvania Railroad in 1861, advancing through the hierarchy to become first vice president. In 1882, at only forty-two years of age, he abruptly resigned from the company, reportedly in a pique over not being elevated to the presidency on the retirement of Thomas A. Scott. Other evidence suggests, however, that Cassatt, as a wealthy man, was indifferent to the blandishments of corporate rank and sought only to satisfy his interests and particular goals.

A severe man, rather arrogant in demeanor, with a downward-slanting moustached mouth and hard eyes under upward-curving eyebrows suggesting a constant questioning of others and his surroundings, he had several overriding passions. One concerned horse breeding—the development of superior horses for the racetrack—from which he earned the title of "patron of the American turf." Another, derived from his civil engineering background, led him to pursue the study of highway development. In this pursuit, he was not prescient; if he had been, he would have recognized the possibility that hard-surfaced roads would damage the very structure of the rail and steamboat network which he had so

carefully husbanded. A third interest consumed his time: the reorganiza-
tion of the way railroads conducted their business, in particular the rate
system and the rebates extorted by shippers, leading to inequality around
the transportation system. This interest brought him back to the PRR as
a director and to its presidency in 1899. He served in that capacity until
his death in 1906.

His last abiding passion was the extension of the railroad service on
the Delmarva Peninsula. His enthusiasm for the enormous undertaking
could not be quelled by discouraging profits, financial difficulties (when
pressed, he advanced his own money), or stages of indecision on the part
of his subordinates. In effect, he was the father of the railroad that ran
down the spine of the peninsula to Cape Charles (with service by
steamer to Norfolk). The New York, Philadelphia, and Norfolk Railroad (NYP&N, or Nip'n' N, as it was nicknamed) was largely his creation,
and he served as its president (without salary) from 1885 to 1889, concurrent with his tenure as a director of the PRR. The "benign" interest of the
PRR in the construction and operation of the NYP&N line was evident,
and in 1904, gossip flowed that takeover by the PRR was imminent. It
occurred in 1908, two years after Cassatt's death.

Remarkably, the NYP&N, with branch lines into Crisfield and several
other communities in Maryland, followed a straight course through the
densest woods of the Eastern Shore of Virginia. Were it not for the curva-
ture of the earth, an observer in Makemie Park near the Maryland state
border, because of the flatness of the land, could see a train leaving Cape
Charles, Virginia, forty or more miles away. The path taken by the builders of the railroad meant that the service catered primarily to "through"
trains from the North to Norfolk. Most of the settlements of Accomac
and Northampton counties of Virginia were left to depend on the creeks
and rivers emptying into the Bay for their source of transport and liveli-
hood. For most of the Eastern Shore of Maryland, this dependence on
the water highways, crisscrossing the peninsula in a canal-like system,
prevailed also, in spite of the existence of the railroads.

In fact, throughout the Chesapeake region on both its western and
eastern shores, rail service to Tidewater was meager, in most areas non-
existent. Rail trunk lines connected the major cities, but few branch lines
reached into the vast areas of the countryside along the tributaries of the
Bay. Exceptions existed in local rail service to Annapolis from Baltimore
and Washington, in the excursion line to Chesapeake Beach, and in
branch line service to Pope's Creek. Vast areas of Tidewater, where the

rivers reached inland, lacked rail service of any sort. Steamboats plying these waters furnished the transportation link deemed unprofitable for the railroads to construct on land. More than two thousand miles of navigable waterways served as the highways of commerce, which the railroads could not feasibly replace.

The importance of these steamboats to the economy of the Bay and the fact that as many as fifty or more steamboats operated out of Baltimore alone in a season (a similar overall total out of Norfolk and Washington) brought the focus of the PRR upon possible acquisition to complete its thesis "that a railroad system could not attain its greatest affectiveness and utility until it had rounded out its contours to include its logical sphere of territory."

Several plump targets had presented themselves. The financial difficulties encountered by several steamboat companies operating out of Baltimore to landings on the Eastern Shore prompted the PRR to work behind the scenes for their purchase. Overtly, the following events characterized the move: The Choptank Steamboat Company sold out to the Eastern Shore Railroad Company on March 9, 1894; immediately afterward, on July 18, both the Eastern Shore Steamboat Company and the Maryland Steamboat Company (totally bankrupt) also yielded their ownership to the Eastern Shore Railroad Company; on October 20, a new company made up of these holdings including the Eastern Shore Railroad Company emerged and was incorporated as the Baltimore, Chesapeake, and Atlantic Railway Company. Its railroad components traversed the peninsula from Bay to ocean, and its initials, BC&A, gained various reverse acronyms—notably "Black Cinders and Ashes" or "Before Christ and Afterwards." With the rail component, the BC&A also gained ownership of wharves and adjoining property plus fifteen steamboats: the side-wheelers *Avalon, Chowan, Eastern Shore, Enoch Pratt, Helen, Ida, Joppa, Kent, Maggie, Pocomoke, Tangier,* and *Tivoli,* and the screw steamers *Cambridge, Choptank,* and *Tred Avon.* (See Appendix B for a listing of representative steamboats mentioned in this chapter with specifications, enrollment, and other data.) These railroad and steamboat acquisitions were the overt manifestations of the move. Covertly, the BC&A, advertised as a "syndicate," was the creature of the Pennsylvania Railroad, which owned the creature, lock, stock, and barrel. To these holdings, the BC&A added steamers of the Wheeler Line, which sold out under BC&A (PRR) pressure: *Chesapeake, Easton,* and *Minnie Wheeler.* Eighteen steamboats now graced the maritime larder of the Pennsylvania Railroad.

The second series of plump prizes targeted by the PRR presented themselves for acquisition in late 1904. One was the Queen Anne's Railroad, founded in 1894 to run from Queenstown and Love Point, Maryland, to Lewes, Delaware, and which in 1904 was a financial disaster. Another was the Chester River Steamboat Company, a small but still prospering line running four old steamers, *B. S. Ford, Corsica, Emma A. Ford,* and *Gratitude,* from Baltimore to Chestertown and Centreville. But these were small pickings; the appetite of the PRR was much larger.

What the PRR saw as a juicier prize was the Weems line, the oldest steamboat line on the Chesapeake—indeed, in the United States. Begun in 1819, the Weems line had prospered in eighty-seven years to become the most respected steamboat enterprise on the Chesapeake. Its steamers, some of the finest on the Bay, provided the essential overnight packet service between Baltimore and the Patuxent, Potomac, and Rappahannock, with links to Norfolk and the James River. The landings along the three major rivers of the western shore reaching inland through the rich farm country of southern Maryland, the Northern Neck of Virginia, and the region south of the Rappahannock to the James, had known the sound of the whistles of the Weems boats for several generations. Whether they liked or disliked the monopoly that the Weems line exercised on those rivers, the planters and the fishermen along their shores accepted the Weems steamboats as part of the economic and social fabric of the region.

The Wilmington banking house of Henry Scott and Company approached all three, the Queen Anne's Railroad, the Chester River Steamboat Company, and the Weems line, with a package deal. For the syndicate it represented, the banking house offered to purchase the three lines for over $3.5 million: the Queen Anne's Railroad for $330,000 in gold bonds, $1.4 million in mortgage bonds, and $600,000 in income-mortgage bonds; the Chester River Steamboat Company (unencumbered) for $200,000 cash; the Weems line for $1,030,966.13. The first two companies quickly accepted. The Weems line, owned by Georgeanna Weems Williams and Matilda Weems Forbes (granddaughters of George Weems), vacillated, until Henry Williams, its much-respected president, considered the options with care and then succumbed. On January 3, 1905, the deal was consummated. The property of all three companies passed to the ownership of a new corporation, the Maryland, Delaware, and Virginia Railway Company (MD&V). The MD&V was owned outright by the Pennsylvania Railroad. The creation of the MD&V and the acquisition of a fleet of steamboats on the Bay marked the last major official act of PRR President Alexander J. Cassatt.

The BC&A and MD&V, together with the NYP&N (after 1908), controlled most of the rail network on the Eastern Shore, connecting not only the North through the Delmarva Peninsula via Cape Charles and Norfolk with the South but also the Chesapeake Bay (via Love Point) with the resorts on the Atlantic Coast. But more importantly, by the purchase of MD&V in 1905, the PRR gained ownership of an additional fleet of fourteen steamboats: *B.S. Ford, Corsica, Emma A. Ford,* and *Gratitude* from the Chester River Steamboat Company and *Anne Arundel, Calvert, Caroline, Essex, Lancaster, Middlesex, Northumberland, Potomac, St. Mary's,* and *Westmoreland* from the Weems line, among them some of the best steamboats on the Bay. With the steamboats went wharves, scows, leased property by transfer, and other valuable assets. By 1906, the PRR subsidiaries operated more than thirty steamers out of Baltimore and several on the run from Cape Charles to Norfolk. Nearly two-thirds of the regularly scheduled steamboats on the Bay flew the flag of the PRR or displayed its red and gold keystone emblem on their stacks, and more than three-fourths of the essential freight and passenger service to and from tributaries of tidewater Maryland and Virginia burdened the decks of PRR vessels. Around the Chesapeake, the PRR had literally acquired a transportation empire.

To this fleet, the PRR added other vessels as the years passed, some to replace older boats, others to match the times, technical changes, and shifting tastes in elegance and novelty. In 1902 and 1903, BC&A had built *Maryland* and *Virginia,* virtual sister ships in appearance and performance, at Sparrows Point. In 1908, the twin-screw *Neuse,* purchased by BC&A, became the *Piankatank* for service on the Piankatank River, and gained a reputation for speed and a particularly appealing appearance. In 1910, *Three Rivers,* named for the Patuxent, Potomac, and Rappahannock, joined the fleet, with staterooms on the top deck and superior passenger accommodations. *Talbot* and *Dorchester,* built at Sparrow's Point in 1912, with inclined engines and a third deck of staterooms, became the queens of the PRR fleet.

Throughout the reign of the PRR on the Bay, the BC&A and MD&V appeared to the public as separate corporations, but in fact they met at the top under the same PRR management (Willard Thomson as general manager with his administrative staff), and they interchanged their steamboats in peak periods of travel or heavy freight. In planning and scheduling, the lines diverged in the tributaries and parts of Tidewater they served, but the separation in management was illusory.

In geography, the PRR steamboat empire began in the lower reaches of the Bay in the transit service from Cape Charles (terminus of the NYP&N) to Norfolk. It continued northward on the Eastern Shore in service from Baltimore to landings around Pocomoke Sound and its tributary creeks, to the Nanticoke River, Wicomico River, Tuckahoe River, Choptank River, Chester River, Eastern Bay (Claiborne), and to Love Point on Kent Island. On the western shore, it continued north-ward to serve the Piankatank, Rappahannock, Potomac, and Patuxent and their various coves, creeks, and ancillary rivers. To this formidable extent of territory and listing of the steamboat lines owned directly by the PRR must be added the prestigious packet lines plying between Balti-more and Norfolk, in which railroads controlling these companies were in turn manipulated by the substantial holdings of the PRR. (For a list of representative steamboats owned by the PRR, together with their specifi-cations and other data, see Appendix B.)

That a huge corporation—one of the largest and most pervasive in U.S. history—held in its grip the transportation system of the Chesa-peake Bay conjures up images of exploitation, greed, indifference, and impersonal services. There existed a certain truth in all of these images. Charges of foreshortened schedules in slack seasons, leaving shippers and passengers stranded, and disproportional rates were often well founded.

It was true, also, that the PRR, like many vast railroad systems, ex-ploited its employees. In October 1906, captains and mates of the BC&A and MD&V tied up their boats at Light Street (an enormous congestion occurred), went home, and refused to return unless their wages were raised 50 percent; salaries at that time were $60–$100 per month for captains, $40–$60 for first mates, and $30–$40 for second mates. Thir-teen days after the strike began, the management gave up the battle and acceded to the officers' demands.

Despite these problems, during its reign over a regime of sleek, white-sided, and picturesque steamboats, the PRR through its subsidiaries maintained a relatively high standard of performance in the elegance of its shipboard accommodations, dining room cuisine, schedule punctual-ity, and general efficiency.

At the southern reaches of the Bay, the dream of Alexander J. Cassatt to connect Cape Charles at the end of the Delmarva Peninsula with Norfolk encountered the harsh realities of crossing the Chesapeake at its mouth. Here the tides of the Bay met the surge and the storms of the Atlantic. Between Cape Charles and Cape Henry (on the southern side of the Chesapeake entrance) stirred a choppy sea, even on a calm day moving in long swells, but in a southeaster, the lashing white-combed seas curled in angry fury at the shoaling depths. Ferry service across the eighty-mile run from Cape Charles to Norfolk meant the building of vessels with sea-keeping capacity.

Even more ambitious, Cassatt envisioned steamers able to load passengers and freight cars directly on deck from the tracks of the NYP&N. He began by trying out a barge, able to carry twelve freight cars, towed by a tug. Success bred confidence. He built a steamer. The *Cape Charles*, built expressly for the NYP&N in Wilmington, arrived in 1885; in addition to Florida-bound passengers, she carried two passenger cars on tracks mounted on her forward deck. However, in the attempt to improve her sea-keeping qualities and to place her overhang high enough for sufficient freeboard in heavy seas, the designers and builders failed in one respect: She proved to be difficult to handle in the small harbor at Cape Charles. In due course, she was joined by *Old Point Comfort*, smaller but more efficient—so efficient, in fact, that her route was extended to include not only the trip from Cape Charles to Norfolk but also a run up the James River to Richmond. Although the route proved to be profitable, it was abandoned for various reasons, notably, competition from the Old Dominion Line out of Norfolk. *Old Point Comfort* went north in 1907 to serve as relief steamer on many BC&A routes.

Over the years, barges towed by tugs ferried freight and passenger cars across the straits; in 1929, the barge-freight terminal shifted from Norfolk to Little Creek, inside Cape Henry. But, most importantly, a number of splendid steamers carried vacation-bound passengers to the terminal in Norfolk for onward travel by rail to the South. In later years, as hard-surfaced roads developed, these steamers transported autos on their freight decks. Among the most venerated of these steamers were the *Maryland, Virginia Lee,* and *Elisha Lee.*

A trip aboard *Elisha Lee* was sea voyage in itself. Crowded with passengers during the war years of the 1940s, she nevertheless preserved an air of elegant nostalgia of the golden years of steamboat travel. A graceful vessel, with a pronounced sheer to handle boarding seas and two buff stacks flaunting the PRR keystone above a well-proportioned white superstructure, she set out for her eighty-mile crossing to the Norfolk terminal from the basin at Cape Charles. The cost of the dredging for the basin had been paid for from the personal funds of A. J. Cassatt. Off the marshes of Kiptopeak, at land's end of the Delmarva Peninsula, *Elisha Lee* would feel underfoot the lift and fall of the long swells of the Atlantic Ocean—subtle in calm weather, lashing in a gale. Breaking each wave with a dip of her sleek bow and a fling of spray from her counter, she lost sight of land in the crossing.

Often the schedule called for a stop at Old Point Comfort on the north shore of Hampton Roads, Virginia. Two hours after the steamer's departure from Cape Charles, the bulk of the Chamberlin Hotel poked through the mist, a luxurious establishment at Old Point Comfort commandeered by the government as officers' quarters in the war years. Beside it sprawled the ancient battlements of Fortress Monroe. Maneuvering alongside the wharf at Old Point Comfort called for skill; the captain often spun the steamer on its heel and with a breast line out let the current sweeping from the sea over nearby Thimble Shoals push the vessel against the dock. There she surged uneasily while passengers and freight were unloaded over the gangplank. Underway again, *Elisha Lee* threaded her way through the anchorage of Hampton Roads, where gray or camouflaged naval vessels of the Atlantic Fleet melded with merchant vessels at assigned anchorages, awaiting formation into convoys to cross the Atlantic. On her way through the anchorage, she crossed the site of the turning point in naval history—the battle between the ironclads *Monitor* and *Virginia* (formerly the *Merrimac)*. Past the Naval Operating Base she steamed, where the docks teemed with naval ships, from destroyers to aircraft carriers, and where the air rattled with the sound of work in the dockyards. At length, she slid into her berth at the Norfolk terminal and poured her human and material cargo on the pier. The voyage, lasting for several hours, caught the scent of the open sea.

In Baltimore, the PRR fleet dominated the wharves along Light Street. The Light Street wharves were a half-mile line of cluttered wooden piers and flimsy street-side fronts thrown up to form sheds for the steamboat lines. Light Street itself was a narrow confine of confusion between the rat-infested wharves on the one side and warehouses and warrens of commission merchants on the other. The street was filled with drays and trucks backed to the piers, clattering wagons, cursing drivers, chanting roustabouts, and terrified pedestrians, all slipping over cobblestones slimy with decaying produce and the dung of horses and cattle.

Over the loading platforms and on the street side of the wooden fronts, for long stretches of the wharves, were advertised the lines of the Baltimore, Chesapeake, and Atlantic Railway Company and the Maryland, Delaware, and Virginia Railway Company. Farther down the line of Light Street wharves toward Federal Hill were the terminals of the Old Bay Line (Baltimore Steam Packet Company) and its rival, the Chesapeake Line. The former was noteworthy for its dark green, rather dignified appearance, with an ornate cupola surmounting its roof, and a bridge across the tumult of Light Street to protect its patrons from the mayhem of the street below.

On the basin side of the piers lay the steamers riding at their slips, smoke wisping from their stacks in preparation for the evening's departure.

Evening sailings began after 4:00 P.M. and continued past 6:00 P.M. At least a dozen steamers in that interval readied for departure, belching black smoke, sounding a plaintive wail on their whistles as they backed one by one into the harbor. As they pivoted about in the basin—their paddle wheels or propellers throwing up a froth at the stern—they caught the glint of the evening sun on gilded paddle-boxes, polished railings, and white superstructures punctuated by rows of windows on either side. Down to the mouth of the Patapsco River they steamed, in a stately procession reminiscent of a century of steamboating on the Chesapeake.

Off the lighthouse at Seven Foot Knoll at the Patapsco entrance, a few split off for destinations on the upper Bay. Most of the PRR boats continued south. In the darkness their cabin lights twinkled. During the late evening and early morning hours, they veered for their destinations.

Toward the Eastern Shore and its canal-like system of rivers the portly side-wheelers took their separate paths: *Tangier* steamed for the Nanticoke River and a forty-mile run from its mouth through narrowing marshland to Seaford, Delaware. *Joppa* headed for the Choptank River and a winding trip through farmland to Denton, thirty miles from the open water of the Bay. *Virginia*'s route took her up the Wicomico River to Salisbury, twenty-three miles upstream, lying at the head of navigation where turning about was difficult. *Eastern Shore* and *Tivoli* traveled the Pocomoke and Occohannock rivers, winding through the byways of Pocomoke Sound to Tangier Island, Onancock, Saxis, and Pocomoke City to Snow Hill, a twelve-hour journey from Crisfield with its fish factories, where the steamer first stopped at dawn on entering the sound.

Toward the western shore and its long, majestic rivers steamed the packets of the former Weems line and vessels added to the fleet. For the

Patuxent River and Bristol forty miles upstream near the bridge and head of navigation ran *Westmoreland,* stately with an eagle mounted on her pilothouse and emblazoned on her gold-trimmed paddle-boxes. The Rappahannock River and Fredericksburg at the fall line ninety-five miles from the Bay were the destinations of *Lancaster.* One of the handsomest of Bay packets, *Lancaster* was a touch of symmetry in motion, an almost poetic expression of the art of steamboat design. For the Piankatank River steamed *Piankatank,* a twin-screw vessel, low-lying, slim, noted for her speed and cargo-carrying capacity. *Dorchester* sailed for the Potomac, with its historic and picturesque tributaries like the Coan or Yeocomico. The steamer was a floating palace, noted for the sumptuousness of its staterooms and dining room. After nearly one hundred miles of travel up the famous river past Mount Vernon and Alexandria, the vessel arrived in Washington at the head of navigation, a two-day journey from Baltimore (an hour's trip by train).

A large fleet of first-class PRR steamers (like the *Anne Arundel, Potomac,* and *Talbot*) ran these routes also. The sound of their whistles echoed around the bends of the rivers for decades and in the memory of the inhabitants for generations.

During the morning hours also, the Light Street wharves were alive with departures. *Cambridge,* a fast propeller-driven boat carrying its cargo of freight as well as vacationers bound for the ocean resorts, departed for Love Point on the northern tip of Kent Island. For the Chester River, with its deep bends and rich history, steamed the venerable *B.S. Ford* to Chestertown or twice-named *Gratitude* (a landing on the route was named for the boat) to Centreville. Other steamers during the day set forth on lesser routes in the service of the PRR.

In the late 1920s, three-fourths of the steamboat service out of Baltimore felt the reins of control by the PRR. This included the fast packet lines for Norfolk: the Old Bay Line with the handsome overnight hotel-like *Alabama* and *Florida* and later the queens of the Bay, *State of Maryland, State of Virginia,* and *President Warfield,* and the rival Chesapeake Line with the palatial *City of Richmond, City of Baltimore,* and *Yorktown.* The former company (owned by the Seaboard Air Line Railroad) and the latter (owned largely by the Southern Railway) found their management decisions circumscribed by the shadowy financial presence of the PRR in the parent companies. That presence of the PRR on the Chesapeake was pervasive.

At the peak of the PRR's supremacy on the Bay, there existed more than three hundred landings in the navigable waters of Tidewater (the

Chesapeake and its vast network of estuarine tributaries), at least three-fourths of which were owned, leased, rented, or otherwise controlled by the subsidiaries of the PRR. Its fleet traversed the Bay—its length and its breadth. (See Appendix B for specifications and other information on some of the steamboats owned by the PRR.)

Certain steamboat lines out of Baltimore managed to escape the grasp of the PRR. The Ericsson line to Philadelphia, with its vessels designed to transit the Chesapeake and Delaware Canal, failed to interest the PRR, simply because the railroad's management could not conceive that steamboat service to the City of Brotherly Love could offer competition to rail service on the main line. Excursion companies serving resorts and amusement parks around the Bay—lines to Chesapeake Beach (or Seaside Park), Tolchester, Fairview, Brown's Grove, and Betterton (served partly by the Philadelphia boats)—thumbed their noses at the PRR. A few small companies tried to keep their independence: the unsuccessful one-year venture of the Baltimore and Southern Navigation Company, the one-steamer excursion line of the *General Lincoln*, the failed attempt of the Baltimore and Richmond Steamboat Company to start a freight route to Richmond, and other sporadic sallies into the steamboat trade that succumbed to competition.

Out of Washington, the major packet steamboat service, as discussed above, operated under the PRR in the guise of the MD&V. The Old Bay Line's steamers from Washington to Norfolk operated under the same management controls as the Baltimore line. Aside from this blanket, a number of excursion routes to Colonial Beach, Marshall Hall, and other resorts flourished without PRR control. But the PRR held its grip on the vital link of Tidewater country, via the Potomac and the Rappahannock, to the major centers of commerce.

Out of Norfolk, a few excursion lines held their own, but the scene was dominated by railroad-owned steamboat companies. The Chesapeake and Ohio Railroad Company, in which the PRR had an interest, operated steamer service between Norfolk and Newport News. The PRR owned the service between Norfolk and Cape Charles, as portrayed in the foregoing discussion of the NYP&N. And the Old Dominion Line, with handsome steamers running the James River to Richmond and oceangoing ships offering service from Richmond to New York, entangled its interests with the Southern Railway, whose status depended on the involvement of the PRR. Even *Mobjack*, paddle-wheeler revered by vacationers, watermen, and farmers in lower Tidewater, sailed for the

Old Dominion Line. Steamboat companies free of the PRR's long reach seemed few indeed.

At the peak of the steamboat era, the Pennsylvania Railroad exercised a virtual monopoly over the essential freight and passenger steamboat services on the Chesapeake. Its empire on the Bay—its railroads encircling the area and its steamboat network reaching throughout the Tidewater country—held the transportation system in its firm grasp. Described as avaricious, grasping, mercenary, or, alternatively, as benevolent, efficient, and caring, the PRR's dominance nearly fulfilled its early dictum to "attain its greatest effectiveness and utility [by rounding out] its contours to include its logical sphere of territory." In the enormity of its scope, that dominion surpassed the wildest flights of imagination of Robert Fulton and Robert Livingston. What John Stevens had envisioned—a total steamboat monopoly on the Chesapeake—almost came to pass with the Pennsylvania Railroad's empire on the Bay.

The Pennsy's dream of a monopoly on the Chesapeake was poorly timed. The ambitions of its management outran its practical assessment of the future. Even in 1905, when the PRR created the MD&V to supplement its earlier creation of the BC&A, indications that events would overtake the steamboat world might have caught the attention of more thoughtful planners. First, the steamboats themselves at that time carried on their decks (for shipment) the first automobiles and primitive trucks seen in the Bay region. Second, hard-surfaced roads appeared in increasing numbers and mileage in the United States, at first in urban areas, but in rural areas on demand, often from local subscription. Why the directorate of the PRR failed to estimate the effect these events would have on steamboats cannot be explained. Alexander Cassatt himself, obsessed with the design and completion of the NYP&N, still absorbed himself in the development of highways, apparently oblivious to what his planning meant to the future of steamboating and railroading. Inexorably came the shift to the automobile and the truck over swift all-weather highways that reached into the byways of the countryside and Tidewater, making slow steamboat service irrelevant.

By 1932, the PRR's steamboat empire had disappeared in the wake of bankruptcy declared by MD&V, its successor (the Baltimore and Virginia Steamboat Company), BC&A, and a number of subsidiaries created in desperation by the PRR as the axe fell. The great "Keystone Fleet" disappeared in sales and simple abandonment. (See Chapter 8.)

Only bits and pieces remained. Ferry service from Baltimore to Love Point continued until 1947, when the old *Philadelphia,* double-ended ferryboat renowned for its rescues of stranded yachtsmen, was sold off for service on the Delaware River. *Elisha Lee* made the last voyage from Cape Charles to Norfolk in 1953 and headed for the scrap yard, thus ending service across the mouth of the Bay. The curtain fell on the era of the Pennsylvania Railroad's ownership of a Chesapeake fleet. Even the shadowy and second-hand interest of the PRR in the Old Bay Line, the Chesapeake Line, and the Old Dominion Line had disappeared through the years with the increasing financial embarrassment of the PRR itself and its effort to liquidate and consolidate its holdings. In 1971 with Amtrak and in 1976 with Conrail, the Pennsylvania Railroad Company as a corporate entity for all practical purposes ceased to exist. The name itself disappeared. The vast transportation empire begun in 1846 to transform the heartland of the country died in a spasm of financial chaos—victim of the highway, the truck, and the automobile. Under the federal controls of Amtrak and Conrail, there was a vast curtailment of passenger travel, an enormous reduction in areas and communities served, and critical regulation of the remaining network. These steps have salvaged the usable remains of what, at its peak, was the greatest railroad system in the world.

The "Keystone Fleet" climaxed the steamboat era on the Chesapeake. The romance of the steamboat will linger in the history of the region and call to mind a time and a way of life that will not return but cannot be forgotten.

8

THREE LONGS AND A SHORT

Little remains around the Chesapeake Bay to remind oncoming generations of the steamboat era that flourished there for a century and a half. In a few places, there are wharves restored to recapture the flavor of the period, like Saunders Wharf on the Rappahannock, rebuilt by the descendants of the plantation owners, and the dock and warehouse below the bridge at Chestertown, Maryland, preserved by the residents. In unexpected places, one can see spears of rotted piling just offshore: at Bristol on the Patuxent, at Grasons on St. Inigoes Creek, at Bushwood on the Wicomico near the Potomac, and at a dozen or so other sites of former steamboat landings.

In the still of a summer evening, when the wind and the sea wax silent, one can almost hear the hint of a wail in the air—a long-drawn-out plaint of a steamer's whistle sounding a ghostly call for the landing—and envision spectral waifs at the dock to catch the line.

But the steamboats have gone, and the vestiges of their presence have also disappeared. Their decline began in the early 1900s, even as they flourished in their glamorous heyday. They felt the pinch, even as they fought to preserve their place in the economic patterns of the 1920s and the 1930s. And they felt the final bite, as the trucks and automobiles eclipsed their role in transportation, and the Great Depression wielded a mighty scepter.

Some analysts have suggested that the years 1904 and 1905 started the downward slope of steamboat travel. Two events in those years—while barely perceptible at the time—had long-range and catastrophic consequences.

One was the *General Slocum* disaster in New York on June 15, 1904. The steamer, with thirteen hundred members of St. Mark's Evangelical Lutheran Church on board bound for an amusement park, caught fire just north of Hell Gate. Starting in a galley located forward on a lower deck, the flames (fanned by the wind) engulfed the tinderlike superstructure in a matter of minutes, even before the steamer could ground herself on North Brother Island. Frantic passengers fleeing to the stern and upper decks perished when forced overboard or when the decks collapsed into the raging inferno. A thousand people died in the disaster. When subsequent investigations revealed serious deficiencies aboard *General Slocum* (broken fire hoses and mains, few fire drills, a poorly trained crew), the wrath of the country demanded national and local legislation to regulate safety requirements aboard steamboats. In the succeeding years, progressive steps in regulations were undertaken. And step-by-step, the steamboat lines felt the financial cost of complying with the rules. Enforcement was not uniform, and some steamboat lines used the local laxity for their own benefit. But when a local disaster occurred, even a minor one, the abrupt reimposition of government controls often taxed the financial abilities of steamboat companies to comply. For them, the requirements for expensive safety measures (sprinkler systems, fireroom sheathing, alarms, fireproof bulkheads) were a slow but strangling encroachment.

The second event seemed less threatening—except to those who were more discerning. In 1904 and 1905, several steamboat lines had transported "horseless carriages" to landings about the Bay. The Old Bay Line had delivered a small shipment of them to Norfolk from Baltimore, where they puttered about the streets, some slightly modified to carry goods. The Weems line carried a few to landings on the Rappahannock, along with barrels of petrol to fuel them. (This went not unnoticed by the shrewd eyes of Henry Williams, then president of the Weems line.) As early as 1900, the Tolchester line delivered one automobile to the resort for a run by its owner to Chestertown in fifty minutes, not much better than the speed of a fast horse and light carriage. Small trucks came to the Eastern Shore by the same means in succeeding years. The press reported that four thousand automobiles had appeared in the United States in 1900, nearly twelve thousand in 1903, and the number was growing astronomically. The federal Office of Public Roads listed 154,000 miles of paved roads in 1904, and the increase portended substantial encroachment on the 2,000,000 miles of unpaved roads in the country. Although slow in arriving in the back country, the trend toward service by automobile, truck, and hard-surface, all-weather roads was inexorable, at least as perceived by those who could forecast the effect on steamboat travel.

Except where they impinged directly on the local transportation links, as around Norfolk and Richmond, railroads did not adversely affect steamboat services to the Tidewater regions of Maryland and Virginia. Instead, the monopoly of the Pennsylvania Railroad and the steamboat network of the Chesapeake tended to complement one another. The steamboats penetrated the tributaries of the Bay and took advantage of the economic potential of areas where the construction of lengthy spurs would have proved unprofitable for the railroads. The railroads, in turn, covered the circumference of the Bay and provided the links to major cities and railheads for the service the steamboats performed locally. But the effects of the macadam (or concrete) highway and the truck and automobile struck the rail and steamer network with equal vengeance about the region as the years, bit by bit, took their toll.

In spite of the factors that seemed to doom the steamboats on the Chesapeake, they thrived for a number of years. The very peak of the steamboat era occurred in 1905, when some fifty-two steamers ran out of Baltimore, and twenty-five or more claimed Norfolk or Washington as their home ports. The Bay and its tributaries were filled with the bustling white vessels, crisscrossing the open expanses and seeking out the three hundred landings on the byways. On a clear day, a wisp of smoke from a steamboat was seldom out of sight. In the inner harbor of Baltimore, steamers crowded the slips along Light Street, and schedules of arrivals and departures provided for an orderly use of the wharf space, which could not accommodate more than a third of the home-ported steamers at once.

As World War I began, the number of steamboats around the Bay dropped to about thirty-seven out of Baltimore, and half that number out of Norfolk and Washington. Surprisingly, the number held firm when the war ended, and the surviving steamboat lines managed to keep functioning with reduced services—but with a wary eye to the future. Most steamboat owners had come to the realization that their vessels were anachronisms, that the colorful drama of steamboating on the Bay was playing out its denouement and resting precariously on little more than nostalgia. It remained for the Great Depression to cut its swath and for days of the 1940s and 1950s, with the changing tastes and appetites of the times, to bring down the curtain.

The overnight packets, probing the rivers of the Bay, were the first to feel the pinch and the ones to hurt the most. Nearly all of these boats had been absorbed by the Pennsylvania Railroad (PRR) in the guise of the

Maryland, Delaware, and Virginia Railway (MD&V) and the Baltimore, Chesapeake, and Atlantic Railway (BC&A) (See Chapter 7). The decision of the PRR to acquire these boats came too soon. Within a few years, the managers of the PRR had good reason to regret the stranglehold they had chosen to exercise over a dying industry. The MD&V from the very start had never prospered. Except for 1910–11, it had suffered operating losses every year, and only the guarantee of the interest on its loans by BC&A kept it afloat. By 1922, MD&V began to abandon less profitable routes, the first being service to the Pocomoke River and the lower Eastern Shore. At the same time, the president of the PRR declared that, in his opinion, both the MD&V and the BC&A were losing enterprises, victims of competition from trucks and highways, and would have to be abandoned. He made it clear that the PRR wanted to cast off what had become a noose around its neck.

On May 7, 1923, in foreclosure proceedings, the MD&V was sold off to a newly formed company, the Baltimore and Virginia Steamboat Company (B&V), itself a creature of the PRR. Still hoping that some modicum of profit could be eked out from a limited packet service on the major tributaries of the Bay and on a steamboat linkage to the rail system down the Eastern Shore, the PRR set about through the new company to buy just the steamers it needed for the restricted projection and to discard the remainder (including both steamers and the landings they served). An attempt to win a subsidy from the State of Maryland to help defray the costs failed to pass the scrutiny of a governor's investigative committee.

Some of the finest steamboats in the MD&V fleet, those of the former Weems line, went on the auctioneer's block: *Westmoreland, Lancaster, Potomac, Northumberland, Calvert, Middlesex,* and *Anne Arundel.* In the end, all were repurchased by B&V (at a marked-down price) except for *Westmoreland* and *Lancaster,* handsome vessels sacrificed to pay for the declining fortunes of the MD&V (see Appendix B for details of the ends of these vessels). A number of steamers were sold to the new B&V: *Avalon, Tred Avon, Talbot, Dorchester, Piankatank, Pocomoke, Virginia, B.S. Ford,* and others.

For a time, service on the Rappahannock and Potomac went on as before, but in 1924 the B&V sharply cut its calls to the Patuxent and a year later curtailed all passenger service to the river. The Chester River route was abandoned, along with steamer service to Claiborne and Queenstown. Step by step, other less profitable landings were bypassed and routes shortened or abandoned. In spite of a spotlessly white appearance, the steamers themselves barely managed with poor maintenance and beckoned for disaster.

The BC&A struggled on under its own name but melded increasingly with the B&V. Like the latter, it reduced its services under the controls of the PRR. Eventually, it had no identity of its own. To the nonobservant public, the white packets steaming forth from the Light Street wharves each evening still embodied the romantic tradition of the steamboats of the Bay, just as they had for generations.

But the profits were not forthcoming, the losses mounted, and the Great Depression and its immediate aftermath brought the climactic end.

In January 1932, the B&V declared bankruptcy. All of its steamers stood on the auction block. March 1, 1932, marked "the blackest day" (as sympathetic observers called it) for steamboating on the Chesapeake— the day that B&V suspended operations. And with that day, the PRR rid itself of what was left of its ill-considered and moribund monopoly and a fleet of steamers that had become a millstone around its neck.

During its last years of decline, the B&V progressively curtailed its services and sold off its steamers, until only nine remained. One by one, in that single week of March 1932, these steamers arrived at Pier 1, Light Street, to discharge a trickle of freight and to say farewell to a few passengers who in passing over the gangplank turned to view them for the last time and to mourn their passing. *Calvert* (from Cambridge), *Eastern Shore* (from a few landings on the lower Eastern Shore), *Piankatank* (from the river whose name she bore), *Potomac* (from the Rappahannock) and *Northumberland*, *Talbot*, *Dorchester*, and *Virginia* (having tied up earlier at other locations about the harbor) from various tributaries—each sounded a long, last dirge on her whistle and settled at her moorings with an air of dejected resignation.

The fires died beneath the boilers and in the galleys, the lights went out, the crews departed, and the captains and pursers locked the last doors and slipped ashore. The boats were left to rot or face their fate, whatever that might be.

One steamer had yet to arrive. *Anne Arundel* had the longest journey to make before completing her life with the B&V: the trip from Washington to Baltimore—the last to be made by a regular packet on the Chesapeake.

Anne Arundel, the last steamer to be built for the Weems line, had been launched on May 14, 1904, by Elizabeth Chew Williams, daughter of Henry Williams (president of the company) and Georgeanna Weems

211

(daughter of Mason Locke Weems), in a festive display of bunting at Locust Point. Named for the Maryland county (there was a question of the correct spelling—two l's or one), *Anne Arundel* was an elegant and sturdy propeller-driven boat, a near counterpart of *Potomac*, born in 1894. *Anne Arundel* was not known for speed (her engines, so it was reported, were originally intended for a tug), but she earned a reputation for seaworthiness in the storms of the Bay and hospitality on her long runs on the Rappahannock and the Potomac.

She left Washington for the last time on Monday, April 30, 1932. At four o'clock on a blustery evening, she pulled away from the Seventh Street dock. On board were a handful of passengers and not enough freight to pay for her fuel. No one was on the wharf to bid a formal farewell. A young black woman, friend of one of the stevedores on board, shouted across the water, "Good-bye, sugar!" and her voice was lost in the wind.

Captain Herbert A. Bohannon pulled the whistle cord and sounded three long blasts and a short toot, nautical language for "Good-bye and good luck." The steamer gathered way and headed down the Washington channel. She sang her mournful tune for each vessel she passed—*Northland* readying for her Norfolk run answered her, then the D.C. fireboat *Firefighter* and an army boat at the War College. As he swung the boat around Hains Point, Bohannon, who had "followed the water" of the Chesapeake for forty-six years, wiped his glasses and murmured, "Good-bye, Washington." An elderly lady nearby in a squirrel-skin coat who was taking the trip for sentiment's sake blinked tearfully.

At Alexandria, approximately fifty people gathered at the Prince Street wharf to witness the quick arrival and departure of *Anne Arundel*. Thirteen delegates of the city's government in their most formal rig lined up on the dock.

"They look like pallbearers," said the woman in the squirrel-skin coat.

Absent from the dock was the Alexandria freight agent, whose feelings at the moment overwhelmed him. Captain Bohannon saluted with the whistle as the steamer departed, and saluted again as he passed Fort Washington and Mount Vernon. The performance was repeated with each landing the steamer had visited on its journeys up and down the Potomac.

Night fell, and the atmosphere throughout the steamer was as dolorous as the darkness surrounding it. In the pilothouse, the only light came from the green square above the binnacle and the glow from the men's pipes. About eight people, including the captain, first mate, and quarter-master at the wheel, crowded the wheelhouse. Long silences punctuated the conversation.

"Well, boys," said the quartermaster, "I've served twenty-five years, and even skippered the *Dorchester*. . . . Now here I am, back to where I was twenty years ago. Steersman. Ain't that something?"

"And ya won't be there long," added the first mate. Aunt Martha, a relative of the captain, said that she thought it was terrible.

Captain Bohannon reminisced. At sixty-four, he looked forward to an unsettled future.

"I don't want to retire," he said. "I wanted to keep on running these boats as long as they would have me, but it looks like it's over now. In these times, I don't know where I can get another berth."

A trim man with square, lined features, a slightly bushy mustache, and wide-rimmed glasses, the captain looked somewhat professorial, in spite of the neatness of his blue uniform with the gold stripes and buttons and skipper's cap, which he wore precisely without a trace of jauntiness. He had been a sailor from age fourteen when he shipped as a deckhand aboard the schooner *William Henry* on the Chesapeake. He served as a deckhand aboard a Norfolk steamer, then became a quartermaster on *Wenonah* when it cruised the Patuxent as a Weems line steamer. Most of his later career was spent on the Potomac as master of steamers of the MD&V.

"Along back around 1907 and 1908," he recalled, "was the heyday of the river service. Once in the month of August I carried 3700 passengers on the old *Calvert*. It was the usual thing then for us to be forced to turn down people who wanted to travel on our line. In order to be sure of a cabin, people would make their reservations a month in advance. And there has been many a gay time on boats I have run. But now that's all gone. During the last year, we have made several trips with not a passenger and with less than $50 worth of freight, though we stopped at every landing on the river" ("Steamer on Final Run," Washington *Star*, March 1, 1932).

He recalled an earthquake in 1897 (lying in the Patuxent, the steamer had all the dishes broken in the galley), Dewey's victory in Manila in 1898 (Washington went wild), Bohannon's rescue of three men at Cedar Point (their skiff was jammed by ice; he climbed to the jibboom of his schooner and caught them as they floated by). Nostalgia caught up with his memories, and he grew silent.

In darkness, the steamer pulled into Colonial Beach, the resort on the Virginia shore, and discharged some window sash weights, lumber, and 196 cases of canned tomatoes. As the vessel steamed away, the captain gave the usual salute, but very softly—for the agent alone—so as not to awaken the town.

The wind rose with dawn, and *Anne Arundel* bucked a choppy sea. Tomato cases skidded about the near-empty freight deck; some broke open and the cans rolled around, making quite a din, until the deckhands cornered them and tethered them in place.

In the morning light, *Anne Arundel* entered the narrow confines of the West Yeocomico River on the south shore of the Potomac for an approach to the dock at Kinsale, the pleasant town with a pungent Civil War history (see Chapter 4). Maneuvering in the narrow channel was difficult enough in quiet weather, but the wind caught her on the beam as she slowed and lost headway. Bohannon called the deck crew to ready an anchor.

At that moment, the voice tube from the engine room to the pilothouse whistled and Chief Eugene Headley's voice sounded: "Circulator pump's busted, sir. Engines got to stop."

The engine stopped. And *Anne Arundel* promptly blew aground. The engineers set to work and in less than an hour the offending pump functioned again. Now Bohannon faced the task of clawing his vessel off the shoals. Backing and filling, forging ahead and reversing, with rudder fishtailing, he edged the steamer out of the mud. The steamer vibrated from end to end with the thrashing of the propeller, and water glasses jiggled in the dining room. Abruptly, the hull broke loose from the hold of the mud, and *Anne Arundel* backed free. "Aground 10:27 A.M." read the log. "Off 11:30."

With much maneuvering and use of spring lines, *Anne Arundel* made the dock at Kinsale and departed. Mrs. Callahan, who lived near the wharf, called out to Bohannon, as the lines were cast off, to tie up again, and she invited everybody on board to come to her house and eat fried chicken. Bohannon waved his thanks and blew a soft farewell on the whistle.

In the open Potomac where the river met the Bay, *Anne Arundel* breasted the nasty chop whipped up by the wind. Once again, the Chesapeake showed its defiance to the inventions of men. The steamer pitched and shuddered. Aunt Martha went below to lie down. Yarn spinning in the pilothouse died off, and *Anne Arundel* in a seaway lined up for the long haul up the Bay to Baltimore. Off Cove Point and the mouth of the Patuxent, the seas quieted, and the storytellers gathered again in the wheelhouse. Captain Bohannon recalled the golden days of steamboating, the period from the turn of the century until the Great War, as he called it.

"Those were the days when there was a bar on every ship," he said, "and thirsts were quenched nightly, especially if the boat put in at a wharf in a dry county. I've seen the bar turn $500 at the end of a trip—which is a lot of beer at five cents a glass. Now there are no bars, and trucks have taken the freight business. Autos have reduced passengers to the vanishing point. . . ." His voice trailed off.

In the early afternoon, *Anne Arundel* slid into her Light Street wharf, her arrival unheralded and unattended. The wharfman's little dog caught the heaving line as usual and carried it to his master. From the freight deck came a few hogsheads and barrels and a lone calf. Appropriately, it had cried all night.

One by one, the crew left the steamer. The fires were drawn in the engine room. The steamer's interior darkened. In his office, Purser C. W. Latimore bundled up his records and account books, locked the door, and disappeared over the gangway. Captain Herbert Bohannon, after a quick look over his shoulder, locked his stateroom, office, and wheelhouse, walked slowly down the staircase to the saloon and to the main deck, and over the gangplank for the last time. To a solitary reporter he said, "Autos have been the ruin of this country—autos, and prohibition" (quotations and narrative from "The Anne Arundel Makes Her Last Cruise," Washington *Daily News*, March 2, 1932).

But nostalgia was hard to kill. A group of steamboat men, along with some Baltimore commission merchants and tradesmen, felt that some form of steamboat service could survive. They cited the landings, with complete wharves and warehouses, dotting the waterways of the Bay and adjoining the agricultural resources of Tidewater, landings that farmers still might want to use in concert with established outlets in Baltimore. And they noted the existence of a fleet of steamers, many like *Potomac* and *Anne Arundel* and some others in serviceable, even prime, condition—all for the plucking at low prices. Led by Captain James Gresham, long a skipper of MD&V steamers on the Rappahannock, they decided to form a small company to salvage what they could of the residual trade on the river system of the Bay.

Initially called the Western Shore Freight Line, Inc., the company in late April 1932 chartered the *Hampton Roads*, formerly owned by the Old Dominion Line in Norfolk, in a venture to provide freight service to the Nanticoke and Choptank rivers on the Eastern Shore (notwithstanding the western slant to the title of the company).The venture proved immediately unsuccessful. At the same time, the company negotiated with the holders of the B&V indenture for the purchase of two steamers, the sturdy and comely screw-steamer *Potomac* and the older side-wheeler *Virginia*. The purchase was consummated in June, and the company advertised sailings—three times a week to Rappahannock and Piankatank landings from Pier 3, Light Street, acquired from the holdings of B&V. Furthermore, exclusive freight service gave way to the encouragement of passenger travel, and weekend excursions to Cambridge on the Eastern Shore and Solomons on the Patuxent were advertised. What the company hoped to capitalize upon particularly was the affection that they supposed Baltimoreans held for the old steamboats.

The name was changed to the Western Shore Steamboat Company to escape the image of a freight carrier. *Hampton Roads*, proving unsatisfactory, had her lease terminated at the end of the season, and *Virginia*, with too many staterooms, too slow a speed, and too high a fuel cost, was exchanged for *Anne Arundel* with the consent of the receivers of the B&V. Now, with *Potomac* and *Anne Arundel* (the best of the old Weems line steamers and nearly sister ships), the new company hoped to forge some sort of trade out of what was left of the old packet routes and, at the same time, cultivate the nostalgia of Baltimoreans for the white steamers of the Chesapeake.

The two steamers scheduled trips to the Rappahannock, the Piankatank, and occasionally to landings near the Potomac mouth, and excursions on "off-days" to Solomons, Annapolis, Oxford, Chestertown, St. Michaels, and Betterton. For the excursion trips, the fare was $1.00 round trip. For the overnight trips to the Rappahannock, the fare ran from $7.50 to $8.50, depending on the number of days involved. The trips to Fredericksburg cost $12.00 for a four-day cruise. All of these fares included all meals and the stateroom.

I remember one trip taken with my mother, who wanted to greet some distant relatives at Tappahannock. The trip took place over the fourth of July holiday of 1935. We boarded *Potomac* at Pier 3, Light Street, about four o'clock in the afternoon. The stewardess showed us to neighboring staterooms, each equipped with a white-enameled iron bed covered with a candlewick spread, washstand, small desk, and a louvered window that could be lowered for ventilation. Each stateroom was immaculate and smelled of disinfectant and a kind of lavender soap. As a young chap, caught up in the fantasy world of steamboats, I bustled about the boat as it lay in its slip, entranced by its graceful shape, the handsome woodwork in the saloon, and the wonders of the pilothouse, where the gold-striped captain and mate and the bearded quartermaster paced about awaiting departure time. At length the deep-throated whistle sounded, then repeated itself five minutes later. The gangway came trundling aboard, lines were cast off, bells clanged and jingled far below in the bowels of the steamer, and *Potomac* shuddered and backed clear of her slip. Three sharp blasts on her whistle signaled her backing. In the evening's glow, she pivoted in the basin, and headed down the harbor, past the sugar refinery, the soap plant, the run-down warehouses, Fort McHenry and the island of Fort Carroll, and the shipyards and docks of Locust Point and Curtis Bay. At the mouth of the Patapsco, where the steel company poured slag in an incandescent mass into the water, she swung around the lighthouse at Seven Foot Knoll and headed down the Bay.

At dinnertime, a white-coated steward strolled the deck and saloon with a bell, and my mother and I were ushered to a linen-covered table gleaming in silver and decorated with a rose nosegay. The table was on the starboard side, at the second window from the dining room entrance. It overlooked the gallery running around the stern and commanded a magnificent panorama of the passing Bay. We had trout for dinner, prepared by an old cook who knew how to extract full flavor from the Bay's harvest and served elegantly by a waiter with a napkin over his left arm. I remembered the location of our table in the dining room, not only because of the sumptuousness of the fare, but also because a later event at that exact spot eclipsed the life of the steamer.

I stood on the upper deck near the pilothouse long into the night, while the steamer forged south, her bow creaming the seas, her jackstaff pointing at the stars overhead. From the bow came the plaintive cry of the lookout man, "All's well," answered by the mate from the wheelhouse, "Very well." Distant lighthouses flickered briefly, and buoys close aboard in the channel boomed their muffled gongs in the passing swell. Some naval vessels beyond the horizon down the open Bay blinked messages to each other by aiming their distant beams at the sky. On the starboard beam, small lights pricked a darkened shore. The sensuousness of the breeze, the whisper of the waves, and the pulsing of the ship seemed utterly romantic, a sensation detached from the world of reality.

I retired to a sleepless night in my bunk, tossing the hours away in this creaking, throbbing, wonderful creature that was a steamboat. Then as light began to filter through the louvered window, engine bells sounded below, the propeller stilled, the vessel rattled and vibrated as the engine reversed, then stilled again. And outside my window, I heard the guard-rails on the main deck squeal and shiver as the steamer pushed her way alongside a dock. Throwing the window open, I leaned out and looked down in the half-light at a landing, where there stood a half-dozen men, a few carts, and an agent with his young son, who caught the steamer's lines and made them fast to the piling. In a moment, the gangplank hit the dock, a few roustabouts from the main deck trundled a couple of barrels and boxes to the wharf, the agent and the purser exchanged a few notes, and *Potomac* slid away into the morning light, beginning a day exploring the landings of the lower Rappahannock.

One after another, the steamer nudged her way into various wharves, her arrival and departure largely uncelebrated by the local populace. In entering the narrow confines of the approach to Urbanna, she churned up the mud of the twisting channel and dug her propeller deep in the bottom when she maneuvered away from the dock.

At Irvington in Carter's Creek, she encountered a rebellion on the part of one of her passengers—my mother. While the steamer lay along-side the dock, I decided that a dollop of ice cream would satisfactorily cool the appetite, and I crossed the gangplank—duly observed by the purser on the dock—to mount the hill and make my purchase at the general store. Believing that the steamer would stay at the dock for a while, there being what seemed to be a fair amount of cargo to load, I took my time in savoring the pleasures of dry land and the sights of the historic village.

Suddenly the sound of *Potomac*'s whistle rent the air. I jumped with alarm. Several blocks of country lane, mostly downhill, separated me from the dock. Hanging onto my ice cream (it had cost me a precious nickel), I sped down the hill, just in time to see the gangplank being drawn aboard and the lines slackened. Sick with fear that I would be left behind, I shouted and ran even faster, losing my valued ice cream in the dirt. Then I saw my mother at the pilothouse—with the captain's nose at the end of her pointed finger—her foot stamping on the deck. The captain threw up his hands. Some water surged under the steamer's stern, the lines tightened, and the rail across the freight deck port opened. I made a flying leap from the wharf to the arms of a stevedore on board, as the mate scowled from the deck above, and my mother flew down the steps to meet me, torn between relief at my safe return and righteous anger for my causing so much trouble.

Throughout that long day, I haunted the environs of the pilothouse, worshipping my idols in the gold braid and brass buttons, until the captain, tired of tripping over the little figure on the wheelhouse steps, grunted, "You might as well come on in. Just stand over there and stay out of the way." So I rode in the wheelhouse, just behind the quartermaster, digested all the orders and conversations as if they were spoken gospel, and felt transported to a realm of untold ecstasy. I was remembered. Years later, an officer from the *Potomac* and a quartermaster recalled that day. "That kid! He spent the whole day up here. Never left! A little more and he'd become a skipper!"

But there were other particulars to that trip that I remember. The fare was $7.50 each, including five meals, two nights of stateroom accommodations on the steamer, and a cruise on one of the most spectacular waterways of the Eastern Seaboard. I noticed other aspects of the trip. Fewer than half the staterooms were occupied, the dining room was unpopulated, and the freight deck was notably empty.

The dreary economic trials of the 1930s did not favor the fledgling steamboat line, and passengers failed to flock aboard its excursion runs or its overnight journeys. Freight failed to materialize. Then a series of events brought catastrophe.

The hurricane of August 23, 1933, which swept up the Bay and devastated shipping, demolished eighteen of the thirty-three wharves used by the company. There was no money for replacement. Then on February 22, 1936, *Potomac*, caught in the ice at Seven Foot Knoll, was rammed by the Bull Line coastal freighter *Jean*. Ironically, that ship had borne the name of *Jean Weems* when owned by the sons of Henry Williams (president of the Weems line), and *Potomac* had been the pride of the Weems line. The steel prow of the freighter struck *Potomac* on the starboard quarter and penetrated through the guardrail into the dining room at the second window from the dining room entrance—the window from which my mother and I had viewed the Bay as we dined. The damage was not extensive—*Potomac* entered the harbor under her own power—but the costs of repair were more than the company could bear. The handsome, sturdy steamer was laid up until 1938 and eventually sold off to become a barge for hauling pulpwood (see Appendix A).

Alone, *Anne Arundel* carried on for another year, even as her owners knew from the bookkeeping that her end was near. Then on July 29, 1937, catastrophe occurred; like the hurricane of 1933 and the ramming of 1936, it was a disaster over which the company had no control. At first, the effect of the tragedy on the Western Shore Steamboat Company was not clear, but the spillover was not long in coming.

On that fateful evening, the *City of Baltimore* of the Chesapeake Line cleared her moorings at Pier 13, Light Street, at 6:30 P.M., bound for Old Point Comfort and Norfolk, and headed down the basin and the Patapsco River toward the Bay. The sun set in a cloudless sky; a brisk breeze came from the southeast. Some forty passengers lounged about the decks to enjoy the scenery, chatted in the saloon or bar, or settled themselves in their staterooms. Some late diners ate leisurely and satisfying meals in the dining room forward of the saloon. Behind them, the mahogany stairs descended to the main deck below, whose forward area was the freight deck with ports on either side for loading.

The *City of Baltimore*, built in 1911, was the steel-hulled, 261-foot, white-sided model for the twin steamers *City of Richmond* and *City of Annapolis* built two years later; the first twin sank the second in a tragic collision in a fog off Smith Point on February 24, 1927 (see Chapter 3). The *City of Richmond* and *City of Baltimore* had continued in service on the packet runs between Baltimore and Norfolk.

As the *City of Baltimore* approached Seven Foot Knoll that evening, her captain, Charles O. Brooks, saw astern the Pennsylvania Railroad steamer *Maryland* en route to Love Point and, farther astern, the competition, the handsome *State of Maryland* of the Old Bay Line, bound also for Old Point Comfort and Norfolk. The *City of Baltimore* had just passed the slow-moving freighter *Arkansan* of the Hawaiian Steamship Company. Anchored nearby was the fishing boat of Captain Z.R. Lewis, with three Baltimore City firemen on board. Also cruising near the Seven Foot Knoll lighthouse was the Love Point pilot boat *William D. Sanner*. On board was Captain Richard B. Wysong, president of the Maryland Pilots Association, who was hosting the Society of Royal Jesters on a pleasure trip on the Bay. The *City of Baltimore* rounded Seven Foot Knoll and headed south. The time was 7:15 P.M.

Suddenly, shouts of "Fire!" rose from the freight deck and rang through the steamer. Waiters in the dining room abruptly abandoned their tables, deckhands rushed to fire stations, and a crew of fifty-five ran about, endeavoring to bring fire hoses to bear and to deal with a hot blaze on the freight deck on the port side between the cargo ports. Passengers gathered on the forward and upper decks, or emerged from their staterooms when roused by banging stewardesses.

In a matter of minutes the flames spread to the dry tinderbox of the superstructure, fanned by the southeast breeze and the motion of the ship. Captain Brooks headed the vessel toward the shoals north of Bodkin Creek, and she grounded—her engines still running, and her propeller still turning and endangering any rescue boats that approached.

Quickly, the flames engulfed the steamer and erupted at various points through the upper decks. They rose to fifty feet above the hulk. In the thickening darkness, they were visible for miles—to points on Bodkin Creek and Gibson Island at the mouth of the Magothy. Residents at Pinehurst on the shore near the site phoned in the alarm to the Coast Guard and fire departments.

On board, efforts to fight the fire proved futile. Flames breaking out forward and amidships through the cabin spaces and upper decks drove back the crew and some assisting passengers. Some later said that water never reached the fire hoses. Others reported that fifteen minutes had elapsed before the first lifeboat was lowered. Three did hit the water, but one carried only four people, another only twenty. One lifeboat got trapped in the falls.

Passengers and crew (a total of ninety-five), some wearing life jackets, others not, simply jumped over the side and hoped for survival in the choppy seas. Amazingly, several passengers carried suitcases with them.

Arkansan, the freighter, approached *City of Baltimore* as the steamer was still under way and bounced along the burning vessel's sides, damaging several of her own plates (she had to return to Baltimore for repairs) in an attempt to rescue passengers huddled on the bow. *Arkansan*'s lifeboat rescued five and transferred them to the pilot boat *William D. Sanner,* which had arrived on the scene and was busily plucking some sixty people from the water. Captain Lewis's fishing boat nearly capsized from the weight of the survivors. *State of Maryland,* commanded by Captain John L. Marshall, stood by the burning vessel for four hours before resuming its run to Norfolk. By the time of its arrival on the scene, a horde of small boats had swarmed around the hulk, the fire so hot and the turning propeller so dangerous that they could not approach too closely, and the seas so choppy that rescuing people in the water was difficult.

A phone call to Annapolis brought the navy tug *Key Wadin* (commanded by Lieutenant R. C. Brown), a Naval Academy crash boat, three fifty-foot motor boats, and other small craft to the scene. The Coast Guard cutters *Apache* and *Carrekasset,* plus other craft, raced to Bodkin Creek.

Captain Brooks and L. J. Harvard, a fruit dealer from Newport News, were the last to leave the ship. They jumped overboard about 8:00 P.M. and were rescued along with Gussie Polikoff of Aiden, South Carolina, by Frank Gensler of Pinehurst, who had manned his powerboat to search for survivors.

Miraculously only two people died in the disaster (a third was discovered later). One was J. R. Polikoff, father of the woman rescued with Captain Brooks. The other was a member of the crew. Two people remained unaccounted for. The survivors included several professional golfers headed for a championship match at the Chamberlin Country Club (they lost their prized possessions, golf clubs) and several Coast Guard recruits, who learned very quickly some basic lessons in the purposes of their forthcoming profession.

The cause of the fire remained a mystery. Captain Brooks reported that the engine room failed to respond to his orders to turn on the fire pumps and that when he attempted to blow distress signals he found the whistle out of commission. He darkly hinted of sabotage. Asked what he based his suspicions of arson upon, he replied, "Only on what has been happening along the water front for the last few months . . . the kind of men we've been having trouble with. We had two CIO [Congress of Industrial Organizations] men go down on our ship as passengers recently. My brother has had trouble on his ship, too." The brother was Captain Archie H. Brooks, master of *Fairfax* of the Merchants and Miners Transportation Company, engaged in coastal trade from Boston and Baltimore to Savannah and Miami. The statements condemning union men made by Captain Charles O. Brooks came under scrutiny and challenge from attorneys for the National Maritime Union and remained unsubstantiated.

But the investigation by federal and state authorities into the burning of the *City of Baltimore* disclosed a litany of deficiencies—so severe that various agencies involved in the formulation and enforcement of maritime safety regulations convened in emergency session.

When *Anne Arundel* arrived in Baltimore from her Rappahannock run on July 31, two days after the *City of Baltimore* catastrophe, she was greeted on the dock by officers of the Bureau of Marine Inspection and Navigation of the Department of Commerce. Just as had happened so many times in the past, amendments of safety regulations to keep up with the times and the enforcement of these regulations had lagged—through indifference, neglect, or lack of funds—until conspicuous catastrophes occurred, when the responsible officials were galvanized into immediate action. As a result of the disaster aboard the *City of Baltimore*, the bureau proclaimed that it would enforce the safety-at-sea regulations passed by Congress on June 30, 1936, to be placed in effect on October 1, 1937. Up to that point, steamboat operators on the Bay had given lip service to these regulations, believing that their enforcement would be given lip service, also. But the episode of the *City of Baltimore* had built new fires, so to speak, under the seats of the mighty.

Under these regulations, all passenger vessels with fifty or more berths were required to install fireproof bulkheads and automatic sprinkler systems or face a restriction that they carry freight only. The Chesapeake Line announced that it would hasten to comply; the *City of Norfolk* (last of the triumvirate) would have the bulkheads and sprinklers installed and be ready to receive passengers by October 15. The Old Bay Line signaled its compliance.

For the Western Shore Steamboat Company, the news fell like an axe. The beleaguered board members knew immediately what the tidings meant. The company lacked the financial resources, even by borrowing, to perform the necessary renovation aboard *Anne Arundel*. After a last painful meeting, they decided that there was no recourse but to cease operations on September 30, 1937.

Captain John Dare Davis of the *Anne Arundel* had one last request. The son of Captain Daniel Davis, master of the former Weems line steamers *Mary Washington, Theodore Weems, Wenonah, Mason L. Weems, Essex, Westmoreland, Richmond,* and *Lancaster,* he had grown up in the heritage of steamboating on the Chesapeake. A short man, friendly and open in disposition, he was both pugilistic if the occasion demanded and intensely sentimental. Much of his steamboat life had been spent on the Rappahannock, and he wanted, for old time's sake, to make one last round trip from Baltimore to Fredericksburg—a sentimental journey to relive very briefly the days of romance aboard the steamers and to say farewell. He planned to retire when the voyage ended, after forty years of service. He proposed to the directors that he fill the passenger list, if necessary, with friends and steamboat lovers and those who had been his loyal supporters through the years. The directors readily agreed.

Little notice attended his decision. On September 8, a small, inconspicuous newspaper advertisement announced the following:

Trip to Fredericksburg. Via Rappahannock River. Steamer *Anne Arundel* leaves Pier 3, Light Street, 2 P.M. Saturday, September 11. No sailing to Rappahannock River Sunday, Phone Plaza 1634. Western Shore Steamship [*sic*] Company.

On the same day, the headlines in enormous bold type announced the Japanese advance into Fukien province of China; the ordered evacuation of American citizens from Tsingtao, Amoy, and Fouchow; and the closing of U.S. consulates in principal ports along the China coast. Other headlines screamed the latest atrocity of Hitler in Europe. When the *City of Baltimore* burned on July 29, the international headlines shocking the world were replaced by the equally shocking news of the disaster off Bodkin Creek. In little more than a day, however, the international news shoved the steamboat's burning aside. Now, on the eve of the departure of *Anne Arundel* for her last trip as an overnight packet, the press had nothing to say about an event so climactic in the life of the Bay.

Ten minutes after the appointed time of 2:00 P.M., on Saturday, September 11, Captain Davis sounded a long blast on the soprano whistle of *Anne Arundel*. The lines from Pier 3 came rattling aboard, backing bells sounded in the engine room, and *Anne Arundel* slid from her wharf, turned about in a froth of spume under her counter, and started her voyage. Bunting and flags whipped from every vantage point. A full complement of the company's friends and steamboat aficionados crowded at the rails, sentimentally reliving many departures from Baltimore in better times. The afternoon glowed with the amber of impending autumn. As the steamer spun on her heel at Seven Foot Knoll and took her departure for the long reach down the Bay, the eastern sky sank into the deeper shades of blue, and the western shore stood silhouetted against the sun setting behind a halo of fluffy clouds. As darkness fell, the horizon on both sides of the Bay winked with tiny lights. Farther south, the loom of the lighthouse at Cove Point marked the entrance to the Patuxent. As the steamer sliced on to the whisper of the seas, the distant flash of the lights at Point Lookout and Smith Point blinked in the night, and still later, the brief flicker of the light at Windmill Point marked the mouth of the Rappahannock. Few passengers turned in early to their staterooms; most jammed around the wheelhouse to stand with Captain Davis. Others sat on folding chairs on the forward deck, just behind the lookout man to hear his "All's well!" and the tap on the bell, and to drink in the mystery and the magic of a night aboard a steamboat cruising down the Bay.

Early Sunday morning, *Anne Arundel* began her sentimental journey up the Rappahannock. One by one, she passed the sites of landings once visited by Weems line steamers and those of MD&V at the turn of the century. Only twelve of these, with sufficient business to justify a call, remained on the schedule of the Western Shore Steamboat Company. Then, after the great hurricane of 1933, which flooded the Rappahannock valley and swept away most of the wharves and their warehouses, leaving only spears of piling in the stream, just six landings remained for regular use: Westland (at the mouth of the river), Urbanna (on the south shore in Urbanna Creek), Irvington (on the north shore inside Carter's Creek), Tappahannock (on the south shore at the town center), and Fredericksburg (at the head of navigation). There were "on call" stops at several other landings. Briefly, *Anne Arundel* pulled in to each of the principal landings, was greeted royally by spectators and nostalgic well-wishers at some, was nearly ignored at others, and then pulled away, sounding softly, as on her last trip from Washington, her whistle lamentation of three longs and a short—"Good-bye, and good luck."

No passengers stayed ashore at the landings, no freight crossed the gangplank. Her cargo of very special excursionists thronged the decks and stood for hours, imbibing the beauty of the upper Rappahannock, where tree-shrouded hills sloped to the narrow river's edge and masked each other in shadowy retreat. The passengers reminisced about former hours spent on the decks of *Middlesex*, when she shaved the banks of the river so closely in hugging the channel that someone amidships on the hurricane deck could grab a leaf from a tree as she passed. They recalled the meals served in her dining room amidships in the saloon between the paneled staterooms, and they remembered the days of leisure and song and a way of life long since gone. As darkness fell, *Anne Arundel* arrived at her wharf below the hill at Fredericksburg, unannounced and unheralded.

Her return trip to Baltimore, with tired and nearly tearful passengers to remember the journey, was punctuated only by the final farewells, the mournful dirge of her whistle at long-gone wharves (Hop Yard, Port Royal, Wilmont, Saunders, Leedstown, Laytons, Naylors, Bowlers, Monaskon, and others), where decaying sheds or rotting piling marked the site. When she crossed the river from Wellfords on the north shore to Bowlers on the south, Captain Davis held the whistle cord and *Anne Arundel* wailed all the way across.

She slid into her Light Street berth, saw her nostalgic passengers cross the gangway with a final look over the shoulder at the white-sided vestige of the past, drew her fires, discharged her crew, and watched Captain Davis leave the steamboat world for the last time, his duties at an end.

With that last voyage of *Anne Arundel* to Fredericksburg, the era of travel through the Tidewater country by the picturesque packets of the Chesapeake came to an end.

On the James River out of Norfolk, the demise of overnight river service had come much earlier. The Old Dominion Line, which operated coastal steamers to New York and, much earlier, a service to the North Carolina sounds, introduced in 1902 two of the finest packets in the region, the thousand-ton steel *Berkeley* and *Brandon,* named for plantations overlooking the James and intended for luxurious travel to Richmond. When economic realities came to bear, the Old Dominion Line was forced to suspend its steamer river service on April 6, 1920. Stranded were a number of its steamers : *Hampton, Mobjack* (beloved boat serving Gloucester and Mathews counties), *Virginia Dare, Hampton Roads, Ocracoke, Smithfield, Pocahontas,* (popular excursion boat), and *Berkeley* and *Brandon.* The last two, graceful two-deckers with lavish accommodations, replicated the sumptuousness of the steamers operated by the Baltimore Steam Packet Company (Old Bay Line) and Chesapeake Line, competitors for the Norfolk trade out of Baltimore.

In 1928, when both the Old Bay Line and the Chesapeake Line launched the last of their splendid packets designed for the overnight shuttle between Baltimore and Norfolk, the appearance of prosperity was deceptive. The two steamers, each representing one of the archrivals, were launched within a few weeks of each other: *President Warfield* of the Old Bay Line on February 6, *Yorktown* of the Chesapeake Line on February 25. The first was much larger than the second.

President Warfield joined the *State of Maryland* (launched in 1922) and *State of Virginia* (launched in 1923) to form a fleet of palatial three-decked vessels, the epitome of express packet travel on the Chesapeake. Each had a steel hull and steel sheathing around the superstructure up the passenger deck; each measured 330 feet in length, 58 feet in beam, with a rated speed of seventeen miles per hour. All three vessels boasted elaborately paneled saloons, smoking rooms resembling British pubs, glass-enclosed palm rooms on the gallery deck, grand stairways, and balconies hung with chandeliers and oil paintings. Each had 170 first-class staterooms, 38 with private baths. Costs of the first two ran to $718,000 each; for the *Warfield* $960,000. Aboard the latter were rather exceptional accommodations for the president of the Seaboard Air Line Railroad (owner of the Old Bay Line) Solomon Davies Warfield.

A rather arrogant man who enjoyed pulling political strings and de-
stroying his opponents, he was both sentimental and illogical, bequeathing $4 million to support the ailing Old Bay Line in a wave of
nostalgia for the "Old South." The steamer was named for him after his
sudden death. The champagne bottle on launching might have been
smashed over the bow by his niece, Bessie Warfield, had she not been
abroad rounding up her second husband (her third nearly brought
down the British throne).

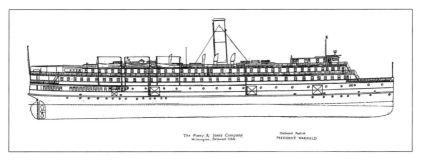

Steamboat *President Warfield,* flagship of the Old Bay Line. From the builder's drawings
of Pusey & Jones.

The *State of Maryland* and the *State of Virginia*—after the retirement of
their predecessors, *Alabama* and *Florida*—ran in bitter competition with
the Chesapeake Line, with its four three-deck vessels setting standards of
speed and excellence. After the sinking of the *City of Annapolis* on February 24, 1927, by her sister ship, the Chesapeake Line was left with the
trenchant sister, the *City of Richmond,* and with the *City of Baltimore*
(doomed to burn in 1937) and *City of Norfolk.* (The latter two steamers
were built as models for the twins in 1911.) To match the competition,
the Old Bay Line built *President Warfield* in 1928. And to meet that challenge, the Chesapeake Line built *Yorktown* and launched her in the same
month as *President Warfield.* Like the Old Bay Line packets, *Yorktown* was
a three-decker in white-walled elegance, well fitted out, and like her competition able to traverse the Bay from Baltimore to Norfolk with railroad
watch precision. Somewhat smaller than her competitors, she nevertheless showed a graceful pair of heels and a comparable luxury.

Out of Washington in the same period steamed the packets of the
Norfolk and Washington Steamboat Company, *Northland* and *Southland.*
Earlier boats included *Norfolk, Washington,* and *Newport News. Northland*
and *Southland* were joined in 1925 by *District of Columbia,* built expressly

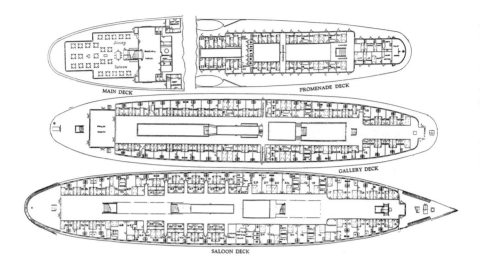

Deck plan of steamboats *State of Maryland, State of Virginia,* and (with slight modification) *President Warfield.* Drawn from brochure of Old Bay Line.

for the Washington–Norfolk route. These three vessels bore the imprint of the Old Bay Line steamers, carrying with them the line's design, accommodations, and appearance.

One other line precariously survived. The Ericsson line, running steamers through the Chesapeake and Delaware Canal to Philadelphia, could not meet the competition of the railroads, particularly the PRR, in the wake of the *City of Baltimore* disaster. In 1937 the line discontinued passenger service, although its stately steamer *John Cadwalader,* with a few small helpers, continued to carry on. The sight of the many-stateroomed, handsome three-decker cleaving the water of the upper Bay brought more than a lump in the throat to those who remembered when the Ericsson line steamers called at Betterton en route to Philadelphia and disgorged their cargo of exuberant vacationers.

The steamers of the Old Bay Line, the Chesapeake Line, and the Norfolk and Washington Line were the undisputed "queens of the Bay." They climaxed the steamboat era on the Chesapeake. Yet, even as they steamed back and forth on their precisely scheduled route, bearing the social elite of the Florida trade, the prosperous vacationers bound for Virginia Beach, and travelers using the steamers as a mode of service, there hung over them a cloud that would not go away. To the observant, steamboats were an anachronism in a changing world of economics and transportation, a romantic illusion resting on little more than nostalgia and a sense of escape. Increasingly, in the late 1930s, the Chesapeake Line felt the pinch from the Old Bay Line and knew that it could not survive the competition.

Obvious to most observers was the fact that the economics of the times would not sustain two lines competing for identical and diminishing trade. With shadows of war on the horizon, the Old Bay Line bought out the Chesapeake Line. Behind the former were the stock holdings of the Seaboard Air Line Railroad; behind the latter, those of the Southern Railway and the Atlantic Coast Line Railroad. And still farther in the shadows were the interests of the Pennsylvania Railroad.

The blow came with the events of World War II and came with abrupt suddenness. On April 1 and 2 of 1942, the *State of Maryland* and *State of Virginia* were requisitioned by the U.S. Army for duty in the Army Transport Service. When they left their berths on Light Street and donned the camouflage of war, they sounded the familiar dirge on the whistle. They performed routine transport service, grew weary in the process, and ended up on the scrap heap.

Other events in April 1942 transpired, including many behind the scenes. In that month, secret correspondence between President Franklin D. Roosevelt and a certain "former naval person" in Whitehall concerned the launching of an offensive on the western shore of Europe. One necessity was the immediate procurement of fast, shallow-draft vessels for inshore transport operations. Under the pressure of this requirement, the War Shipping Administration (WSA) under lend-lease set about to procure some fifteen vessels meeting the specifications and to transfer them to the British Ministry of War Transport. On June 26, representatives of WSA and the British Ministry of War Transport, meeting in Washington, selected suitable vessels from a list of twenty-five. The best were picked. These included *Northland* and *Southland* (Norfolk and Washington Steamboat Company packets), *Virginia Lee* (Cape Charles to Norfolk steamer of the PRR; she was found to be defective and removed from the list), *John Cadwalader* (Ericsson line steamer to Philadelphia; she burned at her dock before sailing). Also included were *Yorktown* and *President Warfield.*

The two Old Bay Line steamers ran with destiny. On a fateful September convoy (RB-1) under British flag, bound from Newfoundland to Britain, both vessels came under U-boat attack. *Yorktown* sank in a torpedo explosion that broke her back. *President Warfield,* dodging torpedoes by skillful maneuvering, reached the coast of Devon. There at Appledore, she served as mother ship for amphibious crews training for a later operation. Suddenly transferred back to the U.S. Navy, she joined a convoy for Normandy. Off Omaha Beach, she took station as a control ship in the landing.

Battered and weary at the end of the war, she returned to Norfolk. In her condition, the Old Bay Line had neither the resources nor the will to accept her back. She was laid up among the discards in the James River. A year later, she was sold under mysterious circumstances, dragged out, and renovated in strange locations around Baltimore and the Delaware River. British intelligence—and then that of the countries of "flags of convenience" under which she took registry—dogged at her heels. When surveillance got too close, she abruptly cleared the Delaware and Virginia capes, appeared on the coasts of France and Italy under various guises and for seemingly odd purposes, and then, outwitting her pursuers, slipped into Sète, France, near Marseilles. There she loaded forty-five hundred Jewish refugees who had struggled across the hidden byways of Europe from detention camps in Germany. Under Haganah, which under front organizations had bought her in the United States, she left Sète and headed east—destination Palestine.

At that point she joined the long march of dilapidated vessels carrying refugees from the Holocaust in their attempts to penetrate the British blockade (erected to prevent Jewish immigration into Palestine as insurrection in that troubled mandate mounted) and to find sanctuary in what they perceived as their homeland promised in the Balfour Declaration.

Just as she cleared Sète, *President Warfield* found *Ajax* (British light cruiser); destroyers *Chequers, Chieftain,* and *Charity;* and several minesweepers or patrol ships on either flank, a formidable force to accompany her all the way to Palestine. She attempted to elude them off the shallow entrance to the Nile, but they joined her when she emerged.

Then, on the night of July 17, 1947, with the searchlights of *Ajax* blinding her, destroyers rammed her, and Royal Marines boarded her. A battle fought with clubs, pistols, and tear gas on the one hand, and potatoes and cans of food and slippery oil on the other raged on her decks.

Suddenly, in the glare of light, her name board on the pilothouse was flipped over and a new name appeared: *Exodus 1947.* Forced into Haifa, her cargo of refugees stuffed into three British transports and returned to the very detention camps in Germany where they had begun their epic journey, the steamer *President Warfield/Exodus 1947* evoked the sympathies of the world and the attention of the United Nations. She became a symbol directly attached to the emergence of the state of Israel.

Left to decay in Haifa, she burned on August 26, 1952. An attempt to salvage her hull on August 23, 1964, failed. (For a more detailed account of the vessel's history, the reader is referred to Holly, *Exodus 1947.*)

During the war years, the Old Bay Line had only the former Chesapeake Line steamers *City of Norfolk* and *City of Richmond* to serve the throngs of soldiers and sailors jamming their decks for passage to Norfolk. The two shuttled back and forth on nightly runs, meeting each other in the ghostly shadows of the Potomac mouth with a brief salute. No time could be spared for maintenance and overhaul, and the steamers suffered. Paint work grew shabby, rust streaked the white hulls, carpets looked threadbare, and canvas covering the open decks cracked for lack of gray paint. At night, the saloons and cabin spaces swarmed with men, unable to book staterooms, who slept in upright chairs or on the carpet itself. The freight decks carried the logistics of war supplied by the factories of Baltimore and needed at the naval and other military establishments around Norfolk. In summertime, a few hardy vacationers managed to book passage for Virginia Beach and other Atlantic resorts, but the expectation for entertainment diminished as gas rationing and other restrictions limited the potential for amusement. At the end of the war, the Old Bay Line had two old and suffering steamers on its hands and bleak prospects for the future.

Then, on October 31, 1948, *District of Columbia* of the Norfolk and Washington Steamboat Company struck the tanker *Georgia* at anchor in Hampton Roads in a fog and sustained enough damage to force her owners out of business. The Old Bay Line bought and repaired her, and maintained the Washington–Norfolk route until September 1957, when operations were suspended. The wharf in Washington, leased from the U.S. Army, had rotted and become unsafe. Its deterioration and the heavy cost of repairs contributed to the end of the Washington–Norfolk service.

A series of unwonted and unwanted blows struck hard at the continuation of the Old Bay Line in Baltimore. Taken singly, each was barely sustainable. Taken in total, they amounted to a major catastrophe from which the Old Bay Line could salvage little.

A fire damaged its Baltimore pier on Light Street in 1949. During the 1950s, successive labor disputes and strikes disrupted the service schedule and increased costs. The pier at Old Point Comfort, becoming increasingly dilapidated, faced condemnation and eventual demolition, thereby terminating a century-old call bringing travelers to Fortress Monroe and Hampton Roads and vacationers to the hospitality of the Chamberlin Hotel.

Furthermore, in the fall of 1950, the city of Baltimore announced its decision to demolish the entire length of the Light Street piers. Abandoned by their steamboat owners, suffering extinction, they stretched from Pratt Street to Key Highway—a mass of rotting, dilapidated, collapsing lumber, bearing nothing but the memories of a generation of steamboat travelers and lovers. Only the wharf of the Tolchester line and the stately but sagging green front with clock tower and cupola of the Old Bay Line remained.

The city planned to convert the wharf into a memorial park to General Sam Smith, commander of Baltimore's defending force in 1814. It became the site of Harborplace, an extravaganza of the Rouse Company —an extensive marketplace of modern pavilions of brick and glass and wide esplanades, with shops and restaurants, space for an outdoor theater, a three-tiered glass aquarium, and a permanent dock for the U.S.S. *Constellation*, frigate of Baltimore's history. To provide space for this construction and for the partial filling-in of the harbor basin, the wharves of Light Street, including those of the Old Bay Line, had to be demolished.

Pressed to find a replacement, the Old Bay Line settled for wharf facilities at Pier 3, Pratt Street, the former terminal of the Merchants and Miners Transportation Company. In its halcyon days, that terminal had bustled with the elite passenger trade for Florida and Georgia in the winter season, and Boston and Cape Cod in the summer. Its tall, black-hulled, white-cabined coastal ships, laden with cargo and bedecked with well-heeled passengers dripping with the latest fashions, always drew a crowd to gape at departures from the well-appointed terminal. In 1950, with the coastal company in the process of forced liquidation, the pier was no more than an adequate mooring platform for the steamers of the Old Bay Line. The line paid twenty-four thousand dollars a year for its use.

With revenues falling and costs rising, the Old Bay Line in the last throes of solvency tried various expedients: sharply reduced schedules, temporary suspension of service in off-season months, restrictions on weekend sailings, limitations on the number of passengers carried to reduce outlays for stewards and dining room help, and even the carrying of freight only. Each move was more desperate than the last. Then in April 1962, the Old Bay Line succumbed, terminating its service completely. Its three vessels stood idle at the Pratt Street terminal.

All three died off in other waters. The *District of Columbia*, renamed *Provincetown*, ran briefly out of Boston and eventually met the scrapper. The *City of Richmond* sank while being towed to the Virgin Islands and the *City of Norfolk* ended up in a New Jersey scrap yard.

With the end of the Old Bay Line, after 122 years of steaming on the Chesapeake, overnight packet service aboard fast and luxurious steamers between Baltimore and Norfolk came to an end.

Excursion steamers had a special history. Some held on tenaciously to the end of the steamboat era. The destiny of others was linked to the resorts they served, while some were replaced with other modes of transportation. All resorts in the Bay area suffered from the accessibility of Atlantic Ocean resorts—Ocean City and Rehoboth—by automobile. The opening of the Chesapeake Bay Bridge from Sandy Point near Annapolis to Kent Island on July 30, 1952, was celebrated with great fanfare but rendered ferry service across the Bay obsolete by bringing the Atlantic resorts within easy range of the major cities. Lesser resorts along the Bay correspondingly withered for lack of patronage.

On the western shore of the Bay several resorts had died much earlier. Bay Ridge at Tolly Point, where the Severn River entered the Bay, had flourished as an amusement park, resort hotel, convention center, and colorful escape for Baltimoreans around the turn of the century. A number of steamboats brought excursionists from the city to its long covered pier: *Jane Moseley* was chartered from the New Bay Line for the 1885 season and a few succeeding years. The small steamer *Bergen Point* ran excursions from Annapolis in the same year, and even smaller *Bay Ridge* began service from Baltimore in 1886. The large, two-stacked *Empire State* arrived also in 1886, so deep of draft that it grounded repeatedly off the Bay Ridge wharf, which required a lengthening of two hundred feet. *Theodore Weems* of the Weems line called in 1887 on her runs to Fair Haven, and *Emma Giles* of the Tolchester line ran excursions to the resort at various times. And the *Columbia*, acquired from New York interests and licensed to carry thirty-five hundred passengers, began shuttling crowds from Baltimore in 1887. At its peak, the park was a spectacular success. A continuous panoply of events, including jousting tournaments, boat races, dances, pyrotechnic displays, concerts, lectures, livestock exhibitions, in addition to the rides in the amusement park and the comforts of the hotel, kept its patrons entertained for a decade.

Competition for the steamboats arrived when the Baltimore and Ohio Railroad (B&O) gained control of the resort in 1887 and pushed through the completion of its Annapolis and Bay Ridge Railroad. By 1890, the line was carrying thousands of people each day, who came from Baltimore and Washington, even Philadelphia. The steamboat shuttle had little purpose, except for its own attraction as a voyage in miniature from Baltimore.

Financial troubles for the resort began in 1899 and continued to the end—the result of mismanagement and diminished patronage. On July 17, 1899, the B&O sold *Columbia* to the Cape May and Delaware Navigation Company. With her departure, regular steamboat services to Bay Ridge ceased. Almost immediately afterward, rail service ended, also. For the Chautauqua Society in June 1900, *Emma Giles* ran a few excursions to Bay Ridge from Baltimore. In 1901, a storm demolished the resort's long pier. The park withered. On March 4, 1915, the hotel burned to the ground. Bay Ridge as the resort it had been ceased to exist. An inn and a major residential area took its place. Nothing remained to recall the color and excitement at Tolly Point.

Farther down the western shore, in the hook of Herring Bay, lay Fair Haven, the resort created by George Weems in 1839. The steamers of his company, particularly *Theodore Weems*, touched at the wharf there en route to Patuxent River landings until 1905, when the last owners of the Weems line, Georgeanna Weems Williams and Matilda Weems Forbes, sold out to the MD&V (PRR). Although the Fair Haven property was not involved in the sale, as a viable resort it ceased to exist, and, sold off in parcels, became a community and an area of residential estates. The memory of the resort faded with the years.

On the Potomac River, steamboats continued to serve the resorts for years. Often their demise did not simultaneously spell the end of a resort. Colonial Beach, a thriving playground with protected water, a sandy beach, and hotels bent on free-wheeling entertainment, started as a developer's dream—as "Classic Shores" in the early 1900s. From 1902, the steamer *St. Johns* shuttled from Washington for many years. When she departed for eventual disposition, Colonial Beach continued to flourish, largely supported by those who drove the miles from Baltimore, Washington, or Richmond in their cars. Then there appeared the big 300-foot three-decker, three-stacker (the stacks were arranged athwartships) with the elaborate decor in her cabin and name bands for dancing; the *Potomac* turned the excursion down the Potomac from Washington into a holiday. When she left the scene in 1948, steamboat service to Colonial Beach ended. Diesel-driven excursion boats sidled up to the dock, but steamboat buffs hankered for the oily smell of the engine room and the soot of the stack, and found diesel fumes obnoxious. The resort continued with diminished patronage.

Diesel-powered excursion boats, like the 220-foot *George Washington* that served Marshall Hall (the amusement park on the Maryland shore opposite Fort Belvoir) into the 1960s, continued long after the beloved *Charles Macalester* of the Mount Vernon and Marshall Hall Steamboat Company made its final voyage. For a time, *Mount Vernon* of the Wilson Line, which had acquired Marshall Hall, journeyed to the park. The site continued as an amusement park and beer hall, until the revelers from the neighboring areas, forced to come by car, diminished in numbers. Little remained to remind them of the pleasures they once enjoyed at Marshall Hall.

Piney Point on the Potomac, where the elite (and not-so-elite) of Washington and Baltimore gathered (brought down by steamboats, at various times, of the Randall line or the MD&V) became a summer colony and a residential area with the decline of the steamboat lines. Eventually, it evolved into a petroleum storage facility, its existence as a playground for the fashionable nearly forgotten.

The most talked-about resort (for diverse reasons) on the western shore was Chesapeake Beach (or Seaside Park, as it was called in its latter days). The automobile and truck, and then the Depression, took their toll early in the 1930s. By 1934, it was clear to the directors of the Washington and Chesapeake Beach Railway that the rail line between Washington and the beach resort could not be resurrected. The inevitable decision brought an end to the dream of Otto Mears. The last train left Chesapeake Beach at noon on April 15, 1935.

The resort, titled Seaside Park, continued to operate under the Chesapeake Beach Hotel Company. While losing its popularity, the resort returned a modest profit until the beginning of World War II. Steamboat service had been suspended with the departure of *Dreamland* in 1925. Only intermittent daily excursions brought steamers to the long pier. Then in 1931, the Wilson Line, a husky operator of successful excursion routes on the Delaware River, elected to inaugurate its business on the Chesapeake. On May 28, 1931, it dispatched the *State of Delaware* from its wharf leased at Pier 8, Light Street, to reopen regular daily runs in season to Seaside Park. Advertised widely, she made a dramatic difference in excursion travel. Broad-beamed, even buxom, for stability, she was a steel-hulled, squared-off four-decker, sleek and trim in black hull, white upper works, and buff stack, with the Wilson insignia flaunted from flags and bunting and displayed on both sides of the stack. Comfortable armchairs graced her open decks; the folding chairs of *Dreamland* were a poor comparison. When darkness fell on the return trip, passengers could watch movies in the open air of the upper deck or dance to a five-piece orchestra below. Like *Dreamland* in the old days, *State of Delaware* steamed out of Baltimore several evenings a week on a moonlight cruise, where in the shadows of the upper decks lovers could croon and coo, or on the dance floor sway to the music of the best bands in Baltimore. In spite of her name (it had an unfamiliar ring), Baltimoreans called her *Dreamland*.

Her replacement, the rebuilt steamer *Dixie*, was placed on the route in 1935. In spite of the fact that she played "Dixie" as her theme song, she, too, was known by her patrons as *Dreamland*. Then in 1941, the Wilson Line developed an ambitious plan to convert an old boat (*City of Washington* launched in 1909) to a totally renovated excursion boat for Seaside Park before the shadows of war engulfed the project. The Wilson Line almost succeeded. Abrupt federal restrictions on the wartime use of petroleum fuel brought an end to the new boat's career as an excursion boat to Seaside Park. Rechristened as *Bay Belle*, she managed a season before surrendering to federal control and other employment.

Steamboat operations to Chesapeake Beach (Seaside Park) ended. The park became a ghost town, haunted by the wail of the last departing train and the deep-throated whistle of *Dreamland* sounding its final farewell.

On the Eastern Shore, the scenario followed that of Chesapeake Beach on the western shore.

Because of its hotel accommodations, the Betterton resort held on through the 1950s, although with steadily evaporating popularity. A variety of steamers brought excursionists to the resort, almost to the very end. In earlier days, the Ericsson line steamers stopped at Betterton on their high-speed runs via the C&D Canal to Philadelphia, but with the failure of the line in 1935, the last steamer, *John Cadwalader*, made its final call. Excursion lines, however, continued to call.

During the 1930s, the Western Shore Steamboat Company sent *Anne Arundel* or *Potomac* with vacationers on "off-days" when not running the

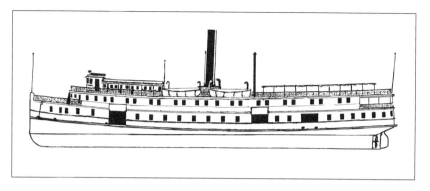

Steamboat *Anne Arundel* as she appeared in the 1930s. Drawn from author's photograph.

Rappahannock or the Potomac. In 1933–34, the Baltimore, Crisfield and Onancock Line ran the screw-driven *Chippewa* to Betterton, but it remained for the Tolchester line and its successor, the Wilson Line, to maintain a modicum of service through the years. After World War II, *Tolchester* (formerly the *City of Philadelphia* and *Liberty Bell*), a big, all-steel three-decker, made special runs to Betterton in connection with her regular excursions to Tolchester Beach. Increasingly, as ownership passed to the Wilson Line, *Bay Belle*, with her ubiquitous appearances at Chesapeake Beach (Seaside Park) and Tolchester, gathered the affections of those who had made Betterton a vacationer's habit. When the Wilson Line of Maryland, final holders of the Chesapeake interests of the Wilson Line, surrendered Tolchester Park and *Bay Belle* to the mortgage holders in 1962, steamboat service to Betterton ended. The pier collapsed in the next ice flow, the resort buildings disappeared for lumber, and the hotels closed one by one, their porches left sagging, their shutters left to bang in the wind, and the view of the upper Bay relegated to a few long-time residents and the passing gulls.

For Tolchester on the Eastern Shore, the end came with twists and turns, hopes and fears. The most revered of the resorts favored by Baltimoreans—and Eastern Shoremen, too—Tolchester suffered from the same changes in tastes, shifts in economic and transportation patterns, and the rush of the times as others, but her owners fought hard, trying as best they could to stem the inexorable course of events that overwhelmed them.

The original progenitors of the Tolchester enterprise culminated in the successful management of William C. Eliason, the respected president who died in 1921, and the somewhat mercurial board that succeeded him. As the 1920s drew to a close and the 1930s arrived in the form of the Great Depression, the board committed several monumental errors in judgment. One was a gamble that motorists and truckers would prefer a trans-Bay steamer shuttle to the long, circuitous route by road around the head of the Bay. In 1925, therefore, the company bought *Express* (formerly *Stapleton*) from New York interests. She was a double-ended, boxlike ferryboat, 225 feet in length, 61 feet in beam, and able to carry fifty cars or trucks and as many excursionists as the old *Louise*, just retiring (since she had no space for trucks or cars). The decision bore little fruit; the company had only the leavings after the established truck lines and the railroads took the bulk of expected freight around the head of the Bay and vacationers took the trains or their cars to Atlantic resorts. Furthermore, *Express* was an expensive failure, losing money in repair and incurring operating costs at twice the rate of *Emma Giles* and *Annapolis* combined (the other two boats of the line). Because of the configuration of her inclined engine and the off-center displacement of her paddle wheels, she ran better in one direction than the other, hence turned around when leaving a slip—thereby confusing motorists in their attempts to figure out how to get off the contraption. Baltimoreans, after the loss of *Louise*, grew to hate *Express*, and many refused to ride her.

Second, the board, in arranging the financing for the purchase of *Express*, underestimated the capacity of the company to repay. The deficit mounted, and the full force of the Depression struck home. In desperation, the board faced the reality of liquidating the property of the company on the tributaries of the Bay that it served, and, in the process, of abandoning the secondary mission of the company—the touching of *Emma Giles* and *Annapolis* at the landings on the Little Choptank, Sassafras, South, West, and Rhode rivers known by a generation of travelers. One by one, the landings were either sold or mortgaged to provide cash, with foreclosure a virtual certainty.

As a last-ditch effort, when the board recognized that its only revenue-producing asset was the beach and amusement resort at Tolchester, *Express* was summarily sold, and the board purchased *Bombay* (formerly *St. Johns*) for twenty-five thousand dollars (twenty thousand dollars' mortgage) with twelve thousand dollars in costs of renovation (the wharves at Galesville and Chalk Point on the West River were used as security). Renamed *Tolchester*, an excursion boat without carrying capacity for trucks or cars, she proved as costly to repair and operate as *Express*. In last desperate moves, the board converted *Emma Giles* into a car-carrying monstrosity and for the first time in the company's history permitted the sale of beer on moonlight cruises and in the park's cafeteria. When *Annapolis* burned at her Light Street moorings, the directors had reached the final impasse. Attempts at refinancing the enormous indebtedness of the company failed, and the directors could find no alternative to bankruptcy proceedings. After a year of legal skirmishing, the completely demoralized Tolchester Beach and Improvement Company ceased to exist on July 14, 1937. *Emma Giles* had made her last calls on the rivers she had served since 1887 and the pier at Tolchester where she had landed thousands of frolicsome excursionists through the years. Sadly, she went off to become a barge and to final oblivion.

Various investors sought control of the defunct company. Two competitors for what remained of the Tolchester beach service fought it out. One was Benjamin Bowling Wills (B. B. Wills, as he was called), a veteran amusement park and excursion entrepreneur on the Potomac. The other was the powerful Wilson Line with widespread interests and steamboats on the Delaware, and, more recently, on the Potomac.

B. B. Wills at thirty-nine was a shrewd and tough fighter, ready to take risks but also ready for innovation. He sought the colorful—in boat appearance and in amusements—to please the public. Somehow the notion of trans-Bay freight service persisted, and B. B. Wills followed the previous owners in leasing a double-ended ferryboat named *Chelsea*, a boat so unsatisfactory that the lease lasted just three months. A little Maine coastal vessel, *Southport*, with a carved-out space in the bows to accommodate twelve cars, lasted two years. *Tolchester* (formerly *St. Johns*) prospered in her summer daily excursions to the amusement park, but on May 15, 1941, she burned to the water's edge, scorching *Southport* in the adjacent berth. Both were scrapped. To replace them, the company chartered (then purchased) the steamer *Mohawk*—none other than the *Anne Arundel*, the last overnight river packet on the Bay. Her cabins and upper decks were torn open for breezy decks and a dance floor, but her graceful sheer and well-proportioned lines were unmistakable in the transformation. She wore an Indian warrior on her stack. Then, to supplement her, B. B. Wills transferred *Francis Scott Key* from Washington. To the delight of those who welcomed her on May 29, 1941, she was none other than the *Susquehanna* renamed, the yachtlike steamer William C. Eliason had built to carry his associates to the Jamestown Exposition in 1908, and one of the best-designed steamers on the Bay. In spite of the restrictions on fuel, when in 1941 war swept excursion steamers from the Bay, B. B. Wills managed to run packed excursions to Tolchester under the guise of furnishing needed commuter service. Although he packed *Francis Scott Key* off to Boston because of her limited size and capacity, his success with her led him to capture *Bear Mountain* from her New York owners, a big, fast side-wheeler with capacity for two hundred passengers. With interruptions occasioned by fuel problems, she ran from 1944 to the end of the war. In 1948, Wills transferred her to Washington for runs on the Potomac.

Captivated with the notion that the immediate postwar years would bring a surge in the excursion trade, Wills replaced *Bear Mountain* with *Asbury Park* (formerly *City of Philadelphia* and *Liberty Belle*), sister ship of *Bay Belle. Asbury Park* promptly became *Tolchester.* Like her sister ship, *Tolchester* cruised the Bay in all-steel, glassed-in, dance-floored, purring, top-deck-movie-showing splendor—unloading a thousand or so picnickers on the pier at Tolchester, steaming slowly back and forth to the light of the moon and the crooning of a smooth orchestra.

Her sister ship ran the Bay, also. The Wilson Line had operated on the Bay, in particular to Seaside Park (Chesapeake Beach), with *State of Delaware* and *Dixie*, then *Bay Belle.* Competition was immediately joined between the two sister ships and the rival lines when the Wilson Line proposed to run *Bay Belle* to Tolchester. In February 1956, the two companies, neither likely to win by bitter competition, agreed on a compromise: *Bay Belle* to run to Tolchester and Betterton, *Tolchester* to operate under charter.

Wills decided that *Tolchester* could be better employed—as a gambling casino (renamed *Freestone*) off Freestone, Virginia (where gambling was outlawed) at the end of a dock (hence in Maryland waters, where gambling was permitted). There she stayed until gambling became outlawed in Maryland; she took the name of *Potomac*, operated on the Potomac sporadically, and made one brief attempt to run an excursion out of Baltimore in late August 1967 without success. The link of B. B. Wills to Tolchester had long disappeared by 1956. Even the Light Street wharves of the Tolchester line had been demolished in the creation of Harborplace.

The Wilson Line, beleaguered by shrinking patronage and failing finances, sold off *Bay Belle* and Tolchester Beach to a completely separate group, the Wilson-Tolchester company, which, in a series of complicated maneuvers designed to liquidate its holdings, sold out finally to Wilson Line of Maryland. Unable to clear itself of fiscal disaster, this company surrendered the park and *Bay Belle* to the mortgage holders, who were, of course, Wilson Lines controlled by the Wilson Line of Wilmington, Delaware.

Tolchester Park under the auctioneer's hammer sold for twenty-five thousand dollars. In 1969, David Bramble bought the tract for one hundred thousand dollars. Demolished were all the sagging buildings and piers of the amusement park, until nothing remained to recall the golden days when Baltimoreans frolicked on its rides and basked on its beach. A marina took its place. Only the gulls flying over or standing guard on top of the piling noted the timelessness of the scene—the groves among the trees where the miniature railroad ran, the slope where the porch-shaded hotel stood, the edge of turf where the twin-towered pavilion offered ice-cream sodas on the lower floor and a panoramic view of the Chesapeake on the upper, and the sandy beach where the wavelets invited the adventurous to dip their toes in the briny waters of the Bay. Memories were hard to put aside.

Bay Belle, sold off at auction to the Wilson Line, was towed off to Wilmington, Delaware. Her departure marked the end of the steamboat era on the Chesapeake. She was the last to run on a regular schedule. The brief appearance of *Potomac* on an attempted excursion from Baltimore in August 1967 could not be construed as part of that era.

Bay Belle scarcely resembled her distinguished forebears on the Chesapeake. Streamlined, with a canted bow, forward-slanting external stanchions on her passenger deck to give a racy thrust to her appearance, and a fat but rakish stack, she was far removed from the stately packets and demure excursion boats of the golden years. Yet she represented all of them in those final days.

Bay Belle bid farewell to Baltimore in May 1963. The date coincided almost exactly with the month in 1813 when the little steamer *Chesapeake* ventured forth in the face of the British blockade to begin her runs from Baltimore to Frenchtown. She was the first steamboat on the Bay. *Bay Belle* was the last. In between, a sesquicentennium marked the steamboat era, never forgotten, but never to return.

Bay Belle, without steam on that final day, could not sound the dirge of farewell on her whistle—three longs and a short—"Good-bye and good luck."

EPILOGUE

Saying good-bye to steamboats on the Chesapeake is not an easy task—particularly for those who rode them. The era was finite. Nothing followed to take its place. Generations coming on who have never experienced the romance and the warmth of that era cannot recreate it.

Time will remove all those who personally experienced the steamboat era. Nostalgia for it will disappear with their passing. I, too, must say farewell to the steamboats and the way of life they represented. My hope is that the era will be recorded as a colorful and visible thread in the fabric of American history.

Like most of those who experienced the latter days of the steamboat era, I shall miss it. I shall be haunted by it, just as reminders of it along the shores of Tidewater have haunted me.

But I am prepared to salute it—if I had a whistle with a long, plaintive wail—with three longs and a short. "Good-bye, and good luck." Only I don't know where to apply the "good luck"—except to those who celebrate the era and wish its memory well.

Appendix A

THE CROSSHEAD ENGINE
AND THE VERTICAL BEAM ENGINE

Background of the Crosshead Engine

The crosshead engine, variously called descriptively, derisively, or affectionately a square, steeple, gallows, or guillotine engine, was built into the hulls of early steamboats on the Chesapeake Bay from 1813 to the early 1830s. Testimony to their sturdiness is the fact that many of the engines built during that period functioned for decades, a few lasting beyond the Civil War. Some design changes occurred in the early years, but by the mid-1820s the pattern had been set, and builders such as Charles Reeder and John Watchman in Baltimore constructed engines of remarkable similarity.

The design of the crosshead engine can be partially understood from the drawings of Thomas Tredgold and treatises by other writers on early steamboat engines (see Bibliography). The general workings of the machinery could be deduced from these sources. But important gaps in information persisted, particularly with respect to dimensions of various components and the mechanism of the valve system.

The resurrection of the engine of the steamer *Columbus* in 1992–93 from the bottom of the Chesapeake Bay off the mouth of the Potomac River dramatically brought to view the parts of a crosshead engine built by Charles Reeder in 1828, the peak time for the production of this type of engine. Here for measurement and analysis were the cylinder, piston and rod, pedestal mountings for the cylinder and paddle wheel, one of the paddle wheel shafts complete with the paddle wheel hub, the condenser, the air pump, and both upper and lower steam chests, with valve and lift rod assembly. Not visible or accessible for bringing to the surface were the complete mechanism for activating the lift rod assembly and the means for alternately admitting steam from the boiler to the cylinder and exhausting the depleted steam to the condenser in both upper and lower steam chests. Missing, also, were the parts to the crosshead itself and the means of effecting its traction through the rails of the A-frame.

In spite of these limitations, the artifacts from the bottom of the Bay, coupled with the Tredgold drawings and other texts, proved invaluable in reconstructing a schematic diagram of a crosshead engine of the period (see figure) and estimating its workings.

General Schematic Description of the Crosshead Engine

Simply stated, the crosshead engine got its name from the crossbar (A), which at the top of a piston rod (F), rode athwartships up and down, guided by vertical rails (G) in the wooden A-frame (B) port and starboard. Suspended from the crossbar were two crankshafts (J), one port, the other starboard. These crankshafts turned cranks (H) on the paddle-wheel shafts (K2, K3), port and starboard, rotating the paddle wheels (K3), which propelled the boat. Steam from the boiler was admitted to the cylinder (C) through a valve system (V2, W2) in the steam chests (V1, W1); the steam pushed the piston and piston rod (D, F) upward on one stroke and downward on the return stroke. Exhaust steam from each stroke left the cylinder (C) via the valve system (V2, W2) in the steam chests (V1, W1) for the condenser (Q1), where a jet stream of cold water from the Bay (Q3) converted the steam to condensate. A so-called air pump (T1) pulled the condensate/water mixture from the condenser (Q1) and forced it into a reservoir called the "hot well" (Q3), where the condensate/water was then pumped back into the boiler as feed water to replenish the loss by conversion into steam. The condenser (Q1) also produced a vacuum, which pulled the piston (D) as the steam pushed it from the opposite side. Various mechanical linkages controlled the valve system for automatic or, alternatively, hand operation by the engineer.

Detailed Description of the Crosshead Engine

In greater detail, the analysis of a crosshead engine of the 1820s as extrapolated from the artifacts of the *Columbus* might begin, as the general discussion above began, with the crossbar or crosshead (A). Its length, extending from port A-frame to starboard A-frame, on such a typical engine would approximate 7 to 7.5 feet. Its end on either side would have shoes riding in the vertical tracks or rails (G) fastened to the A-frame on either side. These rails could not be shorter than the stroke of the piston (D), which in the case of *Columbus* was 78 inches. That measurement of 78 inches corresponded to the enrollment data on the vessel. It also corresponded to the internal distance of the cylinder (C) from the bottom lip of the upper entry (V4) to the upper lip of the lower entry (W4), the distance that the piston (D) traveled on its upward or downward push. This measurement does not include the total interior height of the cylinder (C), since the square entries (or exits) for steam or exhaust (V4, W4) could not be covered by the piston (D) for proper entry or exhaust of steam. On the *Columbus*, the length of the piston rod (F) approximated 78 inches, indicating that the top of the piston rod nearly touched the top of the cylinder (C) on the downstroke (except for the width of the lower entry), and (except for the width of the upper entry) extended nearly its full length on the upstroke.

Given the length of the upward stroke of the piston rod (F), the external height of the cylinder (C), the supports beneath it (E1, E2, E3), the condenser (Q1) beneath these supports, and the necessary framing beneath this very heavy preponderance, the two A-frames on a vessel like *Columbus* could not have been less than 35 feet in height from the floor of the boat near the keel, the height of a three-story building. With a depth of hold of 10 feet and a corresponding cabin height, the A-frame rose 15 feet above the superstructure. Built of heavy timbers and often covered with planking to protect the machinery from the weather, the frames resembled two towers rising from the bowels of the vessel and rearing their bulk above the upper deck.

The cylinder (C) had an internal diameter of 50 inches, corresponding to the enrollment data. Made of cast iron 1 inch thick, it had three openings. At the top, with suitable wrought iron flanges, was a hole through which the piston rod (F) rode on its up-and-down travels. The piston rod (F) approximated 10 inches in diameter and formed a unit with the piston (D). The piston itself (D), of laminated copper construction, consisted of five discs (in sequence from top to bottom: 1 inch, 3 inches, 2 inches, 3 inches, 1 inch, in thickness) fastened together. Spring-like bands surrounded the 3-inch discs, appearing to function much as piston rings operate in a modern internal-combustion engine. Wedged in the interstices of the middle segment were fragments of fiber (hemp or other material), undoubtedly intended as packing to lessen the loss of steam and pressure from the travels of a piston which did not quite fit the interior diameter of the cylinder. Evidence of scoring on the walls of the cylinder and this residue of fiber packing testify to the inability of even a prestigious manufacturer like Reeder to produce tightly fitting castings in the late 1820s.

The piston (D) was about 10 inches thick, 50 inches in diameter, and completely flat on both upper and lower surfaces (in contrast to pistons in later engines, which were slightly convex).

The cylinder had two apertures other than the one for the piston rod. Near the top plating of the cylinder (where the top was fastened to the

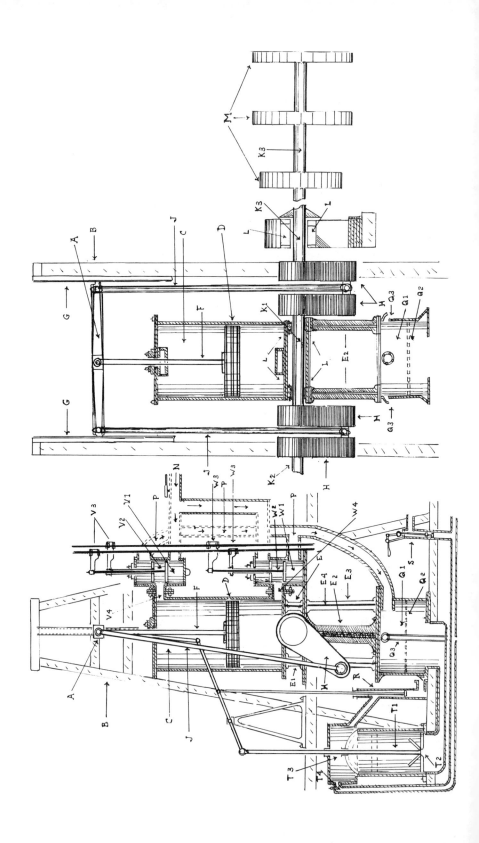

Key

(A) crosshead

(B) A-frame, or "gallows" frame

(C) cylinder

(D) piston

(E1) upper cylindrical pedestal supports

(E2) ornamental pedestal

(E3) lower cylindrical pedestal supports

(E4) tie rod through cylindrical supports

(F) piston rod

(G) rails guiding piston rod

(H) crank

(J) crankshaft

(K1) paddle wheel shaft

(K2) starboard paddle wheel shaft

(K3) port paddle wheel shaft

(L) bearings for paddle wheel shaft

(M) starboard paddle wheel hub

(N) steam intake from boiler

(P) exhaust steam to condenser

(Q1) condenser

(Q2) perforated plate

(Q3) jet intake from Bay water

(R) forced feed pump

(S) hand feed pump

(T1) air pump

(T2) flapper valves

(T3) hot well

(T4) discharge as boiler feed water

(V1) upper steam chest

(V2) upper valves

(V3) upper lift rod system

(V4) upper entry to cylinder

(W1) lower steam chest

(W2) lower valves

(W3) lower lift rod system

(W4) lower entry to cylinder.

Schematic drawing of crosshead engine extrapolated from engine artifacts of steamboat *Columbus* and applied to basic sketch of Tredgold, 1838. Drawing by the author.

circular casting by heavy bolts and wrought-iron nuts), there appeared the rectangular opening for the entry and exit of steam (V4). Near the bottom plating of the cylinder was a corresponding rectangular opening serving the same purpose (W4). These openings, fitted with flanges for attachment to the steam chests, were approximately 10–12 inches in width, 5–6 inches in height. They were rectangular in order to require less space than a round opening—thus, the height of the cylinder could be correspondingly less.

Beneath the cylinder (C) lay a two-tiered support system designed for several purposes: to hold up the tonnage of the cylinder and its contents, to provide a base for the lower steam chest (W1), to channel the paddle wheel shaft (K1) from port to starboard within the bearing surfaces (L), and to cap the condenser (Q1) on which the support system rested. The top tier (E1), just beneath the cylinder (C), served as a spacer, with six hollow tubes 8 or more inches in diameter, 12–14 inches in height, with flanges for attachment. The engine designers of the period knew that tubular forms provided superior strength. Through the top tier passed the paddle wheel shaft (K1), supported by friction bearings (L), through which the shaft rotated. The plating beneath this tier covered a massive cast-iron pedestal structure (E2) and another six tubular spacers paralleling the height of the pedestal structure. The tubular cylindrical spacers both up and down (E1, E3) were held together by the tie rods (E4) passing through them to the plating above and below.

The massive cast-iron pedestal structure (E2) measured 57 inches in height and 60 inches in breadth. Fore and aft, it spanned some 90 inches, its structure forming two feet each 2 feet wide, its center open to provide access to the paddle wheel shaft (K1) running from port to starboard. The top plating was about 3 inches thick.

Most remarkable was the ornamentation on the pedestal structure (E2). On the forward front, it curved gracefully from the top to the distended feet at the bottom. A rodlike or ropelike projection, running down the height of the feet of the pedestal and providing great strength to the structure, was cast in the "reeded" pattern used on furniture of the Empire style, inspired by a classical Egyptian motif much favored in the 1820s and 1830s. That the foundrymen of Charles Reeder's ironworks would go to such lengths in embellishing this casting testifies to the pride they felt in their handiwork. Only the engineers and occasional visitors to the engine room could enjoy it.

The solid paddle wheel shaft (K1), about 10 inches in diameter, passed through the upper tier from side to side beneath the base of the cylinder (C) at its top. Where the shaft went through the side, bearing surfaces (L) held the shaft in place and provided the means for lubrication.

The shaft (K1) was interrupted on each side, port and starboard, with a crank (H), 10 inches thick, 18 inches wide at the hub and 12 inches wide at the end. From the center of the hub to the center of the bearing for the crankshaft (J), the throw measured 39 inches, one-half the stroke of 178 inches.

The connecting rod or crankshaft (J), not among the artifacts recovered from *Columbus*, must have measured 12 inches wide by 6 inches thick, as determined by a residual portion attached to the crank (H). Each crankshaft or connecting rod (J), port and starboard, reached to the top of the piston rod (F), where it swung from a juncture with the crosshead (A).

The crank (H) on each side of the pedestal was matched by a crank connected to the paddle wheel shafts (K2, K3) turning the paddle wheels themselves. Between the cranks a short shaft, about 6 inches in diameter, provided for the movement of the crankshaft or connecting rod (J) as it used the power from the piston rod (F) and the crosshead (A) to rotate the shafts (K1, K2, K3). The paddle wheel shafts (K2, K3) passed through a heavy support and bearing surface (L) to extend 20 feet to the bitter end, port and starboard. These shafts held the paddle wheel hubs (M), to which the framing and buckets of the paddle wheels were attached (not among the recovered artifacts from *Columbus*). The hubs measured approximately 6 feet in diameter.

Beneath the pedestal (E2) and supporting it lay the condenser (Q1), a large cylindrical container, with the same internal diameter of 50 inches as the cylinder (C) and approximately half its external height, in this case about 51 inches. Like the cylinder, it was made of cast iron 1 inch thick. Near the top of the condenser on the forward side, a round opening 8 inches in diameter, properly flanged, connected to the exhaust pipes (P) coming via the steam chests (V1, W1) from the cylinder (C). On each side of the condenser (Q1), small inlet connections (Q3) brought cool water from the Bay to spray inside the condenser (Q1) and reduce the exhaust steam to condensate. A perforated plate (Q2) across the middle of the condenser assisted in the process of collecting water in the bottom to be drawn off by the "air pump" (T1). The condenser functioned not only to reduce exhaust steam to water for return to the boiler but also as an additional source of power, since the vacuum produced when steam condensed pulled the piston from one side while live steam pushed it from the other. Low-pressure, condensing engines worked on this principle in order to gain the needed power.

Condensed water left the bottom of the condenser (Q1) through an opening fully half its diameter. The water was pulled through large pipes by the sucking action of the "air pump" (T1), the purpose of which was to effect the removal of water from the condenser (C) and insure the continuity of vacuum pulling the piston (D) in the cylinder (C). The "air pump" (T1) was a cast-iron cylinder lined with half-inch copper slats 2 inches wide which were intended to provide for expansion. The air pump measured 29 inches in interior diameter, 51 inches in height. The bottom, open to the pipe bringing water from the condenser, allowed a piston to move inside, from bottom to top. The piston of cast iron held four flapper valves (T2) hinged on the piston rod, so that on the downstroke the valves would open and allow water to pass through. On the upstroke, the pressure of the water being carried by the piston would close the flapper valves, and the water would be conveyed to the upper chamber of the air pump; at the same time, the piston with the closed flapper valves would pull water from the condenser via the intermediate piping in readiness for the next downstroke of the piston. A simple analogy of the action of the flapper valves might be the working of an unlatched inverted umbrella with loose spokes thrust into a deep pail of water—closing on a downward stroke, picking up water as it opened on the upward stroke.

At the top of the air pump (T1) there existed a copper dome-shaped cover (not among the *Columbus* artifacts) that rose like the top of a tea kettle and allowed the water raised by the piston to pass around it to the hot well (T3) above. The lowering of the cover on the piston's down-stroke trapped the water in the hot well, from which it was pumped off (R) as feed water for the boiler. The feed water pump (R) operated through an overhead beam attached by linkages to the crosshead (this system not included in the *Columbus* artifacts). When the vessel was in port, or the crosshead was not moving, feed water reached the boiler by a hand pump (S). An engineer's failure to use it beckoned disaster.

The operation of the steam chests (V1, W1) controlled the entire system. On crosshead steamboats of the 1820s, there were two steam chests, upper and lower, each measuring 34 inches in height and 25 inches in diameter, with walls 1 inch thick. Each performed the same function, except that they were at opposite ends of the piston (D) stroke. On the downward stroke, the upper steam chest (V1) admitted steam from the boiler, while the lower steam chest (W1) exhausted the spent steam from the cylinder (C). The reverse took place on the upward piston stroke. The valves

(V2, W2) moved to uncover the pipes bringing live steam (N) from the boiler or those taking exhaust steam (P) to the condenser (Q1).

The valves (V2, W2) of each steam chest consisted of two discs, 23 inches in diameter. These discs were attached separately to the sliding portions of the valve stem. The valve stem itself consisted of two parts, one moving inside the other. One part was a tube passing from the exterior through the top of the steam chest and attached around the center of the upper disc inside. The other part was a rod passing from the exterior through the tube (and hence through the upper disc) and attached to the lower disc inside. Thus arranged, the disc inside the steam chest could be moved separately, by the two parts of the valve stem protruding from the top. The stem extended above the top of the steam chest sufficiently to allow the discs inside the steam chest to travel the required distance to cover or uncover (as needed by the up-and-down passage of the piston in the cylinder) the entry into the cylinder (C) of live steam or exhaust from the cylinder of spent steam. The operation of the valve system was duplicated in the upper and lower steam chests.

Attached to each segment of the valve stem (tube and rod) at its upper extremity was a lift bar, shaped like a pork chop, measuring 16 inches in horizontal width and 3–6 inches in height. At its narrow point, one lift bar was fastened to the upper end of the rod, the other lift bar to the upper end of the tube. At its widest point, one lift bar was attached to a long vertical lift rod (V3, W3) of indeterminate length going above and below the steam chest; the other lift bar was attached to a second long vertical lift rod paralleling the first. One external lift system controlled the admission of live steam; the other controlled the exhaust of spent steam. This system was duplicated in the upper and lower steam chests, except the functions were reversed for the valve stem segments, discs, and attachments to the appropriate lift rods.

From the external appearance of the *Columbus* artifacts, the discs seemed to constitute a simple dual-disc system. The double-poppet system appearing in the late 1820s, as introduced by Robert L. Stevens as a means of assisting in the opening and closing of valves by steam pressure, does not seem to appear in the *Columbus* artifacts. However, with the discs and valve stems immobilized by concretion in such a position as to prevent detailed inspection, their existence cannot be ruled out.

How the valves on the steam chests were activated is subject to both analysis and conjecture. The vertical lift rods (V3, W3) in the artifacts show evidence of cams or projections that were undoubtedly engaged by a rocker arm with corresponding cams or projections. The oscillating movement of the rocker arm, therefore, would cause the lift rods to activate the valve openings and closings.

Among the *Columbus* artifacts was a 40-inch segment of such a rocker arm—tapered, with distended lengthwise ridges designed to be engaged by a hook emanating from a shaft moved back and forth horizontally—and, most significantly, with two cams, clearly intended to raise or lower the cams attached to the lifting rods. This rocker arm, apparently supported by bearings, could be "rocked" by a hooked, horizontal shaft activated by an eccentric attached to the paddle wheel shaft itself.

Remarkably, the Tredgold drawings and other textual materials of the period are silent on the operation of an eccentric, although Tredgold in his text reported that Boulton and Watt engines of a somewhat earlier time used eccentrics to operate the lift valves.

All later engines, that is, the vertical walking beam engines, used eccentrics to activate the valve system (see Holly, *Steamboat on the Chesapeake*, Chapter 12). Such a system could be expected even on a crosshead engine built in 1828, when Charles Reeder certainly was knowledgeable of the mechanism.

Not apparent at first amidst the concretion enveloping the *Columbus* engine as it rose from the deep, such an eccentric indeed appeared as the concretion was removed. It contributed to an explanation of how the valve system probably operated.

An eccentric resembles a wheel mounted not at the wheel's center but instead near the wheel's periphery. The wheel would, therefore, rotate off center. Riding free on the circumference of the wheel (or eccentric, as it would be called) is a collar or ring with plenty of lubrication and adjusting screws to allow it to slide easily in the track provided by the lip of the eccentric. Attached to the eccentric is a bar (or rod) extending forward toward the rocker arm.

The oscillation of the ring or collar around the off-center eccentric translates a rotary motion into a horizontal push-and-pull. At the site of the rocking bar, the eccentric rod would end in hooks which would engage projections on the rocker arm, causing the latter to semirotate. Attached to the rocker arm are cams engaging other cams on the lift rods (V3, W3) activating the valves of the steam chest (the opposing cams are called "wipers" and "toes" on vertical beam engines).

The eccentric on the *Columbus* crosshead engine is mounted on the paddle wheel shaft (H), itself outboard of the paddle wheel crank between it and the bearing surface, or pillow block (L) at the pedestal. The eccentric, moving in line with the crank, is 2⅞ inches wide (bearing width about 1⅞ inches), with a diameter of 26 inches and a throw of approximately 7 inches, sufficient to cause the eccentric rod (not found in the *Columbus* artifacts) to engage the rocker arm by hooks.

If indeed this explanation can be extrapolated from the eccentric and rocker arm found among the artifacts, then there can be hypothesized an answer to another question: What was the means by which the engine could have been operated by hand? Very simply, the eccentric rod with its hooks could have been lifted from the rocking bar by a lever mechanism, and the rocking bar itself moved back and forth by a hand-operated "starting bar," thus activating the valve system as the engineer desired in starting up the engine, in reversing it, and in getting it up to speed. When the last was achieved, he had only to "drop the hooks" to revert the engine to automatic operation.

This system was employed on all vertical beam engines, where usually two eccentrics controlled the entry and exhaust of steam to and from the steam chests. One eccentric was a "reverse eccentric": instead of being mounted to move in line with the crank, it was mounted with the bulbous part of the eccentric in an opposite position on the shaft from the crank, thus reversing the horizontal movement of the eccentric rod.

A second eccentric does not appear among the *Columbus* artifacts, although such an eccentric, more than likely "reverse," may have been expected if the opposite crank and paddle wheel shaft had been recovered. The actual linkage of the single eccentric and its operation in activating the rocker arm and the lifting rods remain matters of conjecture.

Amid the concretion on the valve stems of the steam chests of *Columbus* was evidence of the attachment of some sort of "timing" device to limit the entry of live steam at some point in the drive of the piston (D). The parts of the device could not be distinguished for sufficient analysis. Nevertheless, the evidence suggests that at some time after 1841, when the Sickels/Stevens "cut-off valve" was invented and gained favor, a shipyard engaged in the routine overhaul of the engine of *Columbus* installed the invention—a fuel-saving and efficient device widely respected for its effectiveness.

Particularly interesting is the wrought iron finial appended to the bottom of the upper steam chest (V1) on *Columbus,* an embellishment for the engineer's pleasure, which Charles Reeder and his craftsmen could not resist.

Description of the Vertical (Walking) Beam Engine

By the mid-1820s, vertical (walking) beam engines had begun to appear on the Chesapeake, even as crosshead engines continued to be built. But the demands for larger engines to propel bigger boats spelled the end of the crosshead engine, since its shaft placed beneath the cylinder precluded the mounting of ever larger cylinders above it or correspondingly larger condensers beneath it.

The vertical beam engine separated the cylinder, piston, and piston rod from the crankshaft and crank, and the whole assembly could gain mammoth proportions by placing its components for maximum effect.

The hallmark of the vertical engine was the vertical beam itself (A), a huge, diamond-shaped structure teetering like a seesaw from the top of a steel A-frame (B) (see diagram). Mounted fore and aft, instead of athwartships like the crosshead, this walking beam, in spite of its size and weight (often over 15 tons), occupied proportionately less usable cargo and passenger space than did the crosshead.

The forward end of the vertical beam (A) carried the piston rod (F) as it forced its way up and down from the movement of the piston (D) in the cylinder (C). The after end of the vertical beam carried the connecting rod or crankshaft (J), which swung around the crank (H) to rotate the paddle wheel shaft (K). This shaft, extending from port side to starboard side of the vessel to paddle wheels on each side, was interrupted only at one point, where the single crank swung about the shaft. On the crosshead engine, the shaft was interrupted twice for the two crankshafts.

Many of the components of the vertical beam engine—the cylinder (C), condenser (Q1), air pump (T1), and the hot well (T3)—functioned as they did in the crosshead engine, with only minor variations in dimensions and sophistication. (For detailed explanations of the vertical beam engine, see Whittier, *Paddle Wheel Steamers and Their Giant Engines;* Holly, *Steamboat on the Chesapeake* [Chapter 12]; and other texts listed in the Bibliography.)

Noteworthy are obvious advances in engineering: the convex shape of the lower surface of the piston (D), designed by resort to the calculus in its explanation of the expansive properties of steam; the use of double-poppet valves to enhance the effective operation of the valves, particularly when the engine was controlled manually; the Sickels/Stevens cutoff in the valve system (V2, W2), designed to stop the continuous entry of steam to the end of a stroke, so that the expansion of steam could be

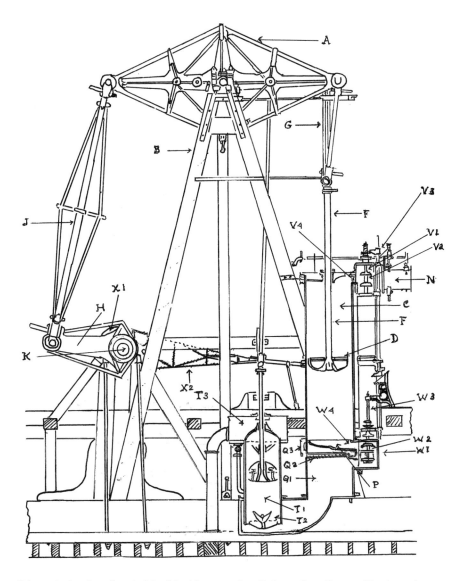

Schematic drawing of vertical (walking) beam engine. Redrawn from Bourne, *Treatise on the Steam Engine,* 1849.

Key

(A) vertical (walking) beam

(B) A-frame

(C) cylinder

(D) piston

(F) piston rod

(G) rails guiding piston rod

(H) crank

(J) crankshaft

(K) starboard paddle wheel shaft

(N) steam intake from boiler

(P) exhaust steam to condenser

(Q1) condenser

(Q2) perforated plate

(Q3) jet intake from Bay water

(T1) air pump

(T2) flapper valves

(T3) hot well

(V1) upper steam chest

(V2) upper valves

(V3) upper lift rod system

(V4) upper entry to cylinder

(W1) lower steam chest

(W2) lower valves

(W3) lower lift rod system

(W4) lower entry to cylinder

(X1) eccentric

(X2) eccentric rod.

utilized without waste; a single steam chest enclosing both upper and lower systems (V1, W1); an eccentric (X1) and eccentric rod (X2) activating "toes" and "wipers" controlling the opening and closing of valves.

The vertical (walking, because the teetering beam seemed to swing from one leg to the other) beam engine, by its rugged bulk and trouble-free operation, propelled the steamers of the Bay for many years. Some lasted for sixty years, often pulled from wrecks to run again. They stood as monuments to the genius of the men like Charles Reeder who built them.

Other Engines

Charles Reeder and his followers, like other engine builders, kept tabs on the developments in marine engineering as they occurred. Compound (two-cylinder)and triple expansion (three-cylinder) engines, not dissimilar in appearance and operation from enormous internal-combustion engines, drove propellers instead of paddle wheels, and fire-tube boilers gave way to water-tube boilers able to develop high pressure, 125 pounds per square inch or even more. These engines, together with steam turbines of a design revolutionary to engineers of the turn of the century, changed the course of marine engineering. But the historical importance of the crosshead engine, the ancestor of steamboat engines in America, remains undeniable and indelible.

Appendix B

SPECIFICATIONS, ENROLLMENT, AND
OTHER DATA ON SELECTED STEAMBOATS

The name of the steamboat is preceded by a letter or letters in parentheses denoting the reason for its inclusion in the appendix: **R** refers to a boat either built totally by Charles Reeder and Sons or whose engine was built by that company; **W** refers to a boat whose engine was built by Watchman or Watchman & Bratt; **P-o** refers to a boat owned by the Pennsylvania Railroad through its various subsidiaries; **P-i** refers to a boat in which the Pennsylvania Railroad had an interest through its investment in a railroad which in turn had substantial interest in the boat or its parent company. In some cases, the name of the steamboat is not preceded by a letter or letters; the boat is mentioned in the text without reference to the items listed above.

The name of the steamboat is followed by three sets of data in parentheses: The first set is the number assigned to the boat on its initial enrollment. Early steamboats were not given numbers. The second set is the date the boat was built. The third set is a sequence of letters describing the boat, with the following abbreviations: **p**, paddle wheel; **s**, screw, therefore propeller-driven; **stbt**, steamboat; **w**, wood hull construction; **i**, iron hull; **s**, steel construction.

The data begin with length, beam, and depth-of-hold figures shown in a series of numbers, separated by a times sign. Thus $154.8 \times 38.2 \times 9.3$ would indicate a length of 154 feet 8 inches, a beam of 38 feet 2 inches, and a depth-of-hold of 9 feet 3 inches. The decimal point usually separates feet and inches. Data from numerous sources, even with documentary materials, is often confusing, even contradictory. Vessels were often lengthened or altered, and data or dates for these changes sometimes went unrecorded. Reporters sometimes arrived at erroneous measurements, but the reader has no way of verifying. Consequently, variations in dimensions are simply listed in sequence in the presentation. There are variations in the way measurements were taken. Hulls of paddle wheel boats, for example, measured on average 25–35 feet in beam. But the main or freight deck reached out another 10–12 feet on either side, to

257

"fair in" the paddle boxes with the sides of the superstructure and provide wide cargo-carrying deck space. Hence the overall beam of a boat 30
feet wide at the hull would be at least 50 feet. In some instances, the exact
measurement is provided and is shown as **oa**, or "overall." Otherwise,
the reader's judgment is required to make the necessary calculation.
Length is similarly necessary to calculate since the main deck extends
beyond the hull at the stern—often by as much as 5 feet. These exten-
sions in both length and beam are referred to in sources as "over the
guards," meaning to the rubbing rail on the edge of the main or freight
deck. Judgment on the part of the reader will prevail in interpreting these
various measurements.

Depth-of-hold is not to be confused with a vessel's draft, which varied
with the load, but instead defined the distance between the floor of the
vessel above its keel and the framing supporting the main or freight deck.

Data on engines are presented in terms of the diameter of the cylinder and the stroke of the piston. Those figures are always in inches. For
a vertical beam engine, the numbers 36×120 would designate a cylinder
36 inches in diameter with a stroke of 120 inches (10 feet). For a compound (two-cylinder) engine used on a propeller-driven boat, the series
$22, 26 \times 42$ would designate an engine whose cylinders measured, respectively, 22 inches and 26 inches, with a 42-inch stroke. For a four-cylinder
triple-expansion engine, the series $24, 36, 40, 47 \times 44$ would indicate an
engine whose cylinders measured, respectively (from high-pressure to
low-pressure), 24 inches, 36 inches, 40 inches, 47 inches, with a 44-inch
stroke.

Boiler dimensions are given in feet. Thus, 18×20 would characterize
a boiler 18 feet high by 20 feet long.

A few place names and railroads are abbreviated in the appendix:
Balto., Baltimore; Phila., Philadelphia; N.Y., New York; N.J., New Jersey;
BC&A, Baltimore, Chesapeake, and Atlantic Railway Company; MD&V,
Maryland, Delaware, and Virginia Railway Company; NYP&N, New York,
Philadelphia, and Norfolk Railroad; B&V, Baltimore and Virginia Steam-
boat Company. Also, USQMD refers to the U.S. Army Quartermaster
Department (Depot), the organization responsible for designating and
chartering steamboats for use by federal forces in the Civil War.

Data came from enrollment or documentation certificates in the National Archives; the files of the Eldredge Collection of the Mariners' Museum (Newport News, Virginia); contemporary newspaper and journal

articles; Emmerson's *Steamboats 1815–1825;* a few secondary sources including Burgess and Wood, *Steamboats Out of Baltimore,* and work by John L. Lochhead concerning vessels out of Norfolk; and *Merchant Vessels of the United States, 1820–1962* and *Merchant Vessels of the United States, 1790–1868,* Lytle-Holdcamper List.

(P-i) *Alabama* (106995) (1893) (s, stbt, s). 293.0 × 54.0 × 16.0, length 305 oa, 40-foot beam at waterline, 43 at main deck, 55 over guards. Triple-expansion engine, 24.5, 40, 47 × 42. Speed 19.5 mph. Built by Md. Steel Co., Sparrows Point, for Balto. Steam Packet Co. (Old Bay Line) for Balto.–Norfolk overnight packet service. 2/6/1908 added 30 new staterooms, overhauled. 1920–21 winter schedule, with *Florida* (Old Bay Line) alternating. Alternate Sundays with Chesapeake Line (tickets of both companies honored). 11/24/1917 on fire off Bodkin Point. 1923 laid up. 4/17/1928 sold to Progress Improvement Co. of Seattle, Wash. Converted to oil-burning by Md. Drydock. 6/16/1928 sold to Edmonds–Victoria Ferry Co. (Capt. J. Howard Payne & Assoc.). Arrived in Seattle via Panama Canal. Began passenger, auto, freight ferry service between Edmonds and Victoria. 5/26/1928 renamed *City of Victoria.* 1943–1945 service as barracks ship for U.S. Navy in Alaska and Aleutians. Scrapped.

(P-o) *Anne Arundel* (201088) (1904) (s, stbt, s). 174.2 (174) × 36.0 × 10.2. Triple-expansion engine, 12.5, 20.5, 36 × 24. Scotch boiler 11.6 sq. Engine reported designed for tug, underpowered for stbt. Accommodated 140 second-class passengers, segregated by sex and race; 39 first-class staterooms, elaborate cabin and dining room decor. Built by Balto. Shipbuilding and Drydock Co., Balto., for Weems Stbt Co. Ran Potomac and Rappahannock rivers. 1/25/1905 sold to MD&V. 4/2/1924 under bankruptcy proceedings to B&V. 9/3/1932 under bankruptcy proceedings to Western Shore Freight Line (Western Shore Stbt Co.). 10/5/1937 sold to Stony Creek Improvement Co. 5/20/1939 name changed to *Mohawk,* modified as excursion boat. 1941 acquired by Tolchester Line; requisitioned by War Shipping Administration, WWII; operated in Hampton Roads. After war, on Boston–Nantasket run. 1948 laid up. 1952 scrapped.

(P-o) *Avalon* (106067) (1888) (p, stbt, i). 190.0 × 30.5 × 8.5; 200.0 × 54.6. Built by Harlan & Hollingsworth, Wilmington, Del. Vertical beam engine, 40 × 120. Launched 2/25/1888, for Md. Stbt Co. 3/19/1890 collided with steamer *Danville* (Capt. James H. Billups) near Seven Foot Knoll; licenses of Capts. Billups and Frank Lambert, pilot of *Avalon*, suspended 5 days. 4/27/1893 ran into Fort Carroll in fog, stem bent ($1,000 in damages). 10/20/1894 sold to BC&A. 12/3/1928 to B&V. 2/9/29 to George W. Brown. 3/9/1936 from U.S. marshall to Balto. Ship Repair Co. and to Acme Amusement Corp. Renamed *Federal Hill*. Abandoned.

(P-o) *B. S. Ford* (3045)(1877)(p, stbt, i). 164.6 × 27.2 × 8.5; 165.0 × 27.0 × 9.0; 164.0 × 29.0 × 9.0. Vertical beam engine, 38 × 108. Boiler, 9.3 × 16.6. Built by Harlan & Hollingsworth, Wilmington, Del., for Chester River Stbt Co. Named for president of Chester River Stbt Co., former member House of Delegates and Senate, Md. One boiler built by Columbian Iron Works, Balto. 5/8/1884 partially destroyed by fire at Chestertown, Md.; rebuilt. (8/20/1884 *Emma Ford* launched; replaced burned *B. S. Ford* on route.) 7/21/1884 from Chester River Stbt Co. to Columbian Iron Works & Drydock Co. as mortgage on repair bills. 4/25/1887 to Chester River Stbt Co. 6/1892 ran to Claiborne in connection with Balto. & Eastern Shore RR. 1894 excursion runs to Chester and Corsica rivers. 1/28/1905 to MD&V; 7/8/1924 to Girard Trust Co., to Manor Real Estate & Trust Co., to BC&A. 12/3/1928 to B&V. 5/22/1929 to Mary E. Mitchell. 1941 converted to barge. Abandoned.

(R) *Baltimore* (3329) (1885) (s, stbt, w). 217.0 × 38.0 × 23.0; 236.0 × 38.0 × 21.2; 252.9 × 35.94 × 22.2. Compound engine by Charles Reeder, 30, 57 × 36. Two Scotch boilers. Built by William E. Woodall, Balto., for York River Line (Balto., Chesapeake & Richmond Steamship Co.). 5/1911 ran between Norfolk and Richmond for Old Dominion Line. 9/1911 sold to Colonial Line with *Danville*. Operated on Long Island Sound, name changed to *Beverly*. Sold overseas and lost in WWI.

(P-o) *Calvert* (127600)(1901)(s, stbt, s). 180.0 × 40.0 × 10.3; 190.0 oa × 38.8 × 12.0. Inclined compound engine, 20, 40 × 28. Scotch boiler, 14.9 × 12.0. Built by Neafie & Levy, Phila., for Weems Stbt Co. A 30-foot stack aft of midships position often cited as awkward. Ran Potomac, Rappahannock, Patuxent rivers. 2/11/1905 sold to MD&V. 7/19/1924 in bankruptcy proceedings, sold to B&V. 10/26/1933 in bankruptcy proceedings sold to Thames River Line, N.Y. 4/12/1934 to Sound

Steamship Lines, N.Y. Modified to oil-burning, then to diesel. 1940 on N.Y.C.–Bridgeport run. 7/8/1942 laid up. 10/7/1942 requisitioned by navy for service in N.Y. Harbor. New commanding officer committed suicide on board. 1947 laid up. 7/16/1957 broken up.

Cambridge (no number) (1846) (p, stbt, w). 210.0 × 25.0 × 8.0. Vertical beam engine, 36 × 120. One boiler. Built for Choptank route of Md. Stbt Co. Later service on the Chester River and to Annapolis, Easton, Cambridge, and Denton. 1850 bought by Rappahannock interests for service on that river. 9/16/1853 burned in Carter's Creek, Va.; engine salvaged and brought to Balto. in schooner towed by *Mary Washington*. Total loss, $25,000.

(P-o) *Cambridge* (126668) (1890) (s, stbt, composite). 184.0 (175.0 oa) × 34.0 × 9.0; 165.3 × 37.5 × 10.1. Compound engine, 20, 40 × 26 built by James Clark & Co. Built by William E. Woodall for Choptank Stbt Co. Speed rated at 18 mph. Crew 31. 10/20/1894 sold to BC&A. Rated as one of the fastest boats of her class, a record 3 hours from Lazaretto Lighthouse (Balto.) to Sharp's Island. Ferry line between Balto. and Claiborne. 1899 went to N.Y. for Dewey celebration. 12/3/1928 sold to B&V. 11/21/1929 to William M. Mills Bros., N.Y. 1937 dismantled at South Amboy, N.J. 11/1/1941 hulk abandoned.

(P-o) *Cape Charles* (126278) (1885) (p, stbt, i). 252.5 × 26.1 × 14.0; 259.6 × 63.6 oa × 14.0; Vertical beam engine, 54 × 132. Built by Harlan & Hollingsworth, Wilmington, Del., for NYP&N to carry passengers and freight between Cape Charles and Norfolk. Had electric lights, first on Bay, and steam steering engine. Bow constructed with two railroad tracks to carry a pullman and one other car, to be delivered to Seaboard Air Line RR terminal. Proved unmaneuverable in Cape Charles Harbor, expensive to operate. 4/1887 generally replaced on Cape Charles–Norfolk route by *Samual M. Felton* and *Old Point Comfort*. Chartered to Central RR of N.J. for run to Sandy Hook. 1/17/1889 purchased by New England Terminal Co. 8/1891 at Harlan & Hollingsworth for change of saloon design and new work on railroad tracks. Scheduled to run between Oyster Bay, Long Island, and Wilson's Point. (South Norwalk). Color changed to terra-cotta. 1899 bought by Gulf & S.I. RR, Shieldsboro, Miss. Converted into dredge. 6/30/1918 abandoned.

(P-o) *Caroline* (136822) (1900) (twin s, stbt, s). 114.6 × 21.0 × 6.0 Built in Milford, Del., as *Emma Reis* for Milford & Phila. Transportation Co. service between Lewes, Del., and Cape May, N.J. 4/1903 sold to Weems Stbt Co. ($17,905); renamed *Caroline*, for service on Rappahannock. 5/15/1903 collided with *Tourist* of People's Line at Port Royal, Va., slight damage. 1/28/1903 sold to MD&V. 6/23/1911 sold to Dover & Phila. Navigation Co., Del.; name changed to *City of Dover*. 6/23/1917 dismantled.

(R) *Chesapeake* (no number) (1813) (p, stbt, w). 130.0 × 22.0 oa × 7.0 (7.5). Crosshead engine, 4.5 stroke. Built by William Flanigan for William McDonald & Son, Balto., for Union Line route Balto. to Phila. 1820 abandoned.

Chesapeake (no number) (1854) (p, stbt, w). Built in Balto. for runs between Washington and Norfolk ($5 one way, $7 round trip). 1854 abandoned.

(P-o) (R) *Chesapeake* (126247) (1884) (s, stbt, w). 140.0 × 25.0 × 8.0; 132.8 × 24.1 × 8.0. Compound engine, 26, 26 × 26. Built by R. W. Waite & Co., Balto., for Wheeler Stbt Co. service on Choptank. 4/7/1901 to BC&A. 5/1/1916 to Charles A. Jording for $5,000 and thence to Bethlehem Steel Co. 9/13/1916 used as barracks there during WWI, then abandoned.

(P-o) (R) *Choptank* (126161) (1883) (s, stbt, w). 136.0 × 25.0 × 8.5. Compound engine, 26, 26 × 26 by J. Clark & Co. Rebuilt by Reeder. Built by William E. Woodall, Balto., for Choptank Stbt. Co. First stbt built for that company. 10/20/1894 to BC&A. 1/8/1924 to Charles A. Jording. 2/10/1927 dismantled.

(P-o) *Chowan* (125363) (1874) (p, stbt, i). 150.0 × 28.0 × 8.9. Vertical beam engine, 36 × 96, from *Ella* (originally built by Henry Esler Co., 1859). Built by Harlan & Hollingsworth, Wilmington, Del., for Albemarle Steam Navigation Co. route from Norfolk to points on the sound. 5/9/1889 to Nanticoke Stbt Co. for $25,000. 6/6/1889 in heavy weather in gale, smokestack rolled overboard, decks swept clean, disabled, drifting, was towed by York River steamer *Baltimore* to Balto. 3/21/1892 to Md. Stbt Co. for $13,500. 1892 first steamer to enter Nanticoke River for Watipqua Creek wharf of Md. Stbt Co. 2/19/1893, with Capt. James Corkrin in command, collided with sloop *Mary* during snowstorm. 10/20/1894 to BC&A. 1899 rebuilt, renamed *Nanticoke*. Elaborate interior furnishings. 1903 resold to Albemarle Steam Navigation Co. 1909 sold to Venezuela.

City of Annapolis (see *City of Richmond*).

(P-i) *City of Richmond* (211710) (1913) (s, stbt, s). 261.6 × 53.0 × 14.0. Four-cylinder triple-expansion engine, 23, 38, 45, 45 × 36. Built by Md. Steel Co., Sparrows Point, for Chesapeake Steamship Co. Sister ship of *City of Annapolis.* 6/19/1915 sank at pier at West Point, Va., and raised. 10/25/1915 sank schooner *James H. Hargrove* in collision off Point No Point in fog. 2/24/1927 sank *City of Annapolis* in collision in fog off mouth of Potomac River. One passenger in path of prow killed. Bow badly damaged. 11/27/1936 collided with S.S. *Evelyn* in Balto. Harbor. Slight damage. 6/10/1941 acquired by Balto. Steam Packet Co. (Old Bay Line) in merger of two companies. Installed radar, first radar-equipped inland waterways vessel. 1941–43 in service on Balto.–Norfolk run with *City of Norfolk.* 1962 sold to B. B. Willis. 10/5/1964 sank off Georgetown, S.C., while being towed to the Virgin Islands for use as a restaurant hotel. Lost.

Columbia (4466) (1828–29) (p, stbt, w). 116.1 × 30.4 × 10.6; 160.0 × 29.0 × 9.0. Vertical beam engine, 40 × 108. One boiler. Built by Andrew Flanigan, Balto., for Balto. & Potomac Steam Packet Co. Plied between Washington, D.C., Alexandria, Va., and Potomac landings for 47 years. Also ran between Balto. and Washington, D.C. 12/7/1878 stranded. Lost.

(R) *Columbus* (no number) (1828) (p, stbt, w). 138.0 × 30.10 × 10.9; 174.0 × 30.1 × 10.9. Crosshead engine by Charles Reeder, 50 × 78; speed 10 mph. Square stern. Man figurehead. One deck, one mast. Built by George Gardiner and James Beacham, Balto., for Md. & Va. Stbt Co. Ran Balto. to Norfolk. 1829 ran aground in James River, floated. 1840 ran between Balto. and Lumpkin's Landing, Mathews County, Va. 3/20/1841 owned by John S. McKim, president of Powhatan Stbt Co. 1/15/1848 went ashore near Magothy River; was assisted by *Thomas Jefferson* and *Planter* (Capt. Weems). 11/27/1850 burned and sank off Point Lookout, mouth of Potomac; loss of 9 lives.

(R) *Constitution* (no number) (1823) (p, stbt, w). Crosshead engine by Charles Reeder. Built in Balto. for Union Line. 1824 came to rescue of

Eagle when boiler exploded, taking crew and passengers aboard. 1830 abandoned.

(P-o) *Corsica* (126023) (1882) (s, stbt, i). 140.0 × 26.0 × 8.6; 145.5 × 6.2 × 7.5. Single-cylinder engine, 26 × 24. Built by Harlan & Hollingsworth, Wilmington, Del., for Chester River Stbt Co. as freighter; altered to carry passengers. 1/28/1905 to MD&V. 5/3/1923 in foreclosure to Girard Trust Co. to Charles Cornard to J. W. Harrison for $12,500. 11/18/1926 U.S. marshall to Ernest E. Fuchs for $1,000. Laid up in Thames River Line pier 30, East River, N.Y. 11/1937 removed and sold for scrap to Federal Iron and Metal Co. of Newark, N.J.

(P-i) (R) *Danville* (157088) (1882) (s, stbt, w.). 210.0 (228.0 oa) × 38.0 × 12.9. Compound engine, 30, 50 × 36 by Charles Reeder & Sons. Two Scotch boilers 7 × 12. Speed 17 mph. Cost $150,000. Handsome saloons and passenger accommodations. Built by William E. Woodall, Balto., for Balto., Chesapeake, and Richmond Stbt Co. (York River Line) for runs between Balto. and West Point, Va. 3/19/1889 collided with *Avalon* near Seven Foot Knoll (damage slight). 5/23/1889 collided with *Samuel J. Pentz* ($200 in damage). 5/25/1898 took First Md. Regiment to Fort Monroe for embarkation for Cuba. 6/1909 chartered to Old Dominion Line while *Berkeley* and *Brandon* were laid up. 9/1911 to William James and to Colonial Navigation Co. 9/12/1911 renamed *Brockton*. 1923 laid up, abandoned.

(R) *Delaware* (no number) (1812–13) (p, stbt, w). 137.0 × 21.0 × 8.0; 130.0 × 20.0 × 7.0. Built by J. & F. Brice, Kensington, Pa. (launched 1813) for Phila.–New Castle, Del., route of Union Line. Ran in concert with *Chesapeake* (Balto.–Elk River route). 1843 abandoned.

(P-i) *District of Columbia* (224391) (1925) (s, stbt, s). 297.8 × 51.0 × 16.3. Four-cylinder triple-expansion engine, 23.5, 37, 43 × 47. Speed 18 mph. Built by Pusey & Jones, Wilmington, Del., for Norfolk and Washington Stbt Co. Sailed alternate nights with *Northland* and *Southland.* 1932 collided with freighter *Yamachichi* at Old Point Comfort, upper works severely damaged. 4/26/1937 in storm after leaving Old Pt. Comfort (65-mph winds, 30-foot waves at broadside), wrecked dining room interior—Vice President Garner aboard. 9/2/1945 *Northland* and *Southland* in government service under War Shipping Administration, *District of Columbia* alone on Washington–Norfolk route. 137 staterooms, 391 berths; in peak season, accommodated an additional 116 first-class and 128 second-class passengers. 1946 resumed service on Washington–Hampton Roads Line. 1948 collided in fog with tanker *Georgia* at Old Point Comfort; female passenger killed in stateroom. Severe damage. Company decided to go out of business. 5/5/1949 sold to Balto. Steam Packet Co. (Old Bay Line) for $287,468. 1961 became spare boat on Balto.–Norfolk run. 4/1962 Old Bay Line terminated service. Steamer sold to B. B. Willis. Operated as *Provincetown* between Boston and Provincetown.

(P-o) *Dorchester* (210650) (1912) (p, stbt, s). 200.0 × 59.0 oa × 10.2; 192.0 × 36.2 × 10.2. Inclined engine, 30, 30 × 96. Speed 15 mph. Feathering, small-diameter paddle wheel. Twin sister of *Talbot*. Built by Md. Steel Co., Sparrows Point for BC&A to replace *Avalon* and *Joppa* on Choptank River route. Later on Potomac route. 6/5/1915 en route from Cambridge to Balto. rammed by fishing steamer *J. R. Palmer* off Annapolis; beached south of Magothy River. 12/8/1928 sold to B&V. 6/3/1932 to American Contract & Trust Co. and 1/14/36 to Fabian P. Noel of Washington, D.C. Renamed *Robert E. Lee* as excursion boat. 1953 scrapped at Bordentown, N.J.

Dreamland (110352) (1878) (p, stbt, i) 272.9 × 37.0 × 10.8; 284.0 × 66.0. Vertical beam engine, 66 × 144. Built by Harlan & Hollingsworth, Wilmington, Del., as *Republic* for excursions between Phila. and Cape May, N.J. Speed 105 miles in 4 hours, 55 minutes. Owned by Dreamland Excursion Co. of N.Y., name changed to *Dreamland*. 1905 ran to Coney Island from West 129th St., N.Y.C. 7/17/1905 collided with ferry *Lackawanna*, both boats damaged. 1907–08, laid up in Bay Ridge Yacht Basin, N.Y. 9/3/1908 sold to Phila. broker to run between Balto. and Love Point by Queenstown & Love Point Transportation Co. in opposition to BC&A. 1909 ran excursions from Balto. to Chesapeake Beach during summer peak. 12/9/1912 sold to John C. Bosley for $30,000. 12/25/1912 prepared for after-season excursion runs between Balto. and Chesapeake Beach. 5/27/1926 John C. Bosley, to Charles A. Jording. 1929 broken up.

(P-o) *Eastern Shore* (135612) (1883) (p, stbt, i). 176.0 × 36.0 × 10.3 (9.5). Vertical beam engine, 36 × 108. Built by Harlan & Hollingsworth, Wilmington, Del., for Eastern Shore Stbt Co. Considered representative of type of steamers on Chesapeake, with many sleeping accommodations and great freight-carrying capacity. 10/20/1894 to BC&A. 12/3/1928 to B&V. 6/3/1932 to New Castle Terminal Co. 10/30-2/4/1937 to American Contract & Trust Co., to Balto.–Trenton Line to New Castle Terminal Co. 1937 changed to diesel screw and freight only. 1948 renamed *Victor Lynn,* one of several vessels by that name. 4/26/1949 burned at Goodwin Inland Boat Industry Dock, Great Bridge, Va.

(P-o) (R) *Easton* (136568) (1896) (s, stbt, i). 154.0 × 30.0 × 9.7. Compound engine, 20, 38 × 28. Built for Wheeler Transportation Co. by Charles Reeder for Choptank and Tred Avon rivers. Launched 5/28/1896. 1901 Wheeler Transportation Co. to BC&A. 5/9/1901 BC&A to H. E. Williams Transportation, South Haven, Mich. ($60,000) for traffic on Lake Michigan. Transferred by ocean, St. Lawrence, and Great Lakes. Dry-docked in Milwaukee; equipped with a new sheriff wheel; galley amidships moved below decks aft; bridge installed side-to-side. Daily trips between Milwaukee, St. Joseph, and Benton Harbor on Lake Michigan. 2/1912 arrived at Duluth Harbor at head of Lake Superior after 200-mile trip from Port Arthur (weather 20–30 degrees below zero; vessel heavily coated with ice and had to break through 6-inch ice for 10 miles). 7/25/1917 to Booth Fisheries and to James W. Elwell & Co. Sold overseas to French interests; name changed to *Apache.*

(P-o) *Elisha Lee* (10971) (1892) (twin s, stbt, i). 300.0 (316.0 oa) × 46.0 (62.0 oa) × 18.6, draft 10.6. Triple-expansion engine, 24, 58, 60 × 30. Four Scotch steel boilers 13 × 12. Speed 20 mph, maximum 23.5 mph. Built as *Richard Peck* by Harlan & Hollingsworth, Wilmington, Del., for the New Haven Stbt Co. for runs between N.Y. and New Haven, Conn. Ran excursions on Long Island Sound. Ornate, elegant interior furnishings. 1/12/1893 sank tug *Charles Allen* in East River. 1/16/1896 struck obstruction in Long Island Sound (5 plates damaged). 6/15/1899 collided with *C. H. Northram* off Norwalk in fog, damaged, dry-docked. 1/1/1941 converted by Tietjen & Lang Drydock to floating barracks to accommodate 1,000 workers where U.S. naval base was being constructed near Bottsville, Newfoundland. 5/20/1943 returned by navy to War Shipping Administration; leased to NYP&N. Renamed *Elisha Lee* after former NYP&N superintendent and general manager.

3/17/1944 began runs from Cape Charles to Norfolk; 2/28/1953 ceased this service. 1954 scrapped.

(P-o) *Emma A. Ford* (135806)(1884)(p, stbt, i). 180.0 × 30.0 × 9.0. Vertical beam engine, 40 × 120. Built by Harlan & Hollingsworth, Wilmington, Del. Named for wife of president of Chester River Stbt Co., for which boat was built. 1892 lengthened by Harlan & Hollingsworth. 1/28/1905 to MD&V. Rebuilt into excursion steamer for service between Balto., Love Point, and Queenstown. 5/9/1906 renamed *Love Point.* 1909 burned at Love Point total loss.

Endeavor (136531)(1896)(twin s, stbt, s). 156.0 × 23.2 × 7.4. Compound engine, 14 × 16. Built by Amos Hillman & Co., Phila., for Denny Bros., Phila. and Seaford, Del., route. 5/14/1898 to Thomas E. Killen, Camden, N.Y. 8/1900 on Lewes, Del., to Cape May, N.J., route. 1904 to Queen Anne Ferry and Equipment Co. 3/1905 to Norfolk & Atlantic Terminal Co. 1915 to Newport News & Old Point Railway & Electric Co., Newport News, Va. 12/20/1916 to Ore Steamship Co., N.Y. 5/1917 to Broadway Ferries Co. Abandoned.

(P-o) *Enoch Pratt* (135371)(1878)(p, stbt, i) 155.0 × 30.0 (48.0 oa) × 8.3; 155.4 × 28.3 × 7.8. Built by Columbian Iron Works (Malster & Reaney) for Md. Stbt Co. to help *Kent* on Great Wicomico and Piankatank routes. *Avalon* built to assist *Enoch Pratt,* which was placed on Choptank with *Ida. Enoch Pratt* took *Kent*'s place on Salisbury route, *Joppa* having been built. 7/19/1879 license of Capt. Edward T. Leonard of *Enoch Pratt* revoked after collision with *Georgiana* off Cambridge in Choptank River. 1892 sank pungy *Ella Lawson* (damage to steamer $200). 10/20/1894 sold by Md. Stbt Co. to BC&A. 7/26/1896 chartered by Old Bay Line to replace *Virginia* sunk in James River. Proved too slow for run. 5/1/1916 BC&A to Charles A. Jording. Dismantled.

(P-o) *Essex* (135855)(1885)(s, stbt, w). 146.8 oa × 27.5 × 9.2; 141.5 × 28.0 × 12.2; 156.0 × 28.0 x × 7.0. Compound engine by James Clark & Co. Accommodated 50 first-class passengers. Built by William Skinner, Balto., for $40,000 for Weems line. 9/1/1887 burned in Balto. ($15,000 in damages); rebuilt. Ran Rappahannock and to Norfolk. 1/28/1905 sold to MD&V. 5/2/1911 partially burned. Rebuilt as fishing boat at

Marine Railway, Machine & Boilers Works, Balto. 5/18/1912 to Indian Creek Fertilizer Co. Sold to N.Y. interests. 9/6/1916 to Northern Transportation Co., Boston; converted into tug. 6/3/1923 grounded at Beach Haven, N.J., total loss.

Express (7063) (1841) (p, stbt, w). 151.9 × 23.0 × 8.3; 172.0 × 23.0 × 8.3; 178.0 × 22.0 × 8.3; 201.0 × 23.7 × 8.3. Crosshead engine, 32 × 120. Built by Lawrence & Sneeden, N.Y., for S. A. Stone of New Haven and W. W. Coit of Norwich, Conn. 1843–46 ran N.Y.C. to Albany on Schuyler Line (to 8/1846) as opposition to N.Y. & Albany Night Line. 6/4/1845 collided with *Empire of Troy* off Barren Island. 1847 Boston to Plymouth. 1/18/1848 arrived at Phila. with bark *Elk* from Boston. 4/1848 lengthened 25 feet by Simpson & Neal, Phila. Carried a horse and rider as wheelhouse ornaments. 8/27/1851 cleared N.Y. for Balto. 6/7/1854 to Alvin J. Cullin and associates of Phila., then purchased by Anthony Reybold from Daniel Drew; was cut in two, lengthened, and rebuilt. 1860 operated by Patuxent Steam Express Co. as opposition to Weems line on Patuxent River; burned and repaired in Balto. 5/31/1861 rebuilt by William Skinner, Balto. 7/19/1861 chartered by USQMD at $175 per day. 2/21/1862 used in prisoner exchange. 1/6/1865 sold by Anthony Reybold to George F. and Asa Needham, Potomac Transportation Line, Balto. 3/18/1865 sunk off Hilton Head by ice, badly damaged above main deck; raised, repaired in Balto. 10/22–23/1878 lost in storm en route from Balto. to Washington. Out of crew of 22 plus 9 passengers, 18 lives lost.

(W) *Fredericksburg* (no number) (1827) (p, stbt, w). Built in Portsmouth, Va.; engine by Watchman & Bratt for Joseph Porter for runs between Washington, D.C., and Potomac Creek. 1845 bought by Balto. & Rappahannock Steam Packet Co. 12/29/1845 sank at Fredericksburg, Va., abandoned.

General McDonald (no number) (1851) (p, steam towboat, w). 222.0 × 29.5 × 9.5. Built in Balto. for service on Chesapeake, but sold to N.Y. as a towboat on Hudson. 12/18/1860 made way to Albany through heavy ice. 9/1/1862 carried 106th Regiment N.Y. volunteers from Albany to N.Y.C. on barges in tow; regiment en route to Washington, D.C. 8/8/1876 owned by Albany & Canal Tow Boat Co. Later broken up.

(R) *George Weems* (10040) (1858) (p, stbt, w). 177.5 × 30.7 (53.0 oa) × 8.6. Vertical beam engine by Charles Reeder, 40 × 120. Built for Weems line. Operated on Patuxent. Excursions to Fair Haven. 8/14/1862 to 3/31/1865 chartered by USQMD ($87.50 to $200 per day). 6/20/1868 burned partially, rebuilt. 6/10/1871 burned at wharf in Balto. ($45,000 in damages). Engine removed and placed in *Theodore Weems.* Scrapped.

(P-o) *Gratitude* (85607) (1880) (s, stbt, i). 124.7 × 20.5 × 7.0; 133.8 × 20.0 × 7.0. Built at Phila. to serve in passenger trade between Phila. and Tacony. Name changed to *Captain Miller.* Burned, rebuilt, renamed *Gratitude.* 7/2/1887 to Centreville and Corsica River Stbt Co. 6/1890 to Chester River Stbt Co. Ran from Balto. to Rock Hall and Centreville. (Town of Gratitude near Rock Hall named for her.) 1897 chartered to Queen Anne's Ferry and Equipment Co. 1/1905 sold to MD&V, service from Balto. to Rock Hall. 1914 sold to H. E. Bennett, Norfolk, Va. Advertised as running excursions from Suffolk to Jamestown, Va., for white people only. 1924 severely damaged in collision with sunken barge in Norfolk Harbor. Sank; 200 passengers, including excursionists of Texas Oil Co., rescued. 6/30/1926 sold to Mateo Garcia of Havana, Cuba. Renamed *Cuba.*

(P-o) *Helen* (95094) (1871) (p, stbt, i). 150.0 × 26.0 × 7.3. Vertical beam engine, 30 × 72. built by Harlan & Hollingsworth, Wilmington, Del., for Eastern Shore Stbt Co. 1/1/1891 offered for sale by Eastern Shore Stbt Co. 10/20/1894 to BC&A. 5/1/1916 BC&A to Charles A. Jording. 7/29/1918 to George D. Wever and associates. 1937 converted to diesel and tanker, owner Petroleum Storage Corp. of N.Y. 1/1/1941 abandoned.

(R) *Hugh Jenkins* (14013) (1849) (p, stbt, w). 165. 0 × 26.4 × 7.8. Built by Meade & Horner, Balto., for owners Hugh Jenkins, John D. Turner, William McCann, all of Balto. for Eastern Shore Stbt Co. Ran to Annapolis, Choptank, and Chester rivers. Ran Talbot County route. 7/3/1861 chartered by USQMD ($100 per day). 9/9/1861 bought by USQMD for $12,000. 3/1/1866 sold at public auction for $4,000; name changed to *Kent Island.* Ran excursions. 1868 available for charters. 1877 abandoned.

(P-o) *Ida* (100281) (1881) (p, stbt, i). 150.0 × 31.0 (50.0 oa) × 10.0; 190.0 × 30.5 × 8.5; 200.0 × 54.6 × 9.8. Vertical beam engine, 40 × 120.

Feathering paddle wheels. Built by Harlan & Hollingsworth, Wilmington, Del., for Md. Stbt Co. 9/20/1881 rammed by *Georgeana* between Oxford and Easton (slight damage). 9/7/1889 collided with scow near Seven Foot Knoll (slight damage). 2/18/1894 burned at James Clark & Co. while undergoing repairs; repaired. 10/20/1894 to BC&A. Ran between Balto. and Choptank River landings 7/1904 sold to N.Y. & Saugerties Line. 9/2/1911 rammed off New Hamburg, N.Y., by *William F. Romer* (ex-*Mason L. Weems* of Weems line) (slight damage). 4/1937 abandoned.

(P-o) *Joppa* (76516) (1885) (p, stbt, i). 190.0 × 31.0 × 9.0; 200.0 × 54.0. Vertical beam engine, 40 × 120. One boiler, 11.2 × 18. Built by Harlan & Hollingsworth, Wilmington, Del. (for $60,000), for Md. Stbt Co. 10/20/1894 sold to BC&A. 12/3/1928 to B&V. 11/26/1929 to Charles A. Jording for $1,500, 2/27/1930 to Julius M. D. Williams, 7/3/1930 to William Fuchs, 12/19/1934 to W. Carroll Redman and A. Wooten. 5/3/1935 renamed *City of Salisbury;* converted by Salisbury Yacht Building Co. to diesel freighter. Abandoned.

(R) *Juniata* (12561) (1848) (p, stbt, w). 136.4 × 25.6 × 7.8. Built by John S. Brown Co., Balto., for Susquehanna Steam Towboat Co. Towing service with *Lancaster* between Balto. and Susquehanna River. Advertised for charter excursions. Ran passenger service in 1850s from Balto. to Susquehanna River. 2/26/1862 chartered to USQMD. 4/13/1880 to Jacob Tome and associates. 7/30/1881 to W. B. Hoyt; refitted in N.Y. Reportedly sold to a railroad in South. 1888 lost (no details).

(P-o) *Kent* (14012) (1854) (p, stbt, w). 155.7 × 24.8 × 7.6; 160.0 × 40.0. Vertical beam engine, 33 × 108. Built by John S. Brown, launched 3/25/1854, for Capt. Edward Sturgeon, owner, to replace *Osiris* of Eastern Shore line. Chartered by USQMD 7/1861 to 9/6/1861 for $200 per day and 2/26/1862 to 9/12/1862 for $125–160 per day. 9/6/1865 sunk by *George Appold,* raised, taken to Balto., repaired. 9/6/1874 sunk by pole going up through bottom, raised, repaired in Balto. 10/8/1897 U.S. marshall for Md. Stbt Co. to BC&A. 1906 abandoned in Balto.

Kentucky (no number) (1832–33) (p, stbt, w). 209.0 × 24.0 × 13.0 Built in Balto. for People's Steam Navigation Co. 1835 sold to Md. & Va. Stbt

Co. Ran from Balto. to Norfolk in 13 hours, reported to be the fastest boat on Bay at time. 1840 abandoned.

Lancaster (14538) (1848) (p, stbt, w). 138.0 × 27.9 × 7.2. Built in Balto. for Balto. & Susquehanna Steam Co. for service from Balto. to Port Deposit. 1860 ran Wye River and St. Michaels route. 2/27/1888 to N. B. Woolford & Co. 2/1/1893 sold to A. Y. Dolfield & M. J. Ash. Rebuilt as barge. 1894 abandoned.

(P-o) *Lancaster* (141217) (1892) (p, stbt, s). 205.4 × 56.1 oa × 10.7; 213.0 × 57.0 × 10.7; 205.4 × 32 × 12.0. Vertical beam engine, 48 × 132. Two Scotch boilers 10.9 × 15.6. Built by Md. Steel Co., Sparrows Point for Weems line. Accommodated 80 first-class and 97 second-class passengers. Elaborately decorated public rooms. Ran Patuxent, Potomac, and Rappahannock routes. 2/1/1905 sold to MD&V. Used as spare boat and freight only. 9/10/1924 sold in bankruptcy to N.Y., Albany & Western Steamship Co., ran to Albany and Troy. 11/4/1925 in bankruptcy proceedings to E. B. Leaf & Co. for $50,000. 1926 laid up. 1927 dismantled; hull used as dock at Hastings-on-Hudson.

(R) *Louisiana* (14509) (1854) (p, stbt, w). 275.0 × 35.0 × 12.4. Vertical beam engine by Charles Reeder, 60 × 132. Built by Cooper & Butler, Balto., for Balto. Steam Packet Co. (Old Bay Line). 1/8/1862 chartered by USQMD ($800 per day), 12/8/1862 to 12/12/1862 ($600 per day), 2/7/1863 to 2/19/1863 ($600 per day), 6/29/1863 to 7/11/1863 ($350 per day). 1/29/1862 grounded in operations with Burnside expedition. 1871 rebuilt by William Skinner & Son, Balto. (cost $50,000). 11/14/1874 rammed and sunk by *Falcon* (Balto.–Charleston run). No lives lost.

(P-o) *Maggie* (90013) (1868) (p, stbt, i). 164.0 × 38.0 × 8.5; 140.0 × 25.0 × 8.6. Vertical beam engine, 32 × 72. Built by Harlan & Hollingsworth, Wilmington, Del., for Eastern Shore Stbt Co. 10/20/1894 sold to BC&A. 2/1/1913 dismantled.

(W) *Maryland* (no number) (1818–19) (p, stbt, w). 137.0 × 26.0 × 5.0; 145.6 × 26.0 × 9.6; 130.0 × 25.0 × 36.5. Crosshead engine, 40 × 56. Built for service on Choptank River to Queenstown, Corsica, and Chester rivers.

1821–24 ran to Annapolis. 1833 ran to West River. 1834 owners became Md. Stbt Co. Ran to Wye River and St. Michaels. 1845 excursion to Worton Creek, Kent County. 1850 operated to Fredericksburg on Rappahannock. 1858 to Potomac Stbt Co. and to Mary Ann Colwin 9/4/1858. 3/8/1862 chartered to USQMD ($200 per day), 8/8/1862 ($160 per day), 10/12/1865 to 9/2/1865 ($140 per day). Abandoned.

(P-o) *Maryland* (93287) (1902) (p, stbt, i). 180.0 × 34.0 × 10.1. Vertical beam engine, 31 × 108. Two boilers. Built by Harlan & Hollingsworth, Wilmington, Del., for BC&A. 1/22/1915 burned to water's edge off Magothy River. 2/19/1915 hulk sold to Arthur L. Spanier and to Md. Transportation Co. 9/1916 Spedden Co. refinished hull, was raised 6 feet, converted into a coasting tow-barge schooner rigged with two pole masts, for Northern Transportation Co. of Balto. from Md. Transportation Co.

(W) *Mary Washington* (16104) (1846) (p, stbt, w). 165.0 × 26.0 × 10.4; 194.0 × 26.3 × 10.35. Built by John A. Robb and associates for Balto. & Rappahannock Steam Packet Co. Vertical beam engine by Watchman. 2/31/1847 sold at auction in bankruptcy proceedings for $26,000 to Md. & Va. Stbt Co. (owners virtually same as previous bankrupt owners). Ran Rappahannock River. 12/22/1854 sold to Weems line. Operated Balto., Fredericksburg, and Rappahannock landings and Patuxent landings. 1/8/1862 to 4/1/1865 chartered by USQMD, rates from $175 per day dropped to $38.30 per day. 1865 lengthened and altered. 1888 dismantled, abandoned.

(R) *Matilda* (116103) (1864) (p, stbt, w). 220.5 × 30.9 × 10.2; 200.0 × 28.0 × 9.0. Vertical beam engine by Charles Reeder & Sons. Built in Balto. for Weems line, served on Patuxent and Rappahannock. Built during Civil War when Weems wanted to keep some service going after 3 vessels seized by USQMD. But *Matilda* was requisitioned, nevertheless. While under government service, boiler exploded in James River, killing engineer. 5/11/1865 discharged from USQMD. 1865–66 ran Patuxent and Rappahannock. 1866–74 operated on Rappahannock for Balto. & Va. Steamship Co., incorporated 2/21/1866 (Weems and Jacob Tome, principal owners). 5/11/1883 to Wesley Ricketts. Engine removed, placed in *Westmoreland*. 6/25/1883 converted to barge. 2/16/1889 assumed lost.

(W) (R) *Medora* (11936) (1842) (p, stbt, w). 180.1 × 23.6 × 9.6. Vertical beam engine by John Watchman, 42 × 126. Built by Brown & Collyer, Balto., for Baltimore Steam Packet Co. (Old Bay Line). 4/15/1842 boiler exploded on trial trip, sank, 26 dead, 38 injured. Worst disaster in Chesapeake steamboat history. 5/9/1842 raised, rebuilt, engine and new boiler by Charles Reeder. Renamed *Herald.* Served in Civil War. 1866 sold to N.Y. and used as a tug. 9/30/1885 abandoned.

(P-o) *Middlesex* (93331) (1902) (p, stbt, s). 200.0 × 36.0 × 12.3; 207.0 oa × 59.0 oa × 11.5. Inclined compound engine, 24, 53 × 84. Two Scotch boilers, 12.9 x × 10.6. Small paddle wheels faired into superstructure; appearance of screw vessel. Built by Neafie & Levy, Phila., for Weems line. Accommodated 45 male, 48 female second-class passengers, segregated; 41 outside staterooms for first-class. Elaborate decor. Ran on Potomac, Rappahannock, and Patuxent. 1/30/1905 sold to MD&V. 11/29/1910 altered at Newport News Drydock for additional 26 hurricane deck staterooms. 4/24/1924 in bankruptcy proceedings sold to B&V. 2/9/1929 sold to George P. Ellis, Somerville, Mass. Name changed to *Plymouth.* 8/20/1930 to Nantasket Beach Stbt Co. (Boston). 5/28/1936 to Marine Operating Corp. of N.J. 4/9/1937 to Sound Steamship Line; name changed to *Manhattan.* 3/13/1939 burned at Tottenville, N.Y. 7/20/1937 to C.G. Willis, Maxwell Co., Norfolk. 5/23/1941 converted into barge. 6/9/1945 sold to Peru.

(P-o) (R) *Minnie Wheeler* (91342) (1881) (s, stbt, w). 130.0 × 23.6 × 8.0; 124.0 × 24.0 × 7.0; 140.0 × 25.6 × 8.0. Compound engine by Charles Reeder & Sons. Built for $25,000 by R. W. Waite & Co., Balto., for Wheeler Stbt Co. for $25,000. Serviced the Choptank. 4/1/1901 sold to BC&A for $8,000. 5/1/1916 to Charles A. Jording for $5,000. 9/13/1916 to Bethlehem Steel Co., Sparrows Point, Md. 1917 used as barracks at Bethlehem Steel Co., then abandoned.

(P-o) *New York* (130450) (1889) (twin s, stbt, i). 207.5 × 31.1 × 12.4. Triple-expansion engine, 18.5, 27, 42 × 24. Built by Harlan & Hollingsworth, Wilmington, Del., for NYP&N for $125,000. Took place of *Cape Charles* in run between Cape Charles and Norfolk. 10/2/1910 most of superstructure destroyed by fire at dock in Norfolk (loss $75,000). Rebuilt. 4/6/1932 sold to William N. Mills, N.Y. 5/9/1932 burned at West New

Brighton, Staten Island; near total loss. Converted to barge, owner W. F. Foreman, Elizabeth City, N.C. 1941 abandoned.

(R) *Norfolk* (no number) (1817) (p, stbt, w) 132.0 × 25.0 × 7.8. Crosshead engine by Charles Reeder. Ran James River, Norfolk to Richmond, 14.5 mph. Served until 1825. 1828 sold to Md. & Va. Stbt Co. Continued James River route. 1840 abandoned.

(P-o) *Northumberland* (130855) (1899–1900) (s, stbt, s). 190.0 × 39.8 (41.0) × 11.0. Triple-expansion engine, 18, 28, 45 × 30. Two Scotch boilers, 9.6 × 20. Berths for 72 second-class passengers, 43 staterooms for first class. Built by Neafie & Levy, Phila., for Weems line for $127,256.49. Intended for Potomac, ran Balto.–Washington route. 1/28/1905 sold to MD&V. 4/2/1929 in bankruptcy proceedings to Excursion Stbt, Inc., Newark, N.J. Ran excursion around N.Y. 3/5/1934 in bankruptcy proceedings to J. A. Cheatham, Norfolk, for $2,500 to carry freight, Norfolk–Richmond. 5/14/1937 to Buxton Lines, Norfolk. 8/5/1937 name changed to *Norfolk.* 9/30/1945 burned on James River at Clermont. Scrapped.

(P-o) *Old Point Comfort* (155122) (1886) (p, stbt, i) 176.0 × 31.0 × 10.1; 183.0 oa × 54.0 oa. Vertical beam engine, 38 × 108. Built by Harlan & Hollingsworth, Wilmington, Del., for NYP&N, service between Cape Charles and Norfolk. 5/12/1904 replaced burned *Pocahontas* on Norfolk–Richmond run. 8/1905 operated by James River Day Line (Va. Navigation Co.) for service between Norfolk and Richmond. 8/13/1907 to BC&A. 8/22/1920 burned in Balto., hulk on bottom. 10/4/1923 to BC&A to Charles A. Jording. 12/24/1923 hull made into barge, renamed *Richmond Cedar Works #5.*

(W) *Patrick Henry* (no number) (1831–32) (p, stbt, w). 172.0 × 25.9 × 9.0. Engine by Watchman & Bratt, 44 × 126. Copper boiler. Built by G. Gardiner for runs between Richmond and Norfolk. Abandoned 1844.

(W) (R) *Patuxent* (5284) (1826) (p, stbt, w). 122.6 × 24.9 × 7.1; 144.9 × 24.9 × 9.1. Schooner hull without bowsprit or mast. Crosshead engine by Watchman & Bratt. Cabin areas with small cubicles separating men and women (men's area used also for dining). Built by Andrew Flanigan for

George Weems. Owners included Weems, John Watchman, John Bratt, and others. 4/23/1835 major modification. Operated on Patuxent throughout Weems's ownership. 8/1828 to 5/1830 served Rappahannock landings to Fredericksburg. 7/1828 ran to Sassafras River. 8/1833 to 10/1834 ran to Fredericksburg. Also, 8/1830 to 10/1841, served Wicomico River to Salisbury and Whitehaven. 1849–50 ran Patuxent for Green Landing. 1849 received new engine by Charles Reeder, 38 × 96. 4/23/1861 to Calvin Taggart and associates, Phila., and Bridgeton Stbt Co., and 12/7/1861 to W. Whildin. 12/18/1861 to 5/1/1863 chartered by USQMD ($100–175 per day). 7/1/1864 bought by USQMD for $16,000. 10/19/1865 sold to S. & J. Flanigan, Balto., for $3,200. Renamed *Cumberland*. 1868 abandoned.

(R) *Philadelphia* (no number) (1816) (p, stbt, w). 116.8 × 23.4 × 8.6. Built by William Flanigan for William McDonald and Union Line. Ran Balto. to Frenchtown. 1841 abandoned.

(P-o) *Piankatank* (130510) (1890) (twin s, stbt, i). 200.0 × 31.0 × 11.0. Triple-expansion engine, 12, 20, 30 × 20. Built by Harlan & Hollingsworth as *Neuse* for Wilmington (N.C.) Steamship Co. 2/20/1899 to NYP&N, one-half conveyed to Norfolk & Southern RR Co. (4/23/1899). 4/6/1908 bought by BC&A for $52,056.16 from Southern RR Co. 5/1911 widened, renamed *Piankatank*, ran to that river and to Great Wicomico River. 3/29/1928 from BC&A to B&V. 6/1932 to New Castle Terminal Co. (Balto., Crisfield and Onancock Line). 1936 to Atlantic States Line, on run between Phila. and Bundicks, Va. 1937 under repair for damage to stack, under lien for nonpayment, laid up. 11/12/1942 scrapped, abandoned.

(W) *Planter* (19543) (1845) (p, stbt, w). 162.5 × 25.8 × 8.6; 168.0 × 25.0 × 8.0; 161.5 × 25.8 × 8.7; 196.0 × 30.9 × 9.4. Vertical beam engine by Watchman, 36 × 120. Single boiler. Built probably by Flanigan, Balto., as partial replacement for *Patuxent*. Main deck enclosed for freight; cabin, dining areas, staterooms, and saloon on promenade deck. Square pilothouse. In hull, boiler room, galley, berths and benches for second-class passengers. Wood fuel on deck. 1857 ran to Green Landing on Patuxent. 1846–47 on Rappahannock, including excursions. 5/17/1855 collided with Fort Carroll, Patapsco River, sank (damage

$9,000). Raised and repaired. 1850 ran to York, East, and Great Wi-comico rivers; 1861 ran to Washington, D.C. From 1/1862 to 6/12/1865 chartered by USQMD ($66–$175 per day). 1866 ran Patuxent River route. 2/26/1881 sold to junk dealer. 6/1881 broken up.

(R) *Pocahontas* (no number) (1828–29) (p, stbt, w). 160.0 × 28.0 × 8.0; 138.0 × 30.0 × 11.0; 116.6 × 35.5 × 11.0. Crosshead engine by Charles Reeder, 50 × 78; 50 × 84. One boiler. Speed 10 mph. Built by James Beacham and George Gardiner, Balto., for Md. & Va. Stbt Co. Ran from Norfolk to Richmond. 1840 offered at auction by bankruptcy of Md. & Va. Steam Packet Co. 9/24/1840 bought by Balto. Steam Packet Co. (Old Bay Line). Service from Balto. to Petersburg and Richmond. 1845 transferred to affiliate of Old Bay Line, the Powhatan Line, for continued service on James River. Chartered by USQMD 1861–62. 1/31/1862 part of Burnside expedition in bringing horses from Annapolis to Hatteras; rudder chain parted off Hatteras; also patch blew off single boiler; other rudder chain parted; grating under boiler gave way; sail set; horses shoved overboard; boat struck bottom, broke up.

(P-o) *Pocomoke* (150516) (1891) (p, stbt, i). 170.0 × 33.0 × 9.6; 175.0 × 32.0. Vertical beam engine, 32 × 108 (same as *Tangier*). Built after model of *Eastern Shore* by Harlan & Hollingsworth, Wilmington, Del., for Eastern Shore Stbt Co. for Balto. to Snow Hill route. 10/20/1894 sold to BC&A. 8/7/1928 collided with freighter *Nantucket* in fog in Chesapeake Bay, extensive damage to bow. 12/3/1928 to B&V. 5/1937 abandoned as a barge.

(P-o) *Potomac* (150672) (1894) (s, stbt, s). 176.8 (180.0 oa) × 35.8 (41.0 oa) × 11.0. Compound engine, 20, 30 × 26. One Scotch boiler, 11.9 × 11.6. Built by Neafie & Levy, Phila., conditionally for Md. & Va. Stbt Co. (Charles R. Lewis), for service on Potomac, Balto–Washington, D.C. 37 first-class staterooms. 1895 sold by Neafie & Levy to Weems Stbt Co. Ran Patuxent, Potomac, and Rappahannock. 2/1/1905 sold to MD&V. 4/24/1924 in bankruptcy proceedings to B&V. 6/13/1932 sold in bank-ruptcy proceedings to Western Shore Freight Co. (Western Shore Stbt Co.). 3/21/1936 to Chesapeake Corp., Newport News, Va., converted to barge. 10/26/1956 dismantled.

(W) *Powhatan* (no number) (1845) (p, stbt, w). 177.0 × 22.0 × 9.0; 175.0 × 20.0 × 8.0. Vertical beam engine, 44 × 128; 40 × 120. One boiler. Paddle wheel, 26 × 8. Built in Balto. for Washington & Augusta Creek. On Potomac River. 4/22/1861 sold to USQMD, Civil War service. Renamed U.S.S. *King Philip.* Scrapped by navy department.

(P-i) *President Warfield* (227753) (1928) (s, stbt, s). 330.0 × 58.0 × 18.6. Triple-expansion four-cylinder engine, 24.5, 40, 47, 47 × 42. Speed 19.5 mph. Crew 69. Luxurious accommodations, with those for president and commodore of the line. Named for Solomon Davies Warfield, president of Seaboard Air Line RR and Balto. Steam Packet Co. (Old Bay Line). Built by Pusey & Jones, Wilmington, Del., for Balto. Steam Packet Co. for Balto.–Norfolk overnight packet service. 1930 chartered to Eastern Steamship Line, N.Y. to Boston service. 1931 chartered to Colonial Line, Boston. 7/12/1942 requisitioned by War Shipping Administration, transferred under lend-lease to British Ministry of War Transport. 9/20 to 9/30/1942 steamed in convoy RB-1, St. Johns, Newfoundland, to Belfast. Under U-boat attack en route. 10/1942 to 4/24/1944, served as amphibious training vessel at Appledore, Devon. Returned to U.S. Navy as IX-169. 7/7/1944 control ship off Omaha Beach, Normandy invasion. 7/25/1945 returned to Norfolk. 11/14/1945 discharged to James River Reserve Fleet. 11/9/1946 sold to Potomac Shipwrecking Co., Washington, D.C., for $6,255, then to Weston Trading Co., N.Y., for $40,000. Panamanian registry. Refitted in secret in Balto. 12/17/1946 transferred to Honduran registry. Outfitted by American crew. 3/1947 to 4/1947 crossed Atlantic to Mediterranean. Until 9/1947 outfitted at Portovenere, Italy. 6/9/1947 left Port-de-Bouc, entered Sète, France; loaded 4,500 Jewish refugees from European detention centers. 7/10/1947 sailed, joined by H.M.S. *Ajax* and British escort vessels. 7/18/1947 attacked on high seas and boarded; battle ensued. Name changed to *Exodus 1947.* Escorted into Haifa; refugees returned to Germany by three British transports. 8/26/1952 burned in Haifa.

(R) *Queen Anne* (20624) (1899) (p, stbt, i). 203.4 × 52.0 oa × 8.6. Vertical beam engine, 46 × 120. Two boilers. Built by Charles Reeder for Queen Anne Ferry & Equipment Co., then to Balto. & Queenstown-Queen Anne RR Co. 5/1906 chartered by Washington & Potomac

Steamboat Co. (Randall Line of Capt. Ephraim Randall). 9/1906 sold to same line for $55,000. 1911 damaged by fire, sold to Fogg & Harris of Salem, N.J. (Salem Freight Co.), to be used between Salem, New Castle, Penns Grove, and Phila. Ran excursion from Phila. to Riverview Beach on Delaware River (adults 35¢, children 20¢), also moonlight cruises. 2/11/1919 sold to Delaware River Day Line. 3/1/1920 chartered to Trenton Transportation Co. 1925 sold to N.Y. interests. Name changed to *Rockaway*. 1926 laid up at Shady Side, N.Y., abandoned.

Queen Caroline (20637) (1901-1902) (s, stbt, i). 200.0 oa × 31.0 × 15.0. Triple-expansion engine, 16, 25, 42 × 56. Four Scotch boilers. Speed 16 mph. Built by Balto. Shipbuilding & Drydock Co. for Queen Anne Ferry & Equipment Co. for service from Lewes, Del., to Cape May, N.J. 9/1/1904 returned to Balto. for winter ferry service across Bay. 6/8/1905 conveyed to Montauk Stbt Co. for $32,500 for N.Y.–Block Island service. Renamed *Montauk*, later *Transport* and *Ramona*. 1933 to Buxton line for freight service between Norfolk and Richmond. Renamed *Richmond*. 1945 laid up, burned, and abandoned.

(W) *Rappahannock* (no number) (1830) (p, stbt, w). 130.0 × 25.0 × 9.0; 133.0 × 26.2 × 9.4. Vertical beam engine by Watchman & Bratt, 40 × 90. Built by John A. Robb for Balto. & Rappahannock Steam Packet Co. Ran between Balto. and Fredericksburg, Va. 1845 in bad repair in Rappahannock. 1/1847 in bankruptcy of company, auctioned off, sold to interests in Delaware River as towboat. 1858 burned below Phila., scrapped.

(R) *Richmond* (no number) (1813–14) (p, stbt, w). 154.0 × 25.0 × 9.0. Built by Charles Browne of N.Y. for Robert Livingston and Robert Fulton (North River Stbt Co.) for James River route. Engine built by Robert Fulton Works. Remained in N.Y. for runs to Poukeepsie, later Albany, operated by North River Stbt Co. Took place of *North River Steamboat (Clermont)*. N.Y. papers advertised: "The public are informed that the old North River Steam Boat is laid aside, and the staunch new boat called the Richmond, with handsome accommodations, substituted in her stead." 7/4/1818 carried remains of Gen. Richard Montgomery (brought from Quebec to capitol at Albany) to N.Y. for burial in St. Paul's Churchyard, N.Y. 10/30/1821 grounded for 4 hours. 6/24/1824 reduced fare from Albany to N.Y.C. ($5). *Richmond, James Kent,* and *Chancellor Livingston* started rate war, lowering to $4 and finally to $2. Motto for steamer: "slow but sure." Took 4.5 days for round trip. Capt. S. Wiswall, who ran *Clermont* in 1808, bought *Richmond* and operated her as independent between N.Y.C., Newburgh, Poughkeepsie, Catskill, Hudson, and Albany; departed from foot of Cortlandt St., N.Y.C. 1843 abandoned.

St. Nicholas (no number) (1845) (p, stbt, w). 180.8 × 26.6 × 9.0. Vertical beam engine, 40 × 132. Two boilers. Paddle wheels, 29.6 × 8.8. Built by William H. Brown as opposition day boat N.Y.–Albany. 1848 opposition boat N.Y.-Norwalk. 8/25/1848 while racing *Cataline* struck rock, sank at Port Chester, en route to Norwalk. *Cataline* received passengers; casks placed under hull, towed off to N.Y. by *Kosciusko* and *Duncan Pell.* 1849 used as towboat and wrecking boat. 4/24/1856 Thomas Clyde to Merchants & Peoples Transportation Co. 8/14/1857 to Samuel Gay. 7/11/1859 to Md. & Va. Steam Packet Co. 5/22/1860 to Washington–Alexandria–Georgetown Steam Packet Line (AWCT&D Navigation Co.). 6/28/1861 seized by Confederates in Potomac River. Purchased by Confederacy for $18,924.17, renamed C.S.S. *Rappahannock.* 4/1862 burned in evacuation of Fredericksburg to prevent capture by Union forces.

(R) *Sassafras* (116539) (1892) (p, stbt, w) 151.0 × 28.0 × 8.0; 165.0 oa × 45.0 oa × 8.0. Vertical beam engine, 36 × 108. Steel boiler, 12 × 15.5. Built by S. W. Skinner & Sons, Balto. Engine by Charles Reeder for Sassafras River Stbt Co. 11/1/1902 lengthened 25 feet by William E. Woodall. Renamed *Annapolis,* sold to Tolchester line. 10/29/1935 burned, abandoned.

(W) *Susquehanna* (no number) (1826) (stern-wheel, p, stbt, w). 82.0 feet long. Stern-wheel 4.5 feet in diameter. Renamed *Baltimore.* Built in Balto. for Susquehanna River service. Drew 26 inches water, with 100 passengers. Exploded, wrecked on maiden voyage; 4 lives lost.

(R) *Susquehanna* (116827) (1898) (s, stbt, i). 157.7 × 38.0 × 9.0. Compound engine, 20, 38 × 28. One Scotch boiler, 12 × 12.6. Built by Charles Reeder for Tolchester Beach Improvement Co. Ran to Port Deposit and Havre de Grace on Susquehanna River. 1923 sold to New Orleans. 1939 operated by Sound Steamship Co., N.Y. During 1941, 1943, 1947–48 operated by Tolchester Lines, Inc., to Tolchester as *Francis Scott Key.*

(P-o) *Talbot* (210704) (1912) (p, stbt, s). 200.0 × 59.0 oa × 10.2; 192.0 × 36.3 × 10.2. Inclined two-cylinder engine, 30, 30 × 9; small-diameter, feathering paddle wheels. Speed 15 mph. Exact sister ship of *Dorchester*. Built by Md. Steel Co., Sparrows Point for BC&A to replace *Avalon* and *Joppa* on Choptank River route. Later ran on Potomac. 12/3/1928 to B&V. 6/3/1932 to American Contract & Trust Co. 2/29/1936 to N.Y. & Keans-burg Stbt Co. 7/1/1936 name changed to *City of New York* at Perth Amboy, N.J. 11/25/1950 driven ashore in heavy gale at Keyport, N.J., scrapped.

(P-o) *Tangier* (145049) (1874–75) (p, stbt, i). 163.0 × 47.0 × 10.0; 169.9 × 29.0 × 8.8; 153.3 × 29.5 × 8.5. Vertical beam engine, 32 × 108. Paddle wheels, 17 feet diameter, buckets 6.9 feet by 34 inches. Sister ship of *Helen*. Built by Harlan & Hollingsworth, Wilmington, Del., for Eastern Shore Stbt Co. 1/12/1889 lengthened 18 feet by Harlan & Hollingsworth, supplied with electricity. 1892 ran to Claiborne with Balto. & Eastern Shore RR, then other Eastern Shore routes, Balto. to Crisfield. 10/29/1889 collided with schooner *George H. Somers* near Lazaretto (slight damage). 10/20/1894 sold to BC&A. 8/1923 laid up at Woodall, in bad shape. 6/3/1927 to Charles A. Jording and 2/4/1929 to James Henry Townsend. Dismantled, as stbt. 11/2/1929 renamed *Suburban* as gasoline screw boat. Abandoned.

(R) (P-o) *Theodore Weems* (24908) (1872) (p, stbt, w). 196.2 (207.0 oa) × 30.0 (50.0 oa) × 9.45; 192.3 × 30.4 × 9.4. Built by William Skinner & Sons, Balto., for Weems line to replace *George Weems* (engine from latter installed by Charles Reeder). Resembled *George Weems*. Hurricane deck extended from stem to stern. Limited number of staterooms and second-class accommodations. Ran excursions to Fair Haven; 1879 initiated excursions to Bay Ridge. 9/10/1889 burned at Light St. wharf (damage $50,000). Rebuilt and renamed *St. Mary's*. 2/11/1905 sold to MD&V. 12/5/1907 burned off Benedict on Patuxent River. Total loss.

(R) *Thomas Jefferson* (no number) (1827) (p, stbt, w). 112.2 × 27.6 × 9.6. Built by James Beacham, Balto., for Benjamin Ferguson, Balto. Ran between Norfolk and Richmond. 1840 owned by Md. Stbt Co., ran to Annapolis and West River. Also, ran on Choptank to Denton, then Wicomico to

Whitehaven and Salisbury. Sold to N.Y., name changed to *Independence.* Abandoned.

(P-o) *Three Rivers* (207131) (1909–10) (p, stbt, s). 180.6 × 36.0 × 9.8; 190.0 oa × 57.6 oa × 9.8. Vertical beam engine, 40 × 108. Two boilers. Built by Md. Steel Co., Sparrows Point, for MD&V. 4/2/1924 in bankruptcy proceedings, to B&V. 7/5/1924 burned to hull off Cove Point; 139 passengers and crew aboard (10 lost their lives, estimated damage $90,000). 10/14/1924 hull sold to Tolchester Beach Improvement Co. 1/12/1925 to Charles A. Jording. 3/23/1925 to Richmond Cedar Works as barge, renamed *Richmond Cedar Works #6.*

(P-o) *Tivoli* (145678) (1894) (p, stbt, s). 175.5 × 53.9 oa × 9.4; 175.5 × 32.0 × 10.9. Vertical beam engine, 38 × 102. Built by Md. Steel Co., Sparrows Point, for Md. Stbt Co. 12/1894 sold to BC&A. 11/26/1915 burned off Kent Island; 58 on board, 5 lives lost. 1/27/1916 to Boston Iron & Metal Co., 2/3/1916 to Charles A. Jording to be converted into barge. 1927 to S. C. Loveland, Phila., as barge. 1/11/1929 as barge renamed *S. W. Burgess,* Phila. 1943 as barge renamed *Richmond Cedar Works #1.*

(R) *Tockwogh* (145523) (1889) (p, stbt, w). 166.0 (175.0 oa) × 36.0 × 8.6. Vertical beam engine by Charles Reeder & Sons, 40 × 120. Paddle wheels 26 feet diameter. Built by William Skinner & Sons, Balto., for Sassafras River Stbt Co. Named for extinct tribe of American Indians. Ran until 1890. Placed on charter at times. Ran to Bay Ridge. 10/5/1889 broke strap on walking beam off Fort Carroll, Patapsco River (damage $10,000). 6/1892 sold to Newport & Wickford RR & Stbt Co. for runs between Wickford and Newport, R.I. 4/11/1893 burned at Wickford dock. Total loss.

(P-o) *Tred Avon* (145390) (1884) (s, stbt, composite) 160.0 × 33.0 × 9.0; 151.2 × 33.3 × 8.4. Compound engine, 34 × 26. Built by William E. Woodall, Balto., for Choptank River Stbt Co. 40 staterooms. 10/20/1894 sold to BC&A. 7/1896 under charter to Old Bay Line to replace *Virginia.* Proved too slow for run, as was *Enoch Pratt.* 12/3/1927 under bankruptcy proceedings sold to B&V. 2/1930 sold and fitted out by Refining Transportation Co. for freight service, Balto. to Norfolk and N.C. sounds.

9/24/1930 to 7/14/1931 transferred by U.S. marshall to Stoney Creek Improvement Co. 1/1/1941 abandoned.

U.S.S. *Tulip* (no number) (1862) (s, steam gunboat, composite). 101.4 × 22.1 × 11.5. Compound engine, 13, 20 × 24. Schooner rigged. Propeller diameter, 7.8. Two fire-tube boilers, each 15 × 6.1 × 8. Pressure 100. Eagle figurehead. Built as *Chi Kiang* for the Chinese navy by James C. Jewett, N.Y.; engine by Daniel McLeed, N.Y. 6/23/1863 financial arrangements with Chinese representatives collapsed, sold to U.S. Navy. 8/1863 modified in Washington Navy Yard, dismantled, armed. Assigned to patrol north of Piankatank to Rappahannock and lower waters of Potomac. 10/1863 under repair in Washington Navy Yard for major boiler and mechanical repairs. 8/1864 major boiler problems; engineers refuse to run steamer. 11/11/1864 steamed out of St. Inigoes under port boiler only. Starboard boiler brought on line in spite of orders not to use it. Boiler exploded, steamer sank (49 of 57 in crew lost).

(R) *United States* (no number) (1817–18) (p, stbt, w). 145.0 × 27.0 × ?; 134.0 × 26.0 × 8.9; 124.1 × 26.5 × 8.9. Built by William Flanigan and James Beacham, Balto., for William McDonald and Union Line. 1834 abandoned.

(W) *Virginia* (no number) (1817) (p, stbt, w). 136.0 × 25.0 × 5.0; 136.0 × 24.9 × 5.0; 158.6 × 25.1 × 8.9; 135.0 × 25.6 × 9.0. Crosshead engine by Watchman & Bratt, 35 × 48. Copper boiler. Like other copper boilers, to maintain 8 psi pressure, burned 20–25 pitch pine logs every 15 minutes. For 24-hour trip, consumed 2,500 logs. Little room for cargo. Speed about 5–7 mph. Equipped with sails. Paddle wheels 20 feet in diameter. Built by William Flanigan, Beacham, for Norfolk & Va. Line (Benjamin Ferguson and associates). 10/21/1822 advertised display of life preserver dress: men can walk, eat, drink, discharge guns, fence with swords, in water with ease—ladies also. Excursions with band music, entertainment: 75¢ each. 9/30/1828 sold to Md. & James River Transportation Co. 9/30/1828 by auction to Md. & Va. Stbt Co. 1840 to Balto. Steam Packet Co. Rebuilt, 3 masts for sailing, with engine used as auxiliary power. Thence to Atlantic Steam Co. for runs between Norfolk and Charleston, S.C. 1843 to William S. Pendleton, Phila. Renamed *Temple of the Muses*, as Hudson River showboat. 1841 abandoned.

(P-o) *Virginia* (161945)(1903)(p, stbt, s). 131.0 × 34.2 × 9.4; 188.0 × 55.6 × 10.5. Built by Md. Steel Co., Sparrows Point. Sister ship of *Maryland*. Built for BC&A. 12/13/1928 to B&V. 6/3/1932 to American Contract & Trust Co. and 6/15/1932 to Western Shore Freight Line (Western Shore Stbt Co.). Too slow for Rappahannock and Piankatank route, too expensive to operate, too many inside staterooms. 10/4/1932 returned to American Contract & Trust Co. in exchange for *Anne Arundel*. 5/26/1936 to Albert F. Paul and associates. 4/13/1937 converted into barge, renamed *Richmond Cedar Works #2*.

(P-o) *Virginia Lee* (228015)(1928)(twin s, stbt, s). Built by Bethlehem Shipbuilding Co., Boston, for NYP&N for service between Cape Charles and Norfolk. 7/10/1942 requisitioned by War Shipping Administration. 9/1942 readied in N.Y.C. for service at sea. Turned over to British for Allied invasion of Europe. Sailed in convoy to St. Johns, Newfoundland, but deemed unneeded and unfit for planned use. Left with skeleton crew. Cold weather caused pipes to freeze. Returned to War Shipping Administration under charter to Capt. John W. Niemeyer of Norfolk. 4/1943 to 5/1943 sailed to Brazil, engaged in rubber trade on Amazon, carrying engineering specialists and native workers to plantations. 5/4/1947 to B. B. Wills, for service on Potomac, but was unable to leave Amazon because of fuel shortage. 5/8/1948 departed Trinidad. 6/15/1948 at Balto. for sale by U.S. Maritime Commission. Sold for excursion runs, Boston to Providencetown, renamed *Holiday*. 9/1949 returned to Balto. for winter use with Tolchester line. In 1950s converted to diesel, renamed *Provincetown*. Freight use only as *Accomac*, scrapped.

Washington (no number)(1813)(p, stbt, w). 130.0 × 20.6 × 7.4. Crosshead engine, 28 × 48. Built by Charles Browne, N.Y., for North River Steamboat Co. Engine by Robert Fulton Works. During 1815–22 owned by Potomac Steam Boat Company (Benjamin H. Latrobe). 5/21/1815 left N.Y. for Norfolk, arrived 5/24/1815. First steamer to enter Norfolk Harbor and navigate Elizabeth River. 6/10/1815 arrived in Washington, D.C. Two trips to Aquia Creek and return. 12/2/1822 to be sold at public auction. 7/19/1823 arrived at Norfolk from Washington, later scrapped.

(P-o) *Westmoreland* (80995)(1883)(p, stbt, w). 199.3 (210.0 oa) × 32.3 (55.0 oa) × 12.5. Vertical beam engine, 48 × 132. Built by William Skinner

& Sons, Balto., for Weems line. Ran Rappahannock and Patuxent rivers. Staterooms in inner and outer banks on passenger deck. 1/26/1905 sold to MD&V. 5/1909 outfitted by James Clark & Co. as excursion boat to replace *Love Point.* Operated by BC&A. 1/4/1924 sold in bankruptcy proceedings to Marine Sand and Gravel Co. 1/30/1925 dismantled.

Appendix C

MAPS OF THE REGION

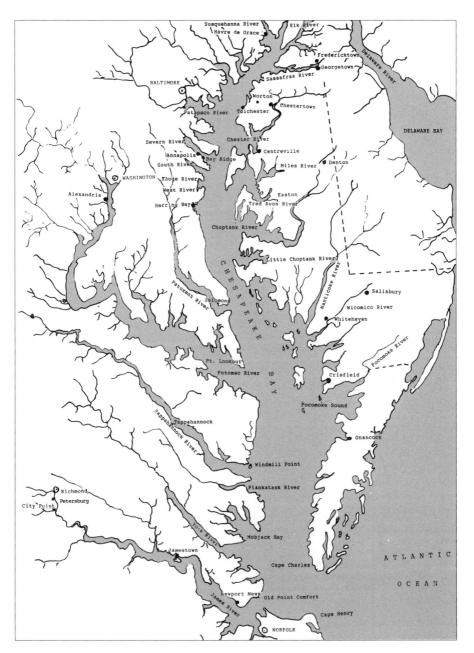

Chesapeake Bay overview

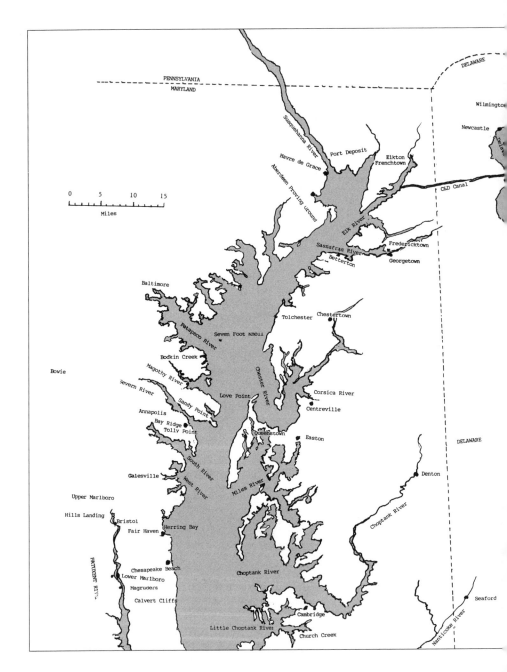

Upper Chesapeake Bay

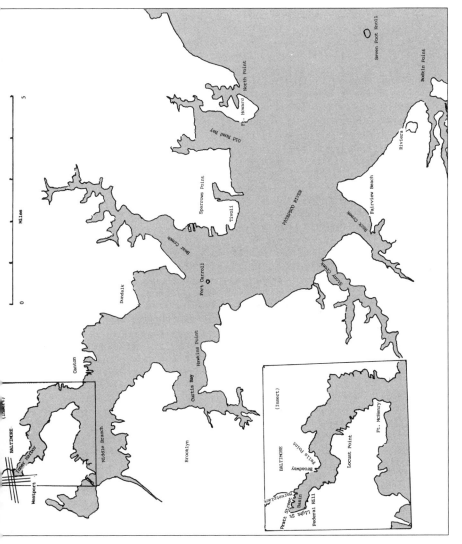

Baltimore and Patapsco mouth

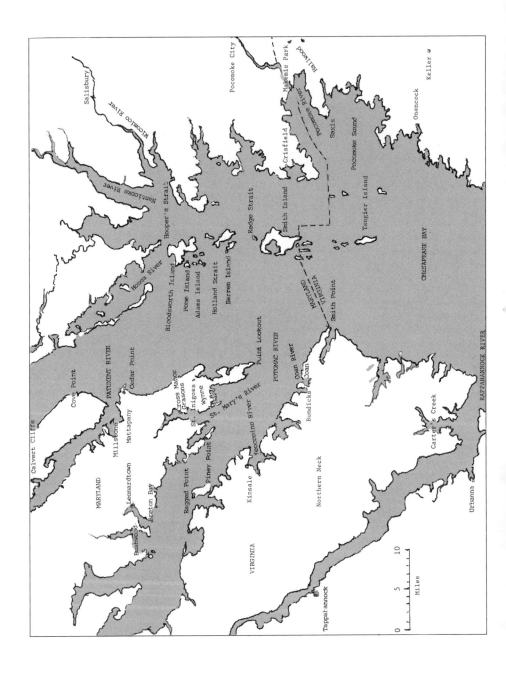

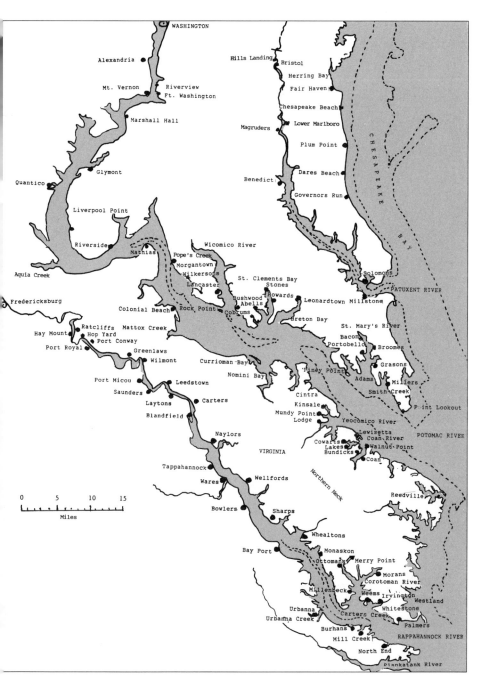

Landings on the Patuxent, Potomac, and Rappahannock

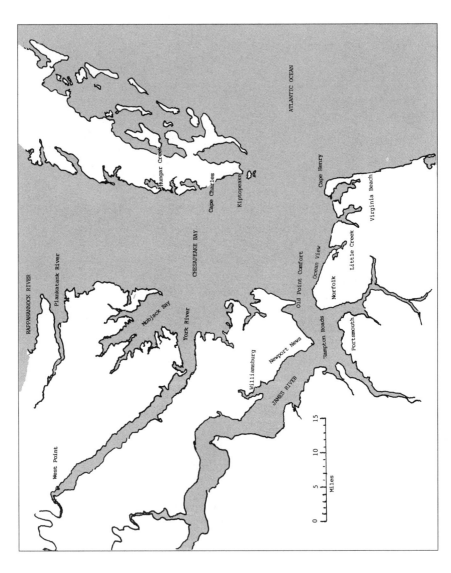

Lower Chesapeake Bay

SOURCE NOTES

This book is intended for the information and enjoyment of the general public. At the same time, it contains material of scholarly interest to the historian. In an attempt to avoid the tedium of footnotes or endnotes to document the text (notes that are seldom read except by researchers bent on further investigation), the author has elected to discuss his sources in the following paragraphs.

Chapter 1 depends to some extent on the references and sources of principal treatises cited in the Bibliography. The works of Dickinson, Latrobe, Philip, Hunter, and Turnbull were of great value in piecing together the roles played by John Stevens, Robert Livingston, Robert Fulton, Benjamin Latrobe, and Nicholas Roosevelt in maneuvering around each other on the matter of monopolistic power and, in particular, a focus on the Chesapeake Bay as a link to the Delaware River. The role of William McDonald appears in these texts, also. This information is balanced against research performed for the author's *Tidewater by Steamboat*. Other citations in the Bibliography contributed extensively to the chapter. Additional materials came from collections on file in the Library of Congress, Washington; Enoch Pratt Free Library (Maryland Room), Baltimore; Dorchester County Historical Society, Cambridge, Maryland; Maryland Historical Society, Baltimore; Mariners' Museum, Newport News, Virginia; and some private repositories. Steamboat data in the National Archives, Washington, proved valuable.

For Chapter 2, sources include materials derived from authoritative historical volumes on engines of the early nineteenth century: Bourne (1849), Marestier (1824), and Tredgold (the 1838 edition has the only known diagram of a crosshead engine). Textbooks on early marine engines, cited in the Bibliography along with Bourne and Tredgold, proved of great usefulness in deducing the engineering of the crosshead and vertical beam engines. Most valuable in tracing the history and accomplishments of the Baltimore steam engine builder Charles Reeder and his competitor, the firm of John Watchman and John Bratt, was the unpublished manuscript in the possession of the Maryland Historical Society: William J. Kelley, "Shipbuilding at Federal Hill . . . Fells Point" (1964), as edited by Randolph Chalfont, who furnished additional notes from his own research on the subject. Details concerning the Rappahannock River controversy came from privately held documentary sources. Additional materials emerged from collections on file in the Maryland Historical Society, the Mariners' Museum, the National Archives, and the Enoch Pratt Free Library

Chapter 3 consists of three segments. For the first segment, the sinking of the *City of Annapolis* by her sister ship in 1927, the author relied heavily on the extensive newspaper coverage of the event, including the investigation that followed.

For the second segment, the foundering of *Express* in the hurricane of 1878, the sources are more detailed. Newspaper coverage from Baltimore, Washington, and Norfolk was extensive and unfolding, and provided a sound basis for the narrative. The *St. Mary's Beacon* proved helpful. Secondary material in Shomette, as well as Burgess and Wood, cited in the bibliography, was less extensive but contributive. Great assistance was given by Grace Anne Koppel, who disclosed her own materials related to the tragedy, in particular the wills of Caleb and Randolph Jones, and important information relating to the background of Randolph Jones. The work of Brown, cited in the Bibliography, served as useful background. Census data were indispensable. Fresco's book on local doctors was especially valuable.

For the Civil War explosion of U.S.S. *Tulip,* the primary source was the article cited in the Bibliography by Schmidt, a scholarly piece of work drawn from his master's thesis on the same subject. Other sources, notably materials from the National Archives, the Mariners' Museum, the works of Shomette, Patterson, Tilp, and Beitzell, and local information concerning the St. Inigoes coaling station and the national monument were important supplements.

For the last segment, the burning and sinking of *Columbus* in 1850 and the resurrection of its engine in 1993, the sources are numerous. Extensive newspaper reports of the incident furnished the narrative. Data in the National Archives and the Eldredge Collection of the Mariners' Museum provided technical information, as well as all the texts and manuals on early engines cited in the Bibliography for Chapter 2. Emmerson listed particulars concerning the steamer. Secondary sources included Shomette and the works by Brown listed in the Bibliography. But the most critical and significant material relating to the crosshead engine came from the author's visit to the site of the wreck as the U.S. Army Corps of Engineers valiantly succeeded, after several attempts, in bringing the engine to the surface from the bottom of the Bay where it had rested for 143 years. The author was able to measure the resurrected component parts after their salvage and deduce whatever was possible about the design and construction of the engine in 1828 by Charles Reeder. The contributions of Mimi Woods, archaeologist of the Corps of Engineers, Dr. R. Goodwin and his associates, and Michael Pohuski, photographer, diver, and archaeologist, were key to understanding the operation and its results. Especially valuable were the efforts of Michael Pohuski, who worked mightily to ensure the preservation of the historic site. Further technical assistance came from Richard Anderson, whose work is cited in the Bibliography and whose knowledge of historic ships and meticulous study of maritime engineering proved invaluable.

For Chapter 4, the primary source is the unpublished scrapbook of newspaper and journal articles, official records, and family manuscripts entitled *The Thomas Brothers of Mattapany*, prepared and photocopied in multiple sets by Armstrong Thomas, 1963. The scrapbook includes a wide coverage of the genealogy and background of the family, the activities of George and James William Thomas in the Civil War, the history of the estates of the Thomas family, as well as an excellent collection of material on Richard Thomas Zarvona. Other documentary sources include the *Official Records of the Union and Confederate Navies* . . . (in the Bibliography) and materials on file in the Maryland Historical Society and in the Library of Congress. Some information on the incident aboard *Mary Washington* came from private sources. Secondary sources of immediate value included Fenwick, Earp, Brooks, Dwiggins, Hammett, Toomey, and Stern. The narrative augments the account in the author's *Tidewater by Steamboat.*

For Chapter 5, the interpretation of Tolchester Beach parallels some material in the author's book *Steamboat on the Chesapeake: Emma Giles and the Tolchester Line,* and its detailed footnotes and bibliography furnished a broad background, supplemented by contemporary newspaper articles and the recollections of the author, his friends, and his relatives who lived the Tolchester experience. For the material on Chesapeake Beach, a debt is owed to Ames Williams for his study of the Chesapeake Beach Railway listed in the Bibliography. His detailed analysis of the development of the railroad from Washington to the resort, a study which constituted most of his book, was put aside in favor of presenting the resort from the entertainment aspect and the view from the perspective of the Baltimoreans arriving by the steamer *Dreamland.* For the latter purpose, the vertical files of the Mariners' Museum, the Calvert Marine Museum, and the Chesapeake Beach Railway Museum disgorged quantities of contemporary newspaper clippings, documents, and photographs (or postcards), all of which constituted an excellent reservoir of primary sources. Newspaper articles in the *Calvert Independent, Prince Frederick Recorder,* and *Calvert County Recorder* were especially helpful. Kunnecke's article cited in the Bibliography was very useful. A paper (typescript) written by a ninth-grader, Laura A. Hanyok, entitled "The Chesapeake Beach Resort," summed up the general background of Chesapeake Beach. Most importantly, extensive conversation in March 1993 with Harriet Stout, curator of the Chesapeake Beach Railway Museum, and Bernard (Bernie) Loveless, volunteer and aficionado of the history of the resort, proved invaluable in combining their deep knowledge of Chesapeake Beach and their enthusiasm for the preservation of its history.

For the interpretation of Bay Ridge, the thorough study and entertaining portrayal of the resort by McWilliams and Paterson was invaluable and was used extensively for picturing the resort and its history. The point of view from the steamboat—the purpose of this volume—placed the material in a somewhat different perspective and occasioned the introduction of data from other sources: contemporary newspaper, documentary, archival, and private.

Sources for material on Betterton include those cited in the author's summary in *Steamboat on the Chesapeake* and from primary newspaper articles. Material on Fair Haven was drawn from the extensive coverage on the resort in the author's *Tidewater by Steamboat.* Piney Point, discussed in Tilp, Hammett, and Bcitzell, was described in various primary newspaper articles and in recollections of those who had visited there. Weikert, McKinsey, and Harris were very useful.

For Chapter 6, a wide range of general treatises on steamboating on the Chesapeake presents a general portrayal of its history and the various characteristics of the steamers. The works of Burgess and Wood, Brewington, Brown, Davison, Elliott, Hain, Heyl, Lochhead, Shanahan, and Stanton furnished a broad background of the era. The author's *Tidewater by Steamboat* used the history of the era to serve as a backdrop to the narrative of the Weems line. That book also surveyed the lives and characters of some colorful figures associated with the steamboats: Mason Locke Weems, Charles R. Lewis, James Gourley, and William C. Geoghegan, described in detail in this chapter. Additional materials came from documentary files in personal collections and biographical articles in such books as *Geneaology and Biography of Leading Families* . . . cited in the Bibliography. Accounts of steamboat masters in the works of Brown, and Burgess and Wood, were useful. For the biographical material on William C. Almy, the personal collection of William D. Almy, the captain's grandson, proved to be a treasure of information.

For Chapter 7, the interlocking of principal treatises on the Pennsylvania Railroad proved to be important, since they interlaced in presenting the intricacies of the railroad's grasping history. Their documentation proved invaluable. These books, which are more in the nature of documentary or primary sources, included Burgess and Kennedy, Schotter, and *One Hundred Years . . . of the Pennsylvania Railroad Company*. Additionally, the works of Holbrook and of Rodgers were valuable. Particularly essential was the book by Hayman on Eastern Shore railroads. For a summary of steamboats of interest to the monopolistic acquisitiveness of the PRR, the author used the general treatment of these vessels and steamboat lines in his *Tidewater by Steamboat* and *Steamboat on the Chesapeake*, as well as the cataloging set forth in Burgess and Wood. In addition, newspaper files were explored extensively. Additional and important materials came from documentary collections and corporate records in the Hagley Library, Wilmington, Delaware; The Mariners' Museum, Newport News, Virginia; the Library of Congress, Washington; and the Maryland Archives, Annapolis, Maryland. Technical data were supplied by the National Archives, Washington, D.C.

For Chapter 8, sources were numerous. Primary sources were newspaper articles covering various aspects of the last days of the steamboat era. Especially valuable were contemporary accounts of the last voyages of the *Anne Arundel* in 1932 and in 1937, the burning of the *City of Baltimore* in 1937, the trials and troubles of the Tolchester line from 1933 to the end in 1938, what was public knowledge of the *President Warfield/Exodus 1947* incident, and the last days of Chesapeake Beach. Articles of the Baltimore *Sun* were particularly thorough. Interviews with those who remembered or participated in the finale were substantive. The footnotes in Elliott's *Last of the Steamboats*, the author's *Steamboat on the Chesapeake*,

Tidewater by Steamboat, and *Exodus 1947* led to additional material for this chapter. These books, in addition to Ames Williams's *Otto Mears Goes East,* Brown's *Steam Packets on the Chesapeake,* and Burgess and Wood's *Steamboat Out of Baltimore,* furnished the essential framework and background for the presentation. Brochures promulgated by the Baltimore Steam Packet Company and the Western Shore Steamboat Company proved useful in schedule information and other descriptive data. Articles in *Steamboat Bill* by John L. Lochhead provided material on the final days of river steamboats out of Norfolk.

Source information for Appendixes A and B is cited in each appendix.

SELECTED BIBLIOGRAPHY

In parentheses following each entry are numbers indicating chapters where the entry applies; the letter *G* indicates that the entry is of general or background interest to the subject matter of the book.

"Ames Williams on the Chesapeake Bay Railway." *Calvert Independent,* May 25, 1979. (5)

Anderson, Richard K., Jr. *Guidelines for Recording Historic Ships.* Washington: National Park Service, 1988. (2, 3)

Appleton's Dictionary of Machines, Mechanics, Engine-work, and Engineering. 2 vols. New York: Appleton, 1850. (2)

Beitzell, Edwin M. *Life on the Potomac River.* Abell, Maryland: Published by the author, 1968, 1979. (3)

Bourne, John, ed. *Treatise on the Steam Engine.* By the Artisan Club, 3rd ed. London: Longman, Brown, Green, and Longman, 1849. (2)

Braynard, Frank O. *S.S. Savannah: The Elegant Steam Ship.* New York: Dover, 1963. (1)

Brewington, M. V. *Chesapeake Bay: A Pictorial Maritime History.* Cambridge, Maryland: Cornell Maritime Press, 1953. (G)

Brooks, Kenneth. "Coinjock Roberts Wasn't Really His Name." *Chesapeake Bay Magazine,* May 1985. (4)

Brown, Alexander Crosby. *The Old Bay Line, 1840–1940.* Richmond, Virginia: Dietz Press, 1941. (3)

———. *Steam Packets on the Chesapeake: A History of the Old Bay Line Since 1840.* Cambridge, Maryland: Cornell Maritime Press, 1961. (3, 7, 8)

Brugger, Robert J. *Maryland: A Middle Temperament, 1634–1980.* Baltimore: Johns Hopkins University Press, 1988. (G)

Burgess, Robert H. "A Bay Link Breaks." Baltimore *Sunday Sun Magazine,* January 23, 1955. (G, 8)

———. "The First Steamboat on the Bay." Baltimore *Sun,* March 26, 1950. (1)

————. "Gone Are the Days—When Spotless Little Steamboats Bound down the Chesapeake Sailed Out of Baltimore on a Summer's Afternoon." Baltimore *Sunday Sun,* July 3, 1949. (8)

————. "Half a Century on the Chesapeake: Capt. John D. Davis Keeps Alive the Name of the Bay's Oldest Steamboating Family." Baltimore *Sunday Sun,* May 23, 1954. (6, 8)

————. "I Remember . . . the Day That 'Real Steamboating' Ended on the Bay." Baltimore *Sun Magazine,* February 27, 1972. (8)

————. "I Remember . . . the Old Sidewheeler Louise." Baltimore *Sun,* July 31, 1955. (5)

————. "I Remember . . . Weekend Steamer Voyages." Baltimore *Sun Magazine,* June 20, 1971. (8)

————. "The Last Days of a Popular Bay Boat." Baltimore *Sunday Sun Magazine,* September 22, 1963. (G)

————. *This Was Chesapeake Bay.* Cambridge, Maryland: Cornell Maritime Press, 1963. (G)

————. "Vanished White Fleet of Tidewater." Baltimore *Sun,* March 30, 1947. (8)

Burgess, George H., and Miles C. Kennedy. *Centennial History of the Pennsylvania Railroad Company, 1846–1946.* Philadelphia: Pennsylvania Railroad Company, 1949. (7)

Burgess, Robert H., and H. Graham Wood. *Steamboats Out of Baltimore.* Cambridge, Maryland: Tidewater Publishers, 1968. (G)

Clark, Charles B. *The Eastern Shore of Maryland and Virginia.* 3 vols. New York: Lewis Historical Publishing, 1958. (G)

Dangerfield, George. *Chancellor Robert R. Livingston of New York, 1746–1813.* New York: Harcourt, Brace, 1960. (1)

Davison, Spencer. "Tolchester Move Recalls Sidewheelers: 'Headstrong' Louise and the Emma Giles." Baltimore *Evening Sun,* January 24, 1951. (5, 6)

Day, Samuel Philips. *Down South.* London: Hurst and Blackett, 1862. (4)

Dayton, Fred Erving. *Steamboat Days.* New York: Frederick A. Stokes, 1925. (G)

Dickinson, H. W. *Robert Fulton: Engineer and Artist: His Life and Works.* New York: John Lance, 1913. (1)

Dollar, Robert. *One Hundred Thirty Years of Steam Navigation.* New York: Charles Scribner, 1928. (1)

Dozer, Donald Marquand. *Portrait of the Free State: A History of Maryland.* Cambridge, Maryland: Tidewater Publishers, 1976. (G, 1)

Durand, William F. *Practical Marine Engineering for Marine Engineers and Students.* New York: Marine Engineering, 1902. (2)

Dwiggins, Don. "The Lady Was a Colonel, but the Colonel Was No Lady." *Argosy,* June 1968. (4)

Earp, Charles A. "The Amazing Colonel Zarvona." *Maryland Historical Magazine,* December 1959. (4)

Ellicott, J. M. "A Child's Recollections of the Potomac Flotilla." U.S. Naval Institute *Proceedings,* 1935; reprinted in *Chronicles of St. Mary's,* September 1962.

Elliott, Richard V. *Last of the Steamboats: The Saga of the Wilson Line.* Cambridge, Maryland: Tidewater Publishers, 1970. (5, 8)

Emmerson, John C., Jr. *The Steamboat Comes to Norfolk Harbor and Log of the First Ten Years, 1815–25.* Portsmouth, Virginia: reported [collected and published] by the Norfolk *Gazette and Public Ledger, American Beacon,* and Norfolk and Portsmouth *Herald,* 1947, 1949. (1)

Fenwick, Charles E. "Mattapany—Sewall Manor." *Chronicles of St. Mary's.* August 1956. (4)

Flexner, James Thomas. *Steamboats Come True: American Inventors in Action.* Boston: Little, Brown, 1948. (1)

Footner, Hulbert. *Maryland Main and the Eastern Shore.* New York: D. Appleton-Century, 1942. (G)

———. *Rivers of the Eastern Shore: Seventeen Maryland Rivers.* New York: Farrar and Rinehart, 1944.

Fresco, Margaret K. *Doctors of St. Mary's County, 1634–1900.* Published by the author, 1992. (3)

Genealogy and Biography of Leading Families of the City of Baltimore and Baltimore County, Maryland. New York: Chapman, 1897. (6)

Gibson, Stuart. "Steamer Louise Passes from Bay After Forty-Three Years." Baltimore *Sunday Sun,* February 1, 1926. (5)

Gilfillan, S. C. "Early Steamboats of the Chesapeake." Baltimore *Sun,* May 31, 1931. (1, 3)

Graham, Frank D. *Audel's Engineers and Mechanics Guide Number 3.* New York: Theodore Audel, 1921. (2)

Gray, Ralph D. *National Waterway: The History of the Chesapeake and Delaware Canal, 1769–1885.* Chicago: University of Illinois Press, 1967, 1987. (1)

Grosvenor, Gilbert. "A Maryland Pilgrimage." *National Geographic Magazine,* February 1927. (3)

Gutheim, Frederick. *The Potomac.* Baltimore: Johns Hopkins University Press, 1944. (3)

Hain, John A. *Side Wheel Steamers of the Chesapeake Bay, 1830–1947.* Glen Burnie, Maryland: Glendale Press, 1941. (G)

Hammett, Regina Combs. *History of St. Mary's County, Maryland, 1934–1990.* Ridge, Maryland: published by the author, 1991. (3)

Harris, R. P. "The Trip to Tolchester." Baltimore *Evening Sun*, July 11, 1949. (5)

Hayman, John C. *Rails Along the Chesapeake: A History of Railroading on the Delmarva Peninsula.* Salisbury, Maryland: Marvadel Publishers, 1979. (7)

Heyl, Erik. *Early American Steamboats.* New York: published by the author, 1964. (G)

Holbrook, Stewart H. *The Story of American Railroads.* New York: American Legacy, 1981. (7)

Holly, David C. *Exodus 1947.* Boston: Little, Brown, 1969. (8, 9)

———. *Steamboat on the Chesapeake: Emma Giles and the Tolchester Line.* Centreville, Maryland: Tidewater Publishers, 1987. (2, 5, 8)

———. *Tidewater by Steamboat: A Saga of the Chesapeake: The Weems Line on the Patuxent, Potomac, and Rappahannock.* Baltimore: Johns Hopkins University Press, 1991. (G)

Hopley, Catherine. *Life in the South.* London: Chapman and Hall, 1863. (4)

Howard, George W. "Charles Reeder, Sr., and Charles Reeder, Jr." In *The Monumental City: Its Past History and Present Resources.* Baltimore: J. D. Ehlers, 1873. (2)

Hunter, Louise C. *Steamboats on the Western Rivers: An Economic and Technological History.* New York: Octagon, 1969. (1)

Hutcheon, Wallace, Jr. *Robert Fulton: Pioneer of Undersea Warfare.* Annapolis, Maryland: U.S. Naval Institute Press, 1981. (1)

Jackson, G. Gibbard. *The Ship Under Steam.* New York: Charles Scribner, 1938. (G, 1)

Jones, Virgil Carrington Thomas. *The Civil War at Sea.* New York: Rinehart and Winston, 1960. (4)

Kcith, Robert C. *Baltimore Harbor: A Picture History.* Baltimore: Ocean World, 1982. (2)

Kelley, William J. "Baltimore Steamboats in the Civil War." *Maryland Historical Magazine,* 1942. (4)

Kunnecke, George B. "When the Dreamland Came to Baltimore." Baltimore *Sunday Sun Magazine,* August 9, 1957. (5)

Latrobe, J. H. B. *The First Steamboat Voyage on the Western Waters.* Baltimore: Maryland Historical Society, 1871. (1)

————. *A Lost Chapter in the History of the Steamboat.* Baltimore: Maryland Historical Society, 1871. (1)

Lentz, Emily E. "History of the Steamboat on Chesapeake Bay." Series of articles, Baltimore *Sun,* January–March, 1908. (1)

Lippson, Alice Jane, ed. *The Chesapeake Bay in Maryland: An Atlas of Natural Resources.* For the Natural Resources Institute of the University of Maryland. Baltimore: Johns Hopkins University Press, 1978. (G)

Lochhead, John L. "Steamships and Steamboats of the Old Dominion Line." *Steamboat Bill,* March, June, September, 1949. (7, 8)

McKinsey, Folger. "Betterton Has Historic Past as Well as Bright Present." Baltimore *Sun,* June 16, 1940. (5)

McWilliams, Jane W., and Patterson, Carol C. *Bay Ridge on the Chesapeake: An Illustrated History.* Annapolis, Maryland: Brighton Editions, 1986. (5)

Marestier, Jean Baptiste. *Mémoire sur les Bateaux à Vapeur des Etats-Unis d'Amèrique.* Paris: Institute of France, Royal Academy of Sciences, 1824. *Memoir on Steamboats of the United States of America.* Sydney Worthington, trans. Mystic, Connecticut: Marine Historical Association, 1957. (1, 2)

Maryland: Its Resources, Industries, and Institutions. Prepared by the Board of World's Fair Managers of Maryland by Members of the Johns Hopkins University and others, 1893. (2)

Mayer, Lewis, Louis C. Fisher; and E. J. D. Cross, comps. *Revised Code of the Public General Laws of the State of Maryland,* Vol. 1. Baltimore: 1879–1904. (6)

Merchant Vessels of the United States. Annual List. Washington: Government Printing Office, annually. (G)

Merchant Vessels of the United States, 1790–1868. Lytle-Holdcamper List. Staten Island, New York: Steamship Historical Society, 1975. (G)

"NESEA Responsible for Upkeep of Country's Smallest National Monument." *Lexington Park Enterprise,* February 16, 1992. (3)

Nock, O. S. *Railways of the USA.* New York: Hastings, 1979. (7)

Official Records of the Union and Confederate Navies in the War of the Rebellion. Washington, Government Printing Office, 1897. (3, 4)

One Hundred Years, the Ninety-Ninth Annual Report of the Pennsylvania Railroad Company. Philadelphia: The Pennsylvania Railroad Company, 1945. (7)

Patterson, Richard Oakes. "Frederick Townsend Ward, the Mandarin from Salem." U.S. Naval Institute *Proceedings,* February 1953. (3)

Philip, Cynthia Owens. *Robert Fulton: A Biography.* New York: F. Watts, 1985. (1)

Portrait and Biographical Record of the Eastern Shore. New York: Chapman, 1898. (1)

Powell, Henry Fletcher, comp. *Tercentenary History of Maryland.,* Vol. 4. Chicago: S. J. Clarke, 1925. (1)

Practice and Explanation of the Principles of the Machinery Used in Steam Navigation. . . . 2 vols. London: John Weale, 1851. (2)

Reigert, J. Franklin. *The Life of Robert Fulton.* Philadelphia: C. G. Henderson, 1896. (1)

Rodgers, William. "Pope's Creek." *Maryland Magazine,* Winter 1986. (7)

———. "Riding the Maryland Rails." *Maryland Magazine,* Winter 1986. (5)

Rowland, K. T. *Steam at Sea: A History of Steam Navigation.* New York: Praeger, 1970. (1)

Scharf, J. Thomas. *History of the Confederate States Navy.* New York: Prager and Sherwood, 1887. (4)

———. *History of Maryland from the Earliest Period to the Present Day.* 3 vols. Hatboro, Pennsylvania: Tradition Press, 1967. (G, 2)

Scharfenberg, Kirk. "If Ghosts Like Amusement, There's Tolchester Beach." Baltimore *Sun,* July 29, 1958. (8)

Schmidt, James S. "Tragedy on the Potomac: History of the U.S.S. Tulip." *Chronicles of St. Mary's,* Spring 1993. (3)

Schotter, H. W. *The Growth and Development of the Pennsylvania Railroad Company.* Philadelphia: Allan, Lane, and Scott, 1927. (7)

Shanahan, John H. K. *Steamboatin' Days and the Hammond Lot.* Baltimore: Norman Publishing, 1930. (G)

———. "Steamboating on the Chesapeake: Advent of the Automobile." Baltimore *Sun,* March 9, 1930. (1, 8)

Sheads, Scott S. *The Rockets' Red Glare: The Maritime Defense of Baltimore in 1814.* Centreville, Maryland: Tidewater Publishers, 1986. (1)

Shomette, Donald G. *Shipwrecks on the Chesapeake.* Centreville, Maryland: Tidewater Publishers, 1982, 1991. (3)

Stanton, Samuel Ward. *Steam Navigation on the Carolina Sounds and the Chesapeake.* Salem, Massachusetts: Steamship Historical Society, 1947. (G)

Stein, Charles Francis. *A History of Calvert County, Maryland.* Published by the author in cooperation with Calvert County Historical Society, 1976. (5)

Stern, Philip Van Dorn. *The Confederate Navy: A Pictorial History.* New York: Doubleday, 1962. (4)

Thomas, Armstrong, comp. *The Thomas Brothers of Mattapany,* 1963. Unpublished manuscript scrapbook on file in Library of Congress, Washington.

Thurston, Robert H. *A History of the Growth of the Steam Engine.* 2nd ed. London: C. Kagan Paul, 1879. (2)

Tilp, Frederick. *This Was Potomac River,* 3rd ed. Alexandria, Virginia: published by the author, 1987. (3)

Toomey, Daniel Carroll. *The Civil War in Maryland.* Baltimore: Toomey Press, 1983. (4)

Tredgold, Thomas. *The Principles and Practice and Explanation of the Machinery Used in Steam Navigation.* . . . 2 vols. London: John Weale, 1838, 1851. (2)

———. *The Steam Engine, Its Invention and Progressive Improvement.* 3 vols. London: John Weale, 1852. (2)

Turnbull, Archibald Douglas. *John Stevens: An American Record.* New York: Century, 1928. (1)

Twain, Mark. *Life on the Mississippi.* 1896. (2)

Usher, Abbott Payson. *A History of Mechanical Inventions.* Cambridge, Massachusetts: Harvard University Press, 1954. (2)

Usilton, William B., III. *History of Kent County, Maryland, 1628–1980.* Published by the author, 1981. (5)

"U.S.S. Tulip Centennial Commemoration Ceremony, November 11, 1964." *Chronicles of St. Mary's,* December 1964. (3)

Walsh, Richard, and William Lloyd Fox. *Maryland: A History, 1632–1974.* Baltimore: Maryland Historical Society, 1974. (G)

Watson, Mark S. "Motor Horns Sound the Bay-Boat's Knell." Baltimore *Sun,* March 6, 1932.

Weikert, Jean Tolson. "Piney Point, St. Mary's County, Maryland." *Chronicles of St. Mary's,* August 1994. (5)

Weston, B. Latrobe. "Guilford: Its Name and Development." Baltimore *Sun,* January 9, 1944. (1)

Whittier, Bob. *Paddle-Wheel Steamers and Their Giant Engines.* Duxbury, Massachusetts: Seamaster Books, 1983. (2)

Williams, Ames A. *Otto Mears Goes East: The Chesapeake Beach Railway.* Prince Frederick, Maryland: Calvert County Historical Society, 1975. (5)

Wilstach, Paul. *Tidewater Maryland.* Indianapolis: Bobbs-Merrill, 1931. (G)

———. *Tidewater Virginia.* Indianapolis: Bobbs-Merrill, 1929. (G)

INDEX

For conciseness, a number of items have been placed in blocks by subject. These include the following: Captains, Engines, Rail lines, Resorts, Rivers, Shipbuilders, Steamboat lines, Steamboats (by name), Steamboats (by topic).